D1270942

HISTORY
through the
OPERA GLASS

HISTORY
through the
OPERA GLASS

FROM THE RISE OF CAESAR

TO THE FALL OF NAPOLEON

by

George Jellinek

Pro/Am Music Resources, Inc.
White Plains, New York

Kahn & Averill
London

FIRST EDITION

Published in the United States of America 1994 by
PRO/AM MUSIC RESOURCES, INC.
63 Prospect Street, White Plains, New York 10606
ISBN 0-912483-90-3

U.S. School & Library Distribution by
PRO/AM MUSIC RESOURCES, INC.

U.S. Trade & Retail DIstribution by
THE BOLD STRUMMER, LTD.
20 Turkey Hill Circle, Box 2037, Westport, Connecticut 06880

Published in Great Britain 1994 by
KAHN & AVERILL
9 Harrington Road, London SW7 3ES
ISBN 1-871082-47-1

for

HEDY

CONTENTS

(CONTENTS)

(CONTENTS)

PREFACE

History and opera have crossed paths at many junctures. They are combined in this book in a heretofore untried manner. But perhaps I should begin by explaining what this book is *not*.

It is not another textbook of history, nor is it a history of opera. But you will find in its pages some world-shaking events over two millennia, and such larger-than-life personalities as Julius Caesar, Nero, Attila, Charlemagne, Henry VIII, Elizabeth, Queen of England, Boris Godunov, and Napoleon, to mention only a few. These extraordinary human beings have inspired countless novels, plays, and operas. As an enthusiastic student of both history and opera, I found it an exciting challenge to place these figures and the events surrounding them — together with nearly 200 operas in which they appear — into a single continuous narrative.

More than 2000 years of history will be reviewed here from the perspective of an opera scholar. It is my aim to separate true history from the kind of history we encounter on the operatic stage, obscured, embellished, or sometimes distorted by the librettists' imagination.

Many librettos are based on important plays by Shakespeare, Goethe, Schiller, Pushkin, Hugo, and other eminent playwrights. It seemed necessary to examine these literary sources, as well, for in many instances departures from true history occurred at the literary, not the operatic, level, with librettists confirming or compounding such deviations from the historical record.

History Through the Opera Glass is, by definition, somewhat slanted history, shaped as it is by the operatic repertoire. From the vantage point of a true historian it is incomplete, for it omits or slights certain historical events not reflected in opera. This is a book that deals more with personalities than with geopolitical trends, the kind of book where Adrienne Lecouvreur, a queen of the stage, commands more space than legitimate rulers, and where — in a chronicle of 18th-century England — Handel rates more mention than Robert Walpole, the Prime Minister, or King George II, for that matter. On the other hand, no mainstream operas that are history-related have been overlooked, and I have included many works that are far off the beaten path but possess genuine historical relevance. (There is, in addition, a reference chronology at the end of the book, which lists a great many of the lesser works besides.)

As opera itself enters the flow of history, the great operatic personalities — Monteverdi, Lully, Gluck, Mozart, *et al.* — become a part of that flow. But they appear on these pages only insofar as they related to historical events: Monteverdi as court musician to the Gonzagas of Mantua, Gluck as the teacher of Marie Antoinette, Mozart in his relationship to the Viennese court, Paisiello as Napoleon's favorite, etc.

Like many opera scholars, I am something of a missionary, or at least a propagandist for the cause. I believe that this book will enrich the experience of opera lovers while offering all readers an entertaining account of grand events and personalities. History as reflected in opera, and opera as enriched by an understanding of historical events — these are the targets of my double-barreled enterprise.

In completing my research, I consulted various branches of the New York Public Library, including the Research Division of the Library at Lincoln Center. Special thanks are due to the staff of the Library of *The New York Times* and the Library at Hastings-on-Hudson, New York.

I owe a note of thanks to Ann Dembner and the late Arthur S. Dembner for their initial encouragement of my undertaking a book that I had been wanting to write for a long time. Professors Charles and Barbara Jelavich of Indiana University and Professor Jaroslav Pelikan of Yale University read portions of the manuscript, and I am grateful to them for their valuable suggestions.

Several friends and colleagues have contributed to my work in various ways. I extend my thanks and appreciation to Peter Allen, Oscar Evans, Mortimer H. Frank, Nimet Habachy, Shirley Hazzard, Francis Steegmuller, and Wanda Van de Water; also to Winnie Klotz and Robert Tuggle of the Metropolitan Opera and Jane L. Poole of *Opera News* for their valued assistance with the illustrations.

My publisher and editor Thomas P. Lewis, dedicated to the task from the outset, gave me his unwavering support and encouragement. His wise and jovial nature served as a welcome antidote to my customary "Type A" approach to things.

Finally, I thank my wife Hedy for her devotion and unsparing help with every phase of this book, for her patience, support, and invaluable professional participation.

GEORGE JELLINEK

INTRODUCTION

LEGEND INTO HISTORY—AND OPERA

Attempting to chronicle some 1800 years of history in approximately 300 pages of *History Through the Opera Glass* is an ambitious undertaking. To keep its scope within reasonable limits, I have confined the "action" within the neatly symmetrical borders of the rise of Caesar and the fall of Napoleon. But one cannot ignore the fact that the Rome of Caesar was already the inheritor of 3000 years of civilization. This introduction briefly sketches those early years where legend and history are intertwined and where archaeology has helped to fill in the gaps between hazily recorded data and full historical documentation.

It is a well-established fact that civilization was emerging some time before 3000 BC in various areas of the Near East, and that the tribes that lived around the Nile eventually formed settlements headed by an absolute ruler. These primitive groupings eventually grew into the kingdom of Egypt, ruled by 30 consecutive dynasties. When the curtain rises on the first act of Verdi's *Aida* (1871) and the young warrior Rhadames dreams of leading a victorious army to "*il plauso di Menfi tutta*"—the acclamation of all Memphis—he is referring to a city founded by Menes, the first Egyptian king, around 3000 BC.

Although the story of *Aida* was loosely based on a sketch prepared by the Egyptologist Auguste Mariette, recent scholarship has left little doubt that Verdi's librettist Camille du Locle and Italian adaptor Antonio Ghislanzoni had taken some ideas from early plays by Metastasio and Racine in developing the opera's plot. While the historical period of the opera's action was never clarified, we know that Egypt did not develop an army until the rule of the eighteenth dynasty (around 1500 BC). That army was powerful enough to repel such invaders as the Hittites and the Libyans, though historical records are silent on any Ethiopian invasion during this period.

The Pharaoh who ruled Egypt during the end of the eighteenth dynasty was Amenhotep IV, who ascended the throne in 1375 BC. He was something of a visionary who was determined to reform the ancient religion of Egypt by establishing the worship of a single universal God called Aton, represented by the image of the sun. He accordingly took the name "Akhnaton". His reforms, however, did not survive him, and Egypt soon returned to the old traditions where the army and the clergy exerted great power. Eleven of Akhnaton's successors in the nineteenth and twentieth dynasties bore the name Ramses. Akhnaton's aspirations are celebrated in Philip Glass's opera *Akhnaten* (1984), a "minimalist" work that perhaps befits its gentle and ascetic subject.

After several millennia of great cultural achievement, magnificent pyramids and luxurious temples, the political disintegration of Egypt began, hastened by the migrations of other Near Eastern peoples. Internal dissensions finally precipitated the breakup of the empire of the Pharaohs after 1000 BC.

* * *

Among the various Western peoples that entered history during the decline of Imperial Egypt were the Hebrews, adherents of a unique religion and descendants of the patriarch Abraham. Eventually enslaved by the Egyptians, they were led into freedom by Moses around 1280 BC and reached Canaan. The miraculous events surrounding the Exodus as related in the Old Testament have inspired musical masterpieces through the centuries. The text of Handel's oratorio *Israel in Egypt* (1739), with its moving narratives and magnificent choruses, was taken from the Old Testament in its entirety. Rossini's opera *Mosè in Egitto* (1818) also follows the biblical line in its essentials but, in an effort to make its subject more "operatic", the librettist Tottola invented a romance between the Pharaoh's son Osiris and Anaïs, the daughter of the Biblical Miriam. The opera ends with the parting of the Red Sea and the destruction of the Pharaoh's army. According to Stendhal's eyewitness account, this scene was greeted by the Naples audience of 1818 with gales of laughter; since *Mosè* is still occasionally revived in Italy, modern stage directors have obviously found ways to handle it. Schoenberg's *Moses und Aron* (1954), to the composer's own text, deals with the mission of Moses, the episode of the Golden Calf, and, primarily, the philosophical conflict between Moses, the thinker, and Aron, the practical man of action. The brothers dominate the drama, but there are many subsidiary roles, a vast chorus, and "four naked virgins", required for the second-act orgy. The Red Sea causes no problem here—Act III remained uncomposed.

Thanks mainly to Handel, the historical aspects of the Old Testament are eloquently treated in such dramatic oratorios as *Samson* (1743), *Jephtha*

(1752), *Saul*—the first king of Israel, 1002-1000 BC—(1739), and *Solomon* (1749), though these eventful biblical centuries were not overlooked by later composers such as Camille Saint-Saëns (*Samson et Dalila,* 1877), Carl Nielsen (*Saul and David,* 1901), and Arthur Honegger (*Le roi David,* 1921). Sadly, the Fall of Troy, monumentally described by Homer and Virgil, cannot be accepted as authentic history, though the period is wishfully placed in the late thirteenth, early twelfth century BC. What fabulous operatic events are conjured up by the mere names of Dido and Aeneas (Purcell and Berlioz), Agamemnon and Iphigenia (Gluck), Electra (Mozart and Richard Strauss), not to overlook the cause of it all: Helena, Paris, and Menelaus (Richard Strauss and, if you will, Offenbach). Metastasio's text of *Didone abbandonata* alone was set by twelve composers between 1723 and 1824!

The Jewish state was conquered around 600 BC by the Assyrian king Nebuchadnezzar II, marking the start of the Babylonian Captivity. The invaders destroyed the Temple of Solomon in Jerusalem (which had been consecrated in 955 BC) in 586, which is the date specified by the Italian playwright Temistocle Solera for Verdi's third opera, *Nabucco* (1842). Two scenes of this opera take place in the legendary Hanging Gardens of Babylon, one of the wonders of the ancient world, founded, according to legend, by the Queen Semiramis (heroine of Rossini's 1823 *Semiramide*). *Nabucco* ends with the blasphemous king's conversion to the faith of Jehovah after a priestly prophecy that Babylon would fall. The figure of the Hebrew priest Zaccaria was clearly inspired by the biblical prophets Jeremiah and Ezekiel. (According to the Book of Daniel, Nebuchadnezzar went mad and died in 560 BC.) The Babylonian state was overrun by the Persians under Cyrus the Great in 538, who allowed the Israelites to return and restore their Temple.

During the span of nearly a century that followed, a succession of Persian kings ruled over the Near Eastern empire. It was the century also of Confucius, Buddha, and Zoroaster, something of a zenith of human wisdom; the Zoroastran teachings, which became the official Persian religion, anticipated in many respects the tenets and practices of Christianity. Cyrus the Great (553-529) is gratefully remembered in operatic history largely due to Pietro Metastasio, the most successful librettist of the eighteenth century, whose *Siroe* was set to music by Vinci (1726), Handel (1728), Hasse (1733), and Piccinni (1759). (Ten other operas about Siroe/Cyrus were written to non-Metastasian texts.) Darius I (522-485) inherited the wisdom of his predecessor. He divided his empire into 30 satrapies (provinces) and introduced far-reaching reforms in the fields of currency and taxation—but these achieve-

THE NEAR EAST AND GREECE

Important cities of Ægean
Civilization underlined, i.e.. Troy

Forest
Woodland, Grass and
Cultivable Land
Steppe
Semi-desert and Desert

CASPIAN SEA
MEDIA
PERSIA
Pasargadae
Persepolis
PERSIAN GULF
ELAM
Ecbatana
Susa
Behistun Rock
ROYAL ROAD
ZAGROS MTS.
SUMER
Ur
Nippur
BABYLONIA
Agade
MESOPOTAMIA
ARABIA
ASSYRIA
Nineveh
Assur
Tigris
Euphrates R.
CAUCASUS MTS.
Caucasian Gates
Kura R.
Aras
Araxes R.
L. Urmia
ARMENIA
L. Van
Carchemish
ROYAL
PERSIAN R.
Trebizond (Trapezus)
BLACK SEA
Bosporus Khani
(Hattush)
Halys R.
ASIA MINOR
Hittites
TAURUS MTS.
Tarsus
Antioch
Damascus
SYRIA
Orontes R.
PHOENICIA
Sidon
Tyre
Jordan R.
Jerusalem
Dead Sea
PALESTINE
Jaffa (Joppa)
Mt. Sinai
PENINSULA OF SINAI
RED SEA
ARABIA
East from Greenwich
Byzantium
Bosporus
Sea of Marmora
Troy (Ilium)
Sardis
Ephesus
Miletus
CNOSSUS
CRETE
CYPRUS
MEDITERRANEAN SEA
ÆGEAN SEA
BALKAN MTS.
Orchomenus
Corinth
Mycenae
Tiryns
Argos
Sparta
Nile Delta
Alexandria
Memphis
L. Fayum
EGYPT
Nile R.
Thebes (Karnak)
Oasis of Siwa (Amon)
Cyrene
Longitude

ments, however worthy, are not the kind to attract creators of opera. That was not the case with Xerxes I (485-465), who fought great battles against the Greeks (including the famous one at Thermopylae in 480) and whose name is immortalized in the operas of Cavalli (1654), Bononcini (1694), and Handel (1738). Handel's *Serse* may be more of a lover than a warrior, but he is also the image of benevolence in the best tradition of Baroque operas. In any case, he has the privilege of singing the beautiful *"Ombra mai fu"* aria early in the action. One notes with regret, however, that the historical Xerxes was assassinated in 465 BC, an event that precipitated the decline of the Persian empire.

With the waning years of that empire came the rise of the Greek states—mainly Athens and Sparta—in terms of military power and cultural achievements. Athens stood for the pursuit of pleasure and knowledge, while Sparta was synonymous with discipline and military strength. Pericles, a visionary leader who ascended to power around 460, embodies the spirit of Athens during its golden period. What posterity recalls as the Periclean Age of Athenian Democracy produced philosophers like Socrates, poet-playwrights like Aeschylus, Sophocles, Euripides and Aristophanes, historians like Herodotus, and artists like Phydias. The dramatic masterpieces of this period, dealing with the legends of Antigone, Medea, Oedipus, and the accursed house of Agamemnon, were the inspiration of countless musico-dramatic works through the centuries. Even a partial list is impressive: Gluck's *Iphigénie en Aulide* (1774) and *Iphigénie en Tauride* (1778), Cherubini's *Ifigenia in Aulide* (1788) and *Médée* (1797), Mayr's *Medea in Corinto* (1813), Richard Strauss's *Elektra* (1909), Leoncavallo's *Edipo Re* (1920), Stravinsky's *Oedipus Rex* (1927), Enescu's *Oedipe* (1936). Perhaps fittingly, the sharp comedies of Aristophanes found later reverberations in operettas like Paul Lincke's *Lysistrata* (1902), a similar fate that befell the sculptor Phydias, a principal character in Suppé's *Die schöne Galathea* (1865).

Pericles fell victim to the plague in 429 BC. A protracted war between the rival city states of Athens and Sparta ended when the Spartans destroyed Athens as a military power, and the disappearance of Athenian democracy was soon to follow. Socrates, a brave philosopher, in re-examining traditional Greek morality held the view that individual conscience was a better guide to conduct than society's demands. His teachings were eventually considered dangerous and corrupting of the younger generation. When brought to trial, Socrates refused to recant and was ordered to drink hemlock. His pupil

Plato, who witnessed the master's death in 399, carried on his teachings, while music remembers the Athenian sage in such divergent works as Telemann's *Der geduldige Sokrates* (1721) and Erik Satie's cantata *Socrate* (1918).

Macedonia, a country which previously had enjoyed some ties with the Greek states but remained relatively backward in trade and culture, came under the rule of the ambitious Philip in 359. Taking advantage of the rivalries between the Greek states, Philip gradually increased his political power by undermining his opponents and later (339 BC) occupied Athens. Within three years of his conquest, however, he was assassinated, and it fell to his son, Alexander (356-323), to consolidate his rule.

Alexander shared his father's admiration of Hellenic culture, and entertained the vision of uniting the entire world in a giant confederation based on Greek models. He himself was a pupil of Aristotle (384-322), from whom he learned to appreciate the arts and sciences. By nature a generous man, Alexander also had a cruel streak which surfaced in 336 when he put down the insurrection of Thebes. His quest for world domination began with the conquest of Persia, a feat achieved in 330 without losing a single battle. As able an administrator as he was a soldier on the field of battle — and, not unmindful of posterity — he founded many cities, including sixteen that bore his own name. The first and most famous among them was the Egyptian city which came to assume great significance in the centuries ahead. His attempts to unite Greeks and Persians into one nation, however, were not successful, and gave rise to several conspiracies.

In 327, after completing his conquest of the Persian empire, Alexander set out to conquer India, defeating the large and well-trained armies of the Indian king Porus. He then continued his march onward without fully realizing the vastness of the country he intended to conquer. Food shortages and a heat so intense that horses could not tolerate it eventually caused Alexander to check his advance. In the spring of 323, on his way home, his robust health could not withstand the fever that struck him, and this great general and conqueror died in Babylon, not yet 33 years old.

Creators of opera in the eighteenth century paid this remarkable ruler an unprecedented homage. The Indian adventure alone, with treatments by the inexhaustible Metastasio, inspired operas by Leo (1727), Vinci (1730), Handel (1731), Hasse (1731, under the title *Cleofide*), Gluck (1745) and Piccinni (1758 and 1774). Handel chose to name his opera *Poro,* after the Indian king Porus, but five years later he created the festive ode *Alexander's Feast* (to a Dryden text) as an additional tribute, having previously written

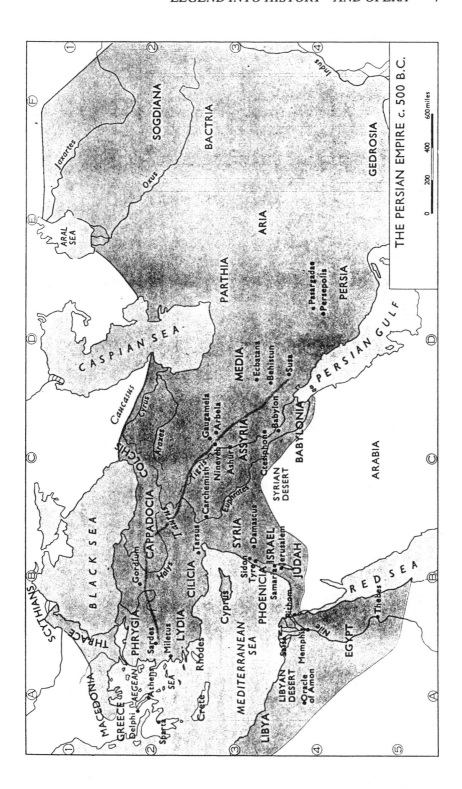

THE PERSIAN EMPIRE c. 500 B.C.

the opera *Alessandro* (1726) to another libretto. Sarti, Johann Christian Bach, Paisiello, Cimarosa, and Cherubini all composed "Alexander" operas. The total number, before the eighteenth century was out, was estimated to have reached a hundred!

With Alexander's death, his mighty empire fell apart. India, Egypt, and Persia reverted to their original rulers; Athens and Sparta again became city states. While politically Greece could never be the same again, the colossal cultural achievements of the sixth and fifth centuries left an overwhelming impact on human nature and imagination, and prepared the world for the emergence of a new age, the Roman Empire.

* * *

According to legends, Rome was founded by the Trojan hero Aeneas, whose mission (as dramatically depicted in Berlioz's monumental *Les Troyens*) was to lead his people to "*Italie*", the promised land. It was Ascanius, the son of Aeneas (still a child in *Les Troyens*), who established the dynasty of the first Roman kings. The city of Rome (named after Romulus, who killed his twin Remus in a fratricidal struggle) was founded in 750 BC according to Tacitus. Several centuries of Roman kings are recorded by Tacitus and Livy, ending with the rule of Tarquin the Proud (534-510 BC). It was the arrogance of this despot that brought an end to the monarchy, an event precipitated by a royal scandal: the violation of Lucretia, the virtuous wife of the Roman prince Collatinus, by the king's profligate son, Sixtus Tarquinius. Handel turned the legendary Lucretia's plight into a passionate cantata in 1707; the same tragic event, ending with the victim's suicide, formed the plot of a French play which, in turn, provided the basis of *The Rape of Lucretia*, an opera by Benjamin Britten (1946).

Rome became a republic in 509, governed by two consuls who held office for one year. That century—a golden age for Greece—was a tumultuous epoch for Rome, aggravated by frequent wars with marauding Gauls and neighboring Latins and Samnites, as well as constant internal struggles between patrician and plebeian factions. The historians Livy and Plutarch relate continuous wars between Romans and their enemies through the fourth and third centuries, including the vain attempts of Pyrrhus of Epirus (credited with the dubious glory of the "Pyrrhic" victories) to break Rome's mastery of the Italian soil.

There followed two bloody wars with Carthage for domination of the

Mediterranean.* The First Punic War (264-241—the word derives from "Phoenician") resulted in the Roman conquest of Sicily, Sardinia, and Corsica. In the Second Punic War (218-202), Rome came close to destruction when the Carthagenian general Hannibal, leading a great army supported by elephants, defeated several Roman armies and menaced the city itself (*"Hannibal ante portas!"*). But after intense battles and successful Roman counterattacks led by Scipio Africanus, the Roman forces triumphed at Zama (202 BC), drove out the Carthagenians, and conquered Spain, which was divided into two Roman provinces. Roman hero that he was, Scipio Africanus received his operatic reward by a host of Italian Baroque composers in now forgotten works by Alessandro Scarlatti, Caldara, Leo, and Galuppi.

Hannibal committed suicide in exile in 182, but a Third Punic War (149-146) was needed finally to destroy Carthage. According to legend the triumphant Roman general Scipio (adopted grandson of Scipio Africanus) wept over the carnage and the tragic fate of Carthage—a city state that once possessed immense power and prestige. This younger Scipio is the hero of Handel's *Scipione* (1726), Galuppi's *Scipione in Cartagine* (1742), an allegory by the child Mozart (*Il sogno di Scipione*, 1772), and Mercadante's *Scipio in Cartagine* (1820).

At the end of the Third Punic War—with Greece already conquered in various Hellenic campaigns—the Roman Empire consisted of seven provinces: Sicily, Sardinia, Corsica, the two Spains, Gallia Transalpina, Africa, and Macedonia. Scipio, the conqueror of Carthage, died in 129 BC. Rome continued to be plagued by internal struggles that claimed the lives of several of its leaders. Meanwhile a new generation of enlightened statesmen was emerging: Cicero (b. 106), Pompey (b. 106), and Gaius Julius Caesar (b. 102). In time they, too, were to meet violent deaths. Their fate—and the operas that record their tumultuous lives—will be related in more detail on the following pages of *History Through the Opera Glass*.

---

*   Located in present-day Tunisia (North Africa), Carthage was originally settled by sea-going traders from Phoenicia.

I

THE ROME OF CAESAR

Norma (Bellini); *Mitridate, re di Ponto* (Mozart);
Giulio Cesare (Handel); *Antony and Cleopatra* (Barber);
Hérodiade (Massenet); *Salome* (R. Strauss)

We are in the opera house. The curtain rises on Bellini's *Norma*, the vigorous closing measures of the Overture still echoing in our ears. The scene before us is the sacred forest of the Druids, in Gaul, about 50 BC. In the foreground, we see a ceremonial oak tree and an altar stone. To stately music, a procession enters: warriors, priests and, finally, the high priest, Oroveso. It is his voice—a solemn bass—that we first hear, announcing that the priestess Norma is about to cut the sacred mistletoe to celebrate the new moon, according to ancient rites. But solemnity turns to anger as Oroveso joins the other Druid priests in a fierce choral outcry:

> Irminsul, awesome God,
> Inspire her with hate
> and anger against the Romans...
> God will thunder from these
> sacred oaks, and will free
> Gaul of the hostile eagles...

Norma and Oroveso are, of course, literary creations—but everything else is history. The Druids were the priestly caste among the Celtic peoples of ancient Britain, Ireland, and Gaul. Roman historians—Caesar and Tacitus, among them—left detailed accounts of Druidic customs, rites, and modes of everyday life. In the face of Roman invaders (58 BC and thereafter), the Druids were the defenders of Gaul's freedom. They retreated into their forests and hiding places, but continued to lead rebellions against the hated conquerors. Their political power was eventually broken by Rome, but the Druidic cult persisted until the dawn of Christianity.

In *The Mysteries of Britain*, historian Lewis Spence relates that "the rite which has been described more frequently than any other was that of the ceremonial gathering of the mistletoe." As Spence further relates, the ritual took place on the sixth day of the moon at which time "a white-clad Druid climbed the tree and cut the mistletoe with a golden sickle." Historical accounts do not point to the presence of high priestesses in the Druid hierarchy. The noble figure of Norma is the creation of the French playwright Alexandre Soumet, whose five-act tragedy *Norma* (1831) was the inspiration for Bellini's opera. However, the heroine's immolation on an elaborate funeral pyre, which ends the opera, was a true Druidic act, amply described by Julius Caesar in his history of the Gallic Wars.

How did Caesar get to Gaul? The Rome of his youth (he lived from 102 to 44 BC) was characterized by a series of victorious campaigns and rapid territorial expansion. A period of almost uninterrupted civil war followed after 78 BC. That year marked the death of the strong-willed and ruthless dictator Lucius Cornelius Sulla (who emerges as a fairly benign ruler in Mozart's opera *Lucio Silla*).

The governmental machinery of the Roman Republic was complex; while the power of the Senate was considerable, executive authority generally rested in the hands of two consuls, elected for a term of one year. Paramount in the power struggle after the death of Sulla were Pompey, a former military aide in Sulla's campaigns, and Crassus, a wealthy aristocrat whose stature was strengthened when he crushed the slave rebellion led by the gladiator Spartacus in 72 BC. The resolution of this struggle was delayed by continual challenges from outlying territories of the Roman Empire. One such challenge came from Mithridates, King of Pontus in Asia Minor, a ruler with ambitions of his own, whose quest for territorial expansion had already brought him into conflict with Rome under Sulla. (Racine's play *Mithridate* was to be the inspiration for the young Mozart's 1770 opera *Mitridate, re di Ponto*, a work dealing primarily with family and amorous conflicts in the king's private life.) Mithridates was finally defeated by the Roman armies under Pompey and he took his own life in 63 BC.

Upon his victorious return to Rome in 61 BC, Pompey found it propitious to form a triumvirate with the wealthy Crassus and the increasingly popular Gaius Julius Caesar, a well-connected, farsighted, and extremely ambitious aristocrat. The alliance was mainly political, without upsetting the existing governmental structure, and it enabled Caesar to become consul for the first time in 59 BC. (Both Pompey and Crassus had served as consuls in earlier years.) For a while, the system worked: all three triumvirs profited from it at the expense of Senatorial power. On completing his one-year term, Caesar emerged as proconsul in Gaul, with an army placed at his disposal for the further expansion of the wealth and glory of Rome.

Gaul, at that time in history, comprised the territory north of the Pyrenees and west of the Alps – all of today's France and Belgium. The Rhine provided the northeastern boundary, but Caesar's legions continued beyond the Rhine to attack the Germans, and went on to defeat the Britons, a people previously unknown to him. His victories brought great enrichment to Rome (and to Caesar) but, unavoidably, his ambitions caused concern to his fellow triumvirs.

When Crassus fell in battle (53 BC), the rivalry was reduced to two powerful men: Caesar and Pompey. The latter, backed by the majority of the Senators, declared Caesar "public enemy." This led to Caesar's crossing the Rubicon – moving his troops beyond the stream bounding his province and marching on Rome. In the civil war between the two powerful and relentlessly ambitious leaders, Caesar defeated Pompey at Pharsalus in 48 BC. Pompey fled to Egypt, but there his luck ran out. He was killed on the spot on orders of the youthful Egyptian king Ptolemy.

One can assume that, on learning about his rival's death, Caesar, a brilliant and eloquent leader of men, must have pondered on the meaning of power and the transitoriness of life – much as the title character does in the famous monologue "*Alma del gran Pompeo*" in Handel's opera *Giulio Cesare*. In other details, too, the Handel opera follows history. Ptolemy (the 12th successive ruler in his dynasty to bear that name) had inherited the throne of Egypt jointly with his sister Cleopatra, and it was indeed Caesar who, defeating Ptolemy's forces in a battle that claimed the young king's life, actually established Cleopatra as the sole ruler. There are few known details about the romance of Caesar and Cleopatra, except for the fact that they had a son named Caesarion. History, however, has linked their names ever since, and Handel's account is as good a substitute for missing historical details as any other.

With Egyptian matters temporarily settled, Caesar, on his way back to Rome, destroyed, in a single engagement, the rebellion of Pharnaces, son of Mithridates of Pontus (the young Farnace in the Mozart opera mentioned earlier). It was after that battle that Caesar formulated his famous terse dispatch "*Veni, vidi, vici*" ("I came, I saw, I conquered"). He also disposed of other discontents in Africa, among them the courageous Cato, a politician deeply committed to republican ideals. An exile in the North African city of Utica, Cato committed suicide to avoid capture. As often happens in Baroque literature, Metastasio's libretto for the Vivaldi opera *Il Catone in Utica*, though stressing Cato's bravery and strength of character, ends on a conciliatory note, not at all in accordance with historical facts.

And so Caesar returned to Rome in 44 BC to celebrate his triumphs, to enjoy his unchallenged leadership and, after so much bloodshed, to pardon his remaining enemies. The importance of the Senate – not much in evidence during the previous decades – was further reduced as Caesar became, in fact, the sole ruler of Rome. Not too wisely, he also accepted certain symbols of royalty, thus incurring the objections of politicians, including Cicero, who still believed in the spirit of the republic.

His grandiose plans for the future of Rome were not to be realized. In a conspiracy headed by Decimus Brutus and Cassius, disgruntled politicians who were frustrated in their own ambitions, Caesar was assassinated in the Senate on the Ides of March, 44 BC.

Shakespeare has made history come alive for us over the centuries in his eloquent tragedy with its wealth of quotable lines. As they did for *Othello*, perhaps Boito and Verdi could have done as much on the operatic stage for his *Julius Caesar*. Unfortunately, Gian Francesco Malipiero, whose *Giulio Cesare* was written in 1936 (because "something in the air we breathe today urged me towards a Latin hero"[*]), was not up to the challenge. Malipiero's libretto reduced Shakespeare's drama to seven scenes (in two or three acts). The last words of the dying Caesar – "*Anche tu, Bruto? Cadi allora Cesare!* (*Et tu, Brute?* Then fall, Caesar!)" – are followed by a choral-symphonic ensemble with scenic episodes illustrating the deaths of the chief conspirators, Brutus and Cassius. By way of an epilogue, the chorus sings appropriate verses from an ode by Horace.

After Caesar's assassination, a new period of bloody struggles followed. The fallen leader's co-consul, Marcus Antonius (Mark Antony), whose part in Caesar's assassination was dubious at best, formed an alliance with Octavian, Caesar's grand nephew and presumed heir, against the conspirators. Cassius and Brutus both perished at Philippi (42 BC) and Octavian and Antony formed a new triumvirate with Lepidus, a political lightweight.

Bloodshed, meanwhile, continued and Caesar's heirs, while ostensibly pursuing conspirators, disposed of their own personal enemies at the same

---

[*]   Raymond Hall, in *The New York Times*, 3/1/36.

Norman Treigle as Caesar in *Giulio Cesare* (Handel)
CREDIT: Beth Bergman

Beverly Sills as Cleopatra in *Giulio Cesare* (Handel)
CREDIT: Beth Bergman

time – among them Cicero (on Antony's orders), who symbolized the enduring spirit of the Republic.

Antony and Octavian did not remain allies very long, either. In 36 BC Octavian ousted Lepidus, while Antony's infatuation with Cleopatra caused him to desert his own army. From historical accounts, Antony emerges as an adventurer and a libertine, less impressive in real life than the foolhardy yet well-meaning character delineated in Shakespeare's *Antony and Cleopatra*. Malipiero, apparently still burning with Mussolinian zeal, transmuted Shakespeare's play into *Antonio e Cleopatra* (1938) within less than two years after the Genoa premiere of his *Giulio Cesare*. It follows Shakespeare rather faithfully, as does Samuel Barber's *Antony and Cleopatra* (1966), but neither has succeeded in proving that Shakespeare's episodic play is a fortuitous choice for an opera.

As the eye-filling spectacle that opened the new Metropolitan Opera on September 16, 1966, the Barber work earned a secure place in the annals of opera, but still has to establish itself in the repertory. Musical setting of Shakespeare's eloquent lines is a tricky affair and, for all the canny condensations by Franco Zeffirelli and, later, by Gian Carlo Menotti, the text essentially remains Shakespeare's. History is well served at any rate: after the battle of Actium, seeing that all is lost, Antony takes his own life; and Cleopatra, fearing humiliation at the hands of Octavian, calls for the lethal asp. Octavian thus becomes the unchallenged ruler – the *"Imperator"* of Rome.

In 27 BC, Octavian ceremoniously announced the reestablishment of the republic, but no one took him seriously, least of all he himself. He knew that a strong hand was needed after so many chaotic years, and the Senate was happy to bestow supreme powers on him along with a new name: Augustus. Thus began a long period of order and relative tranquility in which the arts also flourished. It was the age of Virgil, Horace, and Ovid, and also an age of administrative efficiency, relatively free of internal conflicts. Consequently, it offered virtually no inspiration to creators of opera. One exception was *Arminio*, possibly Handel's weakest opera, glorifying the German chieftain who routed the invading Romans at the battle of Teutoburg in 9 AD. That ill-fated adventure convinced Augustus never to venture across the Rhine again.

This peaceful period ended with the death of Augustus in 14 AD. During his lifetime, he had appointed several younger members of his family to succeed him, but outlived all of them except his youngest stepson, Tiberius. When Augustus died, Tiberius was already 56; nonetheless he ruled for 23 years with "great indolence, excessive cruelty, unprincipled avarice, and abandoned licentiousness," as the historian Eutropius put it. "He died in the eighty-eighth year of his life, to the great joy of all men." Suetonius, too, commented harshly about the bloodthirsty Emperor's rule, marked by a daily rush of executions from which not even holy days were exempted. But the truly significant events that occurred during the reign of Tiberius took place not in Rome and not even in Capri (where he spent his last years in debauchery) – but in faraway Judaea in the Near East.

Judaea, a Roman protectorate, was ruled by Herod, one of the Jewish leaders elevated to royalty by the Roman Senate in 37 BC. Under Herod's rule, the lavish temple of Jerusalem symbolized a growing center of power and prestige. But Judaea was a land torn by internal strife, with sharp divisions along religious lines. At least three schools of religious practice, the Pharisees, Essenes, and Sadducees, opposed one another, to say nothing of various smaller groups, followers of charismatic holy men who went about the countryside teaching and preaching. Jesus of Nazareth was such a man; John, who introduced a new act of purifying immersion called "baptism," was another.

Herod, whom some historians dubbed "Herod the Great," died in 4 BC and was succeeded by his son Herod Antipas, whose historical notoriety gained added dimension in opera literature. His palace in the citadel of Machaerus is the scene of Gustave Flaubert's *Hérodias*, the third of the great novelist's *Trois contes* (1877). The situation Flaubert etches is, above all else, seethingly political. Twenty years before the action, Herod Antipas had divorced his Arab wife to marry Herodias, a Roman married to Herod's brother. Now, ruling over disputatious Jews and fearing unrest from the Arabs, the troubled Tetrarch turns to Rome for support. The Roman proconsul Vitellius arrives and Herod provides lavish entertainment for him. But the palace is astir with turmoil. A loudly abusive Jewish zealot (John the Baptist) is held captive in the cistern, hurling insults at the Tetrarch and his wife. A follower pleads John's case, but he is not without enemies among other Jews. At a banquet (which Flaubert describes in lusty detail), an unknown girl captivates Herod with her dance, reminiscent of Herodias in her alluring youth. She is Salome, the daughter of Herodias from her previous marriage, brought down from Rome by her shrewish mother as an instrument of her schemes. The plan works: Salome has Herod mesmerized; he promises to grant her wish, whatever it may be. As instructed by Herodias, she asks for the head of John, a man she has never seen, whose name she barely knows. Although Herod is averse to committing such a politically controversial act, the gruesome deed is done. By then, the revelers are in a stupor and beyond caring. As the party dissolves, followers of the Baptist enter bringing news about Jesus. They take the severed head with them as they depart to join fellow Nazarenes.

It was Josephus, a 1st-century Jewish historian, who first identified Salome as the captivating dancer; she is referred to simply as the daughter of Herodias in the gospels of Matthew and Mark. Flaubert's novel was at least partially inspired by the sculpture on the front of the cathedral of Rouen, known to the author since childhood. His research on the subject was impressive enough to cause the French historian Hyppolite Taine to remark that Flaubert's "eighty pages teach me more about the circumstances, the origins, and the backgrounds of Christianity than all Renan's work."[*]

Painstaking historical research, however, is not necessarily crucial to the success of a Romantic opera. In Massenet's *Hérodiade*, based on Flaubert's story, Salome is infatuated with the prophet from the outset. She rejects Herod's advances, and it is jealousy, more than any other consideration, that compels Herod to give the orders for John's execution. Herodias is as resolutely vengeful in Massenet's opera as she is in Flaubert's story, but her identity as the mother of Salome is not revealed until the final scene of the opera. Salome then stabs herself. Some of the political undertones of Flaubert's story are retained in the Massenet opera, and the proconsul Vitellius appears in a minor role.

Oscar Wilde's play *Salome*, full of glowing poetic imagery expressed in the rich language of the French symbolists, was introduced in Paris in 1896 and went on to a successful run in the German theaters almost immediately. Richard Strauss saw it in Berlin in 1902 and lost no time in setting it to music, using Hedwig Lachmann's German translation. That Strauss followed Wilde word for word is a widely held misconception; he retained only some two-thirds of the original text. Furthermore, where Wilde's poetic style is languidly decadent, Strauss's music is muscular and frequently brutal; it captures all the story's eroticism, perversity, and horrors with his characteristically graphic powers. Just as startling is the difference between the two operas inspired by the legend of Salome. With Massenet, she is an innocent child; with Strauss, she becomes an amoral nymphet, the perverted daughter of a monstrous mother. In *Hérodiade*, Jean (John the Baptist) is a talky but suave-

---

[*]   Ernest Renan (1823-1892), author of the *Vie de Jesus* and other books.

ly eloquent tenor; he turns into a thundering baritone in *Salome*, while Herod, who is merely an aging and lascivious ruler in the French opera, becomes a frightened and neurotic weakling in the Strauss work.

Although a relatively short (for Richard Strauss) opera, *Salome* yields a gripping view of clashing forces. There is the depravity of Herod's household in the shadow of the Roman presence (to which Salome alludes in her first scene, complaining about "brutal, heavy-handed Romans with their barbarous language"). The five disputatious Jews on stage illustrate the religious strife within a community frightened by the stirrings of an emerging new movement. The unrelenting sternness and accusatory rantings of Jochanaan (John the Baptist) are transformed into a lyrical hymn when he urges Salome to seek forgiveness from the only one who can save her ("*Er ist in einem Nachen auf der See von Galilea...*"). Later, both the Baptist and the First Nazarene firmly proclaim the coming of the Messiah to the mystified Herod.

The spirit of Christ thus permeates both of these operas. Placing Jesus on stage had long remained the province of reverential, oratorio-like pageants, primarily dealing with the Nativity. In 1848, as revolutionary currents swept through Europe, they left a mark on Richard Wagner, and he completed some 50 pages for an opera *Jesus of Nazareth*, envisioning Jesus as a social revolutionary. Eventually Wagner abandoned the project, but saved some of its musical ideas for *Parsifal*.

Anton Rubinstein, a composer blessed with less talent but with more sincere religious zeal, firmly believed in a form of sacred opera *(geistliche Oper)* distinct from secular operas, yet unrelated to church functions. He wrote six such operas, initially on Old Testament subjects (*Moses, The Tower of Babel*), culminating in *Christus*. According to one of his American champions, Henry E. Krehbiel, "only a brave or naive mind could have calmly contemplated a labor from which great dramatists shrank back in alarm." *Christus* was to be Rubinstein's last work for the stage; he did not live to see it staged in Bremen (1895). His six tableaux depict significant episodes in the life of Jesus: his temptations, baptism, the miracles, the Last Supper, the trial, and the Crucifixion. Like other attempts since, Rubinstein's worthy effort has vanished into the sea of forgotten operas, while the great story lives on in passion plays, oratorios, and — most controversially — motion picture epics.

Hérodiade and *Salome* both had problems with censorship. Although smoothly launched in Brussels and Paris, *Hérodiade* had to be slightly cut in London by edict of that city's severe Lord Chamberlain in 1907. The cardinal of Lyon decreed minor excommunication against the opera's authors, with the result that ticket sales increased dramatically. In Vienna, church authorities refused permission to stage *Salome* until 1911. The same was true in London and, even then, only a bowdlerized version was allowed (1910). In New York, too, scandal attended the opera's first performance. Reflecting on these episodes many years later, Strauss observed that the notoriety engendered by *Salome* enabled him to build his villa in Garmisch.

II

ROME AFTER CAESAR'S DEATH

Agrippina (Handel); *L'incoronazione di Poppea* (Monte-verdi); *Nerone* (Boito); *Nerone* (Mascagni); *La clemenza di Tito* (Mozart)

If there was rejoicing in Rome when Tiberius died, it was only because the people did not know what was to follow. The new emperor was Caligula, whose eccentricity was exceeded only by his cruelty and arrogance. He demanded to be worshiped throughout the empire as a god, his extravagance exhausted the treasury, and his various bizarre and monstrous acts outraged all Rome. Finally, his own Pretorian Guard ended the bloody rule by assassinating Caligula in AD 41. One might think that such a monster would be too repellent a subject for an opera, yet it nearly came to be: Gabriel Fauré wrote incidental music for *Caligula*, a five-act tragedy by Alexandre Dumas *fils,* in 1888. As the composer's biographer, Emile Vuillermoz, put it, the music "reveals a sensual and pagan Fauré who so well understood the carnal intoxication of ancient Rome."

Caligula's murder left Rome temporarily without an emperor, but the guard quickly filled the void by appointing his frightened and seemingly helpless uncle, Claudius, and forcing the Senate to ratify its choice. The new emperor — aging, sickly, and ungainly in appearance — surprised everyone by turning into an able and relatively moderate ruler over a politically restless empire. It was under his reign that Britain was conquered and made into a Roman province.

Claudius was less fortunate in his domestic affairs. His scandalously adulterous third wife, Messalina, went so far in her effrontery as to stage a mock wedding with her lover. That was too much even for the tolerant Claudius, who finally had her executed. But, and this may seem hard to believe, his next matrimonial choice was even more unfortunate. It was his own niece, Agrippina, a totally unscrupulous termagant. She began by persuading Claudius to adopt her son, Nero, as guardian for *his* and Messalina's son, Britannicus. She then arranged Nero's marriage to Claudius's daughter, Octavia, as a fur-

Carol Neblett and Alan Titus as Poppea and Nero in
L'incoronazione di Poppea (Monteverdi)
CREDIT: Beth Bergman

ther step toward assuring Nero's accession. Finally, to cap it all, in AD 54 she had Claudius poisoned. Nero thus became emperor, and, true son of his mother, he began to rule with the elimination of Britannicus.

Handel's early opera *Agrippina* deals with the period when Claudius was still alive, with Agrippina's efforts centering on furthering her son's career. Her obvious amorality is somewhat mollified by some of the wonderful music Handel wrote for the character. Claudius emerges from the sophisticated libretto as a pompous bass; Nero, a depraved teen-ager, as a shrill-sounding male soprano. Poppea appears in the plot with her then-lover Otho, as victims of Agrippina's plotting. The opera clearly foreshadows Nero's coming to power.

Creators of opera have found a constant source of fascination in Nero. This is at least partially explained by the fact that this willful, cruel, and tyrannical man had the soul of a true artist. Historical elements, too, served to perpetuate his fame: the persecutions of the Christians, which rose to a violent level during Nero's rule, provided poets, writers, and dramatists with rich material for literary exploration.

Nero became emperor at 16, and in the first five years of his rule, he showed restraint under the tutelage of Seneca, his spiritual mentor, and Burrus, his instructor in leadership and military matters. But Burrus soon died and, as Nero began dedicating himself more and more to artistic and sensual pursuits, Seneca's influence waned. In AD 59, Nero established the *Ludi Juvenalium*, a youth festival for art, music, and dance. This he planned to expand to a larger concept of games that, according to the classic Greek example, would involve arts as well as various forms of athletics, to be convened at five-year intervals. Patrician Romans, unlike Nero, held Greek culture in low esteem, and so did the emperor's mother, Agrippina. Disagreements between mother and son were not limited to this topic alone; in a short time, as Nero's annoyance was fanned by his new lover, Poppea, Nero had his mother assassinated.

Agrippina is no longer around to be part of Monteverdi's great opera *L'incoronazione di Poppea* (1642). The action is set in AD 65. Nero is tired of his wife, Octavia, as is Poppea of her paramour, Otho. Poppea also intrigues against Seneca, who opposes her relationship with Nero. Knowing that his days are numbered, the old philosopher, with great dignity, takes his own life. Nero exiles Otho and Octavia and joins Poppea in the final love duet, as the despicable pair is praised by the chorus. The customary moral point in Baroque finales is absent here: love has triumphed, and apparently,

so has crime. But this is a superficial summation of what Monteverdi and his
excellent librettist Busenello had accomplished. Their aim was to show the
power of love and its fateful consequences. They wrote about Roman history
for an audience of mid-17th-century Venice that was quite familiar with it
and certainly knew that, for all the rejoicing at the opera's "happy" ending,
Poppea, too, would soon be brutally killed by Nero and that the emperor
himself would soon meet with a violent end.

Monteverdi presents a portrait of Nero as a lover and a carouser, rather
shortchanging his artistic side. Actually, he took his art very seriously: he sang
and played his lyre in public whenever he had the opportunity. For most of
the Roman nobles, that was outrageous behavior, and most unseemly for an
emperor. Nonetheless, Nero forced them to attend his recitals, and no one
was allowed to leave before the show was over. Suetonius relates that women
were known to give birth during one of these concerts, and some resourceful Romans feigned death so that they would be carried away.

A great fire, originating in the vicinity of the Circus Maximus, consumed
Rome in AD 64. Although Nero happened to be away at Antium (Ostia) at
the time, rumor had it that he was instrumental in starting it with the view of
building an entirely new Rome. The conflagration lasted for more than six
days and caused enormous losses. The returning emperor lost no time in
opening certain government buildings and his own gardens for temporary
shelters. At the same time, born entertainer that he was, he could not refrain
from appearing on his private stage to perform a dirge that recalled the fall
of Troy. That bizarre act launched the legend inseparable from his name that
"Nero fiddled while Rome burned."

To counteract the rumors that he himself was the instigator of the fire,
Nero stepped up his efforts to persecute the Christians, a rapidly growing
sect of the followers of Jesus, the charismatic prophet executed in Judaea
during the reign of Tiberius. He pursued this with savage cruelty and, with
his all-consuming sense of showmanship, turned tortures and executions into
entertainments. Tradition has it that both St. Peter and St. Paul, a Roman
subject, were executed during this period.

Nero had two confidants during the final years of his reign: the patrician
Petronius and the vulgar Tigellinus, two polar opposites, corresponding to
the clashing contrasts in Nero's own personality. Petronius was a sophisticated intellectual and a cynical voluptuary who disdained Nero's cruelties
but appreciated his artistic attainments. Nonetheless, Petronius became involved in a conspiracy against the emperor's high-handed rule in 65. To avoid

being put to death when the plot was uncovered, Petronius took his own life in a leisurely fashion. Gathering his intimate friends into his home, he had his veins opened by a surgeon and rebandaged them. He then engaged himself in conversation with his friends, opening and closing the bandages depending on his own amusement level. He finally expired, listening to poetry, and enjoying every last moment of his life. Before dying, he freed some of his faithful slaves and dispatched an insulting letter to Nero.

Petronius, dubbed by his contemporaries *"arbiter elegantiae"*, is the hero of the opera *Quo Vadis* by Jean Nougués (based on the famous novel by Henryk Sienkiewicz). The operatic Petronius (an accurate if somewhat idealized image of the historical figure) becomes thoroughly disgusted with Nero's bestial persecution of the Christians. He is also tired of living and chooses to die luxuriously: in the arms of his devoted slave-paramour Eunicia. Before dying, he dispatches a final message to Nero, saying that he may continue burning cities and killing Christians to his heart's content, but for the sake of the art that is treasured by both of them, he must not continue singing! Nero's henchmen come to arrest him, but it is too late.

Boito's *Nerone* also features historical personalities. The ruffian Tigellinus, Petronius's real-life counterpart in Nero's coterie, appears as the emperor's trusted companion. More important is Simon Magus, a shadowy historical figure whom Gregory, bishop of Tours, recalls in his 6th-century chronicle as the man "steeped in evil and a master of wizardry... rejected by the Lord's apostles Peter and Paul." In Boito's opera, Simon Mago reveals Christian hiding places and assists the soldiers in their arrests. Just the same, he dies a spectacular death on Nero's orders. The libretto is of Wagnerian complexity and rich in historically accurate detail, though Boito's main purpose was to contrast the cruelties of pagan Rome with the redemptive force of Christianity. Phanuel, the charismatic leader of the opera's Christians, is modeled on St. Peter; while Nero, first sighted on Via Appia carrying a funeral urn with the ashes of Agrippina, his slain mother, is depicted as a deranged, guilt-ridden man. It is the followers of Simon Mago who, according to Boito, set the famous fires of Rome.

At the height of Mussolini's fascist rule, sentiments similar to those that motivated Malipiero's *Giulio Cesare* inspired the aging Pietro Mascagni to write his *Nerone*, based on Pietro Cossa's tragedy. He was concerned primarily with the artistic and histrionic aspects of Nero's personality, along with his inner torments as poet, actor, and singer. Commenting on the opera's much-touted premiere at Milan's La Scala (1935), the critic Giovanni Cenzato wrote in *Corriere della Sera* that "the exaltation of imperial Rome, which has become a living reality in Italian life today, has given fresh interest to the subject and a vivid spiritual stimulus ... to the musician's faculties, still intensely ardent at 70 years of age." Mascagni's Nero is a full-time devotee of wine, women, and song, and combines it all by singing serenades at his own orgies. But his final flight and suicide on the Via Salaria is reasonably true to history.

In all these operas by Nogues, Boito, and Mascagni, the love interest is present, with the introduction of attractive women, pagan as well as Christian — and usually fictitious. In Anton Rubinstein's *Nero* (1879), it is Chrysa, a secretly converted Christian, pursued by Nero while he is still married to Poppea. Historical elements are peripheral, but Rome does burst into flames in Act III, and true to form, Nero sings. In the final act, surrounded by the rebellious guards, the emperor has himself killed by a courtier.

Nero's death, as history records it, was preceded by widespread rebellions in Armenia, Judaea, and Britain (referred to in *L'incoronazione di Poppea*). But instead of attending to state matters, Nero embarked on a lengthy theatrical tour to Greece. He found appreciative audiences there, and for his own officers that was the ultimate effrontery. Convinced of their murderous intention (Vindex of Gaul, one of the principals in Rubinstein's *Nero*, was one of the rebellious ringleaders), Nero committed suicide. His last words: "What an artist is lost!" It was AD 68.

Within not much more than a year, three Roman emperors were crowned and subsequently killed: Galba, Otho (the former husband of Poppea), and Vitellius. Vespasian, suppressor of the Judaean insurrection, was the surviving fourth. He was proclaimed emperor in 70, confirmed by the Senate, and began a new, relatively peaceful era for the empire. (Some years back, Vespasian had barely escaped death when he fell asleep during one of Nero's recitals.)

Vespasian ruled for nearly ten years and, breaking a long tradition, died of natural causes. The Roman historians credited him with a respect for constitutional rule, firm control over finances, and sound statesmanship. He began building the Colosseum (on the site of Nero's private lake) for public enjoyment, and groomed his son Titus for leadership responsibilities. It was Titus who was ordered to besiege Jerusalem when rebellion broke out again in Judaea in AD 70. Tacitus (in his *Histories*) describes the siege in great detail. Encountering furious resistance, the Romans eventually set fire to the temple, against the wishes of Titus. He was equally powerless to stop the slaughter that followed. The Arch of Titus, erected in 73 and surviving to this day above the Roman Forum, celebrates this event, triumphant in Roman history but tragic in the history of the Jews. (The Wailing Wall in Jerusalem survives as the sole remains of the destroyed Second Temple.)

Titus succeeded his father, Vespasian. His reign lasted only two years, but by Jove, what eventful years they were! Vesuvius erupted in 79, burying Pompeii and Herculaneum; Rome burned again in a devastating fire that lasted for three days, followed by an epidemic of the plague, which devoured more victims. Titus, a humane man of many good qualities, did everything possible to alleviate the hardship of his subjects. (Music was one of his gifts; he sang and played the harp, but did not inflict his art on unwilling audiences.)

The Romans respected Titus, even loved him, but did not always approve of his actions. During his Judaean campaign, Titus had formed a relationship with the Jewish queen Berenice, widow of Herod Agrippa II, a woman ten years his senior. He brought her to Rome, fully intending to marry her. (Titus had two previous marriages.) But the Romans, remembering Cleopatra, did not want another Eastern temptress in their midst, and the emperor gave in. In any case, Titus died of a sudden illness in AD 81 at the age of 42, mourned by his people as an exceptional monarch who was said to have regarded a day without performing a good deed as a day wasted.

If the life of despotic and flamboyant Nero was a rich mine of operatic ore, that of the benevolent Titus also served, in its nonviolent ways, as an example of noble statesmanship. Playwrights in the age of absolute monarchs held him up as a desirable role model. Both Racine and Corneille were drawn to the Berenice episode, while their Italian contemporary, the opera-oriented Pietro Metastasio, focused on the emperor's generosity and forgiving nature. Eighteenth-century monarchs, in particular, enjoyed being flattered by such allegories as Metastasio's drama *La clemenza di Tito* (1734), written when both the poet and the composer Antonio Caldara served in the court of Emperor Charles VI. In subsequent years, Metastasio's text was set to music by many more composers, but only Mozart's opera (1791) attained immortality. That, too, was written for a ceremonial occasion, the coronation of Emperor Leopold II (who barely knew of Mozart's existence) as king of Bohemia.

It is hard to imagine a conspiracy of any kind against a noble ruler like Titus, but Metastasio came up with one. It is instigated by Vitellia, daughter of one of Nero's short-term successors, Vitellius. Already in the first scene of Mozart's opera, she angrily dismisses the widely held belief that this merciful ruler "calls any day useless where he has not made a person happy" *("inutil chiama, perduto il giorno ei dice in cui fatto non ha qualcun felice")*. She accuses Titus of snatching her father's throne, then seducing her and faithlessly turning to Berenice *("una barbara!")* with intentions of making that foreign woman his queen. Before the first act ends, Titus announces the eruption of Vesuvius, and the chorus reports that a horrible fire is engulfing Rome. After such literally earthshaking events, the conspiracy is almost anticlimactic. Titus forgives everyone in sight, but cannot help exclaiming in Act II: *"Ma che giorno è mai questo!* (What a day this is!)" In the obligatory thanksgiving chorus, his subjects honor him: *"Del ciel, degli dei tu il pensier, l'amor tu sei!!* (You are the darling of the gods!)" And, indeed, this is how many Romans called the benevolent Titus.

Titus was succeeded by his brother Domitian (AD 81–96), a man of some gifts, yet one whose savage nature caused many cruelties and ultimately brought him to a violent end. Happier days dawned under the rule of Nerva, an aged jurist whose tenure was short (96–98), Trajan (98–117), and Hadrian (117–138), the last two of Spanish origin. Trajan was a model ruler, just and farsighted. He conquered Dacia (today's Romania), administered the empire efficiently, and introduced a whole series of philanthropic measures not previously known to Romans. The more cautious Hadrian, who followed him, divested the empire of some of its far-flung and constantly rebellious African provinces. It was Hadrian, too, who codified Roman law. But, like Nerva and Trajan, Hadrian was not remembered by the creators of opera, and neither were his successors Antoninus Pius (138–161) and Marcus Aurelius (161–180). These five comprised the period historians call the "five good emperors," lasting nearly a century.

It all ended with the emperor Commodus (180–192), remembered by the 2nd-century historian Dio Cassius as "a greater plague to the Romans than any pestilence or crime." Going even beyond that view, 20th-century historian Moses Hadas believes that "if a date can be fixed for the decline of the Roman empire, it would be the reign of Commodus." A progressively militarized society, wars, and corruption beclouded Roman life under his successors, the most bestial of whom was the fratricide Caracalla (211–217). He, too, was assassinated, but not before bequeathing to Rome his grandiose baths. They were part of an enormous building program for which the emperor was criticized by his contemporaries. And yet, the baths gained Caracalla's name undeserved immortality for, ever since 1937, they have been serving as a spectacular background for Rome's summer opera seasons.

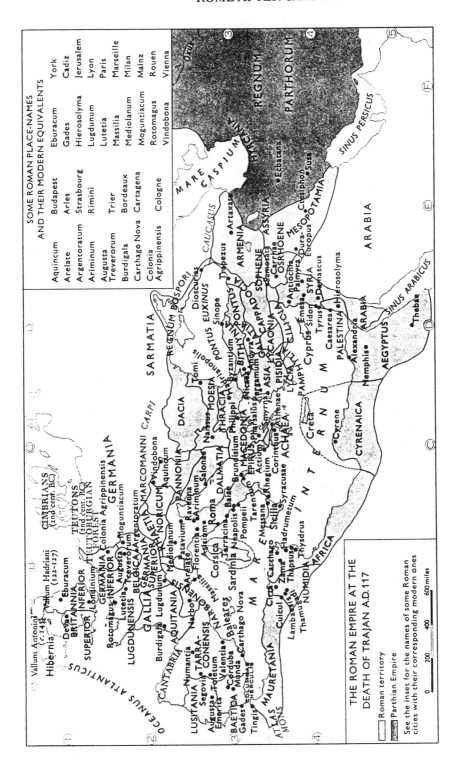

SOME ROMAN PLACE-NAMES
AND THEIR MODERN EQUIVALENTS

Aquincum	Budapest	Eburacum	York
Arelate	Arles	Gades	Cadiz
Argentoratum	Strasbourg	Hierosolyma	Jerusalem
Ariminum	Rimini	Lugdunum	Lyon
Augusta		Lutetia	Paris
Treverorum	Trier	Massilia	Marseille
Burdigala	Bordeaux	Mediolanum	Milan
Carthago Nova	Cartagena	Moguntiacum	Mainz
Colonia		Rotomagus	Rouen
Agrippinensis	Cologne	Vindobona	Vienna

THE ROMAN EMPIRE AT THE
DEATH OF TRAJAN A.D.117

☐ Roman territory

▨ Parthian Empire

See the inset for the names of some Roman
cities with their corresponding modern ones

0   200   400   600 miles

III

THE DARK CENTURIES

Thaïs (Massenet); *Attila* (Verdi); *Belisario* (Donizetti);
La Fiamma (Respighi); *Rodelinda* (Handel)

Corrupt rulers, a weakening economy, and a bankrupt judicial system rushed the fortunes of the Roman Empire irreversibly downward. The depravity of Roman morals increased the appeal of Christianity, an ideology that urged people to turn inward to purge their souls. Despite severe persecutions — Christian worship itself was a capital offense — the movement continued to grow through the efforts of brave bishops and teachers. Under Diocletian (285-305), whose reign was particularly noted for the bloody persecutions of Christians, the faith found a stronghold in Egypt, a troubled Roman outpost ever since the time of Caesar and Cleopatra.

Diocletian's successor, Constantine (306-337), finally recognized the growing strength of Christianity and the futility of the persecutions. After relocating his capital from Rome to Byzantium, newly named Constantinople, he actually gave vast sums to the Christians to build churches throughout the empire. But there was no central organization to bind this growing religion together: individual bishops, who wielded considerable power, at times widely disagreed in their interpretation of the faith.

In Egypt, a deep chasm separated the followers of Athanasius, bishop of Alexandria, from those of a dissident priest named Arius. Anxious to establish unity, Constantine convened the Council of Nicaea in 325. Attended by some three hundred churchmen, the Council established the Nicene Creed, which upheld Athanasius's views, condemned the Arian position, and has remained the core of Christian doctrine to this day.

The land of Egypt was unyielding and poverty widespread. Those hostile to administrative authority chose a monastic life, in communities unified by common discipline, worship, and division of labor. The most ascetic among these were the Cenobite monks, who lived abstemiously and performed acts of penitence every day of their lives.

It is such a monastery in the desert of Thebaid that is vividly described in

Anatole France's 1889 novel *Thaïs*, the inspiration for Massenet's opera. France, an agnostic, saw supreme irony in the tale of a courtesan who achieves near-sainthood, while the Cenobite monk who sets out to "save" her yields to the passions of the flesh. The monk is called Paphnuce in the novel; faced with that inauspicious name, Massenet's librettist Louis Gallet transformed it into Athanaël (a conflation of "Athanasius" and "Nathanael," Christ's devoted pupil).

Anatole France viewed monastic life with unconcealed distaste. "The odor of their virtues rose up to heaven," he observed. Throughout the novel, Paphnuce is presented as a sanctimonious zealot, and the assorted philosophers and theologians appearing at a symposium fare little better. (Their profound but ultimately unrewarding discussions are omitted in Massenet's opera.) It is Nicias, the decadent young Alexandrian, who earns most of France's sympathy. When he observes, "I simply do not see a great difference between the all and the void," it is the novelist talking.

Gallet's elegant libretto softens the novel's cutting edges but, in the end, allows full voice to Athanaël's despair: "God and heaven, all are nothing...nothing is true but the love of two beings." Massenet, who always knew how to combine the sacred and the sensuous in his music, illustrates Thaïs's conversion with an orchestral interlude, the "Meditation," the best known piece in the opera. Its sweet violin melody is plaintive enough to suggest Thaïs's sincerity in embracing a new faith, yet seductive enough to make us remember her passionate past.

Thaïs is an intellectual exercise in sultry surroundings, poised against picturesque Alexandria, *"la terrible cité"* in Athanaël's words. With profound irony, the novel and the opera allow a pagan spirit to triumph at a time in history when Christianity was already a tidal force. Initially, Anatole France resented the changes effected by the opera's authors, but as time went on he was consoled by the knowledge that the opera kept alive his fascinating heroine far beyond the fame of the novel.

* * *

Christianity served as a unifying force within the domain ruled by Constantine. He used religion mainly for political purposes, but did receive baptism in his final year (337) and died a Christian. Except for brief resurgences of paganism, Christianity became a state religion under Constantine's successors. Religious strife, however, continued between various Christian theologies, and the voices of tolerance were often stilled by fanaticism.

This was the age of the great migrations. The vast Roman Empire, divided into East and West under Constantine's successors, was extremely vulnerable to attacks from all directions. Pushed by the Huns, a powerful Asiatic tribe, the Germanic Goths moved into Central Europe and defeated the forces of the emperor Valens in 378 at Adrianople. As the Huns continued their march, the Goths and other peoples moved into territories once ruled by Rome. Rome itself was sacked by the Visigoths in 410, but by then the capital of what still functioned as the Empire of the West had been moved to the well-defended city of Ravenna. Vandals, Burgundians, and Saxons plundered Western Europe, while the Huns consolidated their power over the territories of today's Hungary, Romania, and southern Russia.

Attila, the "scourge of God," appeared on the stage of history around 435, when he and his brother Bleda (or Buda, according to Hungarian legend) inherited the kingdom of the Huns from their father Roua. First they ruled jointly, but eventually feuded, and finally Attila killed his brother. Jordanes, a 6th-century historian, left this account of the fearsome Hun: "He was... a terror to all lands, who in some way frightened everyone by the dread report noised about him... a lover of war, most impressive in counsel.. .and generous to those to whom he had once given his trust. He was short of stature with a broad chest, massive head and small eyes... his complexion swarthy, showing thus the signs of his origins."

In 450, Attila and his Huns crossed the Rhine and laid waste the Gallic provinces. His advance was halted by a combined army of Roman and German forces led by Aëtius (a Roman general who, in their youth, had been Attila's friend). The bloody battle at Châlons (Catalaunum) may have preserved Roman civilization (and Christianity) in Western Europe, but the Huns were only contained and not defeated. Attila reorganized his army and embarked on a new campaign against Rome itself. He began by the devastation of northern Italy and the capture of Aquileia, then a rich and populous city on the Adriatic coast. Its destruction by the Huns was so complete that nearly a century later, according to the 6th-century historian Jordanes, hardly a trace of it remained. The surviving citizens of Aquileia fled for refuge to the seaport of Grado and to the lagoons. There, settlements were formed which eventually led to the federation from which Venice emerged.

To avoid the destruction of Rome, the emperor Valentinian dispatched an embassy headed by Leo, the Bishop of Rome, to meet Attila in 452. What happened at their conference is not exactly known. Attila may have been offered a huge bribe or he may have realized that strategically he was over-extended. In any case, he withdrew from Rome and directed his troops northward, toward Pannonia. Catholic tradition ascribes this dramatic change to a divine miracle. As the 8th-century historian Paul the Deacon relates, "Attila was terrified by the sign of God...he had seen a venerable personage clothed in sacerdotal habit...and that figure held a drawn sword and threatened him with a terrible death if he did not fulfil the Pope's request."

Attila, under the name of Etzel, is part of the Nibelung saga (though not the part Richard Wagner was concerned with). It is undoubtedly this Germanic connection that inspired the playwright Zacharias Werner to write his *Attila, König der Hunnen*, an 1808 play that eventually formed the basis for the Verdi opera *Attila*. But Verdi's librettist, Temistocle Solera, reshaped Werner's drama in a highly Italian mold. As an appeal to Italian patriotism, he made the displaced citizens of Aquileia and the projection of the future glory of Venice a crucial scene in the opera. Also, the line in the dialogue between Attila and Aëtius (Ezio) — "*Avrai tu l'universo, resti l'Italia a me* (You may have the universe, but leave Italy to me)" — resounded with powerful effect in the Italy of the 1840's. Solera also changed the name of Attila's wife from the Germanic Hildegonde to Odabella and that of her lover from Walther to Foresto. In the opera, Odabella, Foresto, and Ezio jointly hatch the plot to kill Attila (in the beautiful, show-stopping trio "*Te sol, te quest'anima*"). In their patriotic zeal, however, Verdi and Solera seem to have lost sight of the fact that they have allowed their Italian characters to behave in a treacherous way, in contrast with the brave, straightforward, and betrayed Attila, who earns the public's sympathy.

In both Werner's play and Verdi's opera, the appearance of Pope Leo attains great dramatic significance. Unlike the play, where Aëtius dies in the battle, the opera follows history and allows him to live for a while. Attila's operatic death at the hand of his wife, on the other hand, is not factually accurate. According to most historical sources, the polygamous Attila took a wife in 453 named Ildico (Ildikó, as Hungarian sources have it), similar in sound to Hildegonde. He died suddenly after a festive banquet, worn out by excessive merriment, from the bursting of a blood vessel. Roman legends, however, subsequently attributed the crime (or glory) to Ildico — acting as the Judith of the Old Testament. It is understandable that this more dramatic variant was used in the opera's conclusion.

According to historical accounts, the body of Attila was enclosed within

Samuel Ramey as *Attila* **(Verdi)**
CREDIT: Beth Bergman

three coffins, gold, silver, and iron, and his precious jewels were buried with him. The captives who had opened the ground were put to death, to keep intruders from such riches, none of which was ever found. The great empire of the Huns quickly disappeared after the death of its mighty ruler. Avars and other oriental invaders settled in the region of Pannonia until the late ninth century, when the Magyars arrived from Asia and occupied what was to become Hungary. Hungarian legends, which sustain Attila's fame as a brave and fearless warrior, credit his slain brother Buda with settling the city that forms the hilly part of today's Budapest.

In Handel's opera *Ezio* (1732), we are allowed a brief glimpse of the general Aëtius, who, surviving the Châlons confrontation with Attila, returns victoriously to Rome, but soon finds himself embroiled in a deadly power struggle. His arch enemy is the patrician Maximus, who covets the throne of the emperor Valentinian III, and frames Ezio so that suspicion for the conspiracy falls on him. Baroque operas being what they are, implicitly bound to a happy ending, Ezio is cleared and Valentinian's throne is secure at the final curtain. The fact, however, is that Valentinian had Aëtius killed in 454. One year later Valentinian himself was assassinated on orders of Maximus, a hated ruler who was stoned to death before the year was out.

Just before Ezio's patriotic outburst in Verdi's *Attila*, he (Aëtius) comments that the ruler of the East (in Constantinople) is old and feeble. That was true enough—the emperor Marcian was to die in 457. In the West, the disgraceful rule of Valentinian and Maximus simply precipitated the inevitable. Their successors came and went, usually meeting violent ends, unable to contain the devastations of foreign armies. Finally, the leader of one of these, Odoacer, deposed the last emperor, Romulus Augustulus, and made himself the ruler of Italy in 476. This was the end of the once glorious empire whose capital was Rome.

Byzantium, the Eastern empire, suffered less from invaders and, under a succession of rulers, was able to preserve its heritage of Greco-Roman civilization. At the same time, the theological dogma of Orthodox Christianity was developed at various church councils during the fifth century, particularly the Council of Chalcedon in 451. Under the reign of Justinian I (527-565), who rose to the purple from common origins, the Byzantine world began to assume its own distinct form. Justinian ruled with a strong hand, fought many battles, but also built magnificent buildings, capped by the great church of Hagia Sophia, one of the most majestic artistic expressions of the Christian world.

Most of Justinian's battles were fought by his great and virtually invincible general, Belisarius, victor over the Persians, Vandals, and Goths in various campaigns (530-540). Despite his bravery and loyalty, Justinian never wholly trusted him, and treated him with ingratitude. On a trumped-up charge, he even imprisoned his loyal general in 562, but eventually restored him to favor. As if fighting heroic battles for an ungrateful ruler were not enough, Belisarius also had to suffer the indignities imposed on him by his adulterous wife Antonina. She intrigued against her husband with the seeming approval of Justinian's wife, the empress Theodora, herself of questionable morals. As related by Gibbon, "the Roman General was alone ignorant of his own dishonor." As for the emperor, while conceding that Justinian was "easy to access, patient of hearing, courteous and affable in discourse," and that "the review of the Roman jurisprudence is a monument of his spirit and industry," Gibbon concluded that "Justinian was neither beloved in life nor regretted at his death."

The pathetic tale of Belisarius, with its grandiose but unappreciated triumphs, misplaced loyalties, and constant humiliations, was colorful enough to inspire a tragic play by Jean François Marmontel (*Bélisaire*, 1766) which, in turn, provided the source for the Donizetti opera *Belisario* (1836). Its action concentrates on the general's imprisonment, pardon, final triumph over the Bulgars (an historic fact, in 559), and death. According to the libretto, Belisarius's sufferings are compounded by his blinding on Justinian's order — a monstrous act much favored in Byzantium, and the fate of many deposed emperors — but historians have refuted it in this particular case. The opera properly charges Antonina for much of the general's misfortunes, but discreetly overlooks her shocking morals. The empress Theodora does not appear at all, Justinian is reduced to a stock operatic bass, and, in the finale, the grieving and penitent Antonina asks for heavenly pardon in words true to *bel canto* formulas: "*Svenatemi... è la morte un ben per me... Ohimé!* [Cut my veins... death is a blessing for me... woe to me!]". The highly melodramatic Salvatore Cammarano, of *Lucia di Lammermoor* and *Il Trovatore* fame, was Donizetti's librettist for *Belisario*.

Justinian initially entertained a dream of restoring the old empire under his rule, but that dream was never fulfilled. Soon after his death, the Lombards, a fierce Germanic tribe, occupied Italy's major cities in a virtually unopposed invasion that, among other things, ended the political importance of Aquileia (nearly destroyed by Attila in the previous century) once and for all. Most of northern Italy came under Lombard rule: Verona, Milan, Pavia,

Brescia, and Treviso. Byzantine supremacy was still retained in the regions of Bologna, Rome, Naples, and Sicily, while the displaced inhabitants of Aquileia, resettled in the lagoons of the northern Adriatic, laid the foundations of the emerging Venice (a century later than the action of Verdi's *Attila* would have it). The Byzantine military governor, given the Greek title "exarch," resided in Ravenna but his authority over the other regions was nominal.

Ravenna's imposing churches with their splendid mosaics were built during this era. Ottorino Respighi, whose tone poems *The Fountains of Rome* (1917) and *The Pines of Rome* (1924) had brought him world fame, became obsessed with Byzantine art, and approached the librettist Claudio Guastalla to collaborate on an opera—*La Fiamma* (1934)—that was to have Constantinople as its setting. The subject they finally settled on was based on a Norwegian play (*Anne Pedersdotter* by Hans Wiers-Jenssen) which deals with the fearful superstitions and the cruel punishment for witchcraft that characterized the sixteenth century. The bleak drama about Norwegian Lutherans was skillfully transplanted into seventh-century Ravenna after Guastalla had persuaded Respighi that Ravenna's churches and mosaics were every bit as beautiful as those of Constantinople. *La Fiamma's* spectacle was further enriched by the rituals of the Orthodox episcopate with its magnificent vestments and processions. The glowing mosaics of Ravenna's basilica of San Vitale (consecrated in 547) provide the background to the horrors of the opera's final act.

There are no historical personages in this opera. As Guastalla related in his diary: "After having explored with great care the period, places, and events, I have allowed myself great liberties, and invented whatever I deemed beneficial to my framework." *La Fiamma* is about Silvana, the daughter of an executed witch, who is married to the exarch Basilio and falls in love with her stepson. On discovering her adultery, the exarch falls dead, and Silvana is condemned to death.

It is an interesting note to early 20th-century Italian opera that this modern retelling of the legend of Phaedra and Hyppolitus was preceded by no less than five torrid plays by the then fashionable Gabriele D'Annunzio, all set by five distinguished Italian composers (Franchetti, Mascagni, Montemezzi, Pizzetti, and Zandonai) *before* Respighi. In *La Fiamma*, the gruesome tale unfolds with music that combines intense passion with the somber colors of liturgical antiquity.

* * *

There were many wars in Italy between the Lombard dukes and the Byzantine forces represented by the Exarchate of Ravenna, while the Eastern emperor Heraclius (610-641) carried on campaigns against the Avars (an Asiatic tribe then occupying Hungary) and the Persians. A new and formidable power also began to assert itself in the East: the Arabs. Mecca was taken in 629 and a Holy War was declared by the prophet Mohammed. The prophet headed his own armies for four years; after his death in 632, his caliphs extended their conquests so rapidly that by 640 the Moslems (called Saracens by the Greeks and the Latin peoples) ruled Jerusalem, Damascus, and Egypt. After the death of Heraclius, the power of Byzantium further declined; its African outposts were lost forever.

During this period, the Lombard kingdom consolidated its power over northern Italy. The Lombards were a warring lot; their various dukes often rebelled against their king. They adhered to the Arian form of Catholicism, considered heretical by the Catholic Church, and Pope Gregory I must have had good reasons to call them *gens nefandissima Longobardorum* ("the most execrable race of Lombards"). With the exception of Rotharis, who ruled for sixteen years (636-652), the Lombard kings were an undistinguished lot. In 661, two rival brothers, Bertharis, duke of Milan, and Godebert, duke of Pavia, inherited the throne. Taking advantage of their rivalry, Grimwald, duke of Benvento, interfered (with the encouragement of Garibald, duke of Turin), killed one of the brothers (Godebert), and had himself crowned as king of Lombardy in 662. Bertharis, the younger brother, fled first to the Avars, then to the Franks.

This is the background of Handel's *Rodelinda* (1725), in which these historical characters are present, with their names suitably Italianized. The opera opens as Rodelinda, the wife of the fugitive Bertarido (Bertharis), believes him to be dead and bemoans his loss. To serve the needs of a conventional operatic plot, Grimoaldo (Grimwald) is smitten with Rodelinda and pursues her with his love. This is one of Handel's greatest operas: eloquent in melody and richly descriptive of mood, situations, and characters. It ends happily, with the reformed Grimoaldo surrendering the throne to Bertarido, the rightful king, and the true villain, Garibaldo, dispatched (discreetly, offstage) by Bertarido himself.

History credits a relative of the slain Godebert with that vengeful killing, but also records the resumption of Bertharis's reign, alongside his noble queen Rodelinda. They erected churches near Pavia, and Rodelinda herself had a cloister built. They were, in short, worthy of being immortalized in opera. Their son Cunibert succeeded to the throne in 688 and ruled for twelve years. But the Lombard kingdom was doomed. Missionaries from Rome gradually removed the traces of Lombard Arianism, and that increased Rome's political influence, as well. On the appeal of Pope Stephen III and, later, Hadrian I, the Frankish armies descended on Lombard territories. They occupied Pavia in 774 and, with its surrender to the Frankish king Charles (Charlemagne), the kingdom of Lombardy ceased to exist.

IV

CHARLEMAGNE

Genoveva (Schumann); *Oberon* (Weber); *Orlando*
(Handel); *Orlando Paladino* (Haydn); *Esclarmonde*
(Massenet)

While the vanishing Lombards could still retain memories of the ancient
Roman cultural traditions, the Franks were alien to them. They were a Germanic tribe that settled along the Rhine in the third century and eventually
moved into Gaul. After much internal dissension, they finally united and accepted Christianity around 500. Subsequent Frankish rulers, members of the
Merovingian dynasty, gradually extended their conquests to include the
kingdoms of Neustria, Austrasia, and Burgundy, corresponding to today's
central France and part of West Germany. Surrounded by hostile peoples in
Europe — the Saxons from the north, the Lombards from the south — by the
early eighth century they faced a new threat from across the sea: Islam.

The Islamic presence in Europe was the result of brutal battles in Africa
for Moslem supremacy between the Abbasid and Umayyad factions. Eventually the former prevailed, and established an Abbasid dynasty that ruled
for 500 years, with Bagdad as the center of the caliphate. The Umayyad forces, meanwhile, sought expansion northward and gained control of the
Mediterranean sea lanes. In 711 they crossed the straits of Gibraltar and
within a few years conquered most of Spain. Abd al-Rahman, their ruler, established Córdoba as the seat of his caliphate, and for centuries thereafter,
Arab civilization flourished in Spain, bringing relative stability and
prosperity to a land that had been torn by conflicts in earlier times.

In 732, bent on further conquests and taking advantage of the unsettled
conditions within the Frankish kingdom, Abd al-Rahman led his forces far
into France. But they were stopped by a powerful Frankish army led by Charles Martel in a battle between Tours and Poitiers and were forced to retreat
to the Pyrenees. This crucial battle provides the background for Robert
Schumann's only opera, *Genoveva* (1848).

Right in the first scene, Hidulfus, bishop of Trier, exhorts an assemblage of knights and squires:

> Take arms to fight a battle that pleases the Lord,
> Against the arch-enemy of our faith,
> Abd al-Rahman, who from Spain
> has broken into France...
> Appalled by his outrages,
> The mighty Charles Martel rises up
> And calls upon the warriors of his realm
> To punish his insolence with the sword

Thereupon the chorus cries out its enthusiasm "to do battle and go to our death for Christ the Lord." And off they march under the leadership of Count Siegfried, Charles Martel's designated general. The Genoveva of the opera is the legendary Geneviève of Brabant, Siegfried's chaste wife, who is falsely accused of infidelity. After she suffers many indignities and is sentenced to death, her innocence is finally revealed in a scene suggesting divine intervention, the guilty are punished, and Geneviève is happily reunited with her husband. The legend had been treated in German literature by Ludwig Tieck and Friedrich Hebbel, and Schumann used both sources to shape his own libretto. But he was not a composer for the stage, and Hanslick's century-old verdict on *Genoveva*, "it suffers from the central incurable condition of being undramatic," sums up its essential weakness.[*]

Charles Martel, who died in 741, did not seek the Frankish throne, but his son Pepin the Short did, establishing the Carolingian dynasty, so named because many of their rulers were called Charles ("Carolus"). The first — and greatest — among them was Pepin's son, remembered in history as Charlemagne.

As his father before him, Charlemagne allied himself with the Pope, and solidified his rule in Italy after the subjugation of the Lombards. He was a strong-minded and farsighted ruler, whose imposing stature, personal

---

[*] Offenbach wrote an outrageous operetta parody called *Geneviève de Brabant,* whose absurd plot defies condensation. It was premiered in 1859. One of its numbers, "*Couplets des deux hommes d'armes*", provided the melody for the United States Marines' Hymn "From the Halls of Montezuma" in 1918.

courage, and bold actions inspired legends that, in all likelihood, further enhanced his historical importance. His battles, however, were real and bloody: he repulsed the invasion of the Avars, defeated the pagan Saxons, and embarked on an ill-fated campaign against Abd al-Rahman. That ended with the withdrawal of the Frankish army, whose rearguard was ambushed at Roncesvalles in 778, with tragic consequences to some of Charlemagne's knights. But since the Roland of legend was one of those who fell, the pass of Roncesvalles was destined to become a peerless breeding ground for poetry and opera.

In 800, Charlemagne was crowned emperor by Pope Leo III. Subsequent popes cited this event as proof of their spiritual dominance over later emperors, while future emperors claimed imperial sovereignty in church as well as worldly affairs. This duality remained an issue for centuries to come. It raised its operatic head in Verdi's *Don Carlos* where the Grand Inquisitor thunders at King Philip:

> You wish to shake with your feeble hand
> The holy yoke extended over the Roman universe!
> Return to your duty! The Church, a kindly mother,
> can again welcome a sincere repentance.

There were historians in Charlemagne's court, and one of them, Einhard, in his affectionate portrait of the monarch, left an account of the friendly relationship that existed between Charlemagne and the equally legendary Harun al Rashid, the Abbasid caliph of Bagdad. The two rulers exchanged emissaries and gifts, most notable among which was the elephant named Abul Abbas, jubilantly received but doomed to a short life in inclement Frankland.

Bagdad, the splendid capital of the *Thousand and One Nights,* cast a spell on many writers of opera. Carl Maria von Weber's one-act singspiel *Abu Hassan* (1811) has Harun al Rashid in the cast as the genial protector of his roguish favorite Abu Hassan. A similarly generous and forgiving caliph (suggesting Harun) appears in Peter Cornelius's *Der Barbier von Bagdad* (1858), an opera with a highly complicated plot in an ingenious musical setting. In an earlier opéra comique, Boieldieu's *Le calife de Bagdad* (1800), the caliph Isauun roams the streets of Bagdad in disguise, falls in love and, after a series

Karl der Grosse (Charlemagne) by Albrecht Dürer
CREDIT: Culver Pictures Inc.

of surprising events, plays Prince Charming to an oriental Cinderella named Zétulbé.

The friendship between Charlemagne and Harun al Rashid gave rise to the fantastic tale of Huon de Bordeaux, as related by the German poet Wieland in his *Oberon* (1780). That literary work, in turn, was the source for Planché's hopelessly inept libretto that kept Weber's opera *Oberon* (1826) from becoming the worldwide success its magnificently colorful and dramatic music would have deserved. In the opera's second act, which takes place in the caliph's palace, Huon abducts Harun's all too willing daughter Rezia with the aid of Oberon, king of the fairies. After a shipwreck and other adventures, Huon takes her to Charlemagne's court and there, having proved his bravery, he is forgiven for an earlier misdeed.

This is, of course, all fantasy, but the Carolingian historians recorded many instances of Charlemagne's generosity during his long reign that assured his empire an enormous prestige in Europe. Its southwestern border placed the Pyrenees (and Barcelona) within the Frankish domain, which extended northward to include all of today's France, Holland, Belgium, Bavaria, Saxony, Lombardy, central Italy, and virtually all of today's Austria. Charlemagne set up a system of "marches" (frontier districts) under local administrators called "margraves" who were directly responsible to him. The emperor administered his vast domain well and dispensed justice with fairness. He admired learning and treated the scholars in his court respectfully. Aachen (Aix-la-Chapelle) became his chosen capital in 800, and he had a royal chapel built there, instructing his architects to take Ravenna's San Vitale as their model.

It is in the subterranean vault of that chapel, containing the tomb of Charlemagne, that the third act of Verdi's *Ernani* takes place. His 16th-century namesake, Charles, King of Spain, awaits his appointment by the electors as the new Holy Roman Emperor, but he is there in the vault to uncover a conspiracy directed against him by political enemies. Moved by the solemnity of the place, the king apostrophizes the dead Emperor Charlemagne:

> *O sommo Carlo, più del tuo nome*
> *le tue virtudi aver vogl'io,*
> *sarò lo giuro a te ed a Dio*
> *delle tue geste imitator...*
> *A Carlo Magno sia gloria e onor!*

O supreme Charles, more than your fame
I wish to have your virtues;
I shall be, I swear to you and to God,
Emulator of your great deeds...
Glory and honor to Charlemagne!

In the spirit of his famed predecessor, the king (the future Emperor Charles V) pardons his political enemies in a grand benevolent gesture, which Verdi turned into a magnificent ensemble finale for the third act of *Ernani*.

To be operatically remembered in works like *Ernani* and *Oberon* is respectable homage by any standard, but Charlemagne's operatic fame pales alongside the mythical image of Roland, the dead hero of Roncesvalles. With the spreading of Christianity over Western Europe, the age of the rough warriors yielded to an era where knightly adventures were glorified in song by the wandering troubadours and trouvères of the twelfth century. Perhaps the greatest epic of the age, the *Chanson de Roland*, transformed the fallen knight into a nephew of Charlemagne and a hero of superlative valor. And, though historians assure us that Roland and his fellow knights were ambushed by the Christian Basques they had come to liberate, the *Chanson* turned their killers into "infidel" Moslems.

Later, in the age of the Renaissance, the poets were still fueling the flames of this anti-Moslem attitude in such epic poems as *Orlando innamorato* by Matteo Boiardo and *Orlando furioso* by Lodovico Ariosto (1474-1533), court poet to the duke of Este, ruler of Ferrara. His monumental *Orlando furioso* was published three times during the poet's lifetime, comprising 46 cantos in its final form. Allowing full flight to poetic fancy, Ariosto's epic places Orlando (Roland) in imaginary circumstances ranging freely across the globe. The central theme is this: Orlando rescues Angelica, an Oriental queen, from deadly danger and falls in love with her. But she loves Medoro, an African prince, and this drives Orlando to raving madness. There is also a romance between the maiden Bradamante and the knight Ruggero, a calculated diplomatic gesture on Ariosto's part, since the powerful Este family was supposed to have descended from the union of these two lovers. Sensual love is the main element in this adventure-laden epic, throughout which Ariosto exhibits a bemused air of superiority.

Orlando furioso's impact on Baroque opera was enormous. Benefiting from the great advances in stage technology, librettists eagerly seized upon the disguises, transformations, and other magic devices the saga of Roland

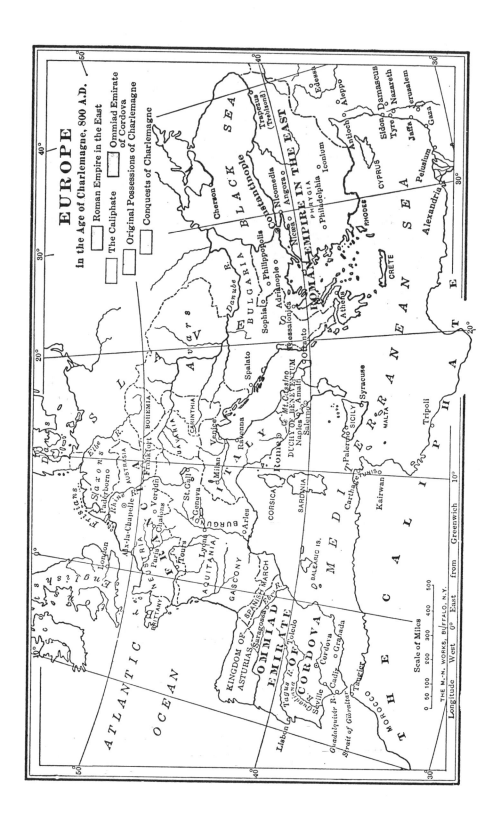

EUROPE
In the Age of Charlemagne, 800 A.D.

☐ Roman Empire in the East
☐ The Caliphate | ☐ Ommiad Emirate of Cordova
☐ Original Possessions of Charlemagne
☐ Conquests of Charlemagne

ATLANTIC

OCEAN

English

London

Frisians

Saxons
Paderborno

Aix-la-Chapelle
NEUSTRIA
Paris
BRITTANY
Tours

AUSTRASIA
Rhine R.
Frankfort o
Verdun
Chalons
St. Gall
Geneva
Milan o
Lyons

BURGUNDY
Arles

AQUITAINE
GASCONY

SPANISH MARCH
KINGDOM OF
ASTURIAS
Saragossa
OMMIAD
EMIRATE
OF
CORDOVA
Toledo
Cordova
Cadiz
Seville
Tagus R.
Guadalquivir R.
Strait of Gibraltar
Tangier
Lisbon

MOROCCO

THE

Danube R.

Elbe R.

THURINGIA
BOHEMIA
BAVARIA
CARINTHIA
Venice

Avars

SLAVS

BULGARIA
Sophia o
Adrianople o
Philippopolis

Danube R.

Ravenna
Spalato
ITALY
Rome o
Mt. Cassino
DUCHY OF BENEVENTUM
Naples Amalfi
Salerno
Otranto

Thessalonica
Athens

BLACK SEA

Cherson

Constantinople
Nicomedia
Nicaea Angora o
ROMAN EMPIRE IN THE EAST
PHRYGIA
Philadelphia o
Iconium

Trapezus
(Trebizond)

Edessa

Aleppo o
Antioch o
Damascus
Sidon
Nazareth
Tyre
Jerusalem
Jaffa
Gaza

CYPRUS

Pelusium

Alexandria o

CORSICA
SARDINIA
Balearic Is.
MEDITERRANEAN SEA
SICILY
Palermo
Syracuse
MALTA
CRETE
RHODES

Carthage
Kairwan
Tripoli
TUNISO

CALIPH

Scale of Miles
0 50 100 200 300 400 500

THE M.-N. WORKS, BUFFALO, N.Y.
Longitude West 0° East from Greenwich 10°

served up for them. There are a generous number of operas based on Ariosto's epic; here a brief consideration of Vivaldi's *Orlando furioso* (1727), Handel's *Orlando* (1733), and Haydn's post-Baroque *Orlando Paladino* (1782) will suffice.

The supernatural elements in the Vivaldi and Haydn operas are provided by Alcina, a sorceress lavish with magic spells that either promote or restrain the ways of love, but invariably complicate the action. Handel supplants her with a prevailingly benevolent male sorcerer, Zoroastro, given to philosophical and even scientific utterances, and clearly the forerunner of Mozart's Sarastro. Early in Handel's *Orlando*, Zoroastro urges the knight to abandon love — which is a courtly Baroque admonition against licentiousness — and seek glory in war. As to Orlando's madness, Vivaldi is content with assigning the hero's ravings to mere recitatives, while the more imaginative Handel contrives an elaborate mad scene for him in Act II, including a passage that the eminent Handel scholar Winton Dean calls "the first appearance in music of notated quintuple (5/8) time." Still, no matter what the misadventures, the honored Baroque convention of a happy ending is duly observed, and that means that Orlando, his sanity restored, accepts the union of Angelica and Medoro with the proper knightly chivalry.

Haydn's *Orlando Paladino* retains Ariosto's basic love triangle, but dispenses with the Bradamante-Ruggero pair. Orlando is already mad when he makes his first entrance and (true to Ariosto's text) savagely strikes and slashes trees and statues during his opening recitative. The happy ending is retained, but this is not an opera bound by old conventions. Calling it a "dramma eroico-comico," Haydn added Pasquale, an earthy, cowardly Leporello-like character, and Eurilla, a Zerlina sound-alike, to the cast. (Musically, too, there are interesting anticipations of Mozart's *Don Giovanni*, to follow within a few years.)

More than a century after Haydn, Massenet wrote his own opera about Roland — *Esclarmonde*. It is not based on Ariosto but on one of the French medieval romances dealing with the same hero. The magic powers exercised elsewhere by Alcina or Zoroastro here reside in the princess Esclarmonde herself, and, like Alcina, she is equipped with her own magic island. The big difference lies in the musical treatment. Where musical tone painting of passionate love in Vivaldi, Handel, and even Haydn was still tempered by classical restraint, it breaks forth in full Romantic splendor in Massenet: the first scene of the second act ends with a *Liebesnacht* of Tristanesque realism, followed by a Scene Two that is all morning-after languor. Music by then had come a long way in terms of suggestive or descriptive power.

* * *

After the death of Charlemagne, his successors could not hold the erstwhile Carolingian empire. A series of partitions occurred among the emperor's various male heirs. By the end of the ninth century, these partitions would pave the way toward the emergence of modern France and Germany, distinctively different nations with their own languages and customs.

V

EMERGING NATIONS — HEROIC LEGENDS

Ugo, conte di Parigi (Donizetti); *Lohengrin* (Wagner);
L'amore dei tre re (Montemezzi); *The King's Henchman*
(Taylor); *Macbeth* (Verdi); *Le Cid* (Massenet)

As the peoples of 10th-century Europe were turning into nations, history—
especially as viewed through the opera glass—became inextricably intertwined with Romantic legends. Well-known places endow these legends with
an illusory historical validity: the Cornwall of Tristan and Isolde, the Spanish
Montsalvat of Parsifal and Lohengrin, and the Welsh Mount Baden where,
according to some sources, King Arthur's battles were fought. Nor does it
help when these legends intersect: Parsifal shows up among the knights of
King Arthur's Round Table, as does Sir Tristram, the Anglicized Tristan. A
true labyrinth is this world of medieval legends—frustrating to the historian,
fascinating to the musical scholar and, of course, entertaining for lovers of
opera. Wagner studied the medieval writings of Chrétien de Troyes and
Wolfram von Eschenbach as he was working on *Parsifal*, and those of Gottfried von Strassburg in connection with *Tristan und Isolde*, adding narrative
twists of his own. The Arthurian saga, which has been with us since the sixth
century, inspired composers from Henry Purcell (*King Arthur,* 1691) to
Ernest Chausson (*Le roi Arthus,* 1895). Noting the wishful, if unsuccessful,
efforts of historians through the ages to lend historical validity to that awe-
inspiring Celtic hero, Winston Churchill, in the first volume of his *History of
the English Speaking Peoples*, summed it up with his inimitable succinctness:
"Let us declare that King Arthur and his noble knights, guarding the sacred
flame of Christianity and the theme of world order, sustained by valour,
physical strength, and good horses and armour, slaughtered innumerable
hosts of foul barbarians and set decent folk an example for all time."
    Charlemagne's legacy combined the enduring vestiges of the civilization
of ancient Rome, the unifying force of Christianity, and the concept of the
Carolingian empire which Franks and Germans claimed as their rightful inheritance. As their awakened national consciousness propelled them toward

distinct statehood, progress was hindered by foreign invasions: the Moslem threat persisted in the south, the Magyars — a new force from Asia — menaced the west, while in the north, pillaging hordes of Nordic tribes, the Vikings, descended on the British Isles and the East Frankish kingdom. Driven by the unyielding climate of their northern homeland, they occupied Scotland, reached Greenland, and penetrated into Russia. Eventually, they amalgamated with the native populations, leaving a strong imprint on all the countries where they settled.

In 870, Charlemagne's empire was divided between his two surviving grandsons, Louis in Germany and Charles (the Bald) in France. Neither Charles nor his successors could achieve much against the Nordic invaders, and their central authority was frequently challenged by powerful native dukes and counts, as well. Royalty became such an elusive phenomenon that at one point as many as five dukes claimed the title of "King of France".

With Louis V, who ruled for only one year, the Carolingian dynasty died out. That one year, though, was eventful enough to be commemorated in an opera, albeit an unsuccessful one: Donizetti's *Ugo, conte di Parigi* (1832). In keeping with his tender age, the king is cast as a mezzo-soprano *travesti*, while Ugo, the tenor here, is none other than the powerful Hugues Capet, Count of Paris and Orleans. Two women love him in the opera, one of them — Blanche of Aquitaine — happens to be the king's ambitious and contriving fiancée. The opera ends well for its hero, but the fate of the true Hugues Capet was even brighter. In 987, upon the death of the youthful Louis V, he assumed the title of King of France. He was rich and politically well-connected: the Duke of Burgundy was his brother, the Duke of Normandy, his brother-in-law. After a rule of nine years, he died in 996 at the age of fifty-four; his successors sustained the dynasty of the Capetian kings in France for more than 300 years.

In Germany, the last Carolingian rulers were just as weak as their French counterparts. Powerful dukes like those of Saxony, Franconia, and Swabia, or churchmen like the bishops of Mainz and Cologne, held the true authority over their regions. They did realize, however, that a leader was needed to combine forces against their common enemies in case of war. Thus, in 911 the dukes elected Conrad, Duke of Franconia, as their king under the principle of *"primus inter pares"*. Although Conrad failed to strengthen royal authority during his seven-year reign, he persuaded the dukes on his deathbed to elect Henry, Duke of Saxony, as his successor. Legend has it that the new king was engaged in trapping birds when news of his election reached him, and the "Fowler" sobriquet has clung to Henry throughout history.

We meet "Henry the Fowler" as König Heinrich in the first scene of Wagner's *Lohengrin* on the banks of the river Scheldt near Antwerp, surrounded by his own Saxon as well as local Brabantian knights and enough common folk to make up a resonant operatic chorus. He tells them that the nine-year truce with the Hungarians is over, a period used wisely "to fortify towns and castles" and "to train an army for resistance." But now the time has come to fight for German honor so that "none will ever offend the German Reich."

This is Wagner, but also history. The year was 933, the end of a humiliating truce Henry had been forced to conclude with the marauding Hungarians in 924 because his ill-organized armies were powerless to contain the enemy's fierce cavalry attacks. The duchy of Brabant was indeed beholden to the German king under such circumstances. But where did those fearsome Hungarians come from?

They came from Asia, as did the Huns before them, during the time of the great migrations, and for a while settled around the river Don, forming a federation called "On-Ogur" from which the Western nations derived the names "Ungar", "Hungarian", "Hongrois". They were nomad warriors, still heathens in the ninth century when they began their westward move, led by seven tribal chieftains. The most populous of these tribes was the "Magyar" (a name that subsequently became identified with the whole nation), and their leader was called Álmos. It was his son — Árpád — who led the Magyars across the Carpathian mountains in 896, to settle in present-day Hungary. (Operatically, the event is noted in *Álmos*, a highly romanticized account by Mihály Mosonyi, a friend of Franz Liszt. The opera was posthumously produced in Budapest, registered a grand total of five performances, stirred patriotic sentiments, and returned to limbo.)

To say that the Hungarians "settled" in the Danube basin under Árpád and his successors would be a gross overstatement. They retained their nomadic ways and, finding their new land somewhat unyielding, regularly raided adjacent territories, pillaging wherever they could. Thanks to the disunity that prevailed in the west, such marauding tactics succeeded and, indeed, they could exert enough pressure on King Henry to exact an annual tribute from him in exchange for nine years of peace.

Henry the Fowler is the only true historical personage in Wagner's *Lohengrin* — the rest of the story comes from the poems of Wolfram von Eschenbach (whom we shall meet at close range in a later chapter) and other epics of German and French origin. There are, however, several episodes that point to Wagner's conscious observance of historical accuracy. In a letter to Hans von Bülow (June 1867), he insists on the presence of horses in the final act. The development of cavalry was one of Henry's main accomplishments during that hard-won nine-year truce. Only with a well-equipped cavalry and with the aid of the Brabantians could the king confront the Hungarians with any hope of success. Wagner's stage directions, in fact, clearly signify the Brabantian acceptance of Henry's leadership (though this may matter little to modern stage directors), even though we are led to believe that this clearly political move was inspired by Lohengrin's shining presence. Finally, though himself a Saxon, from a tribe that once tenaciously resisted Charlemagne's Christianizing attempts, Henry was a deeply religious man, and thus his solemn prayer *"Mein Herr und Gott, nun ruf' ich Dich* (My Lord and God, now I turn to Thee)" before the duel of Lohengrin and Telramund in Act I is fully in character.

Henry did defeat the Hungarians in a battle in 933, but that did not put an end to their attacks. It fell to Henry's son, Otto I, at he head of a large and unified German army, to inflict a crushing defeat on them on the Lechfeld near Augsburg (955). Thereafter the Magyars changed their plundering ways and, though a significant power in central Europe, ceased to be an international nuisance. When Árpád's great-great grandson István (Stephen) became their leader, he married the daughter of the king of Bavaria, became a Christian, and received a crown from Pope Sylvester II especially for his coronation (the very crown that was to become a political ploy after World War II).

Baptized or not, Stephen was a warrior and, once Christianity became a state religion, he ruthlessly destroyed those who opposed the change. Though historians deplored his excessive ruthlessness, strong measures were indeed needed to turn that savage tribe into a member of the European religious and political community. Stephen did accomplish that during his reign (1001-1038), and is justly regarded as the builder of the Hungarian nation. He was also posthumously canonized.

No less a composer than Beethoven brought the life of St. Stephen to the stage when he wrote an Overture and a series of incidental pieces for actors and chorus to accompany a play by August von Kotzebue, commissioned for the opening of a new theater in the Hungarian city of Pest (1812). Devoid of any suggestion of the bloody cost at which the country's internal peace was secured, the work, richly nationalistic in feeling, hails the king and his bride as a "new radiant sun," celebrates his coronation and, in the final triumphal chorus, prophesies Hungary's future greatness. Beethoven was sufficiently impressed by Kotzebue's dramaturgy — an esteem posterity did not share — to request from him a subject suitable for an opera "taken from history and especially from the darker ages, for instance that of Attila" (letter dated January 28, 1812), but, unfortunately, nothing came of the project.

If Henry the Fowler never felt strong enough to seek absolute rule over the German dukes, his successor, Otto I, was determined to revive the Carolingian tradition of hegemony. His decisive victory over the Hungarians certainly strengthened his image, and his contemporaries soon began to recognize him as "Otto the Great". After having himself crowned on Charlemagne's throne in the Aachen Cathedral, he made sure to seek papal sanction for his ambitious plans. Italy, a land in deep moral and political decline since the demise of the Carolingian dynasty, figured strongly in Otto's expansionist plans. When the unpopular and rather immoral Pope John XII turned to him for protection against his local opponents, Otto crossed the Brenner with an army strong enough to secure the Pope's authority. His reward was the imperial crown; the coronation took place on February 2nd, 962. "Thus by the grace of heaven, transmitted through the blood-stained hands of this young ruffian was instituted what was later known as the Holy Roman Empire," in the words of historian H.B. Cotterill.

Those are hard words, but they reflect the Italian view, for Italians regarded John XII as a scandalously corrupt and dissolute prelate. A contemporary chronicler relates that the Roman nobles witnessed Otto's coronation in gloomy silence, for they rightfully perceived that act as a resumption of German domination. That feeling remained unchanged when, two years later, Otto deposed Pope John, for it simply meant that the right to elect their own pontiffs passed from the Romans to the Emperor. Indeed, beginning with the rule of Pope Leo VIII, subsequent popes could not be chosen without imperial sanction.

Sem Benelli's poetic libretto for Italo Montemezzi's sultry *L'amore dei tre re* gives voice to this deep Italian resentment of "Barbarian" rule. Instead of the usual triangle, the opera presents a quadrangle of love: three kings infatuated with the beautiful Fiora, the symbol of Italy herself. Music as well as text is rich in Tristanesque overtones, but the political meaning is unmistakable: in his first-act monologue, the blind old king Archibaldo recalls how, on crossing into Italy forty years before with his army, *"tutti sentimmo ai primi aliti italici il caldo aroma della bella preda* (with the first Italian breeze we all felt the heat of the beautiful prey)", and "*e questa dea, natante fra due mari, ci parve sola* (this goddess, floating between two seas, seemed to be ours)". In the opera, Archibaldo is a foreign king, ruling over the imaginary land of "Altura". He is feared, unloved, and conspired against. The symbolic meaning of the plot is clear: Fiora is Italy herself; she loves and dies for Avito, a prince of her native land, hates the old king and rejects his son, Manfredo, to whom she is united in a loveless marriage. Archibaldo is blind because he cannot see the true feelings of a conquered people. This, in Benelli's vision, is Italy in the tenth century.

For the England of that period, the invasions of the Vikings proved even more disruptive. Although political unity was achieved during the reign of Alfred the Great (871-899), he continued fighting the Danes as Henry fought the Hungarians. Still, his rule was memorable for its reforms of law and its encouragement of learning. The result of his work was, in Churchill's words, "the future mingling of Saxon and Dane in a common Christian England." Alfred's son Edward ruled as an undisputed king (900-924); his grandson Athelstan (924-940) had his three sisters married to three European kings: Charles the Simple (Charlemagne's grandson), Hugues Capet, and Otto the Great.

Peace came to England with Edgar (957-975). He is the hero of the opera *The King's Henchman*, text by Edna St. Vincent Millay, music by Deems Taylor (1927). In the opera, Edgar sends his foster brother Aethelwold to win for him the princess Aelfrida, daughter of the Thane of Devon. The young pair fall in love and marry but, tormented by his betrayal of the king's trust, Aethelwold commits suicide. In the end, the saddened king berates Aelfrida for her role in the tragedy.

The obvious parallel between this and the Tristan-Marke-Isolde triangle is further enhanced by the British-Celtic setting shared by both legends, especially if we remember that Isolde's "*Liebestod*" is Wagner's invention. His treatment of that ageless love story is but a variant of many; in at least one version, Isolde overcomes her grief and marries Marke. As for the Taylor opera, a German historian named Curt Taubner points to various legends of questionable historical accuracy (*Die Edgarsage*, Halle, 1915). In a 12th-century chronicle by William of Malmesbury (d. 1143) Edgar kills Aethelwold in a jealous rage and Aelfrida builds a cloister at the place of the murder. She, like the non-Wagnerian Isolde, ends up by marrying Edgar for, as that unromantic early chronicler observed, she was rather pleased by the thought of becoming queen.

Returning to English history, the Danish King Canute ruled England from 1016 to 1035 in relative peace. His armies invaded Scotland, a divided land where two rival kings, Macbeth of the North and Malcolm II of the South submitted and paid tribute to him. According to bare historical facts, Macbeth was the son of Findlaech, slain by his own people around 1020. He was succeeded by Malcolm, son of Findlaech's brother Malbride. The next ruler, Gillecomgain (Malcolm's brother), was killed in 1032, probably by Macbeth, who then married Gruach, Gillecomgain's widow. Unlike Banquo, Malcolm, Duncan, and MacDuff — all mentioned by name in Holinshed's Chronicle, Shakespeare's source — Macbeth's evil wife is not identified there by name. "Lady Macbeth" was the way she was immortalized in Shakespeare's play, her ominous stature vastly enhanced.

Holinshed's *Chronicles of England and Scotland* (published in 1577) has long been discredited by historians, and Shakespeare dealt freely with the events related therein. Of course, it is somewhat disappointing to students of Shakespeare's drama and Verdi's opera to find their liveliest episodes undocumented in verified historical accounts. The Honorable R. Erskine of Marr in his study *Macbeth* endeavored to discover the real character and to sketch conditions in ancient Scotland before feudalism. According to that author, Duncan, grandson of Malcolm II, became King of South Scotland, and died in a battle against Macbeth in 1040. Macbeth then ruled until 1057, when he was defeated by Duncan's son, the future Malcolm III, and died in the battle of Lumphannan. To trace Scottish history a bit further, Malcolm III (1059-1093) fought the English and achieved independence for Scotland.

Shakespeare and Verdi took the witches, Banquo, and Burnam Wood from Holinshed. But the monologues, Banquo's ghost, and Lady Macbeth's Sleepwalking Scene are Shakespeare's invention. Verdi, who turned these inventions into the most memorable episodes in his opera *Macbeth*, regarded the Shakespeare play "one of the greatest creations of man," and, dedicating his opera to his dearly beloved father-in-law, Antonio Barezzi, called his *Macbeth* "dearer to me than all of my other operas and which I therefore deem more worthy of being presented to you" (1847).

Verdi's early, flawed, yet magnificent opera proved too awesome a standard for Ernest Bloch's later (1910) effort to meet. Composer and librettist Edmond Fleg explored certain Shakespearean episodes not highlighted in Verdi's treatment. Praised at various revivals in Naples (1938), Rome (1953),

Milan (1960), Geneva (1968) and New York (1973) for its combination of Debussyan subtleties and Mussorgskian power, it may yet emerge as a viable theatrical work in the future. At any rate, the thought persists that Macbeth, like other personages of English history in Holinshed's Chronicles, may not have been bloodier than any number of unsung nobles of that turbulent era and, who knows, even Madame Gruach may have been a sane, loyal, and unexceptional queen.

Legends indeed tend to obscure the true image of historical personalities like Macbeth. In the case of Spain's national hero, Rodrigo Diaz de Vivar, better known as "El Cid" (ca. 1043-1099), legends merely enhance historical events. A brief review of medieval Spanish history will place El Cid's accomplishments into their true focus.

During the Carolingian period, the Caliphate of Cordoba (see page 40) was the seat of Moslem-occupied Spain, a substantial region including the cities of Saragossa, Seville, Badajoz, Granada and their environs — greater than the southern half of the peninsula. The northern part was divided into the small independent kingdoms of Castile, León, Navarre, and Aragon. Wars between the Christian and Moorish regions were frequent, but so were hostilities within these groups. Fights among rival Arab dynasties eventually led to the dissolution of the caliphate in 1031, leaving the Moslem-occupied territory broken into principalities. The balance of power in the peninsula began to shift away from the Moslems when the warrior king Ferdinand I united the kingdoms of Castile, León, and Navarre and conquered the Arab province of Toledo.

It was during these campaigns that El Cid began to attract notice, and further fame surrounded him during the reign of Ferdinand's sons, the shortlived Sancho and Alfonso VI. The latter married him to his (Alfonso's) own niece, Jimena Diaz, daughter of the Count of Oviedo. This family connection notwithstanding, El Cid managed to antagonize the king sufficiently to find himself exiled from Castile in 1081.

King Alfonso, Doña Jimena, and Don Diego, Cid's father, are principal characters in Massenet's *Le Cid* (1885), but the opera's librettists allowed their imagination to soar far beyond historical facts. In this they were encouraged by the existence of Guillén de Castro's 17th-century play *Las mocedades del Cid* and by Corneille's classic drama *Le Cid* (1636), which adapted the sprawling treatment of the Spanish predecessor to the exigencies of the Comédie Française. With some skillful incorporation of operatic devices learned from Meyerbeer and Verdi, Massenet's plot basically fol-

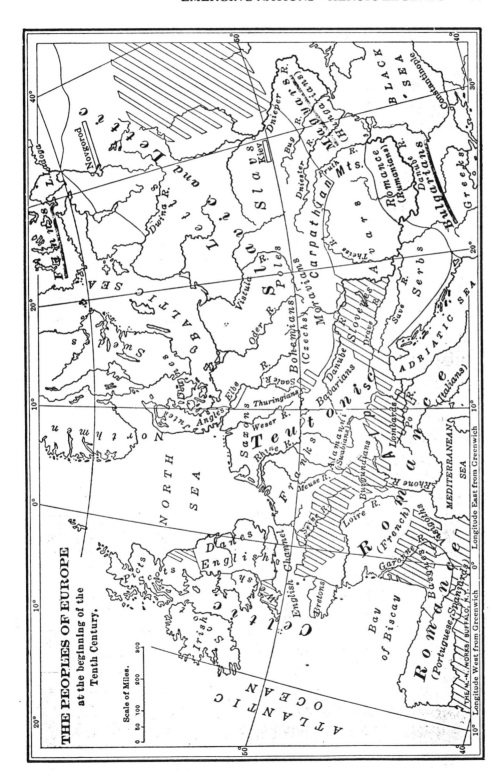

THE PEOPLES OF EUROPE
at the beginning of the
Tenth Century.

Scale of Miles.

lows Corneille. The operatic Cid incurs the king's disfavor by killing one of the royal favorites in a duel defending the family honor. The victim happens to be Jimena's father – a dandy operatic conflict, but with no historical foundation whatever. In due course, the opera allows Cid to perform heroic deeds in battle and to win royal as well as romantic forgiveness.

Exiled from the court, the historical El Cid participated in several campaigns, fighting now on the Christian, now on the Moslem side. (This seeming absurdity was not uncommon in 11th-century Spain. There was, in fact, a great deal of intermarriage between noble houses on both sides.) Although he had enemies aplenty, El Cid was regarded as a valiant and chivalrous soldier, highly respected in Arab circles. (The very name "*Cid*" is derived from the Arabic "*Seid*", meaning "victorious leader".) Eventually, Alfonso readmitted him to royal favors without, however, removing him from suspicion. In 1092, El Cid led the battle that resulted in the reconquest of Valencia, where he lived with his lady Jimena in considerable splendor to the end of his days. His burial place is a monastery near Burgos.

Some of the legends that sprung up about him tend to portray El Cid as a near saint. Quite to the contrary, he was all too human: brave, ambitious, ingenious, with a flair for daring action. In many ways, he was the advance guard for the Crusades, the giant movement that was to inflame part of the world in the years ahead.

VI

THE FIRST CRUSADES

Tancredi (Rossini); *Armide* (Gluck); *Armida* (Haydn); *I
Lombardi* (Verdi); *Euryanthe* (Weber); *Assassinio nella
cattedrale* (Pizzetti); *Rosmunda d'Inghilterra* (Donizetti)

Pope Leo III's crowning of Charlemagne as emperor in 800 alienated the
Eastern Church from Rome and dealt a severe blow to the authority of
Constantine's and Justinian's successors. Nevertheless, the Byzantine empire remained strong during the ninth and tenth centuries. It withstood
several Moslem incursions and enjoyed a period of stability and cultural
flowering which reached its apex under Emperor Basil II (976-1025), an ascetic and stern monarch who reigned over a vast domain after a merciless
campaign against the Bulgars.

But there were signs of trouble for Byzantium, emanating from political
developments in both the Arab world and Italy. Sicily presented a microcosm
of these threatening currents. Much of the island was held by Arabs, but the
various city states — Syracuse, among them — fought for their independence,
distrustful of all foreigners, be they Arab, Byzantine, or Norman.

This is the background of Rossini's early (1813) opera *Tancredi*, based on
Voltaire's five-act tragedy *Tancrède* (1760). It takes place in Syracuse, in
1005. The city's freedom is endangered, and its strength is further undermined by inner dissension. Two rival houses led by Orbazzano (Voltaire's
Orbassan) and Argirio (Argire) reach an uneasy truce, with the former as-
suming leadership and Argirio pledging his daughter Amenaide to him in
marriage. She, however, loves Tancredi (Tancrède), a Norman knight
deprived by Orbazzano of his properties and banished from Sicily. Amenaide
dispatches a letter to Tancredi begging him to come to her rescue. It is intercepted and misinterpreted, causing Amenaide to be accused of treason.
She is sentenced to death, but saved by Tancredi, who returns in disguise.
He kills Orbazzano in a duel, defeats the Saracens in battle, but sustains a
mortal wound.

The opera's libretto lacks Voltaire's political insight and historical detail.

For example, when a subsidiary character in *Tancrède* (Lorédan, missing in the opera altogether) rails against the Arabs for pursuing "pernicious arts" alien to Sicilian customs, it is the historian in Voltaire confirming the documented fact that culture in the Arab-dominated areas flourished at a level attained by few Christian kingdoms of that era. Palermo, in fact, was a splendid city for arts and learning. But dissension between Arab factions continued during the eleventh century, and Sicily remained a battleground between Byzantine and Arab forces. The balance of power tilted again with the rise of a new power in the Arab world, the Seljuk Turks. They occupied Bagdad in 1055 and subsequently crushed the Byzantine army at Manzikert in 1071.

While these clouds gathered over the East, the power of the papacy gained new strength in Western Europe, particularly in France and in England after the Norman conquest of 1066. Pope Gregory VII (1073-1085), a strong-willed man, insisted on the papal right to appoint bishops. The rulers of France and England acquiesced; when the German emperor Henry VII refused to go along, the resulting conflict caused his excommunication. Humiliated, he sought and obtained papal absolution at Canossa in 1077. In Spain, meanwhile, the steady movement of Christian reconquest continued, gaining new impetus with the capture of Toledo in 1085.

When Alexius Comnenus, the Byzantine emperor who took office in 1081, sent a plea to Pope Urban II for unity between East and West in a common effort to drive the Moslem invaders from territories perceived to be Christian, the message fell on sympathetic ears. A strong religious fervor seized Europe toward the end of the century, a sentiment mirrored in the arts, in literature, and in a revival of missionary activities. At a church council held in 1095 at Clermont (near Vichy), Pope Urban delivered a fiery speech, citing Turkish atrocities and urging all the faithful to fight them and to liberate the land holding the sacred monuments to Christianity. Painting an enticing image of a land flowing with milk and honey, the speech was an inspired piece of propaganda appealing to the brave, the poor, the adventurer, and the religious zealot alike. It was received with a roar from the crowd that turned into a battle cry: *"Deus vult!* (God wills it!)". This was the beginning of the Crusades, an undertaking recklessly started and sustained for centuries at the cost of enormous hardships and losses. Ultimately, it accomplished nothing positive; its adverse repercussions are still felt to this day.

Religious zeal was far from being the only motivating force behind the Crusades. The Papacy saw an opportunity to extend its dominion eastward at the expense of the Greek Church. Europe's feudal lords were lured by the prospect of conquest and new riches. Idle armies could be occupied and the attention of the hungry and the malcontents diverted into new directions. Even before armies could be organized under experienced leaders, impatient masses of people surged forth, fired by fanatical enthusiasm. Undisciplined, ill-organized, but large in number, they gathered around a charismatic firebrand named Peter the Hermit. His ragtag army began its holy crusade by massacring the Jewish inhabitants of the German cities of Worms, Speyer, and Mainz. Pillaging their way through Hungary and Bulgaria — and violently resisted by the local inhabitants — they managed to reach Constantinople. Decimated by then, and unenthusiastically received by the emperor, they moved on to the fortress of Nicaea, where the Turks slaughtered what was left of them. Peter the Hermit miraculously survived.

In the meantime, a true army was assembling in France. Its leaders were Godfrey of Bouillon, Duke of Lorraine, and his younger brother Baldwin; Robert, Duke of Normandy (the oldest son of William the Conqueror); Bohemond, a Norman prince from southern Italy and his nephew Tancred de Hauteville, a descendant of the hero of Syracuse. There are conflicting accounts as to the size of the army, but it could have numbered as many as 300,000 soldiers. They reached Constantinople by various routes, frequently ransacking the countryside. But they triumphed. Fighting their way through Asia Minor, and sustaining heavy losses, they advanced through Syria and captured the well-defended citadel of Antioch in 1098. An epidemic in their ranks claimed the life of Bishop Adhémar of Le Puy, the papal legate. Jerusalem fell on July 15, 1099. The Crusaders folded their bloodied hands in prayer when night fell as they knelt at the Holy Sepulchre, sobbing with joy.

With their mission seemingly accomplished, many crusaders headed for their homes and families. Godfrey de Bouillon stayed on as the elected leader of the Christian settlement, and so did Bohemond and his nephew Tancred. But Godfrey died almost exactly a year after the final battle; his brother Baldwin was crowned "King of Jerusalem" on Christmas Day 1100.

Within twenty years, all the leaders of the First Crusade had died, leaving behind a conglomeration of settlements held together in the manner of European feudal societies. The population was predominantly Muslim, with significant minorities of Christians and Jews concentrating in locations like Jerusalem, Nazareth, and Bethlehem. Already factions existed within these groups: Maronite Christians in today's Lebanon, as well as dissident Shiites, an Arab sect from Persia. They coexisted with the rest of the population and tolerated one another, not without a measure of primitive resentment. Hatred came later, with civilization.

The leaders of the First Crusade were men of great valor, but religious propaganda and poetic mythmaking endowed them later with glamor that was larger than life. In his epic poem *Gerusalemme liberata*, Torquato Tasso (1544-1595), one of the great literary figures of the Renaissance, created a fictional history of the Crusade built around a few concrete facts. But his narrative powers were so absorbing, his descriptions so vivid, his language so eloquent, that the spirit of Tasso's poem and his strongly etched characters gave rise to musical masterpieces by Monteverdi, Lully, Handel, Gluck, Haydn, Rossini, Verdi, Brahms, and Dvořák, to mention only the greatest musical creators. Their librettists — for most of these works were operas — were not in Tasso's league, but they were skilled craftsmen who drew liberally and imaginatively on the vast storehouse of Tasso's epic.

Gerusalemme liberata starts its narrative with the crusading armies already approaching Jerusalem in the spring of 1099. The opening lines, recalling Virgil, are:

> *Canto l'arme pietose e 'l Capitano*
> *Che 'l gran sepolcro liberò di Cristo*

> (I sing of the pious arms and the Captain who liberated the great sepulchre of Christ...)

The Captain is Godfrey de Bouillon, who becomes God's chosen leader in the first of Tasso's twenty Cantos. Other historical personalities in the epic are Godfrey's brother Baldwin, Tancred and his cousin Bohemond, Raymond of Toulouse, Peter the Hermit, Solyman, sultan of Nicaea, and Bishop Adhémar of LePuy. Battles are fought and single combat occurs between warriors; the fortunes of war favor now this army, now that one, miraculous things happen as historical and imaginary personages confront one another in conjured-up situations. At last, after raging battles, the Christian victory is complete.

Like his great literary predecessor Ariosto, Tasso was court poet to the powerful Este family of Ferrara, and, like Ariosto, he honored the family by creating an imaginary hero, Rinaldo d'Este, and making him one of the principal figures of the conquest. He, too, like Ariosto's hero, succumbs to the magic spell of a temptress, Armida. Their infatuation inspired Philippe Quinault's libretto for Lully's *Armide* (1686), an essentially pastoral work, but with sufficient sense of atmosphere to paint the magical scenes. Nearly a century later, Gluck provided the sensuality and rage that were not part of Lully's musical arsenal with only minimal alterations of that same Quinault libretto for his own *Armide* (1777). Nor was he wanting in magical evocations, as we note the highflown prose of Hector Berlioz, following an 1843 Berlin performance of *Armide* conducted by Meyerbeer:

> It was a kind of voluptuous languor, a fascinating *morbidezza* that transported me into the palace of love dreamed of by Gluck and Tasso, and seemed to present it to me as an enchanted abode...I seemed to be surrounded on all sides by enfolding arms, adorable intertwining feet, floating hair, shining eyes, and intoxicating smiles.

Quinault's libretto concentrates on the predicament of Armida, caught in her own snare after Rinaldo (Renaud, as he is called here) abandons her to return to the crusading army. Handel's rather inept London librettist, Giacomo Rossi, concocted a different story from Tasso's, short on virtually every essential dramatic element but long on magic. In any case, Handel's magnificent music prevailed, and *Rinaldo* (1711) achieved a triumphant rebirth in the twentieth century.

Haydn's *Armida* (1783), too, has undoubtedly survived on the strength of its music, though the spectacular scenic effects must have helped with its initial success. (Its libretto was concocted from various sources leaning on Tasso.) *Armida* was Haydn's last opera, and Prince Nikolaus Esterhazy, the composer's generous patron, must have had a weakness for rich costumes, marching troops of Christians and Turks, and magic transformations. Without historical personages in the cast of characters, the plot soon becomes tiresome.

Rossini, at least, can be excused on the basis of youthful ambition for accepting a libretto full of sorcery and supernatural happenings dutifully derived from Tasso by Giovanni Federico Schmidt in 1817. That *Armida* was premiered at the San Carlo of Naples, where Rossini was house composer at the time and not in the habit of questioning the judgment of the theater's shrewd impresario, Barbaja. Rightfully judged as an unwanted throwback to the age of outmoded Baroque extravaganzas, the opera failed and eventually disappeared, to be unexpectedly rescued from limbo as one of Maria Callas's virtuoso vehicles in 1952.

And if choosing this much-explored subject by Haydn and Rossini is surprising, what are we to say about Antonin Dvořák? Encouraged by the success of his opera *Rusalka*, in which the supernatural element is provided by a folk tale, he turned to the romance of Rinaldo and Armida to crown his productive life with a Tasso-derived grand opera on a Wagnerian scale. Good Catholic that he was, he wrote a beautiful finale for it — Armida's baptism by Rinaldo (which occurs neither in Tasso nor in any other operatic variant) — and enjoyed the moderate success of its premiere on March 2, 1904. Five weeks later, he suddenly died of a cerebral hemorrhage. There are beautiful passages in his *Armida*, but two Dvořák biographers sharply disagree on its ultimate worth. For Alec Robertson, it represented "his most disastrous wrong turning." But, according to John Clapham, "there is no excuse for the shameful neglect of this fine work today."

The figure of Rinaldo sprang from Tasso's imagination, but the Tancredi of his *Gerusalemme liberata* was the historical Norman knight Tancred de Hauteville who fought bravely, stayed in the Holy Land after the conquest of Jerusalem, but died at the age of 36, probably of typhoid fever, in 1112. One of the most famous episodes in the Tasso epic, however, has no historical basis whatever: he has his Tancredi fall in love with a Saracen maiden warrior named Clorinda. They meet once again in combat, neither knowing the other's identity. After fierce fighting (Tasso credits the brave Clorinda with the death of several Christian leaders including Bishop Adhémar), Tancredi kills the maiden and, at her request, baptizes her so she may die a Christian. Lines 52-68 of Canto XII, depicting this poetic episode, were set by Claudio Monteverdi with the title *Il Combattimento di Tancredi e Clorinda*. A dramatic cantata, it was performed in 1624 at the Palazzo Mocenigo in Venice by a narrator, singers, dancers, and instrumentalists. According to Monteverdi's surviving account, the audience was moved to tears. Fourteen years later the work was published in his collection *Madrigali guerrieri ed amorosi*.

Tasso was a troubled genius, subject to episodes of mental imbalance which led to his confinement in an asylum for several years. But he never lacked friends in high places. Pope Clement VIII was planning to decorate him, but the poet died before receiving that honor on April 25, 1595. His adventurous and tormented life inspired literary works by Goethe and Byron, among others, and — enhanced by fictitious details — it became the subject of Donizetti's opera *Torquato Tasso* in 1833.

A few years later Verdi, too, came into contact with the Tasso heritage. His attention turned to Tommaso Grossi's epic poem *I Lombardi alla prima crociata*, which had been published in Milan in 1826 with some success, though not without a measure of criticism from those who felt that no Italian poet should follow in Tasso's revered footsteps. But Verdi and Temistocle Solera, the librettist of Verdi's hugely successful *Nabucco* (1842), rightly judged the temper of the times: with Italy in patriotic ferment, the public was ready to welcome another canny blend of religious and patriotic sentiment. Actually, Tasso's influence is only tangential; the opera virtually disregards historical personages, concentrating instead on family tragedies within the Lombard contingent. Interestingly enough, the minor character Pirro, a treacherous Lombard, is an exception. He is based on the historical figure of Firouz, a turncoat convert to Islam who sided with the Christians at a crucial moment during the siege of Antioch and facilitated the capture of the city.

Solera pruned Grossi's poem with a heavy hand, and consequently the libretto of *I Lombardi* is full of inconsistencies. Nor is Verdi's music on a par with the powerful and deeply moving pages of *Nabucco*. But there was enough there to stir the Milanese: they identified with their Lombard predecessors. For North Italy in 1843, liberating Jerusalem from the Moslems was a mission no more sacred than their own struggle to free Italian cities from the Austrians.

Four years after the great Milanese success of *I Lombardi*, Verdi adapted his opera for the Paris stage. With the help of the French librettists Alphonse Royer and Gustav Vaëz, the story was totally reworked under the new title *Jérusalem;* the music, too, underwent substantial modifications. In that new guise, removed from the Lombard connection, a French perspective prevails with a closer attention paid to history. The first act of *Jérusalem* takes us to Toulouse in 1095, shortly after Pope Urban's incendiary Clermont speech. Raymond, Count of Toulouse and one of the leaders of the Crusade, plays an important role but in largely fictitious circumstances, and even the papal ambassador (Adhémar) joins the Act I ensemble in a properly inspirational posture. Coincidences and implausible turns plague the French version almost as much as they do the Italian one. Greater historical accuracy has not served to sustain the former on the French stages, while the original Italian version, despite its flaws, is still occasionally revived in Italy.

The Holy Land remained disputed territory despite the establishment of the kingdom of Jerusalem. Internal jealousies among rival princes, the avarice of knights and traders, brutality toward the Moslem population—and their counterattacks—created precarious conditions, but the Christian kingdom managed to last for almost a hundred years of continuous "crusading" activity.

In Europe, meanwhile, there were far-reaching changes in the political balance of power. The Saxon and Franconian dynasties that had ruled Germany died out and were succeeded by the Hohenstaufens, the ducal family of Swabia. Traditionally anti-pope, adherents of the Hohenstaufens were known as "ghibellines" in Italy, the word being a derivation of the Swabian community of Weibling. They were opposed to the "guelphs", descendants and partisans of the Bavarian dukes of Welf, allies of the Pope. The confrontations of these two factions were to cause much bloodshed in Italy during the next century.

In France, King Louis VI (1108-1137) had his hands full fighting the English over disputed territories and carrying on an endless campaign against the feudal lords of his own domain who abused their power. He dealt with them rather ruthlessly, but with the full support of his trusted adviser, the abbot Suger, for the rebel nobles represented a threat to papal power, as well. Louis VI, whom ungracious history provided with the sobriquet *"Le Gros"*, appears as the benevolent ruler in Weber's *Euryanthe* (1823), arbitrating between two rival knights, Count Adolar of Nevers (good) and Count Lysiart of Forêt (bad). A notoriously inept libretto severely compromised the opera's success, but Wagner drew on its plot elements rather liberally, and with great success, when shaping his *Lohengrin* two decades later.

Louis VII, who succeeded his father in 1137, was less lucky. He was married at an early age to Eleanor, Duchess of Aquitaine. Although the substantial territory thus acquired strengthened his rule, Eleanor bore the king only two daughters and no son. When in 1144 Edessa (a county bordering on Antioch) fell to the Moslems, triggering a "Second Crusade," the French royal pair decided (against the advice of Abbot Suger) to follow the example of the German king Conrad III and lead an army to the Holy Land. The campaign, however, was a disaster. It resulted in no lasting conquests and shed Christian blood without in any way weakening the power of Islam. For the hapless Louis VII, it also turned into a severe personal and political misfortune. Queen Eleanor, a vivacious woman who did not conceal her opinion that Louis was "more a monk than a man," divorced him by virtue of a papal decree. She soon married Henry Plantagenet, Count of Anjou and Duke of Normandy. Furthermore, Henry was an heir to the throne of England. When he was crowned in 1152, the military and economic resources of Aquitaine were added to England, thus weakening France.

A 12th-century chronicler, Giraldus Cambrensis, described King Henry II as "a great maker of peace...and a special benefactor of the Holy Land." However, as this obviously clerical scholar further states... "he ventured on many detestable usurpations in things belonging to God... Although he was the son of the church, he either dissembled or forgot the sacramental unction."

Henry's problems with the church revolved around the recurrent issue of the Investiture—whether bishops should be appointed by the Pope or the king, an issue that symbolized the great struggle between papacy and kingdom. When Thomas à Becket, a trusted servant and companion of the king in his youth, became Archbishop of Canterbury in 1163, he opposed the growing strength of royal power, rejected the king's authority and placed himself under the protection of the Pope. He spent seven years of exile in France and when he returned, the big issues were still unresolved. "I go to England whether to peace or to destruction I know not," Becket said; "but God has decreed what fate awaits me."

Meantime, to assure a peaceful succession, Henry had his son Richard crowned by the Archbishop of York. This angered Becket, and the bishops who officiated at the ceremony were suspended by the Pope. Realizing Becket's unbending position, Henry uttered a fateful wish to be rid of the troublesome priest. On December 29, 1170, Thomas à Becket was murdered at Canterbury Cathedral by four knights who decided to interpret their king's words literally, and immediately acted upon them. Henry was deeply shocked by the event and by the repercussions it caused, and was forced to do penance at the tomb of the sainted martyr four years later.

The T.S. Eliot play *Murder in the Cathedral* deals with this sombre episode in two parts, separated by an interlude. In Part I, Becket returns from exile on December 2nd, surrounded by fearful priests. He is approached by four figures who tempt him, in turn, to forget animosities and resume his early, lighthearted relationship with the king, to become the king's ally and powerful chancellor, to turn *against* the king in a conspiracy, and, finally, to yield to his own "sinful pride" and seek martyrdom. This is followed by an interlude consisting of the Archbishop's sermon on Christmas morning, in which his impending death is anticipated. In Part II, Becket is threatened by four knights and the priests are urging him to flee. The knights return and kill him, then address the citizens of Canterbury, attempting to rationalize their actions. The play ends with a prayer, "Lord, have mercy upon us. Blessed Thomas, pray for us," while a *Te Deum* is sung in Latin by a choir in the distance.

There are certain operatic overtones to the Eliot play. Puccini or Mascagni would have given it a wide berth, but Ildebrando Pizzetti, whose neo-classicism was antithetical to verismo, responded to it eagerly and, in the main, successfully. His *Assassinio nella Cattedrale* (1958) follows the Eliot drama faithfully, making good use of Becket's Christmas sermon for a musically supported "interlude". Music, likewise, adds another dimension to the sober rationalizations through which the four assassins attempt to excuse their actions. The total effect, with Pizzetti's austere style of enhanced declamation, resembles a morality tale in music with philosophical undertones. After its Milan premiere (March 1, 1958), a special oratorio performance was given for Pope John XXIII at the Vatican. More recently, the enterprising Bel Canto Opera Company of New York presented the work at St. Bartholomew's Church in November 1987.

Compared to the Canterbury tragedy set off by Henry II that sent shock waves through 12th-century Europe, the story of Rosamond Clifford is of negligible historical importance, yet it too had its aftershocks. It seems that the future King Henry met Rosamond, daughter of Walter, Lord Clifford of Scotland, in 1149 when they were both very young. Their friendship blossomed into a love affair, and a son was born from it. After Henry and Eleanor were married, Rosamond entered a cloister of the Knights Templar. Then, while the king was away in Normandy fighting a rebellion, Eleanor was tempted to kill Rosamond, but ultimately changed her mind on the condition that her rival would never see Henry again. Rosamond then entered the nunnery at Godstow, where she died in 1191, aged 57.

This published historical account is at variance with a play called *Henry the Second, King of England, with the Death of Rosamond* that was performed at London's Theatre Royal in 1693. (The author is presumed to be William Mountfort.) In this dramatically charged account, Eleanor is informed of the affair by an abbot who is seeking vengeance for the death of Becket. After an initial attempt fails, Rosamond is poisoned by the queen and the abbot. The latter is subsequently stabbed by a courtier. This version cries out for an Italian opera, one is tempted to say. And, indeed, there is Donizetti's *Rosmunda d'Inghilterra* (1834), with a libretto by the distinguished Felice

Romani. Other variants, however, are added to the story: Henry, it seems, had wooed Rosamond in disguise, seeking escape from a loveless marriage. In the end, Rosamond is poisoned and in her final aria welcomes the release of death, as a proper *bel canto* heroine should.

Eleanor of Aquitaine, a feisty and forceful woman, continued to play an active part in English and French politics long after her husband's death. She died in 1204 and is remembered as a patron of troubadours and the inspiration for many courtly poems, despite the fact that her life was not always treated kindly by weavers of legends.

VII

THURINGIAN CONTESTS — SICILIAN VESPERS

King Roger (Szymanowski); *La battaglia di Legnano*
(Verdi); *Richard Coeur-de-Lion* (Grétry); *Le Comte Ory*
(Rossini); *Bánk bán* (Erkel); *Tannhäuser* (Wagner);
Oberto (Verdi); *Il Pirata* (Bellini); *Les Vêpres siciliennes*
(Verdi)

In the second half of the eleventh century, coinciding with their conquest of England, groups of warrior Normans were encouraged by the popes to conquer as much of southern Italy as they could govern. Their leaders were Guiscard and Roger, the sons of Tancred de Hauteville, the famous crusader. By 1091, their reconquest of Sicily from the Moslems was completed. Thereafter, Roger, as Count of Sicily and Calabria, ruled the island of Sicily for many years with a relatively liberal firmness that assured the land an era of significant prosperity. Under his son, who was crowned King Roger II and ruled from 1113 to 1154, agriculture and commerce flourished — and so did Christian and Islamic culture, side by side. Roger's revenues were said to have been greater than those of any other European king at the time, and his royal court at Palermo was a haven for Greek and Arab scientists and architects, as well as French troubadours. While the latter wove romantic tales about the ancestral hero Tancred and his companions, the former created splendid edifices for posterity, like the Capella Palatina of Palermo's Royal Palace, with its dazzling Moorish mosaics.

Karol Szymanowski's opera *King Roger* (1926), with 12th-century Palermo as its background, presents a highly original juxtaposition of history and fiction. The king and his brilliant scientist-advisor Mohamed Al-Idrisi (an historical figure) are placed into a mystical plot involving a fictitious Queen Roxane. She comes under the spell of a mysterious shepherd endowed with visionary powers, who is eventually revealed as Dionysos, the god of beauty. The opera's message is that King Roger, a man of reason, must balance the principles of both Dionysos and Apollo to arrive at a happy harmony in life. With its rich orchestral textures and oriental hues, influenced equally by

Richard Strauss and Claude Debussy, the music captures a rare medieval world where Christian and pagan elements and diverse cultures could — however briefly — live in harmony.

King Roger was an independent soul and powerful enough to defy the popes, unfazed by their excommunication that resulted from his actions. His successors tried to maintain his legacy of independence and racial harmony at a time of continuing crusades and growing intolerance. But competition from the increasingly prosperous maritime cities of Italy undermined Sicily's position. With the death of Roger's grandson, William II, the end came to the Hauteville dynasty, and the throne of Sicily was claimed by the Hohenstaufens of Germany by virtue of a politically arranged marriage.

The Hohenstaufens spelled nothing but trouble for Italy. Campaigning against the Lombard city states of Milan, Brescia, Parma, and Modena, the emperor Frederick Hohenstaufen, the famous Barbarossa, virtually destroyed Milan in 1162. In despair, sixteen large cities of Italy formed the Lombard League in 1167. When, after a pause of several years, Barbarossa attacked again in 1176, his forces were thoroughly defeated at the town of Legnano, north of Milan. This disaster finally convinced him of the futility of attempting to subjugate such determined people. At a meeting in Venice attended by Pope Alexander III, Doge Ziani of Venice, and the envoys of King William II of Sicily, a six-year truce was declared with the Lombard states and the emperor was never to return with hostile purposes again.

An Italian triumph over a German ruler was just the subject Giuseppe Verdi needed for the most fiery of all his *risorgimento* operas, *La battaglia di Legnano*, completed in 1848 when the region of Lombardy was still under Austrian rule and revolutionary fever swept through all of Italy. The opera's essential plot situations are fictitious (in fact, they were adapted by librettist Salvatore Cammarano from Joseph Méry's Napoleonic drama *La bataille de Toulouse*), but certain details do convey a great deal of historical verisimilitude. The gathering of the Lombard troops in Act I, representing soldiers from Piacenza, Verona, and Brescia, is clearly based on fact, apart from being effective theater, somewhat in the manner of Rossini's Gathering of the Cantons in the second act of his *Guillaume Tell*. The appeal to the city fathers of Como (Act II) is also historical, for Como, Pavia, and Cremona were late and reluctant joiners of the Lombard League. Barbarossa's sudden appearance in Act II, however, is only a dramatic coup, and his death at the hand of Arrigo, the opera's fictitious patriot hero, is pure fabrication:

Barbarossa was to live for another 14 years. He died, in fact, in the Holy Land, as one of the leaders of the "Third Crusade".

Despite repeated papal urgings, the failure of the Second Crusade dampened enthusiasm throughout Europe for new adventurism. The situation changed, however, when the powerful Moslem leader Saladin overpowered the Christian defenders and captured Jerusalem in 1187. It is sobering to read in Sir Steven Runciman's *History of the Crusades* that "where the Franks 88 years before had waded through the blood of their victims, not a building now was looted, not a person injured." Despite the Moslems' humane behavior, the fall of Jerusalem shocked Europe. Pope Urban III allegedly died of grief, and his successor, Gregory VIII, wasted no time in calling for a new Crusade. This is the call to which the aged emperor Barbarossa responded, as did King Philippe Auguste of France and his ally, Richard I of England — "Lion-Heart". The oldest son of Henry II, Richard had just succeeded to the throne in 1189, the very year the Third Crusade began.

And that was Emperor Barbarossa's last year. He died, not in battle, but by drowning in the river Salef, apparently in a foolish act of bravado. His death shattered his army and ended the German participation in the Third Crusade. German legend, poetry, and song have assured Barbarossa's immortality. Dante, on the other hand, assigned a special place for the emperor in his *Inferno*.

The other leaders of the Third Crusade did not fare much better. Richard the Lion-Heart and Philippe Auguste, two bickering allies, were joined by the army of the kingdom of Jerusalem, and took Acre in a bloody battle, but went no further. Philippe returned to France to attend to state matters, while Richard and Saladin continued battling one another, with severe losses to both armies. Gradually, a feeling of mutual admiration emerged between the two adversaries, illustrated by several acts of gallantry on both sides. On June 9, 1192, they concluded a three-year truce that allowed Richard to return home to deal with his overambitious brother John.

But Richard's return was far from smooth. Shipwrecked in the Adriatic, he was captured by the Duke of Austria and turned over to the new emperor, Henry VI, son of Frederick Barbarossa. After being imprisoned in the castle of Trifels, near Lorraine, Richard was released for a vast ransom raised from his lands partly through the efforts of his mother, Eleanor of Aquitaine.

Such a businesslike transaction, however, did not satisfy Michel-Jean Sedain, whose libretto for André Grétry's 1784 opera *Richard Coeur-de-Lion* contrives a romantic liberation of the king by Blondel, a French troubadour, and Marguerite, a French countess in love with Richard. The opera, which enjoyed huge popularity in the first thirty years of its history – translated into nine languages – was the precursor of a whole series of "rescue operas" in which the plot revolved around the rescue of the hero or heroine from imprisonment or deadly danger. Beethoven's *Fidelio* is the most celebrated example of the genre. Curiously, the name of the fort commander who guards the English king in Grétry's *Richard Coeur-de-Lion* is Florestan!

Richard the Lion-Heart, a brave and flamboyant warrior and the subject of many legends, was to surface again in two operas derived from Sir Walter Scott's novel *Ivanhoe*: Marschner's *Der Templer und die Jüdin* (1829) and Sir Arthur Sullivan's *Ivanhoe* (1891), both earmarked for rapid oblivion after brief initial successes. The history of Sullivan's *Ivanhoe* was, in fact, quite remarkable. The composer had hoped to create a grand opera that would enshrine his name, *sans* Gilbert – an association that had become burdensome for him. He obtained a commitment from impresario Richard D'Oyly Carte for a continuous run, and *Ivanhoe* tallied up 160 performances, unprecedented for an English opera. After that, however, it ran out of steam and was never revived again. According to George Bernard Shaw, it was a good novel "turned into the very silliest sort of sham grand opera." It was a verdict echoed by Sullivan's biographer Arthur Jacobs nearly a century later: "An unhappy and longwinded compromise between the old 'ballad' style and the newer 'Wagnerian' allusiveness made *Ivanhoe* strangely old-fashioned for its period."

Ivanhoe, the opera, was a noble failure, though. By placing an episode from Plantagenet England on the operatic stage, Sullivan accomplished what no other English composer had done before him. The much-maligned libretto by Jilian Sturgis deals with the period of Richard's exile, with his brother, Prince John, usurping power. The king returns disguised as a "black knight", discovers the abuses of the Knights Templar, and dissolves the Order. It is a modest, but not undignified, operatic memorial to a king best remembered for his valorous conduct in battle and for his crusading exploits. The real Richard died on March 26, 1199, not in a major battle but in fighting a rebellious French noble in Aquitaine. He was felled by a shot of a lone crossbowman, and perished when the wound turned gangrenous. His mother, Eleanor of Aquitaine, was at his bedside. Their final resting place – next to that of Henry II – is in the French abbey of Fontevrault, in the heart of the ancient Anjou dominions.

Richard left no heir, so his contentious brother ascended the throne unopposed. King John's rule (1199-1216) was disastrous for England, for it resulted in the loss of most of the vast Plantagenet territories to France. He was an unpopular ruler, and was forced by his barons to proclaim the Magna Carta in 1215, restricting royal power, and by Pope Innocent III (1198-1216) to acknowledge papal supremacy in the matter of clerical appointments. This, ironically, was the very issue that had caused the fatal feud between his father, Henry II, and Thomas à Becket.

The powerful pope's primary concern, however, lay in the persecution of all dissidents from the dogma. He restricted the activities of the Jews in society and extirpated the adherents of the Albigensian sect, a group of pious Catholics who disdained worldly property and certain forms of traditional Catholicism. The system of "inquiring" into the practices of heretical suspects — Inquisition — became institutionalized under the rule of Innocent III and his successors. Naturally, he urged the Fourth Crusade with all the eloquence in his power, which was considerable.

But the Fourth Crusade, too, ended in failure, a more ignominious one than the others. Venice, by then a flourishing center for maritime trade, was designated as a rallying point for the participating armies, but the Venetians were more interested in profitable commerce unhindered by Byzantine hostility. With Venetian support, and taking advantage of chronic Byzantine unrest, the Crusaders first captured the Dalmatian port of Zara in 1202. The port was part of the Hungarian kingdom, but Andreas II of Hungary was powerless to defend it. Then they captured and ruthlessly sacked Constantinople in 1204. Some of the city's priceless Christian relics found their way into Western churches, but the Greek church refused to accept papal authority. Venice benefited from occupying some of the Greek islands, but otherwise the Fourth Crusade accomplished nothing — surely nothing toward reducing the power of Islam.

A crusade that turned Christians against Christians could not help but add to the mounting distrust and bitterness that attended such ventures in Europe, where year after year family life was disrupted when fathers, husbands, and sons went off to battle facing an uncertain fate. There were preachers, like Fulk of Neuilly, who went about the countryside — with the Pope's encouragement — to remind the populace of the sacred mission of the Crusades, to lift sagging morale, and to collect funds. Some of these collections, though, never found their way to the right places. Although tremendous crowds gathered to hear Fulk's fiery rhetoric, his followers soon deserted him.

The outrageous fake Hermit in Rossini's brilliant comic opera *Le Comte Ory* (1828) was probably fashioned after a person like Fulk of Neuilly by the librettist Scribe, who based his account on an old Crusaders' ballad published in 1785. Count Ory is a notorious lecher, a no-good scion of a noble family. Disguised as a hermit, together with companions of his ilk, he locates a castle in Touraine that is inhabited only by women: its lord and all its male occupants are away on a crusade. They gain admittance disguised as nuns but, after some hilariously contrived episodes, their unholy intentions are foiled by the crusaders' sudden return. Despite the unevenness of the plot – it virtually disintegrates with the approach of the crusaders – *Le Comte Ory* is made irresistible by its wealth of musical invention. Berlioz regarded it as Rossini's masterpiece.

The Fifth Crusade, which was launched by Pope Innocent's successor, Pope Honorius III, in 1217, ended four years later – again without accomplishing much. It had among its leaders King Andreas II of Hungary, a reckless and ambitious monarch. Constantly involved in foreign adventures, he neglected internal affairs and allowed his people to languish. During one of his early campaigns in 1213, with the king abroad, his nobles rebelled and assassinated the queen, Gertrud of Meran, whose influence and whose corrupt foreign courtiers were blamed for the country's misfortunes. This assassination, quite extraordinary in Hungarian history, is the central event in Ferenc Erkel's *Bánk bán* (1861), to this date recognized as Hungary's foremost national opera.

Before King Andreas joined the Fifth Crusade in 1217, he sent his daughter Elisabeth, still a child, to marry Ludwig, the son of the Thuringian Landgrave Hermann. It was a tragic match: young Ludwig was marched off to join the foolhardy Fifth Crusade and died in the first bloom of youth. His bride, widowed at twenty, was literally hounded out of the Thuringian castle by her hysterical mother-in-law. She devoted her remaining few years to caring for the poor until death relieved her of her suffering in 1231, at age 24. She was subsequently canonized and became the patron saint of the poor.

Franz Liszt's oratorio *The Legend of St. Elisabeth* (1865) deals with this tragic episode with considerable historical accuracy. In the final scene, the emperor himself, Frederick II, delivers the funeral oration, followed by the march and chorus of the crusaders and the final ensemble. Although not intended for the opera house and certainly lacking in dramatic action, theatrical performances have taken place in both Hungary and Germany, and it was staged briefly by the Metropolitan Opera in 1918. It was also a special favorite of the late conductor Leo Blech, who persuaded the young Dietrich Fischer-Dieskau in 1951 to play the part of the young Ludwig.

It is this saintly figure whom Wagner places on stage for us as Landgrave Hermann's *niece* in his *Tannhäuser* (1845). It is Elisabeth whom Wolfram chastely worships, and who saves the hero from the wrath of the outraged knights in the second act. And, finally, it is she whom Tannhäuser addresses with his dying breath: *"Heilige Elisabeth, bitte für mich!* (Saint Elisabeth, pray for me!)"

Wagner's opera is an ingenious mix of history and fiction. It is supposedly set in 1207, much too early for some of the documented events. Hermann, Landgrave of Thuringia, was an art-loving noble whose court was indeed a haven to minnesingers (troubadours). Wagner mercifully takes no notice of the evil-spirited Landgräfin Sophie, Elisabeth's nemesis. A 14th-century poem, well known to Wagner, tells of a competition — *"Sängerkrieg"* — between six minnesingers: Wolfram von Eschenbach, Walther von der Vogelweide, Heinrich der Schreiber, Reinmar von Zweter, Biterolf, and Heinrich von Ofterdingen. Except for the last named, probably a legendary figure, they were all active poets in that courtly age, and we find them duly plying their trade at the Wartburg under the Landgraf's protection in Wagner's *Tannhäuser*. Wolfram von Eschenbach, portrayed as a man of unbelievable gentleness and selflessness, may not have been all that in real life, but he *was* an important poet, the author of *Parzifal*, the chief source of Wagner's last opera. Both he and Walther — whose role in the opera is limited to a tenor voice in the Wartburg ensemble — left a substantial body of literary legacy. In Wagner's *Die Meistersinger von Nürnberg*, Walther surfaces again as a literary inspiration for young Walther von Stolzing, a fact that does not carry much weight with his rival, Beckmesser.

And what about Tannhäuser himself? He, too, existed: a folk poet, probably Austrian, born around 1200, and something of a drifter known for his songs of a merry and sensual character. Wagner provided him with the first name "Heinrich" in deference to the elusive Herr von Ofterdingen whom he dropped from the opera. The operatic Venusberg also has its equivalent in German legends: it is the mountains and caves of Hörselberg near Eisenach, noted in the tales of the brothers Grimm and others for devilish doings. As for the stern pope who denied forgiveness to the errant knight, he was identified in a folk ballad as Urban IV, and not too respectfully, either, due to his bitter opposition to the Hohenstaufens of Germany.

Legend has it that the real Tannhäuser during his adventurous life also participated in the crusade of 1228, the sixth in the sequence. That was an exclusive Hohenstaufen venture organized by Frederick II, who was crowned in 1215. Grandson of Barbarossa, he was also the grandson of King Roger II on his maternal side and a legitimate heir to the Sicilian throne, which he had inherited while still an infant under the guardianship of Pope Innocent III in 1197. As a creature of Sicily, where Christians, Moslems, and Jews lived side by side and where the arts and sciences flourished, Frederick was an independent thinker, a scientist, and a willful and strong ruler who regarded Italy and Sicily as the center of his domain.

Not a religious man, Frederick did not keep the promise he made to his former guardian to join the Fourth Crusade, thereby earning a ban of excommunication from Innocent's successor, Pope Honorius III. In 1228, however, undeterred by the ban, he decided to proceed to the Holy Land (the Sixth Crusade) and, through the wiles of diplomacy, captured Jerusalem, along with Nazareth and Bethlehem, without bloodshed. Under the treaty he concluded with the sultan of Egypt (whom he played against the sultan of Damascus), the holy places were divided between the two faiths, and were all kept open to pilgrims. Far from appreciating this remarkable accomplishment, Pope Gregory IX urged a crusade — against the emperor. This was the same pope who is "credited" with the first public burning of heretics in Rome — an act that so enraged the populace that Gregory was forced into temporary exile.

Although he displayed an open mind in his dealings with the Moslems, Frederick II ruled his German and Italian subjects with a firm hand. After imprisoning his first-born son for his rebellious acts, he appointed the second, Conrad, viceroy of Germany. And to keep the restless Lombard cities in line, he ceded their control to his vassal Ezzelino da Romano (1194-1259), the very model of a medieval tyrant, ruler of Padua, Mantua, and Verona. (His unusual name, a diminutive of Etzel — that is, Attila — suggests foreign origins as well as Italian antipathies.)

Without appearing in the cast of Verdi's first opera, *Oberto, Conte di Bonifacio* (1839), Ezzelino casts an ominous shadow over its action. *"Ad Ezzelino ascesi, gli stolti abbatterò!* (I have joined Ezzelino, and will destroy these madmen!)"* announces Riccardo, Count of Salinguerra, early in the first act. Riccardo, Ezzelino's ally, is the villainous hero here. Having seduced and abandoned the daughter of Count Oberto, he is courting Cuniza, Ezzelino's sister. Determined to clear the family honor, the aged count challenges Riccardo to a duel and is killed by him. Then, overcome at last by guilt, Riccardo goes into exile. Temistocle Solera, Verdi's librettist, places the opera's action in 1228. History tells us that Ezzelino was the greatest power in Northern Italy for thirty more years. He, too, earned a choice location for himself in Dante's *Inferno*.

Frederick's problems with the papacy did not abate with the death of his old adversary Gregory IX at age 98 in 1241. The new pope, Innocent IV, scion of the prominent Fieschi family of Genova, continued to preach against him relentlessly, and even attempted to have him assassinated through hired killers. When finally the emperor succumbed to natural death in 1250, the unforgiving pope remarked: "*Laetentur coeli et exsultet terra* (The heavens are pleased and the earth should rejoice)". Then he renewed his imprecations against the dead emperor's son, King Conrad IV of Germany.

Conrad and Pope Innocent both died in 1254. There were many claimants to the German throne, but no election took place and an interregnum of almost twenty years ensued. In Sicily, Manfred, Frederick's illegitimate son, had himself crowned over papal objection. The new pope, Urban IV, of French origin, offered the crown to Charles of Anjou, brother of the reigning French king, the pious and chivalrous Louis IX.

King Louis was the leader of the Seventh Crusade (1248-1254), which, after some early successes, ended with his own captivity and subsequent rescue for a large ransom. When another French pope, Clement IV, came to power in 1265, he lost no time in throwing his influence to the Angevins for the rule of Sicily. The armies of Charles of Anjou and Manfred clashed at Benvento, where Manfred perished. He lives on in Sicilian legends as a tragic folk hero and a champion of the island's independence, and was touchingly remembered by Dante (*Purgatorio* III).

This is the turbulent period dealt with in Bellini's *Il Pirata* (1827); the author of the libretto, Felice Romani, sketches in the historical background in his preface. The opera's title character, Gualtiero, Count of Monaldo, was exiled after the battle of Benvento, but continued fighting the Angevins at sea. When his outlawed fleet is defeated in the straits of Messina, he falls into the hands of his mortal enemy, the Duke of Caldora, and is eventually executed.

Charles of Anjou thus became the King of Sicily, and an extremely cruel and unpopular one. His victory strengthened Guelf power in the Northern

Italian cities, notably Florence. Those with Ghibelline sympathies turned to the young German King Conradin, the last Hohenstaufen, for help. But their support was not translated into a large enough military force. The young Conradin bravely confronted the Angevin army, but he was defeated at Tagliacozzo, captured, and, after a mock trial, executed on October 29, 1268.

Pope Clement, unfazed by Charles's cruelty, exulted over the death of the last Hohenstaufen. He died a month later without realizing the severe shock caused by that brutal execution all over Europe. No papal successor was immediately named: the rising power of Charles of Anjou intimidated the cardinals. For a while, indeed, the king's ambition knew no bounds. In 1270, he persuaded his brother, King Louis IX of France, to undertake a new crusade against the Emir of Tunis. It was fruitless, like so many others, and it claimed the life of that saintly king — he died of the plague. Nor did Charles succeed in his dreams to merge the kingdom of Naples and Sicily with the Byzantine empire. Just the same, he was the most powerful monarch in Europe.

In Sicily, meanwhile, the unpopular Angevin rule was enforced by Guy de Montfort, Viceroy of Tuscany. He was the grandson of Simon de Montfort, the exterminator of the Albigensians, and son of Simon, Earl of Leicester, also of bloody reputation. Guy himself had been excommunicated for the murder of his cousin, Henry of Cornwall. Embittered by the cruelties of the French rule, the Sicilians turned toward the Spanish house of Aragon for help. King Pedro of Aragon was married to Manfred's daughter, Constance. It was in their court that the physician Giovanni da Procida, originally from Naples and a Sicilian patriot and onetime confidant of Manfred, found a friendly reception in exile. Both Procida and the queen urged the Aragonese king to lay claim to the Sicilian throne.

His chance came in 1282, at Eastertime: an insult to a Sicilian bride by a French soldier ignited a rebellion, remembered in history as the "Sicilian Vespers", that ended in the wholesale slaughter of the French occupiers. The massacre was horrible indeed, and in the absence of authenticated details it was magnified by posterity into a major political event.

It also inspired a grandiose opera, Verdi's *Les vêpres siciliennes* (1855), created to satisfy the Parisian taste for extravagant spectacles. It was to challenge Meyerbeer's *Les Huguenots* (1836), matching its predecessor length for length, ballet for ballet, massacre for massacre. Eugène Scribe, the tireless arbiter of French operatic tastes and librettist of *Les Huguenots*, was Verdi's collaborator this time.

Scribe's libretto (originally conceived for Donizetti's unfinished *Duc d'Albe,* dealing with another country and another period) enlivened history with many fictitious elements. For one thing, Procida, the fanatical instigator of the rebellion of the opera, may not even have been in Palermo when the massacre occurred. It is true that Frederick, the young Duke of Austria, had been beheaded along with his friend, Conradin, an event referred to early in the action. But the existence of Frederick's sister Hélène, who is dressed in mourning (fourteen years later!), is not substantiated by history. History, furthermore, tells us that Montfort had two daughters but no son. Of course, he may have had an illegitimate son, but the father-son conflict that is a crucial element in the opera's plot is entirely Scribe's invention. In his authoritative study *The Sicilian Vespers* Sir Steven Runciman does not even connect Montfort with the massacre. Contemptuously dismissing Scribe's effort, Runciman identifies Herbert of Orléans, not Montfort, as the governor of Sicily, with headquarters in Messina, not in Palermo.

Departure from historical fact, however, was not Verdi's main concern. As he wrote to Crosnier, director of the Opéra: "It wounds the French because they are massacred; it wounds the Italians because M. Scribe, in altering Procida's historical character, has made him — according to his favorite system — a common conspirator with a dagger in hand...I am an Italian above all and come what may I will never be an accessory to any injury done to my country." Verdi, nonetheless, was unsuccessful in altering the essence of Scribe's text.

Verdi's intuition proved accurate. *Les vêpres siciliennes* never attained popularity in France. In Italy, censorship originally allowed it only under a different title, with the action transposed into an even more inauthentic Portuguese setting. As *I vespri siciliani,* it has enjoyed warmer reception in recent years, even though its Italian version is a pale replica of the original French text. Its survival, and even immortality, is assured not by Scribe's clever mixture of fact and fancy but the emotional power and humanizing qualities of Verdi's music.

In the opera's fourth act, with the conspirators in prison, a letter is smuggled into Procida's hand, informing him that an Aragonese ship in the harbor is ready to come to their aid. This has some basis in historical fact, for Pedro of Aragon did land in Palermo on September 4, 1282, a few months after the bloody Easter, and was acclaimed King of Sicily.

Sicilian historians tend to regard the uprising as a spontaneous patriotic affair. Runciman sees it as a patriotic outbreak made possible by a conspiracy organized by Procida with the decisive participation of Pedro of Aragon and his allies, Emperor Michael of Constantinople and the republic of Genoa. After 1282, Sicily's connection with the Italian mainland was severed. Sea battles between French and Spanish forces continued for many years, but Sicily's fate was to be linked with the house of Aragon and the Iberian Peninsula for several centuries to come.

VIII

THE EARLY HABSBURGS—EUROPE
IN TURBULENCE

Libuše (Smetana); *The Brandenburgers in Bohemia*
(Smetana); *Guillaume Tell* (Rossini); *The King Goes
Forth to France* (Sallinen)

With the extinction of the Hohenstaufen dynasty, whose consistently anti-papal policy had culminated in the lengthy interregnum, the medieval concept of imperial power was undermined. In some regions, the authority of local princes grew; in others, feudal chains that tied peasants to their lords loosened. A new page was turned, however, with the elevation to the German throne of Count Rudolf of Habsburg in 1273. The new ruler set a course designed to strengthen the power of his dynasty through cooperation with the church: the cornerstone of Habsburg policies for the next six centuries.

The Habsburgs—the name derives from their ancestral castle *"Habichtsburg"* or "hawk's castle"—were originally minor counts with lands in today's Switzerland between the Rhine and Aare rivers and Lake Lucerne. By clever politics, they increased their holdings during the eleventh and twelfth centuries, acquiring Alsace and other German provinces. Rudolf was able, ambitious, and ruthlessly pragmatic. He married off his six daughters to various German princes to gain their support, one of them to the Bohemian King Ottokar II, his own greatest political rival. (Incidentally, political marriage remained a powerful tool in increasing Habsburg power through centuries.) In the case of the Bohemians, however, Rudolf's plan did not work. After a brief truce, war broke out again and ended with Ottokar's defeat and death in the battle of Marchfeld on August 22, 1278. His provinces of Austria, Styria, and Carinthia were added to Rudolf's domain, establishing the Habsburgs in the Danube basin, the center of their future empire.

Habsburg triumph, however, meant tragedy for the Bohemians. Ottokar was one of their greatest rulers, descendant of the Premysl dynasty whose origins are the stuff of legends, as immortalized, among others, in Smetana's operatic pageant *Libuše* (1881). Suffused with patriotic zeal, Smetana's tableau ends with a prophetic vision in which heroic figures of future Bohemian history appear, Ottokar II among them. The message, from Smetana's late 19th-century hindsight, is that troubled times lie ahead but the Czech nation endures.

Six centuries after the first Rudolf, with Bohemia still in the Habsburg orbit, *Libuše* was introduced at the inauguration of the Czech national theater in Prague honoring another Rudolf, the Habsburg archduke of Mayerling fame, on the occasion of his wedding to a Belgian princess. In an atmosphere of political amity, the archduke summoned the composer to the royal box and showed great compassion when he discovered Smetana's deafness.

If *Libuše* was "rebellious" only by implication, Smetana's first opera, *The Brandenburgers in Bohemia*, introduced fifteen years earlier, was quite emphatic in its anti-Habsburg sentiments. It is set in the period following Ottokar's defeat and death at Marchfeld in 1278, when the armies of Otto, Margrave of Brandenburg, under Habsburg protection, plundered Bohemia and caused widespread misery throughout that war-torn land. The actual plot by Smetana's librettist, Karel Sabina, is imaginary and somewhat diffuse, but the opera leaves no doubt that the Czech people are the real protagonists, rising against their oppressors. And that was not lost on the 19th-century audience at the time when Czechs (like Italians and Hungarians, as reflected in *their* operas of the period) were anxious to break away from the Habsburg rule and establish their own national identity.

After his victory at Marchfeld, Rudolf further consolidated his power by arranging for the marriage of yet another daughter, Clementia, to the grandson of Charles of Anjou, Charles III ("Martel"). But, for all his artfulness in elevating the dynasty, Rudolf was unable to achieve his goal of becoming the emperor crowned by the pope. After his death in 1291, he was further repudiated when the prince electors bypassed his son Albert in favor of the Rhenish Count Adolf of Nassau. Albert, nonetheless, obtained the German crown by force, defeating Adolf in battle. He was crowned in 1298 and ruled until 1308, when he was killed by his own nephew in a family power struggle.

Meanwhile, storms gathered over the ancestral Habsburg dominions of Switzerland. On August 1, 1291, only seventeen days after Rudolf's death, the three forest districts (cantons) of Uri, Schwyz, and Unterwalden united in creating the Everlasting League for the defense against any attackers. (The date is still celebrated as Switzerland's national holiday.) The Swiss cantons continued to offer resistance to Habsburg authority under Albert, protesting the latter's army of overlords. Finally, Albert appointed two bailiffs (*Landvogt*) over the cantons: Hermann Gessler of Brauneck and Berenger of Landenberg. Both were rude and abusive men, and ruthless in imposing unprecedented taxes.

Gessler appears as the hated villain in Schiller's 1804 drama *Wilhelm Tell* on which Rossini's grand opera *Guillaume Tell* (1829) is based. The second act of the opera – the gathering of the cantons in the pine forest on the heights of Rütli – is a splendid operatic reenacting of a simple but important historical event. On November 11, 1307, 33 men representing the Swiss cantons made a solemn pledge there to free Switzerland. Wilhelm Tell may have been one of them, but modern historians tend to discredit the familiar Tell legend. (Interestingly, Nordic sources describe similar exploits of such a marksman.) The legend began to emerge in the fifteenth century, to be published in Gilg Tschudi's *Chronicum Helveticum* (1734-36). Tschudi was the main source of Schiller's stirring play of a suppressed people fighting for freedom. Gessler's notorious insistence that passersby salute his hat as a symbol of imperial authority (Act III in the opera) is considered by historians as an unpopular but common gesture in that period. Tell's superlative marksmanship and his courage in the face of mortal danger, although unsubstantiated, became an essential part of Swiss patriotic consciousness. And, beyond his stature as a national hero, Tell will always represent a symbol of man's passion for freedom.

During the reign of the ill-fated Albert I and his successors, Habsburg domination was virtually abolished in Switzerland, and a confederation of cantons was established. The measure of self-government, with its progressive laws protecting the rights of the peasant population, was unique in the Europe of that time. And so was the admirable and obsessive neutrality established in Switzerland – the only country that has managed to stay out of all subsequent European wars.

In both England and France, meanwhile, powerful kings like Edward I (1272-1307) and Philip IV (1285-1314) succeeded in consolidating monarchic authority and expanding the powers of royal officials. Economic conflicts created growing tensions between the two countries in the ensuing years. And when the French king Philip VI occupied the disputed territory of Aquitaine in 1337, hostilities broke out that were to last for more than a century and became known as the Hundred Years' War (1337-1453).

In 1346, King Edward III of England scored a great military victory over the French at Crécy, followed by the invasion of Calais harbor and the plunder of Northern France. The French lost 4000 soldiers in the battle, among them their greatest military leaders. This disastrous episode forms the centerpiece of a provocative contemporary opera, *The King Goes Forth to France* (1984), by the Finnish composer Aulis Sallinen, a black satire on the abuses of royal power, the excesses of militarism, and the mindlessness of governments. Although Paavo Haavikko's libretto is an accumulation of bizarre characters and happenings, they are set against the background of carefully studied history. We learn from the opera that the English won at Crécy due to the superiority of their archers using the longbow, a revolutionary weapon perfected by the English after the subjugation of Wales. The French employed mercenary Genoese archers, and slew them when they proved ineffective in battle – another historical fact. So is the presence of the blind King John of Bohemia, one of the 4000 fatalities of the battle. (His son Charles, the future king and emperor, escaped in time.) Jean Froissart, the great chronicler of the period, is a subsidiary character in Sallinen's opera. The ironic implication, one presumes, is that the voices of objective historians are ignored as history is being made.

To the many other misfortunes that befell the fourteenth century – wars, insurrections, feudal excesses, the erosion of papal power and a decline in religious faith – the worst was added: the plague, known as the Black Death, which killed an estimated one third of Europe's population between 1348 and 1350. In her brilliant volume *A Distant Mirror*, Barbara W. Tuchman calls the "calamitous fourteenth century...a distraught age whose rules were breaking down under the pressure of adverse and violent events...a period of anguish when there is no sense of an assured future."

Cruelties did not end with the fourteenth century and, surely, wars and feudal excesses continued. But mankind regained that "sense of an assured future" even before the end of that "calamitous century". For it to happen, dynamic forces were needed to transform medieval civilization. They took shape first in Italy, the land of the Renaissance.

IX

ITALY—THE AGE OF DANTE AND PETRARCH

Gianni Schicchi (Puccini); *Francesca da Rimini* (Zandonai); *Marino Faliero* (Donizetti); *Simon Boccanegra* (Verdi); *Rienzi* (Wagner); *Karlštejn* (Novák)

Italy around 1300 presented a picture of great political diversity. The French house of Anjou ruled the southern region as the kingdom of Naples, involved in constant rivalry with the cities of Sicily under Spanish domination. Much of northern Italy was governed by the German-oriented Holy Roman Empire, while in the central part the political power of the papacy was paramount. Further complicating the situation, various city states emerged in north and central Italy, like Milan and Venice, that went their own way, chose their own government, and frequently allowed local despots to exercise absolute power.

Florence, a flourishing city, had a Guelph tradition, but its entrenched nobility faced constant crises of rebellion stemming from such neighboring Ghibelline strongholds as Pisa and Arezzo. At the battle of Campaldino (June 11, 1289), Dante Alighieri, a young Florentine scholar, fought bravely in the front ranks as the Guelph army led by Corso Donati scored a decisive victory over its Ghibelline opposition. Of patrician family himself, Dante married Gemma Donati—a marriage that brought him political eminence and several children. Nevertheless, it was not his wife but his distant and idealized lady love, Beatrice Portinari, whom Dante immortalized in his *Vita Nuova* and, later, in Canto XXXI of his *Paradiso*. (Beatrice died in 1290.)

Dante was the first great modern poet: his Divine Comedy inhabits a sphere wholly different from that of the gallant troubadours of earlier ages. And with Dante in literature there were Giotto and Cimabue in painting, and Arnolfo di Cambio in architecture—all Florentines, all active in 1299, as the new century was dawning.

Puccini's *Gianni Schicchi* actually takes place in 1299. Librettist Giovacchino Forzano ingeniously evolved the comic opera from a few lines in which Dante (in Canto XXX of the *Inferno*) summed up Schicchi's roguery. Dante and Forzano, however, did not see eye to eye in respect to the main characters. Dante the patrician did not regard Schicchi with the same sympathy the opera's authors did more than six centuries later. In his view, Hell was the rightful place for such cheats. Besides, the person Schicchi had the temerity to impersonate was Buoso *Donati*, the poet's kinfolk. At the same time, Forzano's contempt for the entire greedy Donati clan leaps out of every page of his libretto, right down to his second-guessing of "*gran padre Dante*" in Schicchi's final spoken apostrophe.

The historically oriented spectator certainly should be amused by young Rinuccio's prophetic vision in his brief aria "*Firenze è come un albero fiorito*" as he salutes the "present" glories of Florence in 1299 (the Piazza dei Signori and the Piazza di Santa Croce) and foresees the coming of Giotto, Arnolfo, and even the Medici "*mercante coraggioso*". It is also significant that Rinuccio and Lauretta plan their wedding to take place on May 1, 1300, in the "*ricca e splendida Firenze*" in the new century.

However sternly Dante may have regarded a mountebank like Gianni Schicchi, he had infinite compassion for young lovers. He himself had fallen in love with Beatrice Portinari on May Day of 1283, a youthful love that haunted him all his life. He was still a young man, and Beatrice was still alive, in 1289 when Giovanni (Gianciotto) Malatesta, the Lord of Rimini, discovered his wife Francesca in adulterous union with his brother Paolo, and killed them both. Dante immortalized Paolo and Francesca, placing them in the "second circle" of his *Inferno* (Canto V), among the "malefactors of the flesh who subjugate their reason to desire." (Dante's "first circle" is the abode of great heroes of antiquity— Aeneas, Caesar, Plato, Socrates, Horace, and their ilk— to whom Paradise was closed because they were not Christians.)

Francesca, Paolo, and their killer, Giovanni Malatesta, were historical characters, and Malatesta's murderous act required no penance, least of all in a city where his word was law. That the plight of the lovers moved Dante deeply is shown not only by the compassionate tone of his account but also by the generous length with which he treated the episode. Following him, painters, poets, and composers were inspired to recreate the immortal story, placing the tragic figures of Paolo and Francesca into a pantheon of great lovers that holds Romeo and Juliet and Tristan and Isolde.

In Dante's vision, these lovers, driven in life by storms of passion, were similarly tossed about incessantly by the tempests in the second circle of Hell. This musical whirlwind is magnificently captured in Tchaikovsky's orchestral fantasy *Francesca da Rimini* (1876), a subject he had originally planned to

Renata Scotto and Placido Domingo as Francesca and Paolo in
Francesca da Rimini (Zandonai)
CREDIT: Beth Bergman

treat operatically. Unquestionably, the work had an influence on Sergei Rachmaninoff, a prominent conductor of the Bolshoi in the early 1900s, whose two-act opera *Francesca da Rimini* was introduced there in 1906 (Tchaikovsky's brother Modest was the librettist). Aside from efforts by lesser operatic lights (Ábrányi, Goetz, Napravnik), it was Riccardo Zandonai's treatment (1914) based on Gabriele d'Annunzio's white-hot play that has won worldwide operatic success for the ageless story.

Rachmaninoff ingeniously encapsulates the action between two quotations of the famous Dante lines from Canto V: "There is no greater pain than to remember past joys in misery...," first uttered by the lovers as their ghosts appear to Dante and his guide, the shade of Virgil. The lines are repeated by the chorus in the brief epilogue. As the first act opens, Gianciotto Malatesta resolves to carry out the pope's command and destroy his Ghibelline enemies.

In his broader treatment (four acts against Rachmaninoff's two), Zandonai devotes the entire second act to a clangorous battle that ends with the Guelph victory. In the first act, which takes place in the courtyard of Francesca's home, the palace of the Polenta family of Ravenna, we learn of the political machinations that ultimately bring about the tragedy: Francesca was tricked into a politically desirable marriage with the unattractive Gianciotto—she believed that the handsome younger brother Paolo, who came on Gianciotto's behalf as a suitor, was to be her intended. This historical fact is only mentioned in Rachmaninoff's more concise treatment as part of Gianciotto's angry monologue in Act I, while he is preparing for battle.

The deadly struggle between Guelphs and Ghibellines that caused so much bloodshed in medieval Italy was particularly destructive in Dante's Florence. It did not help that the city was traditionally Guelph; the ruling party split into two factions: the Blacks (accepting the domination of Pope Boniface VIII) and the Whites (opposing it). Soon after entering political life and elected prior, Dante, no friend of the pope, found himself condemned on trumped-up charges of bribery, perjury, and other offenses, and in 1301 was banished from Florence for life.

One of Dante's companions in exile was a certain Francesco di Petracco, whose first-born son Francesco Petrarca (Petrarch, 1304-1374) raised Italian lyric poetry to an exalted level. Born in Arezzo, he spent his youth in Avignon, the temporary seat of the papacy, and visited Florence only in middle age. His abiding dream was the unification of all Italian peoples.

In his political writings Dante advocated the need for two guides for human beings: the spiritual and the temporal. Recognizing Rome as the center of Christianity (while remaining vociferous in his denunciation of papal excesses), Dante fervently wished for a Roman Empire united under a single ruler. For a while Henry of Luxembourg (who succeeded Albert of Habsburg as emperor in 1308) embodied Dante's hopes. In three letters addressed to Henry, Dante urged him to subdue the "Florentine vipers". It was not to be. Henry died in 1313, shortly after being crowned in Rome by a papal legate, in the absence of the pope.

The Papal State at that time was in a state of flux. Dante's antagonist, the generally unpopular Boniface VIII, died in 1303, and when his successor, Clement V, a French prelate and a submissive underling of the French King Philip IV (The Fair), removed the seat of the papacy to Avignon (1305), papal authority in central Italy dwindled to a shadow. Clement died soon thereafter, after presiding over the massacre of the Templars in France.

Dante, playing no favorites, found an infernal destination for both popes, Boniface and Clement, in the *Divine Comedy*. He completed that literary masterpiece in exile—an honored guest in the palace of the Polentas in Ravenna, the birthplace of the unfortunate Francesca da Rimini. He died there on September 14, 1321 on returning from Venice, where he had been sent as Guido da Polenta's ambassador. He was fifty-six years old. During the centuries that followed, Florence has asked Ravenna repeatedly to return the remains of its native son, but always in vain. In a little chapel on the Via Dante in Ravenna, a monument bears this inscription:

> *Hic claudor Dantes patriis extorris ab oris,*
> *Quem genuit parvi Florentia mater amoris.*

> (Here I am enclosed, Dante, exiled from my native land,
> Whom Florence bore, the mother, that little loved him.)

* * *

Before settling in Ravenna, the exiled Dante had been cordially welcomed by Bartolomeo della Scala, the podestà of Verona, under whose rule in the early 1300s the tragedy of Romeo and Juliet allegedly took place. Lack of historical substantiation—tour guides in Verona notwithstanding—has failed to prevent operatic immortalization of that irresistible story. Among those who could not resist: Georg Benda (1776), Nicola Zingarelli (1796),

Nicola Vaccai (1825), Vincenzo Bellini (1830), Hector Berlioz (a "*symphonie dramatique*", 1839), Charles Gounod (1867), and Riccardo Zandonai (1922). Shakespeare could not have been far from any of the respective librettists' efforts, but Giuseppe Foppa (for Zingarelli) and Felice Romani (for Vaccai and Bellini) took as their principal source Gerolamo della Corte's *Storie di Verona*. (The legend also appears in a story by Matteo Bandello, published in 1554.)

Only the Bellini and Gounod operas have stood the test of time. In Gounod's *Roméo et Juliette*, the spotlight is rarely removed from the lovers, and the language of the libretto (by Barbier and Carré) makes an honest effort to match Shakespeare in rapture and eloquence. Bellini's *I Capuleti e i Montecchi* calls for a smaller cast, removes the Shakespearean characters of Mercutio, Benvolio, and the Nurse, turns Friar Lawrence into a doctor, and eliminates the historically inaccurate figure of the "Duke of Verona". On the other hand, Bellini's librettist Felice Romani takes the trouble of clarifying that Juliet is the daughter of Capellio, a Guelph leader, while Roméo Montague (Montecchio) is a Ghibelline. They are separated not so much by personal enmity but by the very same tragic conflict that was tearing most of Italy apart in the thirteenth and fourteenth centuries. The mention of the tyrant Ezzelino da Romano as an ally of the Ghibellines in the 1300s, however, appears to be an historical inaccuracy on Romani's part — that tyrant, who ruled Verona for more than thirty years, had been dead since 1259. The Scaligeri (Bartolomeo della Scala and his heirs) ruled Verona for more than a century after Ezzelino's fall. In 1405, the city came under the domination of the Venetian Republic.

* * *

The development of Venice was unique among Italian cities. The close connection between the city and the Byzantine Empire introduced wealth, luxuries, and certain ideas that were not favorable to democratic thinking; hence Venice became a patrician rather than a democratic city state with a doge (duke) as its elected head. This form of government was already established by the early 8th century. The doges were then powerful men, often linked by marriage to royal families. Doge Sebastiano Ziani (1173-1178)[*]

---

[*]   See page 71.

played an important role in Barbarossa's containment. But, while the doges were elected for life, the growth of private wealth as a result of Venice's exceptional position as a trading center created a broader ruling class that was reluctant to give them limitless power. After several constitutional changes curtailing the doges' monarchical powers, a Council of Forty was established from among members of patrician families, charged with the election of future doges.

Meanwhile, Genoa emerged as a serious maritime rival to Venice in the prosperous Mediterranean trade. In 1298, a Genoese fleet led by Lamba Doria defeated the Venetians, who suffered great losses in vessels sunk and personnel killed or taken captive. Among the latter was Marco Polo, just three years after his return from the East. It was during his Genoese captivity—of relatively short duration (he was released within a year)—that he wrote the story of his fabulous travels.

In 1310, a conspiracy against doge Pietro Gradenigo was crushed. Among its leaders, all of whom were executed, was a member of the prominent Badoero family, whose 17th-century descendant plays a prominent part in Ponchielli's *La Gioconda*. It was against the danger of such conspiracies that the feared and notorious Council of Ten was established. Acting on denunciations placed in a prominently placed receptacle called "*Bocca del Leone*" (The Lion's Mouth), the Council of Ten conducted its investigations in secret. As set forth in one of its statutes: "When the Tribunal shall have determined the death of anyone as necessary, the execution shall not be public. The condemned shall secretly be drowned during the night in the Orfano Canal." The informer Barnaba in *La Gioconda*—a fictitious character shaped by Arrigo Boito after a Victor Hugo model but all too realistic in that historical context—offers a sinister portrait of the Venetian hierarchy in his first-act monologue, "*O monumento!*"

> Ducal palace and infernal hole...
> Your base are the *pozzi*, your peak, the *piombi*
> Before your facade of marble and gold...
> Joy and horror are alternating here...
> There sits the doge, an old skeleton
> With his ceremonial headdress,
> Above him is the Grand Council,
> A fateful assemblage of nobles
> But above *them*, the most powerful of them all —
> A king: the spy.

The *pozzi* (wells) and *piombi* (lead ducts) were dreaded dungeons where light never penetrated, and from which captives rarely emerged alive.

The dreaded procedure by which justice was served in 14th-century Venice was soon to claim a head of state as its victim. In the background lay the city's perennial bloody rivalry with Genoa. Hostilities ceased only briefly in 1348, when the Black Death decimated the population of Venice; they resumed the following year despite the passionate pleas of Petrarch, acting as a Milanese envoy, begging both rivals to end their fratricidal wars. In 1354, the Genoese scored a major victory that caused one of the noblest of the Venetian doges, Andrea Dandolo, to die of a broken heart. (His friend Petrarch composed his epitaph.)

The new doge was Marin(o) Faliero, scion of a prominent family that had given two doges to the republic, and himself a distinguished military hero of many wars. Nonetheless, his reign was brief and it ended with his secret trial and decapitation. In 1820, George Byron wrote his deeply moving tragedy *Marino Faliero, Doge of Venice*, paying meticulous attention to documented history. A French play by Casimir Delavigne was also written on the same subject. Librettist Emanuele Bidera drew on both literary works for Donizetti's opera *Marino Faliero* (1835), a worthy effort almost immediately overshadowed by his *Lucia di Lammermoor*, which followed it a few months later.

Faliero was

> one who has done great deeds, and seen great changes:
> No tyrant, though bred up to tyranny;
> Valiant in war, and sage in council; noble
> In nature, although haughty; quick, yet wary;
> Yet for all this, so full of certain passions,
> That if once stirr'd and baffled, as he has been
> Upon the tenderest points, there is no Fury
> In Grecian story like to that which wrings
> His vitals with her burning hands, till he
> Grows capable of all things for revenge....
> — BYRON

He was insulted when an arrogant noble named Michele Steno cast aspersions on the virtue of his young and beautiful wife. Outraged when the Council of Forty let the offender off with a minor punishment — and also frustrated by the limited power of his office, and what he perceived to be a corrupt city government—he joined a conspiracy instigated by a group of disgruntled plebeians. Had the conspiracy succeeded, Faliero himself would have emerged as a ruler with monarchical powers. But one of the conspirators, Beltramo, fearful of the wholesale bloodshed the rebellion would have created, alerted a patrician named Nicolò Lioni with a view of saving his life. The plot was thus exposed, the Council of Ten went into action, the doge was tried, sentenced to death, and, on April 17, 1355, was executed. Byron follows history to a remarkable extent; Donizetti's opera embellishes historical truth with a fictitious secret romance between the *dogaressa* and Faliero's nephew—an element taken from Delavigne's play seized upon by the practical Donizetti to create a showy tenor part for the celebrated Rubini. (Lablache sang the title role at the opera's Paris premiere in 1835.)

In the opera, the doge's wife is called Elena. Byron identifies her as Angiolina Loredano, of a patrician family that gave three doges to the republic. A century later, another Loredano was to prove a mortal enemy to a doge named Francesco Foscari, another victim of Venetian intrigues, and a hero of yet another Byron play and Verdi opera.

* * *

Like Venice, Genoa became a great commercial power through its sea trade with the Byzantine empire, though its strength was frequently undermined by fratricidal wars with Venice and Pisa after the twelfth century. There were civil feuds, too, between the aristocracy—the families Spinola, Doria, Fieschi, and Grimaldi—and people of humbler origin. As the wealth of the population increased, the populists were able to attain a measure of self-rule and keep aristocratic excesses in check. One of their leaders, Guglielmo Boccanegra, actually governed the city council as "*primo capitano*" from 1257 to 1262. But he was unable to curb the power of the nobility, chose exile, and Genoa continued its ancient struggles: nobles against plebeians, Guelphs (Fieschi and Grimaldi) against Ghibellines (Spinola and Doria), brother against brother.

The rule of the noble families continued well into the fourteenth century, but Genoa rarely enjoyed internal peace. Eventually, widespread discontent exploded into an uprising in 1339. It drove the patricians from power and created a new head of state with wide authority and the title of "doge", following the Venetian model. It was specifically mandated that no one of noble birth could carry that high office. The first doge of the new Genoese republic was Simone, nephew of Guglielmo Boccanegra.

He was a reputable citizen and not a *corsaro,* as he is often referred to in Verdi's *Simon Boccanegra* (1857). It was actually his brother, Egidio, who chose the sea for his career and distinguished himself in several sea battles against the pirates who threatened Genoa's commercial lifeline. Staying clear of the city's internal politics, Egidio Boccanegra eventually lent his services to Alfonso XI, King of Castile, became an admiral of Spain, and presumably died of natural causes.

Not, alas, his brother Simone, the tragic hero of Verdi's opera. He ruled wisely and managed to curb excessive agitation on both sides while maintaining the city's defenses against her enemies. Nonetheless, the nobles remained hostile to his rule, forcing Simone to relinquish his power in 1344 and to go into exile. Genoa soon found itself embroiled in wars against Venice and against the Turks—adventures that were draining the city's resources.

Always devoted to the cause of Italian unity, Petrarch appealed to Doge Andrea Dandolo of Venice in 1351, calling for a cessation of hostilities. A year later, he turned to the Genoese with a similar appeal, to no effect. In 1356, finally, Simone was returned to power. This time, he resolved to use stronger measures against his enemies, all the while successfully containing the Visconti forces of Milan, who had been threatening the Ligurian coastline. Nonetheless, Boccanegra's enemies could not tolerate his rule. At an opportune moment—a banquet to honor a royal visitor—they poisoned him. On March 14, 1363, the doge died a slow death while his enemies gloated over his agonies.

For all its faithfulness to the spirit of history, the Piave-Boito libretto had to be condensed to capture three turbulent decades of Genoese politics within the limitations of a three-hour opera. This, of course, necessitated many departures from historical fact. Combining the two Boccanegra brothers into one operatic character had already been accomplished by the Spanish playwright Antonio Garcia Gutierrez, whose drama was the source for the libretto. To tighten the action, the opera simply ignores the two separate periods in the doge's reign. Petrarch's appeal, which actually reached the Genoese during Boccanegra's exile, is read in the Council Chamber in the opera by the doge himself—an effective dramatic *coup* that creates a great emotional effect.

Verdi's own love of the Ligurian coast enriches his music with several felicitous maritime allusions. The orchestral prelude to Act I is a musical seascape of shimmering delicacy. And in the final act, Boccanegra, already weakened by the deadly poison, longingly recalls his youthful adventures and wishes that he had found death "in the sea's friendly bosom." As for Jacopo Fiesco, the exiled Grimaldi brothers, and Gabriele Adorno—they are all historical characters logically and convincingly placed into the opera's action.

Two footnotes may be added to the operatic events: Gabriele Adorno, who indeed succeeded Boccanegra, turned out to be a weak ruler and was forced to resign in 1370. Happier circumstances attended the family of his wife, Amelia Grimaldi. By the fourteenth century, the Grimaldis were established as rulers of the tiny principality of Monaco. We have Boito's word for it (in *La Gioconda*) that their 17th-century descendant named Enzo Grimaldo was a most unwelcome visitor in Venice. But the family continued to rule Monaco in a luxuriant manner far beyond territorial modesty: today's Prince Rainier is a Grimaldi.

Rome was not spared the strife that tore the rest of Italy apart. When Pope Clement moved the papal seat to Avignon in 1305, he left the eternal city without effective government. During the seven decades of the so-called "Babylonian Captivity", lawlessness prevailed in Rome. The powerful noble families of Colonna and Orsini maintained private armies and abused the populace. Human life had little value: corpses floating in the Tiber were a common occurrence.

Into this state of anarchy stepped Cola (Nicholas) de Rienzi, a well-educated young plebeian, gifted with a rhetorical flair and obsessed with the bygone glory of ancient Rome. As one of the Roman delegates to Avignon in 1342, he befriended Petrarch, who was taken by his eloquence. He returned to Rome as a papal notary and, displaying innate leadership qualities, began agitating against the abusive nobles. With rapidly increasing multitudes rallying around him, he had himself elected Tribune, restoring to currency the ancient office of the Roman republic. He ran an orderly and efficient government, and secured the patronage of Pope Clement VI (1342-1352), who rejoiced in the fall of the all too powerful aristocrats.

But, Latin scholar that he was, Rienzi should have remembered the warning of Tacitus: "The lust for power, for dominating others, inflames the heart more than any other passion." The success of his domestic reforms and his great personal popularity with the masses inspired in his mind a vision of a unified Italy, with *his* Rome as its center. In this, he was enthusiastically supported by Petrarch, by then the poet-laureate of Rome, welcome at various Italian courts, and fired by the same dream of Italian unification.

Power eventually corrupted Rienzi, as it had corrupted many Roman predecessors. His ornate garments, the luxurious trappings of his parades, and his ever-growing arrogance eventually undermined his popularity. Exiled in December, 1347, he tried to enlist the support of Emperor Charles IV, who, instead, delivered him to Avignon. There, again with Petrarch's rekindled friendship, he obtained the patronage of Pope Innocent VI (1352-1362). He returned to Rome in 1354, but the old magic was gone. Riots broke out against him and, incited by the nobles, his implacable enemies, a mob stormed the Capitol and set it on fire. Rienzi was killed, his body mutilated and abandoned in the wreckage, to be consumed by the flames. "Posterity," writes Gibbon, "will compare the virtues and failings of this extraordinary man; but in a long period of anarchy and servitude the name of Rienzi has often been celebrated as the deliverer of his country and the last of the Roman patriots."

The figure of Rienzi fired Richard Wagner's imagination when he read Bulwer-Lytton's romantic novel in 1836. Wagner was young, poor, and impressed by revolutionary ideas. Furthermore, he rightfully recognized a subject worthy of a spectacular opera in the then fashionable manner of Meyerbeer, Auber, and Spontini. It was Wagner's dream to have his *Rienzi* introduced in Paris, where such grandiose operas were grandly staged and warmly received. But he had to wait until 1842, when the premiere finally took place in Dresden. The opera's future was limited to sporadic revivals, mainly in Germany, a fate not entirely due to its excessive length.

Rienzi's grandiose ideas are aptly conveyed in his opening monologue *"Dies ist eu'r Handwerk..."* (Act I Scene 1), and the conflict between nobles and plebeians is dramatized with a sure hand. But then Wagner departs from history by introducing the character of Adriano (interpreted by a mezzo-soprano) as the unconvincingly rebellious son of Steffano Colonna, the powerful leader of the nobles. Moreover, the operatic Adriano is in love with Irene, Rienzi's sister, and a fictitious one at that. Ignoring the fact that the historical Rienzi had a wife, his operatic counterpart is portrayed in a near-incestuous relationship with sister Irene, who heroically stands by his side as the final conflagration engulfs both of them. (The elements of incest and immolation were to re-emerge in Wagner's Ring.)

"The Capitol was yet stained with the blood of Rienzi when Charles the Fourth descended from the Alps to obtain the Italian and Imperial crowns," writes Gibbon. The following year (1356), Emperor Charles IV of Luxemburg, hereditary king of Bohemia, promulgated the "Golden Bull" which established a new method of electing emperors: seven princes — four secular, three ecclesiastical — comprised the electoral body. Charles was an outstanding ruler, founder of Prague University, a well-educated master of many languages. Though his realm embraced many lands, foremost in his mind was the cultural enrichment of Bohemia, where he is still reverently remembered. Charles was a cerebral man who occasionally liked to immerse himself in meditation. On such occasions, he would compel members of his court to join him in a remote castle, devoid of all female distraction. How this extremely unpopular royal edict was outmaneuvered and eventually nullified is the subject of Vitézslav Novák's charming opera *Karlštejn* (1916), still in the repertoire of the Prague National Opera.

X

CRISIS IN THE PAPACY — TURMOIL IN SPAIN, BOHEMIA, AND ITALY

La favorita (Donizetti); *La Juive* (Halévy); *Beatrice di Tenda* (Bellini); *Il trovatore* (Verdi); *I due Foscari* (Verdi)

There were many achievements to benefit mankind during the first decades of the Renaissance: Boccaccio completed his Decameron; Brunelleschi and Donatello created enduring masterpieces; Guillaume de Machaut wrote his *Messe de Notre Dame*, Chaucer, his *Canterbury Tales*; and Heidelberg University was chartered. It is something of a miracle that all these things could happen in a period otherwise marked by wars, massacres, and persecutions, often under corrupt popes and unprincipled princes.

The terrible Black Death of 1348 left an inescapable imprint on people's outlook on life. The pious were engulfed by fear of God's punishment, while others questioned religious beliefs and turned with mounting zeal toward worldly pleasures. Little progress was made toward conciliation between rival nations. England and France poured their energies into the Hundred Years' War; the papal residence in Avignon caused new problems that eventually created a tragic schism, and the two countries where papal influence was normally strong — Italy and Spain — remained divided.

By the fourteenth century, the Moorish element on the Iberian peninsula was limited to the kingdom of Granada, but its strength, in combination with Granada's Moroccan allies, was still powerful enough not to be discounted. Christian Spaniards were fired by their priests with a crusading zeal against the Moslems, but the inspiration they drew from religion was not enough to make them seek unity among themselves; thus the three belligerent kingdoms of Castile, Aragon, and Portugal fought each other in constant wars.

The ruling house of Aragon had, of course, exercised power over Sicily and much of southern Italy ever since the Sicilian Vespers (1282). In Castile, Alfonso XI, who had inherited the throne still in infancy under the regency of his strong-willed and efficient grandmother, managed to solidify his reign against some powerful nobles. In 1340, allied with Portugal, he defeated a strong Moslem army at the battle of Tarifa.

That battle is the historical event around which the fanciful tale of Donizetti's *La favorita* (1839) was woven by the various authors who shaped its libretto. As the operatic King Alfonso eloquently puts it in the first scene of Act Two (Italian version):

> *Sì del Marocco il re e di Granat' insieme*
> *vider la luna a Tarifa crollar.*

> (Yes, the king of Morocco and the king of
> Granada, both saw the crescent moon set at Tarifa.)

Fernando, the opera's naive tenor hero, decorated for his valor by his historical baritone king Alfonso XI, is himself a fictitious character. His tragic romance with Leonora de Guzman, the king's mistress, is equally fictitious. Doña Leonora, however, was a real person — real enough to have borne the king nine illegitimate children. Alfonso would have wished to make her his queen, but could not gain the Pope's approval to divorce the one to whom he was married, Maria of Portugal. The favorable light in which the opera presents Alfonso — aided by some attractive *bel canto* melodies — is not undeserved: he is remembered among the worthiest of the Castilian kings. Alas, the Black Death, no respecter of royal blood, claimed him in 1350 while he was besieging Gibraltar.

His successor, Pedro I (1350-1369), was only sixteen when he inherited the throne, but ruled long enough to be remembered by history as "Pedro the Cruel". Among his numerous victims was Leonora de Guzman, and this turned his half-brother Enrique de Trastamara (son of Alfonso and Leonora) into a lifelong enemy and a dangerous rival. With French and Aragonese support, Enrique finally confronted Pedro and defeated him at Monteil in 1369. Pedro was killed and the throne of Castile passed to Enrique and his heirs — the heirs of Leonora, Donizetti's *La favorita*. Civil wars continued to plague the kingdom until a convenient marriage was arranged between the legitimate and illegitimate heirs of Alfonso XI, reconciling the two branches in 1388.

Neighboring Aragon, too, found itself in a state of turbulence following the death of its king Martin I in 1410. Three pretenders sought the throne: Ferdinand de Trastamara, a Castilian prince and nephew of the late king,

Count Fadrique de Luna of a powerful noble house, and Jaime, Count of Urgel. A council of electors settled on Ferdinand as a compromise choice, but Urgel refused to abide by their decision. He was defeated in the ensuing civil war, and surrendered in 1413.

Manrico, the romantic hero of Verdi's *Il trovatore* (1853), champions the cause of Urgel. His operatic adversary, Count di Luna, reviles him in no uncertain terms (Act I, Scene 2):

> *Insano, temerario, d'Urgel seguace,*
> *A morte proscritto, ardisci*
> *Volgerti a queste regie porte?*

> (Madman, rash fool! A follower of Urgel,
> Condemned to death; how dare you
> Come to these royal gates?)

In the Spanish play *El Trovador* by Antonio García Gutierrez, Manrico's enemy is identified as Don Nuño. In his operatic adaptation, librettist Salvatore Cammarano injected an historical name but confused the issue. Who was Manrico's rival (and operatic brother)? Was it Fadrique de Luna, himself a claimant to the throne, or Antonio de Luna, who was an avid partisan of Urgel and thus should have been Manrico's brother-in-arms? Or was he Alvaro de Luna, powerful advisor to the art-oriented and politically indecisive King Juan II of Castile (1406-1454)? The Luna family wielded great power in Spain, with a cardinal member to lend extra weight to the family's political clout. *Il trovatore,* with its exchanged infants, hammering gypsies, and fiery but fictitious principal characters, will not yield the answer. History is poorly served by Cammarano's flaming and thunderous poetry, but that has not interfered with the opera's success.

But for all the civil wars that disrupted Spanish life, an internal evolution eventually propelled the land toward unity. By the middle of the fifteenth century, Castile, Aragon, and Navarre were all ruled by members of the house of Trastamara. Castile and Aragon were finally united when Ferdinand, son of Juan II, married Isabella of Castile in 1479.

* * *

Meanwhile, the Hundred Years' War, dissipating the energies of England and France, wore on and on, and the papacy, the one potential source of conciliation, was of little help. In England, the heretical activities of John Wycliff (c. 1330-84), an Oxford philosopher who thundered against papal abuses, gained enough sympathy in high places to prevent his arrest. And in France, Pope Gregory XI, though of French birth, resisted all the discouragements of King Charles V when he left Avignon for Rome in 1376, ending seven decades of the "Babylonian captivity". But he was already in ill health and died fifteen months later.

Pope Gregory's death caused a major crisis in the church. A conclave of sixteen cardinals met in Rome, bitterly divided, and in a heated atmosphere aggravated by noisily demonstrating Romans elected the Archbishop of Bari as Pope Urban VI. The new pope was instantly rejected by the pro-Avignon cardinals, who regarded him as a tyrant and Anti-Christ, among other things. They elected the Cardinal of Geneva as the Anti-Pope Clement VII, who promptly moved the papal seat back to Avignon in 1379. The great "schism", which was to last for nearly twenty years, was on.

Wycliff in England regarded both popes as Anti-Christs and advocated the elimination of the papacy. But his king, Richard II, recognized Urban, as did the rulers of Bohemia, Poland, Hungary, and Scandinavia. France naturally supported Clement, and was joined in this decision by both Spanish kings, Juan I of Castile and Pedro IV of Aragon. Incidentally, Cardinal Pedro de Luna (of the *Trovatore* Lunas) had been a member of the contentious Roman conclave.

Urban VI, who was a cruel and violent man, unfit for high office, died in 1389, followed by Clement VII in 1394, but the schism continued, depriving the Church of needed revenues and forcing both papal successors to make concessions to various monarchs for their continued support. Wycliff's teachings, meanwhile, were carried on by a Czech theologian at Prague University named Jan Hus. Aside from being a religious reformer, Hus was a Czech nationalist, a committed fighter against German domination. The growing strength of the various dissident groups led to a series of church councils designed to reestablish religious unity. After the failure of the Council of Pisa (1409), the Emperor Sigismund (who refused to be crowned while the papacy was divided) prevailed on the rival popes — John XXIII of Rome and Benedict XIII of Avignon (the former Pedro de Luna) — to convene the Council of Constance in 1414.

At Constance, with 300 bishops and abbots and as many theologians in attendance, the Council first dealt with the issue of heresy. Jan Hus had been summoned to state his views, and he came with a safe-conduct provided by the emperor. An impulsive man, reportedly unwilling to wait for the personal presence of the emperor, who might have saved him, Hus faced the church authorities, who ignored the safe-conduct and burned him at the stake in 1415.

It is the Council of Constance that serves as the background to Halévy's *La Juive* (1835), a cruel tale of persecutions, hatred, revenge, and martyrdom. In his libretto, the indefatigable Scribe captured the ferocity of the age without too much regard for historical accuracy. A five-act opera with a ballet, in conformance with the Parisian opera conventions of the period, *La Juive* has as its central figure the fanatical Jew Eléazar, fairly obviously modeled on Shakespeare's Shylock. His adopted daughter, the trusting and devoted Rachel (echoes of Scott's Rebecca) commits the mortal sin of consorting with a Christian prince in disguise (possibly modeled on Hugo's François I). Eléazar could save her by revealing that she was born a Christian, were it not for his implacable hatred of Cardinal Brogni, Rachel's biological father, and the church authorities he represents. Except for Rachel, none of the characters emerges in a sympathetic light, and the opera ends with the gruesome death of Rachel and Eléazar.

"Au bûcher les Juifs, qu'ils perissent! La mort, la mort pour leurs forfaits! (To the stake with the Jews, let them perish! They well deserve to die!)" Thus one of *La Juive*'s enthusiastic choral outbursts, and they do ring with the strength of historical truth. Branded as outcasts and Christ killers by many early churchmen and victimized during the Crusades, the Jews faced renewed and violent persecutions following the horrible plague of 1348 all over Europe. They were burned in Basle and in the French communities of Narbonne, Carcassonne, and Strasbourg in 1348 and 1349. During the same years, similar outrages occurred in Brussels and in the German cities of Mainz and Erfurt, while at Worms, 400 Jews chose self-immolation rather than being killed by the townspeople.

This hostility soon spilled over to Spain, where the Jewish population had enjoyed a period of tolerance and tranquility under the earlier rulers. Enflamed by the agitations of a fanatical priest named Ferrand Martinez, riots broke out protesting growing Jewish wealth and influence and demanding the cancellations of debt to the Jews. In 1391, these riots culminated in four days of murder, pillage, and forcible conversions in Barcelona. Together with deep-seated religious intolerance in Spain and elsewhere went the powerful motive of greed. Full participation in their communities was denied them, but banking and money-lending were considered permissible Jewish occupations: cancellation of debts and expropriation of Jewish property were widely desired objectives. In Spain, although the violence eventually subsided, precedent had been established for even more sordid events to follow a century later.

The anti-Semitic outbursts newly fueled by the reaction to the heretics are faithfully reflected in Halévy's *La Juive*. However, the philandering Prince Léopold, hailed in the opera as the leader who "has chastised the insolence of the Hussites with the help of God," is historically nebulous. He is honored by a pageant in the third act, attended by Emperor Sigismund himself, but the latter is reduced to silence in the otherwise prolix libretto.

The papal schism ended in 1417 with the election of Martin V, but the burning of Hus caused great shock waves in Bohemia, and the followers of the victimized reformer continued to carry on his fight against papal authority. Despite frequent military reverses, their struggle continued for at least two decades. Theirs was the first reformist movement to effectively challenge the supremacy of Rome. Remembered as Czech patriots, the Hussites were celebrated in literature and music during the Czech nationalist movement of the nineteenth century. References to their struggles and to their warrior strongholds of Tabor and Blanik resound in Smetana's choral works, in his great symphonic cycle *Ma Vlast* (*My Fatherland*), and in the fourth tableau of his opera *Libuše*, as well as in Dvořák's Hussite Overture. Neither Smetana nor Dvořák was concerned with religious issues; they were keeping alive the flame of Czech nationalism that Hus had ignited centuries before them.

* * *

During the years of the papal schism, the city states of northern Italy were constantly at war. In Florence, under the rule of the powerful banking house of the Medici, commerce and the arts flourished, but in 1402 the city was seriously threatened by the expansionist intentions of Milan's aggressive overlord, Gian Galeazzo Visconti. By then, the Visconti ruled over most of Lombardy, including the cities of Como, Piacenza, Cremona, Bergamo; also over Bologna, Siena, and Pisa. Florence was saved by Gian Galeazzo's sudden death and by the inability of his son Giovanni Maria to consolidate his father's holdings. Unpopular from the outset, Giovanni Maria was assassinated by his enemies in church — a convenient setting for Renaissance assassins. His younger brother, Filippo Maria Visconti, succeeded him and began his reign by torturing and executing his brother's killers.

Filippo Maria was a neurotic man, obese and ugly, and he rarely appeared in public. To consolidate his power, he entered into marriage in 1412 with the widow of the powerful *condottiere* Facino Cane, thereby neutralizing the latter's troops. The widow's name was Beatrice Lascaris di Tenda, of noble birth and probably excellent character. But she was older than her new husband by twenty-two years, and Filippo soon grew tired of her. Six years after the wedding, he accused her of infidelity with Michele Orombello, a court musician, subjected both to torture, and had them beheaded at the castle of Binasco near Milan. Under torture, the parties had confessed but, after the condemnation, Beatrice proclaimed her innocence, claiming that only torture had made her confess. Not satisfied with executing the allegedly guilty pair, Filippo also had the two court ladies beheaded who had testified against them. Such was the power of an oligarch; the episode undoubtedly caused dismay and terror, but life went on.

Bellini's opera *Beatrice di Tenda* (1835) gives a fairly true account of these happenings, but it ignores the difference in ages to appeal more effectively to Romantic sensibilities. Also, Filippo's romance with Agnese di Maino appears to be the librettist's invention. Interestingly, the librettist was the same Felice Romani who had supplied Donizetti with the libretto of *Anna Bolena* five years previously. The plot similarities involving the tyrannical Filippo (see Henry VIII), the betrayed Beatrice (or Anne Boleyn), the ambitious Agnese (Jane Seymour), the innocent Orombello (Smeaton, a court musician like Orombello) are too noticeable to be coincidental.

During the reign of Filippo Maria Visconti (who never remarried), Milan and Venice were frequently at war. Francesco Bussone, a *condottiere* known as Carmagnola, was responsible for most of Milan's successful campaigns. But, rebelling against what he regarded as Visconti's ungrateful attitude, Carmagnola abandoned him and offered his services to Venice – a step that was to bring tragic consequences.

The doge of the Venetian Republic at that time was Francesco Foscari. When he was elected in 1423, he was already fifty, of noble birth, forceful and ambitious, but not without influential enemies, the most vocal among whom was the candidate he had defeated, Pietro Loredano. Foscari's first major crisis involved Carmagnola. Foscari had entrusted the Milanese defector with command of the Venetian forces, but the Council of Ten, faulting Carmagnola's conduct of the war, suspected him of treason. Under the pretense of summoning Carmagnola to a conference, they captured and beheaded him in 1432, over Foscari's objections.

Then later, when Pietro Loredano and his brother Marco died under suspicious circumstances, Pietro's son Jacopo accused the doge of their murder and swore vengeance. How his relentless enmity brought about Foscari's downfall is the subject of Byron's unrelievedly gloomy drama *The Two Foscari*, and the opera that matches its darkly tragic mood, Verdi's *I due Foscari* (1844).

In 1445, Jacopo, the last surviving son of Francesco Foscari's five sons, was accused of conspiring with Filippo Maria Visconti, the Milanese enemy of Venice. His wealth was confiscated, and he was exiled. Although Jacopo's banishment was lifted two years later, he was exiled again in 1450 for his alleged complicity in a political murder. Five years later, desperate to return to his home and family, he wrote to Duke Francesco Sforza of Milan, successor of Filippo Maria Visconti, asking for his intercession with the Venetian government. His letter fell into the hands of the Council of Ten and, although the two cities were at peace at the time, the incident enabled Loredano to have Jacopo returned and tried. He was put to torture and sentenced to be exiled again. Broken in body and spirit, Jacopo died shortly thereafter, and his aged father, deprived of his throne, soon followed him. All this is faithfully documented in Byron's play.

In his effort to condense that rather verbose play, Verdi's librettist Piave may have gone too far. Loredano, the relentless nemesis of the Foscari, is reduced to an ominous but very much diminished presence. And when Jacopo Foscari, languishing in his prison (Act II), is terrified by the vision of the executed Carmagnola, the meaning of the scene is lost on listeners unacquainted with Byron's play or with that cruel episode in Venetian history. The opera faithfully records the old doge's helplessness and his humiliation at being stripped of his office. (His enemies had to change the constitution of the republic to accomplish this.) The historical Foscari died in 1457 a week after receiving word of his son's death in exile. Verdi, with his theatrical instinct, has him collapse at the instant he receives the tragic news. But that the doge's death occurs just as the tolling bells announce the election of his successor, Pasquale Malipiero, seems to be historically accurate. Thus was Loredano's deadly account with the Foscari settled — *"Pagato io sono,"* as the villain's tersely sinister final words have it in the opera. To please the Venetians who still honored him, the old doge was given a sumptuous funeral.

His was the longest reign in the history of the republic, and it was "crucial", in the summation of H.R. Trevor-Roper: "After 1457, the republic no longer feared the doge... The Venetian Republic survived intact through the era of native princes. It kept its independence when the other Italian states fell under foreign rule; it resisted the Papacy during the Counter Reformation; and it was to be praised, in the seventeenth century, as the most perfect model of government for any mercantile state which aspired to be free, effective, and independent."

In Milan, the Sforzas ruled in relative stability for half a century and even in a period of splendor under the art-loving Ludovico Sforza, when Leonardo da Vinci and Bramante flourished. But then, in 1494, the armies of the French King Charles VIII (who was distantly related to the Visconti) crossed the Alps and occupied Milan. From that time until 1859, Lombardy ceased to be part of Italy.

XI

THE SAINT (Joan of Arc) and THE SINNER (Bluebeard)

The Maid of Orleans (Tchaikovsky); *Giovanna d'Arco* (Verdi); *Iolanta* (Tchaikovsky); *Falstaff* (Verdi); *Ariane et Barbe-Bleu* (Dukas); *Bluebeard's Castle* (Bartók)

> England, bound in with the triumphant sea,
> Whose rocky shore beats back the envious siege
> Of watery Neptune, is now bound in with shame,
> With inky blots and rotten parchment bonds:
> That England, that was wont to conquer others,
> Hath made a shameful conquest of itself.
> Ah, would the scandal vanish with my life,
> How happy then were my ensuing death!
> — Shakespeare: *King Richard* II,
> Act II Scene 1

So speaks the dying John of Gaunt, Duke of Lancaster, uncle and chief advisor of King Richard II. Shakespeare's plays are only sporadically accurate history, but these lines, with their inimitable poetic ring, faithfully echo conditions in the England of 1399. Notwithstanding the decisive victories over the French at Crécy (1346) and Poitiers (1356), it was an exhausted land. The doctrines of Wycliff undermined people's attitudes toward Church and King; a violent peasant revolt shook the country in 1381, and the reaction of the feudal lords was brutal. Richard II had become king in early childhood; reaching 20 in 1397, he embarked on a cruel and despotic rule. Two years later he was overthrown by his cousin Henry, son of John of Gaunt, and died in prison. With Henry IV, in 1399, the rule of the Lancastrian kings began.

Henry's reign was brief (1399-1413), beset by rebellions and by his progressive illness. He was succeeded by his young and vigorous son, who, in the words of Winston Churchill, "led the nation away from the internal discord to foreign conquest; and had the dream, and perhaps the prospect, of leading all Western Europe into the high championship of a Crusade." That was Henry V, who, alas, also ruled briefly from 1413 to 1422.

In 1415, at Agincourt, a numerically outnumbered English army dealt a crushing blow to France, causing enormous casualties. The battle, in which Henry V heroically participated, is said to have wiped out half a generation of France's nobility with a devastating effect, morally and strategically. Henry V, on the other hand, emerged from it as an outstanding European figure. He was, as the historian William Stubbs observed, "a true Englishman, with all the greatnesses and none of the glaring faults of his Plantagenet ancestors."

France at that time was a bitterly divided country ruled by the intermittently insane Charles VI (1380-1422). The bitter division between the "Burgundians" and the "Armagnacs" culminated in 1419 in the assassination of the Duke of Burgundy, an act that precipitated an alliance between Burgundy and England. By the treaty of Troyes (1420), Henry V was to marry Catherine, daughter of Charles VI, to become heir to the French throne upon the latter's death, uniting England and France in a double kingdom — and disinheriting Charles's own son, the Dauphin. It was a simple plan, too simple for the unpredictable currents of history.

Henry V died in 1422 in the full flower of manhood. Shakespeare's idealized account of his reign found a modest echo in Saverio Mercadante's opera *La gioventù di Enrico V* (with a libretto by Felice Romani), that was introduced in Milan in 1834 and thereafter disappeared virtually without a trace, for it was not even published. And what about the colorful character of Sir John Falstaff, the rotund knight who enlivened three Shakespeare dramas as a boon companion of the young prince in *Henry IV, Part I,* to be dismissed from the King's service as he ascends to the throne and mends his youthful ways and, finally, as the inveterate skirt chaser in *The Merry Wives of Windsor?* Was this knight, made immortal in literature and opera, an historical figure?

In a way he was, because Shakespeare fashioned him out of two historical personalities. One was Sir John Fastolf (1380-1459), named "Falstaff" in some accounts, a career soldier, knighted around 1415. He distinguished himself in many battles against the French, lived well, but died an irascible old man, childless, and surrounded by rapacious relatives. The other was Sir John Oldcastle (c. 1378-1417), who was indeed a friend of the young Prince Hal in his younger years. Shakespeare even kept his name in the first version of *Henry IV* but changed it to Falstaff when the play was registered in 1598.

Unlike Shakespeare's Falstaff, Sir John Oldcastle came to a very tragic end. As head of the Lollards, a group of dissident Catholics, he proved to be unbending in his "heresy". He was captured and condemned to death in 1417; Henry V granted him a stay of execution, allowing him time to repent. Instead, Oldcastle escaped, but he was recaptured, and he was hung above a slow fire that consumed him and the gallows, as well.

Shakespeare's Falstaff dies sadly but peacefully, as we learn from *Henry V*, Act I, Scene 3. The *operatic* Falstaff lives on lustily and mischievously in two masterpieces: the underrated *Merry Wives of Windsor* by Otto Nicolai (1849), and the dazzlingly brilliant *Falstaff* by Giuseppe Verdi (1893), to which audiences do not respond with the enthusiasm they lavish on many a lesser Verdi work, and in respectable but less successful accounts by Salieri (1799), Holst (1928), and Vaughan Williams (1946).

* * *

Charles VI, King of France, also died in 1422, the year that claimed Henry V. By virtue of the peace treaty of Troyes, the infant King Henry VI was to rule France as well as England. But the adherents of the Dauphin would not accept his rule, and the war between the two countries was resumed. With the English siege of Orléans — desirable as a strategic base for a decisive attack against the Dauphin, who had proclaimed himself Charles VII — a turning point was reached with the dramatic, indeed miraculous, intervention of Joan of Arc.

She was a simple peasant girl, the daughter of Jacques and Isabelle d'Arc, born in the village of Domrémy, near the Vosges forest. As she was tending her sheep, she had visions of the saints St. Michael, St. Margaret, and St. Catherine, and heard their voices urging her to deliver France from the English invaders. Convinced of the rightness of her mission, Jeanne/Joan overcame her father's objections and rode away, in male attire, across France to the Castle of Chinon, where the helpless Charles VII was staying. Legends about a miracle had preceded her coming, and she convinced the king and his council that heaven was on her side. The leadership of the French army, theretofore headed by Dunois, the bastard son of the late Duke of Orléans, was turned over to her. With supernatural heroism and inspiring leadership, she lifted the siege of Orléans and led the French forces to other triumphs over the demoralized English armies. She then urged the king to move on to

ENGLAND AND FRANCE IN 1429

English possessions
Lands of the French crown
Feudal holdings of the French crown
Church lands
Burgundian lands
Joan of Arc's campaign

0   50   100   150   200 miles

Rheims, deep in enemy territory, and there, in the Cathedral of Rheims, he was crowned King of France on July 17, 1429.

With her mission completed, Joan was ready to return home and resume her former life. But there was more fighting to be done, and during one expedition at Compiègne she was captured by the Burgundians, who ransomed her to the English in May, 1430. In English eyes she was not only an enemy but a witch possessed of occult powers, and she was turned over to a religious inquisition headed by Pierre Cauchon, the Anglophile Bishop of Beauvais. After a lengthy trial, she was convicted of heresy and initially sentenced to life imprisonment. When she continued appearing in male attire — the only kind of clothing she owned — she was pronounced a defiant heretic, and burned at the stake on May 30, 1431, not yet 20 years old. Records of her trial, testifying to her courage and ready wit in answering her judges, survived in astonishing detail.

After Joan's death, the gradual reconquest of France from the weakened English forces continued. A truce was finally signed between the two countries in 1444 at Tours, strengthened by the marriage of the English King Henry VI to Charles VII's niece, Margaret of Anjou. Even so, French troops continued the reconquest of Normandy, occupying Rouen, its capital, in 1449. It was only then that the "victorious" Charles VII was able to investigate the fate of the peasant girl who had saved his kingdom.

At his urging, and with the Pope's approval, Joan's rehabilitation began somewhat haltingly in 1450 with the rounding up of the surviving witnesses. Bishop Cauchon and other members of the shameful 1431 inquisition were no longer living, but Joan's mother Isabelle was still alive, as were Dunois and other French generals, as well as countless ordinary people who testified enthusiastically in the Maid's defense. A commission of high church officials headed by the Archbishop of Rheims pronounced the 1431 verdict "...null, invalid, without effect, and annihilated." The date was July 7, 1456.

It took centuries, however, to establish Joan's blameless reputation. In Shakespeare's early three-part *Henry* VI, she is presented crudely from a near-contemporary and biased English vantage point. (Although part of the First Folio, these plays are not considered authenticated Shakespeare by scholars.) No less damaging to her reputation was Voltaire's lengthy epic poem *La Pucelle*, a wicked pseudo-historical parody dealing rather obsessively with the issue of Joan's virginity in an almost pornographic manner.

It was Friedrich Schiller's 1801 play *Die Jungfrau von Orléans* that reversed the trend of irreverence. Beyond serving as an inspiration for several operas, the Schiller drama also paved the way toward major 20th-century theatrical treatments by George Bernard Shaw, Maxwell Anderson, and Paul Claudel, coincidental with her complete rehabilitation by church authorities and eventual canonization in 1920.

In his usual fashion, Schiller used history as a background against which personalities — historical and fictitious — act out events shaped by the author's lofty mind and Romantic impulses. After presenting the Maid with reasonable accuracy in the play's early scenes, Schiller paints a highly idealized picture at the castle of Chinon. He further romanticizes history in the battle scenes by having Joan fall in love with Lionel, an English knight, thus casting the heroine into a burning conflict between earthly love and heavenly mission. The eloquent dying scene in Schiller's play for the defeated English general Talbot is a high dramatic moment, but it ignores the fact that that gallant soldier lived many more years, to perish at age 82 in 1453 in quite another battle. Another vividly dramatic but false historical touch is Joan's denunciation by her father at Charles's coronation. Finally, Schiller's Joan dies not at the stake but on the battlefield, after being granted a vision of heaven. Full of noble sentiments and eloquent lines — and eminently stageworthy, to boot — the play nevertheless no longer appeals to modern audiences. Nor did it appeal to Napoleon, for he banned it despite its pro-French attitude. (Schiller's views on invasions of other countries were obviously not shared by Napoleon.)

Tchaikovsky's sixth opera, *Orleanskaia Dieva* (*The Maid of Orleans*, 1881), follows Schiller's rewriting of history rather faithfully, allowing for the necessary condensations involving operatic adaptations from literary works. Joan's beautiful aria in Act I ("Farewell, hills and meadows") distills a 50-line monologue in Schiller about Joan's mission. Act II — the castle of Chinon with Agnes Sorel, the king's mistress, shown in a more favorable light than the king himself — is also true to Schiller, as is Act III, with its historically absurd love scene and the father's angry denunciation at the coronation. In the opera's fourth act, Lionel (here a Burgundian, rather than English, knight) is slain and Joan is captured by the English with an excessive operatic rapidity. At the end, however, Tchaikovsky abandons Schiller in favor of history: Joan suffers her martyrdom, welcomed to heaven by an angelic choir.

By the time Tchaikovsky got around to the subject, the story of Joan of Arc had been placed onto the operatic stage by several composers familiar with Schiller's play, among them Vaccai (1827), Pacini (1830), and Balfe (1837). While undoubtedly more enduring than any of these, Verdi's ninth opera, *Giovanna d'Arco* (1845), cannot be counted among the masterworks of that genius. Somewhat hurriedly written to a libretto by Temistocle Solera—a playwright who rather proudly assured Verdi that he would not be "imposed upon by the authority of either Schiller or Shakespeare"—the work makes a real hash of history. It dispenses with Schiller's generous array of historical characters (many of whom Tchaikovsky was to retain for his "grand opera" dimensions) and creates something very much like a domestic tragedy for a cast of five. Then, to carry Schiller's license to the point of absurdity, Verdi's Joan (Giovanna) falls in love with the king (Carlo) himself. Solera's libretto properly records the coronation in Act II, but fails to explain how Joan gets into the English camp in Act III. Here, too, Joan is denounced by her non-comprehending father (Giacomo), but later that same father, now repentant, loosens the Maid's chains, helping her to freedom. (It was hard for Verdi, who was so good at it, to miss an opportunity for a father-daughter scene.) After her release, Joan rejoins the battle and dies a hero's death (à la Schiller), comforted by celestial voices. Schiller's romantic vision was no doubt the main culprit in leading Verdi and Tchaikovsky so far from historical truth, but their *métier* was opera, not history, and both works deserve enduring fame on their musical merit.

Arthur Honegger's *Jeanne d'Arc au bûcher* (1935), though not an opera, is an oratorio for the stage. Based on a modern mystery play by Paul Claudel, it concentrates on the martyr's final moments. Joan's spoken lines, intensely delivered against the singing voices of the saints, the judges, and choral echoes of her early life, add up to a work of great emotional impact which captures the spiritual essence of Joan of Arc, this miraculous and mystifying phenomenon of French history.

* * *

One of the valiant French officers who fought in the Maid's battles against the English was Gilles de Rais (1404-1440). He was the firstborn son of an aristocratic family, orphaned at eleven and brought up by an autocratic grandfather of great wealth and obsessive greed. From him Gilles learned the abuse of power, but that was a quality he shared with many French nobles of the period. Gilles was present with Joan and the Dauphin at Chinon, fought at the siege of Orléans, and was made Marshal of France at twenty-five, after the Dauphin's coronation. Then his life took a violent turn. Apparently unable to adjust to the relative peace that followed, and gaining even more wealth and power upon his grandfather's death, he embarked on a life of debauchery and sadistic violence. His victims were children, procured for him by servants and villagers whom he terrorized, and others who shared his perversions. Although rumors about his atrocities circulated, such was his power that for a while no one dared to challenge it. His violent temper eventually brought Gilles into a confrontation with church authorities, while his insane luxuries precipitated his financial ruin. He was arrested by the Duke of Brittany on charges of witchcraft, sodomy, and murder on September 15, 1440. At first, Gilles denied all charges but, when he realized that punishment was inescapable, his attitude changed into calm acceptance. He was condemned to death by hanging and burning, and the sentence was carried out in Nantes on October 26, 1440.

Soon thereafter, the horrible deeds of Gilles de Rais, the homosexual child abuser whose victims numbered in the hundreds, passed into legend. Eventually, these legends turned him into a murderer of women and endowed him with a blue beard. It is as "Bluebeard" that he appears in a fable by Charles Perrault (1697), which then led to a wealth of varied operatic adaptations by Grétry (1789), Morlacchi (1811), to an operetta parody by Offenbach (1866) and, more significantly, to two modern psychological explorations by Paul Dukas (1907) and Béla Bartók (1911).

Both are enigmatic works, not in the least bloody and, curiously enough, neither presents Bluebeard as a monster. In Maurice Maeterlinck's drama that is the basis for the Dukas opera *Ariane et Barbe-Bleu*, Ariane, Bluebeard's new wife, discovers her predecessors in Bluebeard's gloomy castle. Alienated from life and reconciled to their bondage, they resist Ariane's efforts to free them. In Bartók's *Bluebeard's Castle*, with poetic text by Béla Balázs, which is even more enigmatic, the former wives are silent characters and — unlike Dukas's "liberated" Ariane, who escapes — Bartók's Judith willingly shares the fate of Bluebeard's other wives in limbo, or perhaps death.

Both Maeterlinck and Balázs were symbolic playwrights; both operas attempt to explore such eternal issues as male-female relationships, the secretiveness of the former and the subjugation of the latter, and the tragedy of loneliness. They are open to multifold interpretations and, surely in the case of Bartók — if its recent stagings are a criterion — to frequent misinterpretations. One thing is certain: there is not a trace in these two operas of the monstrous Gilles de Rais of history.

* * *

An altogether exceptionally benign figure for those troubled and cruel times was René, Duke of Anjou and self-styled King of Naples and Sicily. Although related to the battling kings—he was the brother-in-law of Charles VII of France and the father-in-law of Henry VI of England—he managed to keep away from their hostilities. René (1409-1480) was an artistic soul, an outstanding illustrator of manuscripts and also a musician. In his Provençal courts of Aix and Tarascon, he organized knightly tournaments and surrounded himself with artists. (The poet François Villon was among those to enjoy his hospitality.) A peaceful man, René could always find the right solutions to his conflicts. Challenged for the land of Lorraine by Antoine de Vaudémont and defeated by him in battle, he proposed a marriage between Antoine's son Ferry de Vaudémont and his own elder daughter, Yolanda. The two were married in 1445, the same year René's younger daughter, Margaret, married Henry VI of England.

Such an arranged marriage may have restored peace and avoided bloodshed, but hardly satisfied the Danish playwright Henrik Hertz. His play *Yolanta, or King René's Daughter*, depicts the young princess, blind from birth, but shielded from the truth by order of the king. She is wooed by young Vaudémont, who risks his life for her. The two fall in love, and love's mysterious powers restore Yolanta's sight.

Tchaikovsky discovered the play in 1883 and chose it for the subject of his last opera, assuring his brother Modest in a letter that "I shall write music that will bring tears to everyone's eyes." Sharing a remarkable double-bill at St. Petersburg's Mariinsky Theater on December 6, 1892 with the *Nutcracker* ballet (world premiere for both), the opera left the critics remarkably dry-eyed, though they did appreciate the ballet. Virtually unknown in the West to this day, *Iolanta* has remained fairly popular in Russia, especially on the strength of a beautiful bass aria sung in the opera by the character who is lovingly remembered in many French legends as "*le bon roi René*".

King René lived out his life in serenity, ruling over his faithful subjects in old Provence, which is a great deal more than can be said about his son-in-law, Henry VI of England. He was an unstable man, ruling over a restless kingdom torn by murderous hostilities between the ruling house of Lancaster and the opposition, headed by Richard, the Duke of York. Among mounting pressures, aggravated by military defeats by the French, Henry VI fell into a period of insanity in 1453. During the next few years, his strong-willed wife

Margaret (daughter of King René), with the aid of resolute Lancastrian nobles, did everything to protect his throne. But "The Wars of the Roses" between the rival houses of Lancaster and York exacted severe losses on both sides. Finally, the Yorkists prevailed: on June 28, 1461, Edward, son of Richard, the Duke of York (who had been beheaded by the Lancastrians), was crowned Edward IV, King of England.

Except for a brief period (1470-71) when the deposed and temporarily sane Henry VI regained his throne, Edward IV ruled peacefully until his death in 1483. Although a peace treaty between England and France was never signed, a truce in 1475 virtually marked the end of The Hundred Years' War.

On Edward IV's death, his brother Richard, Duke of Gloucester, had the king's two infant sons imprisoned in the Tower and, presumably, murdered. Crowned as King Richard III, he ruled for two years until his enemies, which were legion, destroyed him in the battle of Bosworth. Henry Tudor, crowned in 1485 as Henry VII, united the houses of York and Lancaster. He was the grandson of Catherine de Valois, widow of Henry V, and her second husband, Owen Tudor, one of the countless victims of the Wars of the Roses.

It is a pity that the turbulent reign of Richard III, immortalized by Shakespeare, was never transferred onto the operatic stage. Much of its blood and thunder, however, was captured in Smetana's Shakespeare-inspired tone poem *Richard III* (1859).

XII

A RUSSO-TURKISH INTERMEZZO

Sadko (Rimsky-Korsakov); *Prince Igor* (Borodin);
Alexander Nevsky (Prokofiev); *Tamerlano* (Handel);
Maometto Secondo (Rossini); *Le siège de Corinthe*
(Rossini)

In the early middle ages, the vast land of Russia was inhabited by Slavic peoples who formed settlements along the area's rivers — Pskov, Novgorod, Smolensk, Kiev. They were at the mercy of various nomadic tribes until 862, when Rurik, a Varangian (Viking) prince, became their ruler. With Novgorod as his initial base, Rurik protected the settlers from hostile incursions. At the same time, two other Varangian leaders, Askold and Dir, established their rule in Kiev.

It was Rurik who founded the dynasty that ruled over the people of Rus (as they were known at the time) for nearly eight centuries. His son Oleg (879-912) had Askold and Dir assassinated and, uniting the northern and southern tribes, established Kiev as the center of his domain. (This episode of early history is captured in *Askold's Tomb*, the first successful Russian opera, by Alexander Verstovsky, introduced in 1835 and performed about 600 times in Moscow and St. Petersburg.)

Oleg — "the Wise" — with his aggressive politics strengthened *Kievan Rus* and established trade with Byzantium. In 988, under the rule of Prince Vladimir, it became a Christian nation; Vladimir married Anna, the sister of the Byzantine emperor, and the head of the Russian Church thus came under the jurisdiction of the Byzantine patriarch.

Following the death of Vladimir in 1015, his son Yaroslav began his lengthy rule after several years of fratricidal strife. He established Kiev as an ecclesiastical as well as political capital, formulated a basic legal code (*Pravda Russkaya*), and laid the foundation for the government of the country by establishing a council of the prince's advisors (the duma) whose members were elected from among wealthy landowners and merchants (the boyars). But after Yaroslav's death, central government fell into a decline as the northern princes refused to accept Kievan supremacy. Trade with Byzantium suffered due to Arab attacks in the Mediterranean, and Kiev became vulnerable to invasions by the Polovtsi and other nomadic tribes.

Novgorod, meantime, out of range for such threats, enjoyed a position similar to that of the Italian city states. Ruled by prosperous boyars, it was a city governed in a relatively liberal manner. As the chorus of merchants sings in the opening tableau of Rimsky-Korsakov's *Sadko*:

> Kiev has its noble and glorious prince
> And the bold exploits of its heroes,
> But our Novgorod is greater still,
> For it is the seat of liberty...
> Man has no master, after God, but himself.

Sadko (1898), a blend of ancient history and fantasy (much of its action takes place in the depths of the sea), evokes the glories of 11th-century Novgorod, a bustling port where merchants gathered from many lands. Lively choruses by the local populace celebrate the city's blessings but, not to be outdone, three illustrious visitors from foreign shores rise in the second act to sing the praises of their respective homelands. These are the arias known as "The Song of the Varangian (Viking) Guest" (bass), "The Song of India" (tenor), and "The Venetian Song" (baritone).

It was during the Kievan period that the first Russian literary classic was created: *The Tale of the Host of Igor (Slovo o polku Igoreve)*, a poetic account of the burning of Putivl and the defeat of Prince Igor of Novgorod-Seversk by the Polovtsi, a nomadic Turkic tribe, in 1185 near the Kaiala River. In 1869, Vladimir Stasov, a major literary figure of 19th-century Russia, suggested to Alexander Borodin that an opera might be written on the subject. Borodin began writing his *Prince Igor* but, woefully disorganized that he was, he left the opera unfinished at the time of his death nearly twenty years later. It fell to Rimsky-Korsakov and Glazunov to finish the orchestration and prepare *Prince Igor* for publication and performance in 1890.

The final libretto of *Prince Igor* (by Borodin himself) represents a generous expansion of the material related in the ancient *Tale*. The opera's fascinating and flamboyant Khan Konchak displays no signs of gallantry in the *Tale*, nor do we find any trace of the love episode between the operatic Prince Vladimir (Igor's son) and the young Konchakovna. But the baptized Polovets Ovlur, who helps Igor in his escape, was already present in the an-

cient source, and Yaroslavna's lament (Act IV, Scene 1) is a virtually verbatim transfer from the *Tale*. The cruel Khan Gzak, prominent in the ancient
document, has a silent role in the opera's third act, frequently omitted in performance. Borodin was clearly captivated by the epic's oriental elements; it
is no wonder that the fiercely brilliant *Polovtsi Dances* tend to overshadow
his opera's many lyrical scenes.

The decline of Kiev coincided with the westward drive of Mongol hordes
from Asia, led by their ferocious and brilliant leader Temujin, who assumed
the title "Ghenghis Khan" (All-Encompassing Lord). In 1223, he embarked
on a drive through Turkestan and conquered southern Russia, only to
withdraw mysteriously. But under Batu Khan (the grandson of Ghenghis) an
equally strong Mongol army moved westward in 1236, overran Kiev and occupied all of Poland, Lithuania, and Hungary, leaving devastation in its wake.
In 1242, Batu withdrew his forces to assure his rule over the Mongols on the
death of his father. No army in Europe could have withstood the "Golden
Horde" (the name Horde derives from the Mongol *ordu*); had it continued
in its forward impetus, the consequences for the history of the western world
would have been incalculable.

For another century and more, the Russian princes of Novgorod, Kiev,
and Moscow paid tribute to Mongol overlords. Prince Alexander of Novgorod, accepting Mongol suzerainty, concentrated on fighting the invaders
from the north. He defeated the Swedes at the river Neva, earning the sobriquet "Nevsky", and two years later confronted the Teutonic Knights, a crusading order that was formed in the Holy Land. The battle was fought on the
melting ice of Lake Peipus and, after many hours of fierce fighting, the
Teutonic invaders were routed, many of them perishing in the icy lake.

This "Battle on the Ice" was one of the most striking episodes in Sergei
Eisenstein's film *Alexander Nevsky* (1938). Sergei Prokofiev, who created the
film score, extracted a dramatic cantata for mezzo-soprano, chorus, and orchestra from it a year later. The first of its seven sections is an orchestral
depiction of "Russia under the Mongol yoke"; the second glorifies Alexander
Nevsky, the victor over the Swedes; the third introduces the Teutonic invaders in pseudo-liturgical music that sheds an acerbic light on their
"crusade". The fourth section sounds a rallying cry for the Russians, and it is
followed by the graphically etched carnage of "The Battle on the Ice". In the
sixth section, we hear the mezzo soloist's lament, portraying a Russian
woman searching among the dead soldiers. The cantata ends with the ringing of bells and jubilation greeting Alexander Nevsky's entrance to Pskov.

The film and the music gave Russia a powerful anti-German propaganda vehicle during World War II.

Alexander Nevsky died in 1263. Under the reign of his successors, the territory and principality of Moscow constantly grew in importance, while all Russian princes still remained subservient to Mongol rule. Not until the reign of Dmitri Donskoy (1359-1389) were they strong enough to challenge the Mongols in battle. Although their success was short-lived, the Mongols — like other great powers before and after them — soon became the victims of dissension from within.

Another fearsome Asiatic conqueror, Tamerlane, defeated the Golden Horde in 1395, pressed into Russia and reached the vicinity of Moscow, to withdraw suddenly for strategic reasons. His decision was attributed to divine intervention:

Tamerlane (Timur I Leng, "Timur the Lame") was partially paralyzed as a result of a battle wound, and his injury contributed to his cruel and misanthropic personality. A Moslem, educated by eastern scholars, he knew little about the West, and thought little of exploring its riches. He established his capital in Samarkand and ruled over an empire that at its height included Central Asia, all of the Middle East, and the Caucasus. Invading Persia and India, he destroyed entire cities and massacred their inhabitants. Similar massacres occurred in Baghdad and Damascus, cities which Tamerlane occupied in 1401.

By that time, the Ottoman Turks had absorbed most of the Byzantine empire and had their sights set on Constantinople. But against Tamerlane's armies they were helpless. He crushed the Turks at Ankara in 1402 and captured their sultan, Bajazid I. The sultan died in captivity, treated with surprising kindness, which only increased his humiliation. (Legends about his confinement in an iron cage are discounted by historians.) Tamerlane himself was 69 when he died on January 19, 1405 in Samarkand, preparing for the invasion of China.

It comes as something of a shock to reconcile history's grim and intimidating portrait of that great conqueror with the cultivated tones of the countertenor who impersonates him in Handel's opera *Tamerlano* (1725). Dating from the composer's peak London period, the work was written in less than three weeks, based on a libretto by Nicola Haym. The basic plot is derived from various sources, but all traceable to a French play called *Tamerlan, ou la Mort de Bajazet* (1677). Before Handel, the conflict of these two oriental conquerors had already been treated by several Italian composers: Gaspar-

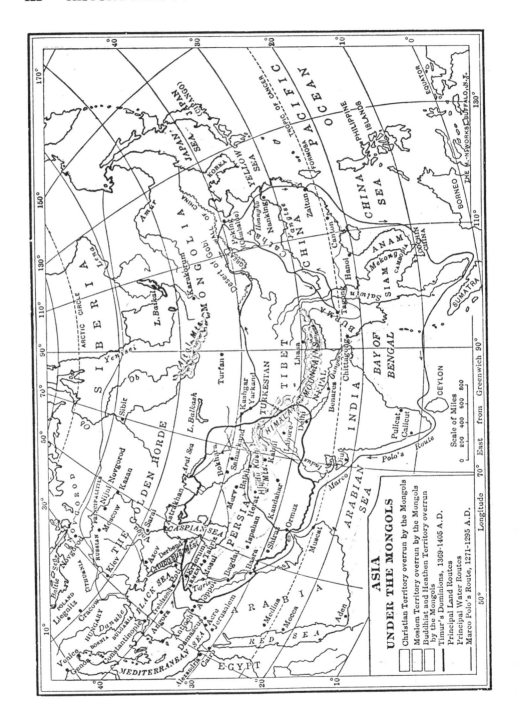

ASIA
UNDER THE MONGOLS

Christian Territory overrun by the Mongols
Moslem Territory overrun by the Mongols
Buddhist and Heathen Territory overrun
   by the Mongols
Timur's Dominions, 1369-1405 A.D.
Principal Land Routes
Principal Water Routes
Marco Polo's Route, 1271-1295 A.D.

ini, Leo, and Alessandro Scarlatti, among them. Handel's opera not only gives credence to the legend of Bajazet's suicide; it makes that event the cardinal episode in the tragedy. Unable to bear his humiliation, the captive Bajazet takes poison and dies after a raging monologue unprecedented in Handel's earlier operas for its overwhelming dramatic intensity. The role, incidentally, is regarded as the first great tenor (as distinct from castrato) part in opera. Otherwise Handel's *Tamerlano*, with its traditional amorous entanglements, adheres to the kind of Baroque conventions that smoothen the rough edges of true history; its jubilant conclusion finds the fearsome Tamerlane in a forgiving disposition rarely ascribed to him by historians.

After the death of Tamerlane, the Ottoman Empire resumed its drive on Constantinople under the various squabbling and fratricidal sultans and carried on separate campaigns against the Venetian Republic, as well. Efforts of the Byzantine emperor John VIII to seek Western help against the Turks was temporarily successful as a crusading army of Hungarians and Poles under János Hunyadi defeated them at Belgrade (1440), but eight years later the tide was turned. The Turkish army under Sultan Murad II defeated the crusaders at Varna (where the Hungarian King Vladislav fell in the battle) and at Kosovo. Murad died in 1451, leaving his young son Mohammed II (1451-1481) with an obsessive determination to capture Constantinople, perceived to be the major threat to Turkish rule.

With a well-trained army of janissaries (young men from Christian families converted to Islam and raised as crack warriors), he began the siege of Constantinople on March 23, 1453. Surrounded by land and sea and subjected to heavy artillery attacks, the city fell on May 29 after a heroically fought battle, which claimed the life of the last of the Byzantine emperors, Constantine XI Palaeologus.

Thus an empire that had stood for more than a thousand years, the empire of Constantine and Justinian, passed into history. The traditions of its civilization survived in the rituals of the Greek Orthodox Church, and were passed on to Russia. Dynastically, too, the connection was strengthened in 1472, when the Russian Prince Ivan III married Sophia, the niece of the last Byzantine emperor. Subsequently, Russian rulers traditionally bore the Byzantine title of "Autocrat" and were crowned according to Byzantine traditions. This continued through the centuries up to the coronation of the last Russian Czar, Nicholas II.

Mohammed II, the conqueror of Constantinople, proceeded to solidify his empire. He repopulated the devastated city with Moslems, Christians, and Jews drawn from all parts of his realm, and gave his subjects considerable religious freedom. Byzantine Constantinople became Istanbul, the Turkish capital, the center of the vast Ottoman Empire. But battles still had to be fought and, in most of them, Mohammed succeeded. He occupied Greece, Serbia, Bosnia, and Albania, and took several maritime outposts from the Genoese Republic between 1456 and 1468. In 1470, a huge Turkish force took Negroponte (now the Aegean island of Euboea) from the Venetians.

The opening scene of Rossini's early (1820) opera *Maometto Secondo* establishes its historical relevance as Negroponte's governor, Paolo Erisso, addresses his Venetian officers:

> Venetian heroes, for two months now,
> Byzantium's arrogant conqueror has surrounded
> These walls with a powerful and savage army....
> The walls are crumbling, and Mohammed
> Threatens us with fire and death
> If the gates are not opened tomorrow...

From this historical premise emerges a libretto (by Cesare della Valle, based on a Voltaire play) that is pure fabrication: cliché operatic situations revolving around an unconvincing romance between Erisso's daughter Anna and the disguised Maometto himself. The ill-fated girl stabs herself in the final scene, and the operatic Maometto is left to find consolation in the highly effective florid music Rossini wrote for his basso interpreter.

Choosing Negroponte as the scene of the opera's action was a decision calculated to appeal to a Neapolitan audience. The Voltaire drama *Mahomet, ou Le Fanatisme* (1742) revolved around the Turkish capture of the Greek city of Corinth, the link between the Peloponnesian Peninsula to the mainland of Greece. In that battle, which occurred in 1459, eleven years before the capture of Negroponte, Mohammed massacred the city's defenders, a fate rather strongly implied in the conclusion of *Le siège de Corinthe*, the opera Rossini refashioned from *Maometto Secondo* for Paris in 1826. At that time, the Greeks were fighting for their independence from the Turkish Empire, and their struggle evoked widespread European sympathy. This at least partially explains the enthusiastic reception Paris accorded to Rossini's opera in its revised form with its frequent references to heroic sacrifices for "*la patrie*".

Mohammed II died in 1481, leaving the Ottoman army well prepared and poised for further European conquests. His Russian contemporary, the Muscovite Prince Ivan III, who ruled from 1462 to 1505, annexed several principalities, including Novgorod, and terminated the long-held threat of the Mongol yoke. The first Russian ruler to be addressed "Czar", Ivan had some difficulties with the powerful boyars who resented his autocratic rule. Their opposition was to be dealt with by the Czar's grandson Ivan IV, better known in history as "Ivan the Terrible".

XIII

CONQUERORS AND EXPLORERS

La cena delle beffe (Giordano); *Caterina Cornaro*
(Donizetti); *Otello* (Rossini and Verdi); *Hunyadi László*
(Erkel); *Ritter Pásmán* (Johann Strauss); *Cristoforo
Colombo* (Franchetti); *Christophe Colombe* (Milhaud);
L'Africaine (Meyerbeer); *Juana la Loca* (Menotti)

The fall of Constantinople and the end of the Byzantine Empire (1453), coinciding with the ascent of Ivan III and the beginning of the new, Muscovite, phase of the Russian state (1462), brought vast changes to Eastern Europe. How was Western Europe shaping up during the last decades of the fifteenth century?

The medieval Holy Roman Empire still existed in name, with the Habsburgs returned to power after the death of Sigismund (1437), the last male heir of the Luxembourg dynasty. Frederick III (1440-1493), an ineffectual ruler, was the last emperor to be crowned by the Pope. His nephew, the infant Ladislas, ruled Hungary and Bohemia through the regency of two powerful local nobles: János Hunyadi in Hungary and George Podiebrad in Bohemia.

This part of Europe lived in constant fear of the ever-growing Turkish power. Hunyadi succeeded in repulsing the Turkish army at Belgrade in 1456, but it was only a temporary triumph for Christendom — the ringing of church bells at midday dates from this event. Hunyadi himself died on August 11 of a fever contracted on the battlefield. His death had tragic consequences.

Powerful men have powerful enemies, and Hunyadi's enemies quickly acted to prevent Hunyadi's older son László from benefiting from his father's enormous popular acclaim. Cillei, King Ladislas's uncle and principal advisor, urged László's arrest but the Hungarian nobles rallying around László assassinated him on November 9, 1456. Deprived of his trusted uncle and intimidated by the Hunyadi family's widespread popularity, the young king reneged on his previously proclaimed safe conduct. He had László and his younger brother Mathias arrested, and two days later (March 14, 1457) László was executed.

Ferenc Erkel's opera *Hunyadi László* (1844), an intense example of Hungarian musical *risorgimento*, captures these tragic events with reasonable faithfulness. A product of the revolutionary surge of the 1840s, this opera sends the message — as does Erkel's later *Bánk bán*[*] — that dire events occur when the country's leadership falls into foreign hands.

Young Mathias Hunyadi appears in a subsidiary role in the opera that centers on the tragic fate of his older brother. A much greater role awaited him in the vortex of history. Fearful of facing the outrage that followed László's execution, King Ladislas sought refuge in friendlier Prague and carried Mathias with him. There the king died under mysterious circumstances. The Hungarian Diet convened and on New Year's Day, 1458, elected Mathias Hunyadi, then age fifteen, King of Hungary.

He soon gave evidence that he was his father's son: heroic, as well as ambitious. Encouraged by Pope Paul II — who was disturbed by the Hussite strength in Bohemia — Mathias invaded that neighboring land and had himself declared King of Bohemia in 1469. Subsequently he found himself at war with Poland, whose ruler also coveted the Bohemian throne — a dispute eventually settled with the division of the territories and both rulers claiming the title "King of Bohemia". By then, Mathias had built what may have been the strongest "regular army" in Europe, largely composed of mercenaries. In 1485, he felt powerful enough to take on the forces of Emperor Frederick III and occupied Vienna. His adventurous and stressful life took its toll: Mathias died in 1490 at the age of 47, and his territorial conquests did not survive him.

Ambitious and frequently reckless in his foreign pursuits, Mathias ruled his country wisely and efficiently through a well-organized central administration. Married to an Italian princess, Beatrice, daughter of the King of Naples, he maintained a luxurious court that welcomed Italian artists and scholars. Perhaps his greatest cultural achievement was the creation of a library of more than 10,000 books and manuscripts called the "Corvina". (The raven — corvus — is the Hunyadi family crest.) Although only a portion of the library survived into modern times, many humanist scholars benefited from its volumes. The legal reforms Mathias instituted seeking justice for the common man earned him the surname "The Just". "King Mathias died — there is

---

[*]   See page 75.

no more justice" is a well-known Hungarian saying, and he is still remembered as Hungary's last native king with melancholy pride.

When not pursuing his expansionist ambitions, Mathias frequently traveled around the countryside in disguise, observing his people at close range and seeking to stamp out injustice. One such event is captured in Johann Strauss's only opera, *Ritter Pásmán* (1892) — a charming story but totally lacking in essential dramatic ingredients. Despite the Waltz King's enormous popularity, the opera was a resounding failure; a rousing orchestral *Csárdás* from it has remained an enduring and much-recorded favorite.

After the dynamic Mathias, the Hungarian nobles wanted a weak ruler, and found him in Ladislas II, King of Bohemia, married to a Habsburg princess. (No one could surpass the Habsburgs in the field of dynastic marriages: with the marriage of Frederick III's son, Maximilian, to the daughter of the Duke of Burgundy, that duchy — comprising today's Belgium, Netherlands, Luxembourg, and northeastern France — was added to the Austrian Habsburg holdings.)

Ladislas II, the new Hungarian king, was no more popular in Bohemia than he was in Hungary; the oppression under his rule gave rise to the legend of Dalibor, the champion of abused peasants, who was tortured and executed when the king sided with the nobles against the people. Smetana's opera *Dalibor* (1868), which abounds in dramatic similarities with Beethoven's *Fidelio*, resounds with patriotic sentiments against royal abuses far beyond its specific medieval relevance.

Peasants revolted in Hungary, too, in 1514, led by György Dózsa, a folk hero in modern Hungary and the central figure in the unsuccessful eponymous Erkel opera (1867). The revolt was put down by the nobles with barbaric cruelty. When the ineffectual King Ladislas died in 1516, he was succeeded on the Bohemian and Hungarian throne by his ten-year-old son Louis II — a helpless pawn in the hands of the nobility. The country was thus totally vulnerable to increasing Turkish attacks under the new Ottoman Sultan Suleiman I ("The Magnificent"). After capturing Belgrade in 1521, the Turks defeated the ill-prepared Hungarian army at Mohács in 1526. King Louis perished in the battle, and the 150-year occupation of Hungary by the Turks began.

* * *

Removed from the imminent danger of Turkish attacks, Western Europe, though frequently suffering from internal strife, enjoyed a high level of economic and cultural activity. Great banking and trading enterprises were built up in Germany, goods were produced with a high degree of craftsmanship in many towns (like Nürnberg), and the ventures of the Hanseatic merchants flourished. Also, the development of the printing press with movable type by Johann Gutenberg of Mainz, which was supplemented by further improvements in Italy, exercised an enormous influence on the cultural climate of the Western world.

Little moral leadership was provided, however, from Rome. Pope Sixtus IV (1471-1484) built the Sistine Chapel and began the beautification of the city, while actively meddling into the affairs of the other city states, at times with bloody results. After appointing the Medici of Florence as the Papacy's banking house, he withdrew his patronage in 1474 in favor of the rival house of the Pazzi. A conspiracy of the Pazzi (in all likelihood encouraged by the Pope) resulted in the assassination of Giuliano de'Medici in church. His brother Lorenzo survived and proceeded with the virtual extermination of the Pazzi house. For this he was excommunicated in 1478.

Lorenzo de'Medici ("*Il Magnifico*") is justly remembered as a great patron of the arts, whose court welcomed a brilliant circle of painters, sculptors, architects, poets, and thinkers. But his foreign policy was costly, and he was not above appropriating state revenues for private purposes. The restlessness caused by the decline of Florentine prosperity, and the wanton licentiousness of the city's aristocracy, is grippingly captured in Umberto Giordano's opera *La cena delle beffe* (*The Feast of Jests*, 1920), based on Sem Benelli's play. Without focusing on a specific event, the opera's gruesome plot is played out against a keenly observed historical background: The brothers Chiaramantesi are political enemies of the "magnificent" Lorenzo — Neri, the older brother, curses the "*maledetta gente di Medici*" in his drunken stupor. Giannetto Malespini, a Medici crony, contrives — with Lorenzo's tacit approval — to settle his feud with the brothers. By clever manipulation of a sinister plot, he draws Neri into a lurid situation where he inadvertently kills his own brother, Gabriello. Neri loses his mind and staggers out, demented, when the curtain falls. It was this kind of moral laxity that the stern Dominican friar Girolamo Savonarola inveighed against. After Lorenzo's death, the opposition summoned the troops of the French King Charles VIII in 1494. Thus began the subjugation of northern Italy that brought both Florence and Milan under French rule. Savonarola supported the French invasion but continued haranguing against corruption and papal abuses. Unwilling to cease his preaching in defiance of the papal ban, he was burned at the stake in 1498.

The Venetian Republic, which included such major cities as Padua, Verona, Brescia, Vicenza, and Bergamo, found itself involved in several wars with Ottoman Turks during these decades. After losing the harbor of Negroponte (1470),* Venice was obliged to pay an annual tribute for Turkish permission to trade in the Black Sea. Limited in her maritime expansion by the Turkish occupation of Greece and Albania, she was blocked on the Italian mainland by the French. In 1489, however, Venice succeeded in acquiring the Island of Cyprus by putting extortionist pressure on its widowed queen, the former Caterina Cornaro, daughter of a prominent Venetian noble. Caterina ended her life in seclusion in 1509, still clinging to her obsolete titles as "Queen of Cyprus, Jerusalem, and Armenia". Remembered for her many charitable deeds and for being the victim of Venetian greed, she attracted enough sympathy among *litterateurs* to have inspired at least three operas—by Fromental Halévy (1841), Franz Lachner (1841), and Gaetano Donizetti (1844). Wagner bestowed uncharacteristically high praise on Halévy's *La Reine de Chypre*, admiring its affinity with the German spirit but, of the three, it was Donizetti's treatment that best stood the test of time.

In 1565, less than eighty years after the Venetians acquired Cyprus, a novel by Geraldo Cinthio was published under the title *Il Moro di Venezia*. Shakespeare gave the Moro a name, "Othello", in the play he fashioned from that source with considerable alterations around 1604. Rossini's early (1816) opera *Otello, ossia Il Moro di Venezia*, was enormously successful in its time. As for its faithfulness to Shakespeare, here is a report from Byron, who attended a performance in Venice on February 21, 1818: "They have been crucifying *Othello* into an opera (*Otello*, by Rossini): the music good, but lugubrious; but as for the words, all the real scenes with Iago cut out, and the greatest nonsense inserted.... Scenery, dresses, and music very good." A year later, no doubt, Byron also learned that for a Rome performance of his *Otello* Rossini prepared an alternate happy ending!

Verdi's masterful *Otello* (1887) relegated Rossini's early effort to curio status. Byron would have probably approved Boito's inspired libretto despite the necessary departures from the Bard. There is, for example, no

---

*   See page 124.

Shakespearean equivalent to Othello's exultant announcement of the defeat and dispersal of the Turkish fleet in the opera's first act:

> *L'orgoglio musulmano sepolto è in mar,*
> *Nostra e del cielo è gloria!...*

> (The Moslem pride is buried in the sea,
> Ours and heaven's is the glory!)

Whether by Cinthio, Shakespeare, or Boito, Othello's story is fiction, but this sea battle *could have* taken place in the last decade of the fifteenth century.

Cyprus remained a Venetian outpost for nearly a century, but it soon became powerless against "the Moslem pride" as Venice assumed a non-belligerent attitude toward the steady advance of the Turks.

* * *

Meanwhile, there were signs of a new awakening in the Iberian peninsula—in Portugal as well as in the newly unified kingdoms of Castile and Aragon. There the fall of Constantinople gave rise to a new crusading spirit, and it was enthusiastically supported by Isabella of Castile and Ferdinand of Aragon, the new rulers of Spain. The two—the intelligent, devout, but rigid and intolerant Isabella and the pragmatic, cunning, and Machiavellian Ferdinand—formidably complemented each other. The final Moorish hold over Spanish territory was broken on January 6, 1492 when, after decades of fighting, Granada was liberated from Moorish rule. A brief period of moderation ensued, during which religious freedom was respected. But eventually intolerance prevailed and the Moors were forced to choose conversion or exile.

Even more acute was the plight of the Spanish Jews and *marranos* (converted Jews who observed their ancient rites). Enforcing a papal authorization of 1478 to root out heretics, Tomás de Torquemada (1420-1498), the Inquisitor General, pursued his task with a cruel and fanatical zeal. Thousands were executed or condemned to lengthy imprisonment before, finally, on March 30, 1492, less than three months after the Moorish surrender, the Catholic kings signed an edict ordering the expulsion of all Jews from their kingdoms.

1492 was a momentous year for Spain. On August 3, Christopher Columbus, a Genoese sea captain in the service of the Spanish rulers, sailed with his three ships, the *Santa Maria* (his flagship), the *Niña* and the *Pinta,* from Palos in the Canary Islands on his first voyage in search of the Indies. On October 12, all three ships anchored off the Watlings Islands in the Bahamas. A new world had been discovered.

It was a great decade for discoveries, and Spain's not too friendly neighbor Portugal had pioneered them. Portuguese explorers, carrying out most of their voyages in secret, had already crossed the equator, established trade with Africa, and obtained papal sanction for claiming exclusive rights to their discoveries in the 1480s. In 1487, the Portuguese Captain Bartolomé Dias rounded the southern coast of Africa, the great promontory thereafter identified as the Cape of Good Hope.

It was the Portuguese King John II whom Columbus first approached with his plan to reach India by striking out westward. The king turned him down in 1483 or 1484, partly because he was unimpressed by Columbus's geographical knowledge and partly because he was already financing Dias and other Portuguese explorers. In 1486, Columbus found a more favorable reception in Spain, particularly on the part of Isabella, who was impressed by the Genoese's religious fervor. The plan was nonetheless rejected by the queen's advisors. Only after the conquest of Granada did the captain's tenacious efforts bear fruit: he was named admiral and sailed out as the prospective viceroy and governor general of all lands to be discovered.

Although the lands discovered in 1492 included Cuba and Hispaniola (Santo Domingo), Columbus was still under the mistaken belief that he had reached the Far East when he returned to be received with royal pomp at the court in Barcelona in April 1493. It was the highest point of his life; never again was he to experience so much universal praise and enjoy complete royal favor.

Losing no time, King Ferdinand appealed to Pope Alexander VI (the former Rodrigo Borgia of Aragon) to obtain his blessings on the new Spanish possessions. After entertaining a counterclaim by Portugal's equally determined John II, the Pope sanctioned the remarkable Treaty of Tordesillas (June 7, 1494). By simply drawing a vertical line at longitude 46° 30', Portugal was to take possession of all the lands to the east, and Spain, those to the west. (This arbitrary division gave Portugal the gift of Brazil a few years later. For some 50 years, the treaty went unchallenged until England began making discoveries of its own and Queen Elizabeth's court served notice on the Spanish ambassador that "the pope had no right to partition the world.")

Steadfast in his pursuit of the Far East, Columbus embarked on two more voyages, adding new discoveries (Puerto Rico, Trinidad, Honduras) to Spain's glory. But he failed as an administrator, and the king replaced him as governor of Hispaniola with Bobadilla, a Columbus antagonist, who had the great explorer put in chains. His longtime champion, Queen Isabella, died on November 26, 1504, and, though quickly set free, Columbus vainly asked that his rank and titles be restored: the king ignored all his requests. Thus the man who laid the foundation for the future Spanish empire died in virtual obscurity. The "New World" he inadvertently discovered was named after Amerigo Vespucci, a representative of the House of Medici in Florence. It is unlikely that he was a better seaman, and he certainly benefited from his predecessor's discoveries, but Vespucci had a firmer grip on geography, and knew how to attract favorable publicity.

A life of grand adventure ebbing into pathetic failure — surely there is the stuff for opera here and, not surprisingly, the *Oxford Dictionary of Opera* lists some 35 operas about Columbus. Of these, Alberto Franchetti's *Cristoforo Colombo* proved most stageworthy. It was commissioned by the city of Genova in 1892 for the 400th anniversary of America's discovery. Toscanini conducted a number of performances all over Italy and in Buenos Aires, as well, with such great Italian baritones in the title role as Giuseppe Kaschmann, Pasquale Amato and Titta Ruffo. The latter sang the role in the opera's U.S. premiere in Philadelphia in 1912, with Rosa Raisa as Queen Isabella.

Franchetti's opera starts with a historically faithful account of the initial rejection of Columbus's project in Salamanca by the Queen's council headed by Cardinal Talavera. It then records, with passionate and highflown eloquence, the Queen's enthusiasm for the adventure. The second act takes place on board of the *Santa Maria*, with the crew in a near-mutinous state after 36 days at sea, and it culminates in the grand moment of the landsighting. The last act is melodramatic: Columbus, aged and weary, is grieving over the departed queen. Then, in a supremely operatic dying scene, he collapses and dies on her tomb.

Three more modern operatic treatments of the life of Columbus deserve mention. *Christophe Colombe* by Darius Milhaud (1930) is on a grandiose scale, employing a large orchestra, a double chorus, and a cast of fifty. The text by Paul Claudel, heavy with symbolism, moves back and forth in time, with a strong dose of allegory and mysticism imposed on the historical facts. Given that Milhaud's music is at times "frustratingly dense" (in the view of

Titta Ruffo as *Cristoforo Colombo* (Franchetti)
Author's collection

one of the opera's producers), the opera's future, if any, is likely to be limited to the concert stage. Such a performance, broadcast to 14 countries, took place in Marseille in 1984.

Far less ambitious is *Christopher Columbus* (1939) by the Hungarian-American composer Eugene Zador with an English text by Lionel Barrymore (Zador's onetime composition pupil) based on a Hungarian play by the Archduke Joseph Franz of Habsburg, a Columbus scholar. Short on specific historical detail, this opera moves on a highly spiritual plane. It concentrates on the dramatic unrest on board of the *Santa Maria*, culminating in the joyous discovery of the new world and ending with an appropriate choral hymn of thanksgiving.

Barcelona, where the triumphant voyager was received by their Catholic Majesties, was the scene nearly 500 years later (September 24, 1989) of the premiere of *Cristobal Colon*, a new opera by the Catalan composer Leonardo Balada with tenor José Carreras in the title role and soprano Montserrat Caballé as Queen Isabella. The future will pass judgment on its durability; in historical matters it is noteworthy that the text of Antonio Gala depicts Columbus as a fuller human being than do his predecessors. Furthermore, it takes notice of two important personages in the discoverer's life: Martin Alonso Pinzón, one of his captains and at a time his antagonist, and Doña Beatriz de Peraza, with whom Columbus was amorously involved.

* * *

In 1495, during the second voyage of Columbus, Portugal's King John II, patron of the explorer Bartolomé Dias, died and was succeeded by his brother, Manuel I. The new king was also eager to follow up previous discoveries, to increase trade and to develop Portugal into a colonial power. He chose for the next expedition a 37-year old seaman named Vasco da Gama, a nobleman known for daring, iron discipline, and a certain cruel and temperamental streak. Charged with a mission to reach India and spread the Christian faith, Da Gama started on his quest from Lisbon on July 8, 1497. His route followed that of Dias, rounding the Cape of Good Hope. Then he proceeded northward along the East African Coast up to Mozambique. There, with the aid of an Arab pilot, his fleet left Africa and reached Calicut at the southern tip of India's Malabar Coast in the spring of 1498.

It was a dangerous journey, and the reception the voyagers encountered from the African natives and the Hindus — whom they mistook for Christian

Beniamino Gigli as Vasco da Gama in *L'Africaine* (Meyerbeer)
CREDIT: Metropolitan Opera Archives

outcasts — was rarely friendly. Nor were the Portuguese explorers successful as traders, seldom able to offer the natives the goods they wanted. When Da Gama returned to Lisbon in September 1499, only 44 of his original crew of 170 survived. But the way was open to an entirely new era of world trade. King Manuel was jubilant, but imposed tight secrecy on the details of Vasco's route.

In 1838, the indefatigable Eugène Scribe prepared a libretto for Giacomo Meyerbeer, ostensibly based on Vasco da Gama's voyage. Actually, what he had was a fairly generic plot into which he managed to place a few incidents of Vasco da Gama's scantily documented life. Composer and librettist disagreed on many points, and completion of L'Africaine was delayed until 1860. Nearly five more years passed before the opera's premiere — an event Meyerbeer did not live to witness.

Not only is the plot of L'Africaine pure fabrication, but it also does a disservice to Da Gama's character, for he is depicted here as a selfish and ungenerous man, vacillating between two women — and singing love duets with both. The absurdities of the opera's action need no further comment save for the fact that one of Vasco's ladies, Selika, is an Indian rather than an African princess. Indian rites, with specific mention of the Hindu deities Brahma, Vishnu, and Shiva, are observed in Act IV, suggesting that L'Hindoue would have been a more appropriate title for the opera.

Shaky though his geography was, Scribe was a solid student of literature, and he must have consulted the great Portuguese epic The Lusiads by Luis de Camoëns (1524-1580) for his libretto. This literary classic encompasses the voyage of Vasco da Gama and much of Portugal's early history. It was Camoëns who created the mythological character of Adamastor, once a mythical being whom a deceitful nymph transformed into a forbidding cape at the bottom of the world. It is to this terror of all seamen that the native Nelusko refers to in the third act of L'Africaine when he sings the rousing ballad "Adamastor, roi des vagues profondes." The subject is, of course, the Cape of Good Hope, no longer feared thanks to pioneering Portuguese navigators.

Camoëns himelf is an important operatic character in Donizetti's last opera, Dom Sebastien de Portugal (1843). Scribe was once again the librettist, but here the historical liberties are less offensive. King Sebastian I (1557-1578) undertook an ill-advised crusade against the Moroccans. On August 4, 1578, his forces were defeated at Al Kasr al-Kabir, and the king perished.

The crucial battle forms the opera's last act. (Camoëns, who fought in that battle, lost one of his eyes.)

In contrast to the melancholy fate of Columbus, Vasco da Gama ended his life properly recognized and rewarded for his achievements. Portugal's fortunes continued to expand with the discovery of Brazil in 1500, and its King Manuel resisted the efforts of Spain's King Ferdinand to unite the two nations. The dynastic marriages of the two daughters of Ferdinand and Isabella both ended in tragedy. Isabella, the older, married to the Portuguese king, died young; Juana, the younger, was mentally unstable. She was married to the Archduke Philip of Habsburg, whom the grandees of Castile preferred to Ferdinand, but he, too, died prematurely in 1506. Thereupon, with his daughter Juana declared insane, Ferdinand continued to rule Castile until his death in 1515.

Giancarlo Menotti's opera *Juana La Loca* (1979) relates with admirable historical accuracy the tragic fate of this unfortunate daughter of the Spanish royal pair. She was kept in confinement for nearly fifty years by the connivance of her father, her husband, and her son. That son, however, was marked for greatness. Designated by the will of his grandfather Ferdinand to succeed him, he ascended the throne in 1516 as Charles I, later to become famous in history as the Emperor Charles V.

XIV

MACHIAVELLI'S "PRINCES"

Lucrezia Borgia (Donizetti); *Ernani* (Verdi); *Benvenuto Cellini* (Berlioz); *Montezuma* (Graun / Sessions); *Fernand Cortez* (Spontini); *Rigoletto* (Verdi); *Karl V* (Krenek)

"Nepotism" is a term that owes its origin to medieval popes who maintained their power and influence by placing their nephews (and other relatives) into prominent positions. Rodrigo Borja, a young man from a prominent Aragonese family and nephew of Pope Calixtus III, became a cardinal at 25. Playing clever priestly politics, he served three subsequent popes while enhancing his own position. So when he himself was elected as Alexander VI to the high office 37 years later, on August 11, 1492, his accession would have seemed a reward well earned. But that was not the view of the first great historian of Italy—Francesco Guicciardini of Florence (1483-1540)—who regarded the election of Alexander VI a foul and shameful act, achieved through bribery.

Alexander Borgia, a libertine whose mode of life was not altered by his exalted position, provided for his nephews, but his children came first. He had nine of them, some actually fathered during his papacy, but the dearest to his heart were the four resulting from his unsanctified liaison with Vannozza Catanei: Cesare (b.1475), Juan (b.1476), Lucrezia (b.1480), and Joffre (b.1482). None reached old age, and two of them met violent deaths, but they achieved unparalleled notoriety during Alexander's years of power (1492-1503) and continued to survive in bloody legends even after they faded from view.

Juan was the first to die, in 1497, at the hands of assassins in the service of his older brother Cesare, who considered Juan a rival in his limitless ambitions. Their father the Pope accepted the outcome as a price to be paid for Cesare's unchallenged leadership of the papal army. And Cesare was a born leader: tall, strong, fearless, and cruel. As he marched through the Papal States, taming and subjugating the rebellious towns, legends about his cruelties struck terror in Italian hearts. Unscrupulous in political matters and deceitful as an ally, Cesare Borgia became Duke of Valentinois and Duke of Romagna, and owner of vast holdings. But he could not kill all his enemies and, driven from power when his father died, he escaped back to his ancestral Spain. There, fighting in the service of the King of Navarre, he was killed in a skirmish in 1507, at thirty-one.

Cesare's sister Lucrezia was not yet fourteen when she was married to Giovanni Sforza. When, four years later, that political alliance no longer served Borgia purposes, the marriage was annulled on the grounds of non-consummation—an absurdity but not impossible to achieve with Pope Alexander having the final word. Her second husband, Alfonso, Duke of Bisceglie, was soon murdered by Cesare's henchmen—an event that shocked all Rome and gave rise immediately to rumors about incestuous relationships. (Similar gossip linked Lucrezia with the Pope, as well.)

So by the time Lucrezia married for the third time, to the dissolute but powerful Alfonso d'Este, Duke of Ferrara, she brought to that marriage a thoroughly besmirched reputation. Modern historians tend to question Lucrezia's reputation as a poisoner on a grand scale, but Victor Hugo's 1833 *Lucrèce Borgia* gave full credence to those legends. Shrewd playwright that he was, however, he made the heroine of his drama an intriguing mixture of good and evil: a devoted mother as well as a cold-blooded murderess. The coexistence of vice and virtue in the same character fascinated Victor Hugo, but he had to take leave of historical facts to make his drama work in the case of Lucrezia Borgia.

The play—and Donizetti's opera *Lucrezia Borgia* (1833), which faithfully follows it—hinges on Gennaro, a fictitious son from an earlier marriage, whom Alfonso d'Este mistakes for a rival. Lucrezia did have a son named Rodrigo from her second marriage to the unfortunate Duke of Bisceglie, but that son was barely two years old when she married Alfonso in 1501. Although she bore Alfonso four children, the marriage was anything but happy. In fact, Lucrezia did have a love affair with the Venetian poet Pietro Bembo, who would have made an interesting operatic character. To carry poetic—and operatic—license even further, the operatic Lucrezia collapses (and perhaps dies) over the dead body of Gennaro. The real Lucrezia died in 1518, after spending her last years in seclusion and religious meditation. She was not yet forty.

As a relentless enemy of the House of Borgia, the great historian Giucciardini faithfully recorded every scandal that attached to the hated name.

But that attitude was not shared by Niccolò Machiavelli, who, as an envoy of the Florentine Republic, was fascinated by Cesare Borgia's leadership qualities and political skill. Although the pattern of his own life may suggest otherwise, in his writings, and particularly in his notorious book *The Prince* (c.1513), Machiavelli cynically states that mankind in general is selfish, stupid, cowardly, and gullible. Therefore, he contends that a ruling prince should use every means in his power, specifically cruelty and deceit, to maintain his dominant position. To be hated, according to Machiavelli, should be a matter of no concern to a prince; to be feared is essential.

Whether Machiavelli intended his book as a guide for tyrants or a bitter pre-Orwellian satire on absolute monarchy, Cesare Borgia was the very embodiment of his hypothetical "Prince". And, in many ways, the qualities urged by the wily Florentine were also shared by three powerful rulers who left their decisive imprints on 16th-century Europe: Henry VIII of England (1509-1547), Francis I of France (1515-1547), and Charles I of Spain, who became the Holy Roman Emperor Charles V (1519-1556). The English ruler involved himself relatively little in foreign relations, but the French and Spanish kings clashed frequently over territorial claims. Being absolute monarchs, they eventually became ready targets for the fiery republican pen of Victor Hugo and leading principals in two Verdi operas, *Ernani* and *Rigoletto*.

When Charles ascended the Spanish throne in 1516 at age sixteen to succeed his grandfather Ferdinand,[*] he was received with deep distrust. A native of Ghent, he spoke Flemish only, was distant and taciturn by nature and ungainly in appearance, with his aquiline nose and protruding Habsburg chin. But he was, by dynastic inheritance, the ruler of Spain, Naples, Sicily, the conquered territories of Spanish America, and a logical aspirant to the emperor's throne — an honor Francis I of France also coveted. Nevertheless, it was Charles whom the seven German electors chose as emperor in 1519 — an election secured by vast sums in bribery, sums largely obtained from the powerful Fugger banking house, an important ally of the imperial Habsburgs for generations to come.

After his coronation as emperor in Charlemagne's Aachen (Aix-la-Chapelle) on October 23, 1520, Charles V immediately found himself beset with problems. In Germany, Martin Luther was attacking the papacy and formulating his doctrines of the Reformation that found favor with several

---

[*]   See page 138.

German electors. And in Spain, where Charles was never popular and even less so as a result of his imperial ambitions, an insurrection broke out uniting aristocratic and bourgeois elements against the authority of the king.

Victor Hugo's grandiose and eloquent, if highly improbable, play *Hernani* takes place in the crucial year of 1519. Charles is first seen in the unlikely role of the romantic wooer pursuing the noble Doña Sol. Later he appears, more convincingly, as a strong ruler who magnanimously pardons the rebellious nobles. There is drama aplenty in the play, the kind that appealed to 19th-century opera librettists. Bellini and his favorite author Felice Romani seriously considered it in 1831 but, anticipating censorship problems in Naples, they abandoned the project. The challenge was taken up later by several minor composers and, more significantly, a major one: Giuseppe Verdi, whose *Ernani* was introduced in 1844.

Ernani glorifies the image of the noble outlaw so favored by the Romantic poets and playwrights of the period, with political issues taking second place to the obsessive Spanish sense of gentlemanly honor. The improbabilities of Hugo's play are rendered downright absurd in the libretto by the necessary condensation that turned Hugo's fervent poetic lines into Francesco Maria Piave's decently serviceable verses. The play's Doña Sol appears more euphoniously as "Elvira" in the opera, where the king (Carlo) is the only true historical character. In the third act, which takes place in Aix-la-Chapelle, he is duly and melodiously elected emperor, uncovers the conspiracy of the nobles and has its leaders arrested with expedient operatic fleetness. Then, overcome by the majesty of the moment and remembering the stature and wisdom of Charlemagne, he announces *"Perdono a tutti!"* The opera's bandit-hero Ernani has a brief hour of bliss before taking his own life, obeying the dictates of his obsession with "honor".

The magnanimity of the historical Charles had its limits. After decisively defeating the rebels at Villalar (April 23, 1521), he pardoned many of them but had Juan de Padilla and several other leaders executed. The experience taught him to deal cautiously with the traditional rights of the nobles. Realizing, too, that he could not govern his vast empire without delegating responsibility, he made his brother Ferdinand ruler of the Habsburg lands around the Danube. This, in effect, divided the Habsburg empire: Charles and his descendants ruled over Spain and the Netherlands; Ferdinand's heirs—the

"Austrian Habsburgs" — became the rulers of Austria and its dominions. (However, much of Hungary came under Turkish rule after the disaster at Mohács in 1526.*)

* * *

The Reformation, which began with Martin Luther's first public protest against priestly abuses and his challenge of papal authority in 1517, was undoubtedly the most momentous event of the sixteenth century. Its grave consequences were not fully grasped by Pope Leo X (1513-1521), who was a great patron of the arts and more of a politician than a churchman. His successor, Adrian VI, a Flemish prelate and once regent for the young Charles V, attempted to eliminate the abuses that caused the reform movement and tried to reconcile the rival monarchs, Charles V and Francis I of France, to unite in a crusade against the Turks. But he died without achieving his goals, and the two kings and their heirs fought each other for decades to come.

The next pope, Clement VII (who was Giulio de'Medici, the natural son of Giuliano de'Medici, Lorenzo's murdered brother**) supported Charles against French attempts to seize Italian territories. At the battle of Pavia (1525), Francis suffered a humiliating defeat and fell into captivity. Under duress, he was forced to sign a disastrous treaty, renouncing his claim to Naples, Milan, and other cities. But he went back on his commitments upon release, and the war continued.

The increasing power of Charles was viewed with concern by Pope Clement, as well as by Henry VIII of England. Matters took an ugly turn when an army of German and Spanish mercenaries led by the Constable of Bourbon devastated Italian territories and mercilessly sacked Rome in 1527. The Constable lost his life but he was cruelly avenged: the leaderless mob pillaged the city, destroyed countless works of art and brutalized its inhabitants. The Pope himself was forced to seek refuge in the then impenetrable Castel Sant' Angelo. Later Charles, though disclaiming responsibility for the outrageous actions of his troops, nonetheless did penance for the sacrilege.

Sharing captivity with Pope Clement VII in the Castel Sant'Angelo was his fellow Florentine, Benvenuto Cellini (1500-1571), goldsmith, sculptor, and

---

*　　See page 128.
**　See page 129.

one of the most colorful figures of the Renaissance. (In his famous autobiography, one of the significant literary documents of the period, Cellini credits himself with the shooting of the invading Constable of Bourbon.) Trouble usually followed Cellini wherever he went; he was imprisoned several times, once for killing a rival goldsmith named Pompeo in a fight. His art, nonetheless, earned him the forgiveness of Pope Clement, as well as that of his successor Paul III. Cellini's adventurous life soon returned him to Florence, then took him to the Gonzaga court in Mantua, to the service of art-loving Francis I in Paris, and eventually back to Florence. There, in the service of Cosimo de'Medici, he completed his best-known sculpture, the bronze Perseus, in 1548. (It is still one of the major ornaments of Florence's famous Loggia dei Lanzi.) He completed his autobiography in 1562 and died in Florence in 1571.

In his *Memoirs*, Hector Berlioz recalled that in 1838 "I had been greatly struck with certain episodes in the life of Benvenuto Cellini, and was so unlucky as to think they offered an interesting and dramatic subject for an opera. So I begged Léon de Wailly and Auguste Barbier... to make me a libretto on the subject." His *Benvenuto Cellini* was introduced at the Opéra on September 10, 1838, at which time "the overture received exaggerated applause, and the rest was hissed with admirable energy and unanimity." After three more performances, the opera disappeared from the repertoire, to be resuscitated periodically since then, championed by such eminent conductors as Liszt and Mahler and, more recently, Sir Colin Davis, Sir John Pritchard, and Georges Prêtre.

The Berlioz opera failed because in 1838 Parisian taste favored either Meyerbeerian spectacle or *opéra comique* à la Auber or Boieldieu. *Benvenuto Cellini* is an uneasy mix of both, and its musical riches cannot quite overcome its theatrical shortcomings. The librettists Wailly and Barbier played fast and loose with history. The casting of Perseus is central to the story, but the authors placed that event into the artist's early Roman period, crediting Clement VII, not Cosimo de' Medici, with its commission. Accordingly, the Pope makes several appearances in the opera, now humoring now castigating Cellini, the unruly "*maitre drôle*". The deadly fight with Pompeo, described in Cellini's autobiography, is retained, as are the true-life figures of Ascanio, his assistant, and Balducci, the papal treasurer and one of Cellini's enemies. The artist's operatic romance with Teresa Balducci, however, is fabrication. He was something of a libertine who gleefully recounts his dalliances in his autobiography. Apparently, though, he settled down in Florence and married Piera di Salvatore Parigi, the mother of his two legitimate children.

* * *

The spread of Luther's reformist movement in the German lands eventually forced Charles V to grant religious freedom to Protestants, and temporarily halted his warlike activities against France. But Spain under his rule — and, initially, even without his knowledge — became a world power. In the spring of 1519, Hernan Cortés, a high official in the service of Diego Velásquez, governor of the conquered land of Hispaniola, set out on an expedition with eleven ships and some 600 men toward the yet unexplored land of Mexico. Within one year of political moves, dangerous adventures, and much bloodshed, the conquest of Mexico was completed and its politically divided Indian inhabitants became the subjects of the emperor. Montezuma, the noble and generous Aztec ruler, who greeted Cortés as the divine presence Quetzalcoatl whose arrival had been foretold by prophecy, was stoned to death by his own kinsmen.

There is a fascinating story here: Christianity clashing with ancient Indian rites (which dealt with sophisticated theories of astral science yet practiced human sacrifice and even cannibalism); the contrast between mercenary Spaniards and trusting and ultimately betrayed natives. No wonder it caught the imagination of European literary minds early on. The Mexican conquest was related in admirable detail by Bernal Diaz de Castillo, one of Cortés's officers, who saw it all. His *Historia Verdadera de la Conquista de la Nueva España* was completed in 1568 and published posthumously in 1632.

It is unlikely, though, that Vivaldi, Sacchini, and Zingarelli — all of whom wrote operas about Montezuma in the eighteenth century — consulted that extraordinary document. Of special interest is *Montezuma* by Karl Heinrich Graun, court composer to Frederick the Great of Prussia, because it was the king himself who provided the opera's Italian libretto. That enlightened monarch left no doubt whatever that his sympathies were on the side of Montezuma and his ancient civilization as opposed to Cortés, the embodiment of tyrannical authority.

Bernal Diaz's chronicle, however, is definitely the basis for the *Montezuma* that followed two centuries later (1964) combining the efforts of G. Antonio Borgese (libretto) and Roger Sessions (music). Diaz, in fact, has a major role as narrator in the opera, devoted to Cortés but an outspoken ad-

mirer of Montezuma, as well. The opera casts a favorable light on both personalities but, imperiled by the Scylla of a severely dissonant score and the
Charybdis of a verbose and obscure text, its future course is not encouraging.

Quite a different case is Gasparo Spontini's *Fernand Cortez* (1809), which
portrays the conquistador as a hero in the Bonapartist mold. (The opera was
intended to glorify Napoleon.) According to Edward J. Dent, "War is the
background of the whole score; from beginning to end it is little more than
a string of military marches, interspersed by a few dances in the polonaise
style." The opera ends with Cortez's triumphant entry into Mexico City on
horseback and, not to spoil the heroic/romantic mood, the life of Montezuma
is spared. When the Metropolitan staged *Fernand Cortez* in 1888, a contemporary observer noted that "the people employed in the representation
rivaled in numbers those who constituted the veritable Cortez army, while
the horses came within three of the number that the Spaniards took into
Mexico." One of the opera's principal characters, wholly fictitious but beauti-
fully written for the soprano voice, is Amazily, the Aztec princess converted
to Christianity, who nobly mediates between the two camps. Renata Tebaldi sang it when the work briefly returned to circulation in Naples (1951).

Since Cortés undertook his Mexican campaign without the approval of
his superior, Diego Velásquez, he could have been tried for insubordination.
Such ideas, however, were soon dispelled by the success of the enterprise
and by the riches resulting from it. In 1522, Charles V formally recognized
the conquest, Mexico became part of his empire, and Catholic missionaries
began to spread the faith. In 1528 Cortés was made a Marquess by Charles
but, to his great disappointment, the monarch appointed another noble as
governor of Mexico. Although a wealthy man, Cortés encountered frustrations similar to those of Columbus in his later years. After Pizarro's conquest
of Peru in 1535, which yielded even more treasures than Mexico to the empire, he became an anachronism. With both his health and his influence at
court in decline, Cortés died on December 2, 1547.

* * *

Few were the years when these two Machiavellian monarchs, Charles V
and Francis I, were not at war with one another, while the third, Henry VIII,
formed alliances now with one, now the other, according to what served his
purpose of the moment. Save for his attempts to invade France itself, Char-

Francis I: The King Amuses Himself
CREDIT: Culver Pictures Inc.

les usually gained the upper hand in these encounters. Concerned with his growing power, Francis formed an important alliance with Pope Clement in 1533, under the terms of which his son and heir, the future Henry II, married the Pope's niece Catherine de' Medici, a union of grave historical significance.

If he could not rival Charles as a statesman or a commander, Francis enjoyed life the way his austere contemporary never did. Brought up in luxury by a mother who idolized him, he became king in 1515 at age 21. His wife died in 1524 after bearing six royal children, leaving Francis to a life totally dedicated to pleasure. He was six feet tall, strong, athletic, and — save for an over-prominent nose — handsome. He loved beauty in every form and showered poets and artists in his court with generosity. (Leonardo da Vinci and Benvenuto Cellini were among them.) Legend probably exaggerated the number of his mistresses, but it is safe to say that he paid more attention to them than to his counselors. According to the 17th-century historian Pierre de Bourdeilles Brantôme, "He loved greatly and too much; for being young and free, he embraced now one, now another, with indifference."

This brings familiar lines to the mind of the operagoer:

> *Questa o quella, per me pari sono*
> *A quant' altre d'intorno mi vedo...*

> (This one or that, they are all the same to me
> As are the others I see around me...)

The dissolute Duke of Mantua who utters these lines in the very first scene of Verdi's *Rigoletto* (1851) is modeled on Francis I, as portrayed in Victor Hugo's savagely anti-royalist play *Le Roi s'amuse* (1832). (The play was instantly suppressed by King Louis-Philippe, a survivor of previous assassination attempts.) Verdi's admiration for Hugo's dramatic gifts had always been keen, and *Ernani's* success only increased it. His enthusiasm came to a near-boiling point in a letter to Piave, the future librettist of *Rigoletto*: "Oh, *Le Roi s'amuse* is the greatest subject and perhaps the greatest drama of modern times. Triboulet is a creation worthy of Shakespeare!! Just like *Ernani* it's a subject that can't fail...."

Rigoletto was commissioned by the Teatro La Fenice in Venice. Therefore, in turning the play into an opera, Venetian censorship had to be considered. After protracted negotiations, during which concessions were made on both sides, the locale of the drama was transferred from Paris to Mantua. Hugo's principal characters, all historical figures, assumed Italian identities: Triboulet, the French king's jester, became Rigoletto; Diane de Poitiers, the king's mistress, Gilda; Monsieur de St. Vallier, Monterone; and Monsieur de Cosse, Ceprano. The operatic Marullo is none other than Clément Marot, court poet to Francis I and a major figure of the French Renaissance. (Piave pays tribute to a fellow literary man when he has Rigoletto, taunted by the "vile courtiers", turn to him in despair, searching for Gilda in the second act:

> *Marullo, signore,*
> *Tu ch'hai l'alma gentil come il core...*

> (Marullo, my lord
> You, whose soul is as gentle as your heart...)

Today it may seem odd that the Venetian censors in Verdi's time objected to placing a French sovereign into such an unfavorable light while allowing an Italian duke to appear under similar circumstances. However, Venice was under Austrian rule at the time and casting aspersions on any royal person was a touchy issue in a monarchy. No such concern plagued the Venetian censors regarding Mantua, an independent duchy that had been ruled by the Gonzaga family for centuries.

The Gonzagas were generous patrons of the arts and some of the ruling dukes were notorious womanizers, as well. Although never mentioned by name in the opera, the most logical model for the opera's "Duke of Mantua" appears to be Vincenzo I (1587-1612). He was married to a Medici princess, a circumstance that did not keep him from siring several illegitimate children. On the other hand, he was the patron of Torquato Tasso, Peter Paul Rubens and, above all, Claudio Monteverdi, the first genius of opera, whose *Orfeo* (1607) and *Arianna* (1608) were introduced at the Mantuan court.

Venus—whom Vincenzo Gonzaga cultivated with even more enthusiasm than he did the muses of art—made him pay with an untimely death for his pleasures. Francis I, Gonzaga's royal alter-ego by way of Verdi and Piave, came to a similar end. The last years of the fun-loving king were darkened by progressive illness, probably syphilis, that ended his long reign in 1547 at age 53. In addition to his kingdom, his son Henry II inherited the royal favorite, Diane de Poitiers, and, politically, the lasting hostility toward Charles V.

That, however, was one of Charles's lesser headaches. Already in 1531, the Protestant princes of Germany formed a league against his authority which forced the emperor into local wars against them; the Council of Trent, which he convoked in 1545, failed to resolve the religious issues. Nor was Charles lucky in his dynastic endeavors. In 1543 he married his son and heir Philip to Maria of Portugal, who died two years later in giving birth to the ill-fated Don Carlos. The second wife Charles picked for his son, Mary Tudor (daughter of Henry VIII and Catherine of Aragon), could have served in a grand design to link the continental empire to England, but Mary died childless in 1558. By that time, Charles, turned into a prematurely aged man by his many frustrations, had abdicated in favor of his son Philip. But Philip II would rule only Spain and the Netherlands; the imperial office went to his uncle Ferdinand I (1556-1564) along with the Habsburg dominions.

Charles spent the last two years of his life in Spain, the country from which he had been absent for a dozen years. There in the monastery of San Yuste he spent his time in meditative seclusion. Ernst Krenek's 12-tone opera *Karl V* (1938) presents the dying emperor in this final phase of his tumultuous life. He hears the voice of God and ruminates over the many crises of his reign:

the sack of Rome, Luther's challenge, his rivalry with Francis I, and his confrontations with the Pope. But, while Charles is the central character of that little-known opera, he is far more familiar to operagoers as the shadowy figure who plays a mystifying role in Verdi's *Don Carlos*.

XV

THE REFORMATION AND ITS AFTERSHOCKS

Mathis der Maler (Hindemith); *Le Prophète* (Meyer-
beer); *Hans Sachs* (Lortzing); *Die Meistersinger von
Nürnberg* (Wagner); *Palestrina* (Pfitzner); *Soliman II*
(Kraus); *Zaide* (Mozart)

In a sense, Martin Luther was the spiritual heir of Girolamo Savonarola, who
was burned at the stake for his fiery speeches urging church reform.[*] During
his pilgrimage to Rome in 1510, Luther was shocked by the corruption there.
It was seven years later, as a teacher at the Augustinian University at Wittenberg, that he posted his ninety-five theses on the local church, attacking
the priesthood on the issue of indulgences. These and further writings by
Luther caused wide repercussions, for they appealed to German national
consciousness and reinforced long-held German desires to be freed of the
discredited power of Rome. As his polemical tone, encouraged by German
humanist scholars, grew ever more aggressive, Pope Leo X issued a ban of
excommunication against him in 1520, an action Luther countered by declaring in one of his pamphlets that salvation could be attained only by renouncing the rule of the papacy.

The political and social consequences of Luther's actions were far-reaching. The German princes, encouraged by the possibility of confiscating
church wealth, were quick to embrace Luther's teachings, and the emperor
(Charles V), mindful of his French entanglements and the ever-present
Turkish menace, had to be cautious in dealing with them. Hoping to achieve
at least a compromise solution, he convoked an Imperial Diet at Worms, to
which he invited Luther to state and defend his views. Armed with a safe-
conduct but haunted by the memory of Jan Hus,[**] Luther appeared before
the emperor, six electors, and a vast array of princes and churchmen; he held
firmly to his theories, and when given an opportunity to retract such doctrines

---

[*]   See pages 129-130.
[**]   See pages 102-103.

as were considered contrary to the Church, refused to do so. *"Hier stehe ich, ich kann nicht anders!* (Here I stand, I can do no other)" These are the words attributed to Luther at that great moment, words that are engraved on the Luther monument in Worms. Backed by four electors (two abstained), Charles V declared Luther as a heretic to be persecuted, but he honored the safe-conduct for the withdrawal of the indomitable priest. The Saxon Elector Frederick chose to detain Luther for his own safety at the castle of Wartburg, the scene of the famous song contests and Tannhäuser's adventures three centuries earlier.

All these events, of course, caused wide repercussions in Germany. Preachers began to denounce their bishops as oppressors. Many of them married and some, going far beyond Luther's teachings, urged a complete breakdown of religious authority. Several secular princes, even members of the emperor's family, embraced the Lutheran faith. Freedom of religious thought soon fanned the flames of resentment that long embittered the peasants of Germany. By the end of 1524, refusal to pay feudal taxes and church tithes was rampant, and many peasant leaders advocated even stronger measures: confiscation of church property and division of feudal wealth.

Initially, Luther supported the rights of peasants to seek just government but later, outraged by the extreme actions some radicals had taken, he firmly disassociated himself from the rebellious activities, saying "rebellion brings with it a land full of murders and bloodshed, makes widows and orphans, and turns everything upside down like a great disaster." In that same startlingly vehement pamphlet (May 1525), he urged Catholic and Protestant rulers alike to stifle rebellion with immediate and cruel action, to kill the "devilish" rebels without mercy. One particularly ugly episode caused widespread shock: Count Ludwig von Helfenstein, an unpopular feudal lord, was tortured and murdered in front of his wife on Good Friday, April 15, 1525. Retaliation was swift, the peasant leaders responsible for the deed were put to death and, by the summer of 1526, the peasant revolt was crushed.

The killing of Count von Helfenstein is an important episode in Paul Hindemith's opera *Mathis der Maler* (1938). Author of his own libretto, Hindemith made the 16th-century painter known as Mathias Grünewald the central figure of this troubled period. In the opera, he is a man facing several crises, sympathetic to Luther's reforms yet unwilling to break with the Catholic Church. He is devoted to his art but is tormented by doubts about what art can mean in a land torn by revolt, where misery and cruelty reign.

The real Mathis gained immortality through his beautiful Isenheim altarpiece in Colmar, France. Scholars are still dubious about certain details of his life, including his place of birth. The artist, whose real name appears to have been Mathias Gothart Nithart, was born around 1475 and died in Halle in 1528. For many years, he served Cardinal Albrecht von Brandenburg of Mainz, an able man but strongly addicted to worldly pleasures, himself drawn to Luther's reforms, yet unable to break with Rome. From the meager documentation available Mathis emerges as a melancholy man caught in an unhappy marriage. There is a brief mention of him in the writings of Philip Melanchthon, Luther's associate, but nothing to link him to the tragic events of the Peasants' War. In Hindemith's opera, nevertheless, Mathis stands in the middle of these events because, according to the composer... "I cannot think of a more vivid, problematic, human, and artistically moving dramatic figure in the best sense than the creator of the Isenheim Altar, the Karlsruhe Crucifixion and the Stuppach Madonna. This man...was obviously afflicted by all the torments of hell endured by a doubtful, searching soul." With one exception, all of the opera's main characters are historical personages. Hindemith, who wrote this opera in Switzerland as an exile from Nazi Germany, clearly identifies with the thoughts Mathis expresses in the opera's First Tableau:

> *Ich plage mich einsam, suche nach Gleichnis und Lösung*
> *Was kann Ich noch tun? In aller Not, was soll Ich?*
> *Wo ist des Schaffens Boden, wo Wachsen und Reifen?*

> (Mine is a lonely search for parable and resolution
> What else can I do? In extreme need, what can I do?
> Where is the soil for creation, where are growth and
>   maturing?)

The peasant uprising took a horrible toll in terms of lives lost and property destroyed. Georg von Truchsess, the general who makes a brief appearance in the Hindemith opera, executed most of the peasant leaders, burned cities and massacred inhabitants even after they had peacefully surrendered. (One noted exception was Götz von Berlichingen, immortalized in Goethe's play, who surrendered in time, changed sides, and lived to the age of 82.) No comforting words came from Luther, who, faced with the bloody consequences of a social revolution he himself had initially encouraged, condemned that tragic episode in the strongest terms.

Feeling betrayed by Catholic and Protestant hierarchy alike, the populace turned toward the radical fringe. The most extreme among the new sects were the Anabaptists, who advocated renewed baptism ("born again" Christianity) and observed utmost severity in morals and manners. Some of them advocated anarchy, as well, along with polygamy and communal living. Originally an offshoot of Zwingli's brand of Protestantism, the movement started in Switzerland, but the Anabaptists' militancy soon led to their expulsion. In Germany, they organized largely underground, subject to persecution and constant threats of death, yet in certain regions they were sheltered by feudal lords who regarded them as industrious workers and farmers.

An inspired apostle of the Anabaptist creed was a young Dutch tailor and innkeeper named Jan Beuckelszoon, to be known later as John of Leyden. His handsome appearance and vivid rhetoric earned him an invitation in 1534 to preach in Münster, the prosperous capital of German Westphalia, a town seething with unrest and hostility against its unpopular feudal bishop Franz von Waldeck. Grouped around the charismatic John of Leyden, the rebels drove away the bishop and his circle, but could not govern. Dazzled by his sudden power over the populace, John had himself declared king and ruled, splendidly gowned and presiding over regal processions, in a strange combination of religious fanaticism and communistic principles.

Though attracting wide sympathy from disgruntled elements of society, the Anabaptist movement could not cope with the enmity of emperor and clergy, Catholic as well as Protestant. Special taxes were levied by the bishop to regroup the feudal army, which surrounded and eventually occupied Münster on June 24, 1535. The defenders were massacred *en masse*, and John of Leyden and his principal aides were tortured and put to death with unspeakable cruelty.

John of Leyden is the hero of Meyerbeer's opera *Le Prophète* (1849) with a libretto by Scribe, and that guarantees wholesale departures from history. The operatic John is initially a decent but gullible person, manipulated by three unscrupulous Anabaptists who use and eventually betray him. He is devoted to Berthe, a hometown girl—a far cry from the real and enthusiastically polygamous John. The remarkable Fidès, prototype of the contralto mother figures predating Azucena and Erda, is Scribe's invention, as is the spectacular explosion-immolation that ends the opera—a transparently exploitative stage device that nonetheless delighted the Paris of 1849. And yet, to a degree Scribe was mindful of history: the spirit of the Peasants' War echoes from the chorus in Act I:

Ces oppresseurs indignes,
Ces vils, ces vils tyrans,
Cruels, cruels seigneurs!
Ah!vengeons-nous sur nos tyrans
Qu'ils meurent tous!

(These infamous oppressors,
These vile, vile tyrants,
Cruel, cruel lords!
Ah! let us avenge ourselves on our tyrants!
Let them all die!")

And when the children's chorus intones (Act IV, Scene 2)

Le voilà, le Roi Prophète,
Le voilà, le fils de Dieu!
A genoux, courbez la tête
A genoux devant son sceptre de feu...

("Here he is, the Prophet King,
Here he is, the son of God!
On your knees, bow your head,
On your knees before his fiery scepter...)

they expose the sentiments of disillusioned multitudes accustomed to the sight of false prophets and eager to hail them as Messiahs.

Astrology and occultism also found the sixteenth century a fertile ground, and the emergence of the Faust legend serves as its most remarkable manifestation. In the middle of the sixteenth century, it took shape in representing Faust as a dabbler in the occult, in league with Satan. Religious zealotry chose to suggest that scientific knowledge that dared to go beyond the teachings of the Bible could lead a man to hell. Goethe's *Faust*, rejecting the narrow medieval interpretations, reconciles a thirst for knowledge with humanistic principles and with the ultimate triumph of the soul. A literary masterpiece of profound significance, it was also the inspiration of songs, orchestral works, and operas and major choral pieces by Liszt, Berlioz, Schumann, Gounod, Boito, and Mahler.

Martin Luther, stern, unbending, and intolerant to the end, died in 1546. Already in his lifetime, the Reformation he began became a European movement, spreading quickly through Switzerland (through the teachings of Zwingli), Sweden, Denmark, and Norway (then under Danish domination), and England, due to the despotic will of Henry VIII, who, with the help of his advisers, succeeded in separating the English Church from Rome.

* * *

Amidst all the religious strife and territorial struggles that spread misery and massacres throughout 16th-century Germany, the city of Nürnberg seemed like an oasis of peace and prosperity. Already an important trading center in the thirteenth century, with a rich tradition of artisans, it enjoyed the status of a free city, liberated by imperial decree from territorial governments. By the sixteenth century, Nürnberg owned considerable land and was governed by a council of 42 members, chosen mainly from patrician families. Taxes, police, judicial powers, and religious matters were all in the hands of the council, as was the direction of the various guilds. The council had full autonomy in religious matters and it accepted Luther's reforms with readiness.

This was the Nürnberg where Hans Sachs was born in 1494 and where his extraordinary activity began in 1516 after the completion of his years of wandering as a *"Geselle"* (apprentice). He was an enthusiastic student of poetry, an art he learned from a master weaver named Leonard Nunnenbeck. Sachs, too, was a *"Meister"* — a master shoemaker — married to a local girl, Kunigunde Kreutzer. The circumstances of their courtship and wedding in 1519 — embellished by highly romanticized details such as the intervention of the Emperor Maximilian — are the subject of Albert Lortzing's opera *Hans Sachs* (1840). The opera was not particularly successful even in Germany, and was eventually consigned into oblivion by Wagner's *Die Meistersinger von Nürnberg* (1868). Interestingly, in the Lortzing opera it is Sachs who is severely criticized by the Masters for not following the established rules of poetry.

Kunigunde Sachs died in 1560, as did all their seven children eventually, possibly from the plague. Thus Wagner's Sachs reveals an historical fact when he tells Eva (Act II, Scene 4): *"Hatt' einst ein Weib, und Kinder genug* (I had a wife once and lots of children)". Indeed, Wagner, who painstakingly studied Christoph Wagenseil's 17th-century Nürnberg chronicles, faithfully adheres to many historical details in his *Meistersinger*. Virtually all the names of the Masters came from that source, though it was Wagner who assigned the various trades to each. The institution of the *"Merker"* (adjudicator) had been established as Wagner observed it, and the pedantic rules of the "*Tabulatur*" by which the construction of each song is strictly regulated by the Guild were precisely as they are related by Fritz Kothner with such unctuous gusto (Act I, Scene 3).

The historical Sachs called attention to himself with his poems praising Luther, whom he called "The Wittenberg Nightingale". An unbelievably prolific versifier, he was credited with more than 4000 songs during his long life — an activity that may have indeed affected the quality of his shoemaking and justified the adverse criticism expressed by the operatic Beckmesser. In any case, it is a historical fact that Sachs was rebuked by the city council in 1527 when it seemed that his literary activity interfered with his concentrating on his "proper trade".

Hans Sachs was not a great poet by any means, and yet he was a major literary figure at a time when 70 per cent of the books written in Germany were published in Latin. Goethe hailed him as one of the pioneers of German poetry. Unlike the "*Minnesänger*" of the courtly centuries, the Nürnberg Masters did not concern themselves with romantic matters. Their subjects, strictly regulated, were limited to religious themes and observations of nature and domestic life. There was, however, an enlivening sense of humor in Sachs's poetry, and the famous Cobbling Song ("*Jerum, Jerum...*") in the second act of *Die Meistersinger* is perfectly in keeping with the kind of "*Meisterlied*" the real Sachs might have written. More importantly, the hymn performed by the choral assembly in the festive second scene of *Die Meistersinger's* third act

> *Wach auf! es nahet gen dem Tag*
> *Ich hör' singen im grünen Hag*
> *ein wonnigliche Nachtigall....*

> (Awake! the dawn of day is nearing
> I hear the song of an enchanting nightingale
> In the green meadows...)

is set to the actual words with which the historical Sachs had hailed Martin Luther, the nightingale voice of the Reformation.

Wagner portrayed him as a melancholy widower, yet clearly attracted to young Evchen Pogner and bittersweet in his renunciation. The historical Sachs, in fact, did marry for the second time, in 1561. His bride, named Barbara, was 27, and they lived happily until Sachs's death (1576) at age 82. Im-

Friedrich Schorr as Hans Sachs in
Die Meistersinger von Nürnberg (Wagner)
CREDIT: Metropolitan Opera Archives

mortalized in music perhaps beyond the worth of his artistic attainments, we must nonetheless recognize him, in Will Durant's words... "not a great poet, but...as a sane and cheerful voice in a century of hate."

* * *

That "century of hate", however, produced many notable musicians, primarily in church-related activities, who did not lack patrons in high places. The Flemish Adrian Villaert was director of music at Venice's famous San Marco, where he taught the even more famous and more prolific Andrea Gabrieli. Another Flemish master, Heinrich Isaac, enjoyed the patronage of Lorenzo de' Medici and, after the latter's death, was pensioned by music-loving Pope Leo X. His pupil, Swiss-born Ludwig Senfl, enjoyed the patronage of the Duke of Bavaria. These were all masters of church polyphony, while in Italy the madrigalists Philippe Verdelot and Cipriano de Rore perfected their art setting the secular poems of Petrarch and Tasso to music. Quite independent in character and direction, the courtly *chansons* of France, as cultivated by Pierre Attaingnant and Clément Janequin, found enthusiastic reception in the hedonistic reign of Francis I.

Martin Luther responded to church polyphony with enthusiasm:

> When natural music is sharpened and polished by art, then
> one begins to see with amazement the great and perfect wis-
> dom of God in His wonderful work of music, where one voice
> takes a simple part and around it sing three, four, or five other
> voices, leaping, springing round about, marvelously gracing the
> simple part, like a square dance in heaven...He who does not
> find this an inexpressible miracle of the Lord is truly a clod,
> and is not worthy to be considered a man.

But, in time, there came a reaction to all this, and it was a severe one. The Council of Trent, initially convoked by Charles V in 1545 [*] and adjourned without decisive action, was reassembled in 1562, and the service of the Mass came up for consideration. Severe criticism was voiced on the elaborateness of contrapuntal music that caused words and meaning to be obscured and

---

[*]   See page 149.

rendered unintelligible. Pope Pius IV appointed a special commission to study the matter.

According to a long discredited account by the Abbé Baini published in 1828, Cardinal Carlo Borromeo, head of the Papal Commission, entrusted the highly respected Giovanni Pierluigi da Palestrina with the composition of a Mass to be known as the *Missa Papae Marcelli,* which ultimately cleared the air and restored polyphonic music to an honored position within Catholic liturgy.

The Bavarian composer Hans Pfitzner was fully aware of the shaky historical foundation of Baini's account. But he was inspired by the spiritual associations—the saintly character of Pope Marcellus II (Paul IV's predecessor), who died after only three weeks in the Holy Office, the contrasts between the tempestuous outside world and the inward life of a creative artist like Palestrina—so that he used the legend for the basis of his opera *Palestrina.* The work was introduced in Munich in 1918 under the direction of Bruno Walter and has retained, to this day, a highly respectable position in the musical culture of Bavaria and Austria.

The historical Palestrina (who took his name from his birthplace, some 20 miles from Rome) had been appointed choirmaster of St. Peter's in 1555, but lost that position a year later when Paul IV dismissed all married men from his pontifical staff. Palestrina subsequently found employment with other Roman churches, and his growing fame as a composer would have justified Cardinal Borromeo's commission "to save church music." According to Abbé Baini's account, the Marcellus Mass was publicly performed on June 19, 1565 and was received with enthusiasm. No documented proof for Baini's conjecture has been established, and it seems likely that the subsequent fame of the Marcellus Mass is due to its musical merit rather than to the events Baini benevolently recounted.

Pfitzner's opera, however, uses many elements of the legend to good operatic purposes. His large cast is generously populated with historical personages, and several incidents are based on the records of the Council of Trent, which the composer (who was his own librettist) had studied in detail. Cardinal Borromeo has a major role in the opera, eloquently and forcefully urging the composer to pursue his task, and Pope Pius IV himself makes a solemn appearance, announcing that "his ear was ravished by the sublime beauties of the Mass" and inviting Palestrina to return and to lead the Sistine Choir to the end of his days, *"Fürst der Musik aller Zeiten!* (Prince of Music through all ages!)"

Here, again, Pfitzner embellished history. In 1567, Palestrina published his second book of Masses and dedicated it, not to his benefactor Borromeo, not even to the Pope, but to King Philip II of Spain. That same year, he entered the service of Cardinal Ippolito d'Este, where he continued to compose prolifically. He did return to lead the Sistine Choir in 1571, but by then the Pope was Pius V, and he remained in the service of the latter's successor, Gregory XIII (1572-1585), as well.

Four more ancient and short-reigned popes passed on before Palestrina himself died on February 2, 1594, survived by his son Iginio, who has a fairly important role in the opera. His wife Lucrezia, whose spirit, accompanied by angels, makes an appearance in the reveries of the operatic Palestrina, did not, in fact, die until 1580. Palestrina then married a rich widow and ended his life in productive contentment. His huge legacy includes more than 100 masses, about 450 motets, and a large number of hymns and madrigals with religious and secular texts. Verdi regarded himself and all Italian composers of opera the "heirs of Palestrina".

* * *

As if the challenge of Martin Luther and the Protestant German princes, as well as the abiding enmity of Francis I, were not enough reasons to agitate the imperial mind of Charles V, there were the Turks, a major force in Europe ever since the ascension of Suleiman I, dubbed, not at all undeservedly, "The Magnificent" (1520).* After the battle of Mohács, he held most of Hungary; in 1529, he laid siege to Vienna, and in 1536 he entered into a formal alliance with Francis I, while his navy ruled the Mediterranean and the entire east coast of the Red Sea. After a peace treaty with Ferdinand, who succeeded his brother as the new emperor, Suleiman was the most powerful monarch in all of Europe, commanding the strongest army in the field. Within his own domain, he practiced a kind of religious tolerance unmatched by the West: Spanish and Portuguese Jews safely fled to his empire from the persecutions of the Inquisition. When the new emperor, Maximilian II, refused the payment of tributes agreed to by his father Ferdinand, Suleiman went on a new campaign leading an army of 200,000 men. He died besieging the Hungarian fortress of Szigetvár on the night of September 5, 1566.

---

*   See page 128.

Julius Patzak as *Palestrina* (Pfitzner)
Author's collection

It is entirely possible that there is an opera in Turkish musical literature that represents the warrior sultan in all his magnificence. In Western music, two 18th-century comic operas, only faintly related to history, concern themselves largely with the love life of his later namesake Suleiman II (1642-1689) – Mozart's *Zaide* (1779) and Joseph Martin Kraus's *Soliman II* (1789). Both revolve around the activities in the sultan's harem.

Mozart never really finished *Zaide*, though he lavished some wonderful music on it. He set it aside to concentrate on a better libretto with a Turkish subject, which eventually became his *Entführung aus dem Serail*. The similarities between the two operas are obvious: European lovers caught in the sultan's harem are freed by the magnanimous Soliman (tenor) despite the machinations of the harem-keeper Osmin (bass). In *Die Entführung*, the role of Osmin is enlarged and his character becomes more villainous, while Soliman is transmuted into the equally magnanimous Selim Pasha, a speaking role.

German-born Joseph Martin Kraus (1756-1792) was court composer to Sweden's King Gustav III. His *Soliman II*, with a libretto based on a French text by C.F. Favart, was introduced in Stockholm in 1789 and revived two centuries later at the Drottningholm Theatre, which Gustav founded. The opera follows French models in that music is interspersed with dancing and a generous amount of spoken dialogue. Both the Sultan and his harem-keeper (named Osmin, of course – Kraus must have known his Mozart) are spoken roles. Three ladies of the harem are vying for Soliman's affections, with the temperamental Roxelane winning the contest and becoming Sultana.

The seraglio was a busy place indeed – for the "magnificent" Suleiman as well, who may have had at least 300 concubines. But actual happenings in his harem were hardly fit for comic opera. The longtime favorite of the Sultan was a Circassian beauty named Gulbehar, who bore him a son. Eventually, she was succeeded by a Russian captive named Khurrem (Roxelane, as she was called in the West), whom he married in 1534. Eventually, the ambitious Roxelane prevailed on the aging and lovesick Sultan to have Gulbehar's son Mustafa killed, thereby assuring that *her* son Selim should inherit the throne.

There were many other barbarous aspects to Suleiman's rule, particularly since Turkish traditions easily acquiesced to a ruler's prerogative of eliminating all pretenders to his throne. But Suleiman lived in an age of despots; he actually appears no more cruel or autocratic and vindictive today than his Christian contemporaries Charles V and Henry VIII, and surpassed both of them, as well as that gallantly decadent Francis I of France, as an efficient ruler of a vast domain.

XVI

A TIME FOR MASSACRES

Don Carlos (Verdi); *Egmont* (Goethe-Beethoven); *Les Huguenots* (Meyerbeer); *Le duc d'Albe* (Donizetti); *Le Roi malgré lui* (Chabrier)

The Reformation, which began as a spiritual movement, eventually caused wide repercussions in European power politics. The spread of Protestantism in Germany forced the Emperor to accept the Peace of Augsburg (1555), which assured the territorial princes the right to choose either the Catholic or the Lutheran religion. By then England, through the actions of Henry VIII, had created a state religion of its own. In France, the easygoing rule of Francis I, relatively tolerant in religious matters, allowed the disciples of Calvin, called Huguenots, to organize and to spread their leader's austere tenets.

Reaction to Protestant growth set the Catholic Church on a course to reform itself and combat its enemies. The tone of this Counter-Reformation was set by the stern Pope Paul IV (1555-1559), who said, "If my own father were a heretic, I would gather wood to burn him." King Philip II of Spain, devout and intolerant, who ruled over a nation with long anti-heretical traditions, stood in the forefront of this movement.

Spain was the most powerful European nation during the nine-year period 1559 to 1568 when the dramatic action of *Don Carlos*, Schiller's play and Verdi's opera, takes place. Relying on pseudo-historical sources long since discredited, Friedrich Schiller completed his play in 1787, at the dawn of the French Revolution. Its fascinating conflicts, reflecting Schiller's strongly anti-clerical and fiercely anti-absolutist sentiments, captivated the mind of Giuseppe Verdi nearly eighty years later. Condensing Schiller's unwieldy plot and, if anything, removing it even further from historical accuracy, Verdi completed his opera in 1867. The play, a literary classic, is still staged in German-speaking lands; the opera is justly admired the world over. Both are populated with historical personalities but play fast and loose with some historical facts. What mattered to Schiller was the enduring nobility of his liberal ideas; the more realistic Verdi was primarily concerned with the creation of a viable, successful, and enduring opera.

Unlike his father Charles V, a native of the Netherlands and more cosmopolitan in his outlook, Philip was thoroughly Spanish in his background, upbringing, and tenacious dedication to the Catholic faith. When his father died in 1558, Philip was 31, short in stature but elegant in bearing, with a neatly trimmed, pointed beard and a protruding Habsburg jaw, as shown in Titian's painting of the time. He was a sombre and morose man, methodical in his manner, with a dedication to paper work that caused him to be remembered as *"el rey papelero"*.

Despite his youth, he was already widowed twice. His first wife, Princess Maria of Portugal, died giving birth to the ill-fated Don Carlos in 1545. His second marriage, to the Catholic Mary Tudor, daughter of Henry VIII, could have realized Charles V's cherished ambition of uniting the Spanish and English empires under one ruler. But that dream ended when Mary died in 1558. The union produced no heirs, but the fanatically anti-Protestant Mary's views reinforced Philip's conviction that his empire was threatened by the spread of Calvinism.

Meantime the military entanglements between Spain and France, begun during the reigns of Charles V and Francis I, continued under their sons Philip II and Henry II. With English support, the Spanish armies defeated the French in the battles of St. Quentin (1557) and Gravelines (1558). Count Egmont of the Netherlands, a loyal general in Philip's army, was the victor at Gravelines—enjoying transitory glory in light of later developments.

By that time, French and Spanish treasuries were both exhausted as a result of incessant wars. Internally, too, France was torn by Catholic-Protestant (Huguenot) dissension. With the peace treaty at Cateau-Cambrésis (April 3, 1559) both sides welcomed the end of hostilities. To assure lasting peace between the two nations, Philip, in the Habsburg tradition of advantageous dynastic marriages, briefly entertained the thought of a union between his 15-year old son Don Carlos and Elizabeth of Valois, the older daughter of Henry II, a mere thirteen in 1559. But the young prince, sickly and already known for erratic and even cruel behavior, could hardly be regarded as a guardian of lasting peace. Thus Philip, still a young man of 31, proposed himself as Elizabeth's future husband.

In the first act of the Verdi opera, the engagement is announced to the dismay and heartbreak of the young operatic lovers. That scene at Fontainebleau, however, is mere operatic invention. Don Carlos was nowhere near the place.

The marriage between Elizabeth and Philip took place by proxy in June 1559. The king was represented by his brave general and trusted confidant Fernando Alvarez de Toledo, the Duke of Alba (1507-1582). Two weeks later, Elizabeth's father, King Henry II, sustained a fatal wound in a tournament and died. (During the seemingly innocent exchange of courtly gossip between Rodrigue and the Princess Eboli in the opera's second act, Rodrigue mentions that everyone at the French court talks about "a tournament in which, they say, the king will take part" — an historical touch by Verdi's French librettists that was certainly not lost on the opera's Paris audience.)

Philip's hair was prematurely graying when he first met Elizabeth in 1560, a fact that was noticed by his child-bride, according to some chronicles, though without the tragic overtones suggested by Philip's great soliloquy in *Don Carlos*:

> *Je la revois encore, regardant en silence*
> *Mes cheveux blancs, le jour qu'elle arriva de France.*
> *Non, elle ne m'aime pas! Elle ne m'aime pas!*

> (I see her again as she looked in silence
> At my white hair, the day she arrived from France.
> No, she does not love me! She does not love me!

Quite the contrary. What began as a political marriage grew into love, and the surviving documents prove that Philip, for all his political ruthlessness, was a caring and tender husband and a good father to the two daughters Elizabeth bore him.

It was the son born of his first marriage, Don Carlos, who continued to plague the royal house, and Elizabeth had nothing to do with it. Signs of cruelty and an uncontrollable temper had been evident for years, and the prince's behavior took a dangerous turn in 1562 when he injured his head in a fall down a flight of stairs. Still hoping that Carlos would some day succeed him on the Spanish throne, Philip tried to involve him in positions of some responsibility, but without success. Instead, Carlos — possibly on the urging of Flanders extremists — insisted on going to the Netherlands. Mindful of the dangers to the cause of peace if the unstable prince should attain leadership, even as a figurehead, in that restive country, Philip had him arrested on

January 19, 1568. Carlos was never seen again in public, and died on July 24 of the same year. The fact that the circumstances of his death were never revealed later provided opportunities for the king's enemies to charge him with his son's murder. Actually, this secretiveness may have been motivated by Philip's reluctance to shed light on the streak of insanity in Don Carlos, the great-grandson of the "mad" Juana La Loca.[*]

Tragedy continued to pursue Philip, for in September of that year his wife died following the birth of a third daughter, who also failed to survive. A beautiful and popular queen, she was deeply mourned by her subjects. One of them, a budding young poet named Miguel Cervantes Saavedra (1547-1616), was moved to pour his grief into an ode in Dante-esque *terza rima* which begins:

> Fair spirit, deserving of heaven
> See how the hapless earth darkens
> Without the sight of you to light it...

It was published in 1569 in a Madrid collection and came to the attention of Diego de Espinosa, Spain's Inquisitor General. Through him, the future author of *Don Quixote* made the acquaintance of the papal nuncio, who then took him to Italy for further studies.

Cardinal Diego de Espinosa (1502-1570) was far from the cruel and forbidding figure of Verdi's terrifying Grand Inquisitor, whose operatic character was probably inspired by the dreaded Torquemada of the earlier century. The grave conflict originally dramatized by Schiller and further intensified in Verdi's grand confrontation scene between the two representatives of monarchic and church powers is largely invention: Philip was a faithful servant of the Church who believed in the Inquisition — not at all popular with Spanish society at large in the sixteenth century — and upheld its excesses.

While the king's closest confidant, the Duke of Alba, represented a position of uncompromising rigidity in political matters, Don Gomez Ruiz de Silva (1516-1573) stood for moderation. Heir of an ancient noble house (an ancestor appears in Verdi's *Ernani*), Gomez de Silva was also Prince of Eboli, married to a princess (Doña Ana de Mendoza, 1540-1592) known for her wit and beauty, despite the loss of one eye. Immortalized in Verdi's opera, the princess was doubtless familiar with courtly intrigue, but historians reject the

---

[*]   See page 138.

notion of her affair with the king or her infatuation with the unfortunate Carlos. The princess did take the veil briefly on the death of her husband, but soon returned to court. Many years later, with her then lover Antonio Perez, she became involved in dangerous high-level intrigues. Perez escaped abroad and the princess spent the remainder of her life confined to her estates.

Thus history, though the essence of both the Schiller play and the Verdi opera, is history as transformed by Schiller into his own private vision. When he needed a spokesman to address the conscience of mankind in the blind and hate-filled sixteenth century, the poet invented Rodrigue, Marquis of Posa, a visionary who voices late-18th-century sentiments:

> *Que pour l'Espagne un homme meure*
> *En lui léguant de jours heureux*
> *En lui léguant l'avenir radieux!*

> (Let one man die for Spain
> Bequeathing her days of happiness
> Bequeathing her a radiant future!)

Schiller's play, which endows Don Carlos with the brave character and noble intentions the real prince never possessed, concludes with his arrest and implied violent death. In the opera's confused ending, the orchestra thunders forth a theme that symbolizes the triumph of the Inquisition over liberal spirits like Posa. And yet it is the forbidden ideas of Posa—the sole invention among the opera's true historical characters—that lend Verdi's *Don Carlos* the eternal timeliness that keeps the opera so unfailingly relevant in modern times.

* * *

Flanders, so prominently featured in *Don Carlos*, had not represented a problem for the Emperor Charles V. He was a native of Ghent and remained, to the end of his days, a revered figure to his Flemish countrymen. For his son Philip II, Spanish to the core, the Low Countries (originally ruled by the dukes of Burgundy, and acquired by the Spanish Habsburgs through one of their dynastic marriages), were a "*damnosa hereditas*" (an accursed legacy). The feeling was mutual, for the Netherlanders always regarded the austere figure of Philip with a mixture of distrust and fear.

The seventeen provinces that comprised the Netherlands received news

Philip II of Spain (portrait by Titian)
CREDIT: Opera News

Nicolai Ghiaurov as King Philip in *Don Carlos* (Verdi)
CREDIT: Opera News

of the peace at Cateau-Cambrésis (1559) between France and Spain with great rejoicing. Margaret, the Duchess of Parma and Philip's stepsister, was appointed regent, assisted by a council of leading Dutch aristocrats, including Prince William of Orange and the Counts Egmont and Hoorn. But the real power rested in the hands of Cardinal Granvelle, whom Philip endowed with special authority, and he lost no time in introducing the cruel procedures of the Spanish Inquisition against the local "heretics". Spain in those days was isolated from much of Europe, while the Netherlands, centrally located and a nation of free traders, was open to Calvinist influences and thus a target for the forces of the Inquisition. Cardinal Granvelle pursued his task with a fanatical zeal: people were butchered and homes were burned for minor "crimes" and even the suspicion of heresy. Aggravating the situation was the presence of looting and murderous Spanish soldiers.

At the urging of the Prince of Orange and the Count of Egmont, both Catholic nobles who had done great service for Philip's empire – and, in fact, had been part of the 1559 delegation to ask for the hand of Elizabeth of Valois for Philip – the hated cardinal was removed. Repressive measures against Protestants, however, continued. Enraged by constant persecutions, Protestant mobs sacked the Antwerp Cathedral in 1566.

This is the background of Goethe's *Egmont,* a play for which Beethoven wrote his famous incidental music, heard in Vienna's Burgtheater for the first time on June 15, 1810. The struggle for freedom against tyranny was foremost in Beethoven's mind – his opera *Fidelio*, five years earlier, had been inspired by the same ideal – but the composer's own Flemish ancestry may have provided additional stimulus.

As the play unfolds, details of the Spanish oppression are revealed along with the despair of the populace. We learn that Duchess Margaret, the regent, has resigned and that the Duke of Alba has been charged by Philip to succeed her. (The historical Alba landed in the Netherlands in August 1567.) The cautious Prince of Orange, rightly appraising the situation, decides to leave the Netherlands for safety. Prior to his departure the prince warns Egmont to do likewise, but the latter – mistakenly placing his trust in false conciliatory gestures by Philip, and clinging to the belief that his past service to the king will not be forgotten – decides to remain. (The historical Orange departed on April 11, 1567.)

In the play, Egmont, whom history regards as an uncommonly brave if exceedingly vain patriot, also fails to heed the warning of Alba's own son, Don Ferdinand de Toledo, who appears as an idealistic Posa-like character. He pays with his life for his stubborn pride. History tells us that Egmont and Hoorn were arrested as Alba's first move in what eventually was to become a reign of terror. A tribunal, aptly named "Council of Blood", was established to judge and execute alleged heretics and Protestant leaders, confiscating their wealth. The massacres soon claimed rich and poor alike, and the cruel tortures sanctioned by the tribunal matched the most violent excesses of the Spanish Inquisition.

On June 5, 1568, with 3000 Spanish soldiers surrounding the great square of Brussels, the counts Egmont and Hoorn were publicly beheaded. The Goethe play — admirable in its historical accuracy (save for the romantic invention of Clärchen, Egmont's mistress, who poisons herself in the end) — concludes with the doomed count walking toward his execution as the music (Beethoven's!) intones a victorious strain. In his final monologue, he exhorts all oppressed peoples with words Schiller's visionary Posa might have uttered:

> *Und wie das Meer durch eure Dämme bricht*
> *So brecht, so reisst den Wall der Tyrannei zusammen*
> *Und schwemmt ersäufend sie von ihrem Grunde*
> *den sie sich anmasst, weg!*

> (And as the sea bursts through your dikes,
> Break and tear down the wall of tyranny
> And, in a drowning floodtide, wash it away
> From the ground it has claimed!)

Alba's bloody strategies ultimately failed and he was recalled in 1573, replaced by the more humane Luis de Requesens. The insurrection led from the outside by William of Orange and his brother Louis continued unrelentingly against the Spanish powers. The seven northern provinces proclaimed their independence in 1581, but hostilities continued long after the passing of Philip, Alba, Orange, and all the original principals of this great historical drama. The independence of the Netherlands did not become a reality until the Treaty of Westphalia in 1648.

The Duke of Alba's last campaign, and a victorious one, took him to Portugal. He died, at age 75, loyal and unbending to the end. Justly remembered as a cruel mass murderer in Dutch history, the duke nonetheless earned the distinction of having an opera named after him. (Caligula, Nero, Attila, and

Ivan the Terrible were recipients of similar "honors".) It was the inexhaustible Eugène Scribe who presented the libretto of his *Le duc d'Albe* first to Halévy in 1838 and later to Donizetti. The latter began composing the music but, as other subjects were claiming his attention, periodically laid it aside until his deteriorating health forced him to abandon the project altogether. It fell to a minor composer named Matteo Salvi to complete the opera and, with an Italian text, arrange *Il Duca di Alba* for performance in 1881.

Scribe's original story deals with conditions in Brussels after the execution of Egmont. At its center is the fallen leader's daughter, Amelia, party to a conspiracy against the hated Alba and the Spanish oppressors. When in 1854 Verdi was looking for a French libretto to execute a commission for the Opéra, Scribe got him interested in the plot of his yet unperformed *Le duc d'Albe*, transplanted into a different setting. As he explained to his collaborator, Charles Duveyrer... "the action should be placed in a climate less cold than that of the Low Countries; a climate full of warmth and music such as Naples and Sicily." Thus the hated Alba became Monfort, the hated oppressor of Sicily, and the conspiring Amelia (Egmont's alleged daughter) was transformed into Hélène, sister of Frederick of Austria, an earlier historical martyr. To top it off, while Donizetti's *Le duc d'Albe* could only *voice* the murderous hatred of the Dutch against their oppressors, that hatred was to burst into a massacre under the warm Sicilian skies in Verdi's *Les Vêpres siciliennes*.[*]

* * *

Continuing his efforts to prove himself the champion of Christendom, Philip was determined to remove the Turkish threat from the Mediterranean. A revolt by the Moriscos of Granada (Christian converts who remained Moslem in their speech and traditions) provided him with an opportunity to undertake a punitive campaign against them in 1570. Under the leadership of Don Juan, Philip's half-brother, it was pursued with utmost ruthlessness and ended with mass deportations and the repopulation of Granada with Christian settlers.

What followed was the formation of an alliance between Philip, the Doge of Venice, and Pope Pius V to end the Turkish menace once and for all. While

---

[*]   See page 80.

these allies faced a common enemy, they pursued different aims: Philip
wanted to expand his empire to North Africa, Venice sought to destroy the
Turkish fleet to assure her untroubled commerce, and the Pope aimed to
recover the Holy Land. Their "Holy League" was doomed to be short-lived,
but achieved a decisive victory at Lepanto on October 17, 1571, where 40,000
Moslems were killed, 8000 captured, and some 12,000 Christian captives
were freed. Among the Spanish wounded was Cervantes, then 24. For his distinguished services, his commander Don Juan commended him to Philip but,
unfortunately, the young author fell into Moslem captivity and had to serve
as a slave for five years before he was able to return to Spain. After Lepanto, the League was soon dissolved but, due to the ineptitude of Turkish
leadership, the Moslem threat was indeed removed from Philip's empire.

There still remained the threat posed by Calvinism, the threat that had
brought about the treaty of Cateau-Cambrésis in 1559, establishing peace between Spain and France. Conditions in France, however, changed radically
after the premature death of Henry II following that fateful tournament.* His
son, Francis II, also died suddenly in December 1560, to be succeeded by a
brother, Charles IX, only ten years old at the time.

The young king ruled under the regency of his mother, Catherine de'
Medici, a vital, energetic, and extremely ambitious woman, playing risky
politics in dangerous times. The Calvinist movement had made substantial
inroads in French life despite all efforts to contain its progress. By 1560, it
was estimated that 25 per cent of the population were Huguenots (Cal-
vinists), with even heavier concentration in certain towns. And they had
powerful leaders like Prince Louis de Condé and Admiral Gaspard de Coligny, with influence at court. Catherine tried to maneuver between two hostile
groups that were growing steadily more aggressive, but could not prevent the
outbreak of religious wars that exacted a heavy toll on both sides. Other
European powers were soon involved; in 1562 Philip sent Spanish reinforcements to the Catholic armies while Queen Elizabeth of England supported
the Protestants.

The situation grew even more precarious in 1567 as Alba began his reign
of terror in the Netherlands. When word came of the execution of Egmont
and Hoorn, the French Huguenot leaders feared that Catherine, Philip's ally,
would plan a similar fate for them. Unwisely, they decided to take preemp-

---

* See page 167.

tive action and attempted to seize the young king. Catherine promptly abandoned her policy of moderation, and a new religious war broke out in the fall
of 1568 that deteriorated into bestial atrocities on both sides. After the loss
of such powerful leaders as Duke Francis de Guise on the Catholic side and
Prince Louis de Condé of the Huguenots, an uneasy truce was signed in 1570.
Coligny, now the undisputed leader of the Huguenots, briefly managed to
capture the trust and affection of young King Charles IX, guiding him toward
an alliance with the exiled William of Orange and against the Spain of Philip.

Enraged by the prospect of losing her influence over the king, Catherine
decided that the Huguenot threat must be met with radical means. With her
encouragement, an assassination attempt was made against Coligny on
August 22, 1572. This happened four days after the marriage of Catherine's
younger daughter Marguerite to Henry of Navarre, a Huguenot prince of
royal blood. It was an event attended by all the Huguenot leaders, and the
timing seemed opportune for Catherine to persuade the young and unstable
king to sanction the extermination of all Huguenots. As August 24 – St.
Bartholomew's Day – dawned, the order was given and the massacre began.
It is estimated that the wanton slaughter, sparing neither age nor sex, claimed
three to four thousand victims in Paris alone. Not all were Huguenots, for
such wholesale atrocities have always created prime opportunities for settling scores.

The news of the St. Bartholomew's Day Massacre shocked Europe, but
the official reaction varied along religious lines. Philip of Spain rejoiced at
the news and dispatched a letter to Catherine praising her for an act that
"brought glory and honor to God and universal Christendom." Pope Pius V
assembled all the cardinals for a festival *Te Deum* and had frescoes painted
at the Vatican to commemorate the event. There was, of course, indignation
in Protestant circles in England and Germany, but not the kind that would
upset existing diplomatic alliances.

Meyerbeer's opera *Les Huguenots* (1836), with libretto by Scribe, uses the
political events as background to a tragic romance between Raoul de Nangis, a Protestant noble, and Valentine St. Bris, daughter of a Catholic leader.
Marguerite de Valois, newly married to Henry of Navarre and not party to
her mother's sinister plotting, is the only historical character among the
opera's principals, though some of the minor characters – De Tavannes, De
Retz – appeared in contemporary chronicles and, in fact, some of the plot
ingredients found their way into Scribe's panoramic libretto from Prosper
Merimée's *Chronicles of the Time of Charles IX*. For all his wide-ranging im-

agination, Scribe remained true to form: his text is generously dotted with historical allusions. While in her famous aria Marguerite dreamily sings "*O beau pays de la Touraine,*" she interjects a note of realism:

> *Que Luther ou Calvin ensanglatent la terre*
> *de leurs débats réligieux;*
> *des ministres du ciel que la morale austère*
> *nous épouvante au nom des cieux!*

> (Let Luther or Calvin drown the earth in blood
> With their religious squabbles —
> Ministers of heaven whose stern morality
> Frightens us in the name of heaven!)

Already in the first act, the Count Nevers, representing the moderate and conciliatory factions of the Catholic nobles, sounds an optimistic note:

> *Notre roi...avec les protestants il se réconcilie*
> *Coligny, Médicis ont juré devant Dieu*
> *une eternelle paix...*

> (Our king...is making peace with the Protestants
> Coligny, Médicis have both sworn before God
> Everlasting peace...)

His statement is received with skepticism by his fellow Catholics, who are not yet, at this point, in a violent mood. Far more aggressive is the old soldier Marcel, a fanatical Huguenot who, when invited to join the company in a drinking song, not only refuses to do so but brusquely launches into Luther's hymn "*Ein' feste Burg*" — which is, of course, a wildly inaccurate touch on Scribe's part for the Calvinist Paris of 1572. Later actions in the opera reflect the sinister events in high places that set the brutal massacre into motion. The final act opens as a grand ball is in progress with the royal newlyweds, Marguerite de Valois and Henry of Navarre, in attendance. Raoul de Nangis rushes in, haggard and bloody, announcing the murder of Coligny and urging his fellow Huguenots to avenge their comrades. The very last scene of the opera — frequently omitted when *Les Huguenots* was still part of the standard repertoire — is sheer horror, with corpses lying all over the stage, though surely no librettist, not even Scribe, could adequately capture the true horrors of August 24, 1572. The opera ends as the soldiers of Charles IX intone

> *Par le fer et par l'incendie*
> *exterminons la race impie!*
> *Frappons, poursuivons l'hérétique!*
> *Dieu le veut, Dieu veut leur sang!*
> *Oui, Dieu veut leur sang!*

> (With sword and fire let us exterminate the impious
>   breed!
> Let us strike and pursue the heretic!
> God wills it, God wants their blood!
> Yes, God wants their blood!)

It is estimated that the Massacre claimed thirty thousand victims all over France and yet it failed to annihilate the Calvinist movement in the country. The court of Catherine de' Medici, still the real power behind the throne in 1573, remained ripe with dissension. That year, her foreign policy produced unexpected results when she succeeded in obtaining the vacant Polish throne for her son Henri de Valois, the younger brother of Charles IX.

The bizarre developments were nothing short of operatic and, indeed, form the background of Emmanuel Chabrier's *Le Roi malgré lui* (1887). Henry of Valois was elected by the Polish Diet on May 11, 1573 because the Polish nobles preferred an unknown candidate to his rival, a Habsburg prince and thus an anathema to the Poles. Accordingly, Henry was sent away from his beloved Paris—indeed *malgré lui*—to be crowned King of Poland with great ceremony at the Cathedral of Crakow on February 21, 1574. His reign lasted only four months. When the death of his brother Charles IX—only twenty-four but long suffering from different maladies and nervous disorders—made him the heir to the French throne, Henry quickly escaped from uncongenial Poland.

Chabrier's sparkling opera places the reluctant Henry into several amorous intrigues, has him disguised and also threatened by a not too dangerous conspiracy. The opera ends as he is acclaimed king with no hint of the brief duration of his reign. The solemn promise Henry extends in the opera's finale, however, is very much in keeping with the fun-loving nature of the historical Henry III:

Je ne veux pas qu'on connaisse l'ennui
A la cour du Roi malgré lui

(I do not want anyone to know boredom
In the court of the reluctant king.)

His lighthearted nature, which eventually led him into dissolute excesses, ill equipped Henry III to deal with continuing problems in France. He had powerful enemies in the Guise family who were related to Mary Stuart, Queen of Scots, and represented the implacable exponents of Catholic zealotry. In December 1588, the king had Duke Henry of Guise murdered in the royal council chamber.

Three weeks later, Catherine de' Medici—long a powerful presence behind the rule of her sons—was dead. She was saved by fate from witnessing the violent death of her third and most beloved son, Henry III, who was murdered on August 1, 1589 by a vengeful Guise partisan. Thus passed the last Valois king; his successor, Henry of Navarre, was crowned Henry IV, the first Bourbon to rule France. A Huguenot at the time of his coronation, he was compelled to embrace Catholicism four years later, to save the peace. ("Paris is well worth a Mass" was the saying attributed to him.)

The Spain of Philip II remained unaffected by this bloody decade of French history. In 1570, Philip was married for the fourth time—to his Habsburg niece Anna—a marriage that finally gave him a son who would eventually succeed him on the throne. The building of the monumental Escorial, a mausoleum for his father, himself, and the future Spanish kings, was completed in 1584, the same year an assassin's bullet eliminated William of Orange, one of Philip's oldest enemies. Yet peace would never endure long in his empire. Four years later, Philip's "invincible" Spanish Armada sailed off to be soundly defeated by the English fleet.

XVII

TUDOR ENGLAND

Henry VIII (Saint-Saëns); *Anna Bolena* (Donizetti);
Elisabetta, regina d'Inghilterra (Rossini); *Maria Stuarda*
(Donizetti); *Mary, Queen of Scots* (Musgrave); *Roberto
Devereux* (Donizetti); *Gloriana* (Britten)

Henry VII, the first Tudor king,* brought relative calm to England after ceaseless wars, established respect for law and order, and strengthened royal authority over the nobles. He was, in the words of Sir Winston Churchill, "probably the best businessman to sit upon the English throne," and he laid the foundation for a more powerful England.

His son, Henry VIII, was eighteen years old when he ascended the throne in 1509. Handsome and athletic, he excelled in hunting and tennis, and appreciated the arts, particularly music (seventeen songs and various hymns are attributed to him). He was a cunning politician from the outset, but initially left the business of government to his Lord Chancellor, Thomas Wolsey, a brilliant and ambitious man of common origins (for which English nobility never forgave him).

Even before his father's death, Henry was betrothed to Catherine of Aragon, aunt of the Emperor Charles V. She was the widow of Henry's older brother, Arthur, the Prince of Wales, who had died in 1502. It was a political marriage, intended to foster the Spanish-English alliance against France. The marriage took place in 1509, shortly after the accession, with special papal dispensation that allowed Henry to marry his brother's widow.

During this period, the power struggles between the Habsburg (Charles V) and Valois (Francis I) houses dominated the European scene. Henry and Wolsey pursued a cautious policy that promoted a balance of power between the two and strengthened England's own position. They also maintained good relations with the Vatican, denouncing Luther's activities, and for this Henry VIII was granted the title Defender of the Faith.

---

*   See page 117.

Henry VIII
CREDIT: Culver Pictures Inc.

Henry remained with Catherine of Aragon for nearly twenty years. Their union produced a daughter, Mary, but grew progressively more languid as the king consoled himself with various mistresses. Anxious for a male heir and infatuated with Anne Boleyn, niece of the Duke of Norfolk and one of the ladies at the Court, Henry urged Wolsey to obtain a papal annulment of his marriage to Catherine on the grounds that it was illegal — papal dispensation to the contrary. All this happened at the worst of times, in 1527, when the imperial troops savaged Rome, forcing Pope Clement VII into hiding. He reluctantly charged Cardinal Campeggio and Thomas Wolsey (he, too, a cardinal by that time) to investigate the intricacies of the case. Under pressure from Charles V, Catherine's nephew, the Pope, eventually refused to agree to the divorce. With a temporary reconciliation between Spain and France added to his frustrations, Henry blamed Wolsey for everything. Anne Boleyn detested him, and the nobles of the realm hated his wealth and lavish living style. His years of loyal service forgotten, Cardinal Wolsey fell from grace.

He was arrested and charged with treason, but death saved him from the executioner's axe in 1530.

In 1532, the King's new minister, Thomas Cromwell (also of lowly origins, conforming to Henry's preference in advisors) expedited through parliament the *Supplication against the Ordinaires*. This and another document called *Submission of the Clergy* in effect ended papal authority in England. It established the Archbishop of Canterbury as the leading ecclesiastical figure, and subjected all ecclesiastical decisions to royal approval. Accordingly, Archbishop Thomas Cranmer declared the king's marriage to Catherine illegal, and Henry married Anne Boleyn, by then the Marchioness of Pembroke, in 1533, amidst great pageantry. Catherine of Aragon died in seclusion and relative poverty in 1536.

Catherine, rather than Henry, is the true hero of Camille Saint-Saëns's opera *Henry VIII* (1883), a work that retained its popularity in France for a quarter century or so, with great baritones like Lassalle, Renaud, and Battistini in the title role. (In America, it was revived for Sherrill Milnes in 1983.) The action deals with the final phase of Catherine's reign relating, with reasonable operatic accuracy, Henry's infatuation with Anne, his subsequent negotiations for divorce, and the papal refusal. In Act III, Henry delivers an angry monologue:

> *Ah, ce pouvoir de Rome qui met l'Europe entière*
> *Aux genoux d'un seul homme*
> *Pèserait-il toujours sur la tête des rois?...*
> *Être maitre d'un peuple et d'un vieillard esclave...*
>
> (Ah, the power of Rome that makes all Europe
> genuflect before an individual.
> Will it always weigh on royal heads?...
> To be the master of a people and slave of an old man...

He then proceeds to end his marriage to Catherine and, rejecting the arguments of the papal Legate (Campeggio), he announces Anne as the next queen with appropriate theatrical flair: "*A moi l'amour, à moi la liberté!*"

In the preceding act, there is an angry confrontation between Catherine and her successor, followed by a ballet *divertissement* that survived the opera's eventual disappearance from the repertory. There is no Wolsey in the cast, but history is represented by the Duke of Norfolk and the Earl of Surrey—father and son—in subsidiary roles. (Faithful servant of the king for decades, the earl was eventually executed "for high treason" and only Henry's own death in 1547 saved the duke from the same fate.)

The most jarring departure from history in this opera is the presence of "Don Gomez", the Spanish ambassador, to whom Anne is betrothed and whom she abandons when royal marriage beckons. (*"Reine, je serai reine!"*) Catherine knows of this relationship, but nobly destroys the correspondence that would incriminate her successor. She then dies an operatic death – and an effective one – that anticipates her actual passing by some three years. But the operatic selflessness matches the forgiving nature of the historical model. The real Catherine, in her final letter to Henry, recalls "the care and pampering of your body, for the which you have cast me into many calamities and yourself into many troubles. For my part, I will pardon you everything, and wish to devoutly pray God that He will pardon you also."

By the time Catherine died, Henry's ardor for Anne Boleyn had already cooled. She had given birth to the future Queen Elizabeth but was unable to provide the male heir Henry was determined to obtain. With the connivance of Thomas Cromwell, Anne was convicted of adultery and incest and executed on May 19, 1536. By then, Henry's roving eye was focused on Jane Seymour, a 25-year old, attractive lady-in-waiting. With Archbishop Cranmer's eager assistance, he married her with unseemly haste within days after Boleyn's execution.

Henry VIII's despotic rule claimed other victims too. When the breach with Rome was formalized with the Act of Supremacy (1534), redirecting papal revenues to the king's treasury and declaring Henry Tudor as "Supreme Head of the Church of England", a number of prominent churchmen registered dissent. Among them were Sir John Fisher, Archbishop of Rochester, and Sir Thomas More, the philosopher and political thinker who, in Churchill's words, was "the defender of all that was finest in the medieval outlook." Some years earlier, Henry had the Duke of Buckingham executed on trumped-up charges. The duke was of royal lineage; Henry perceived him to be a potential claimant to the throne against his own offspring.

Executions thus being far from uncommon, Anne Boleyn's violent end failed to stir the masses. Her overemotional nature and extravagant habits had made her unpopular, in any case. Cromwell used the opportunity of her indictment to rid himself of political opponents when he accused Anne of adultery with five persons, including the court musician Mark Smeaton (who corroborated the accusation under torture) and George Rochford, Anne's own brother. All of them perished with her.

In Felice Romani's libretto for Donizetti's *Anna Bolena* (1830), Henry VIII (Enrico), acting on rumors about his wife's infidelity and already infatuated with Jane Seymour (Giovanna), decides early on to be rid of Anne:

> *M'ingannò pria d'esser moglie*
> *Moglie ancora m'ingannò...*
> (Act I, Scene 1)

> (She deceived me even before she married me,
> And she deceived me as my wife...)

The libretto gives no hint of Anne's unpopularity with her subjects. She ruefully admits to a fatal ambition...

> *Ambiziosa, un serto io volli, e un serto*
> *ebb'io di spine...*

> (I was ambitious and I wanted a crown...
> A crown of thorns is what I got...)

Nonetheless, the operatic Anna Bolena is a tragic innocent, cruelly victimized and destroyed by her unfeeling husband. Her music is passionate and affecting, rich in highly emotional confrontations with her admirer Percy and her rival Seymour (whom she forgives, blaming only Henry for her misfortune) and culminating in a fiery scene with touches of operatic madness. (The true Boleyn conducted herself with admirable courage and grace in her final moments.).

Unlike the fictitious Don Gomez concocted by Saint-Saëns's librettists as the love interest in the later opera, Donizetti's character Percy is an historical figure. He was Lord Henry Percy, heir to the Duke of Northumberland, and was, as in Romani's libretto, indeed betrothed to Anne, but their engagement was terminated by Wolsey on the king's orders. He was not included in Cromwell's indictment and presumably eluded execution.

Jane Seymour (Donizetti's "Giovanna") is rather sympathetically treated in the opera: a woman of decent intentions caught in sinister royal machinations. She did not live long enough to refute her operatic characterization:

Maria Callas as *Anna Bolena* (Donizetti)
CREDIT: Museo Teatrale alla Scala

her marriage lasted only eighteen months; she died on October 25, 1537, almost immediately after giving birth to the future Edward VI.

Thomas Cromwell, the king's powerful minister, had been a willing executor of Henry's political moves, which called for the dissolution of the monasteries — and confiscation of their properties — and the ruthless oppression of a rebellion that arose in the north of England against excessive taxation. But when world politics created a situation where an alliance between England and the German Protestant princes became desirable (1540), Cromwell made a deadly mistake. He advised his king to marry the Princess Anne of Cleves. She was an animated lady, but thin and quite unattractive, captured, not flatteringly, in Holbein's painting. Accustomed to more alluring sights, Henry refused to have anything to do with her; Parliament promptly declared the marriage void and the princess was given a royal pension that enabled her to spend her last seventeen years in the English countryside. Henry blamed Cromwell for the fiasco and made it possible for Cromwell's many enemies in high places to seal his doom. He was executed on July 28, 1540, the day Henry married his fifth wife, Catherine Howard.

She *was* attractive and, at twenty-two, thirty years younger than her by then bloated and goutish husband. Involved in a reckless love affair, she was beheaded on the same spot where Anne Boleyn had met her death, in February 1542. A wiser choice, in all respects, was Henry's sixth wife, Catherine Parr, a respectable widow. She patiently attended a king who was a far cry from his vigorous and fun-loving days. A protracted war with Scotland also beclouded the king's final years. It claimed the life of the Scottish King James V, leaving a newborn infant, Mary, the tragic future Queen of Scots, as the queen in name. In 1546, a truce was arranged, but Henry's health steadily declined. On the night of January 27, 1547, the strong and despotic but extremely able monarch who had ruled England for thirty-eight years died.

Henry VIII's achievements were substantial, even apart from the significant break with Rome. He incorporated Wales into England, laid the foundation for the great English fleet, and secured a comparatively peaceful period for England while continental Europe was torn by bloody strife. He respected the functions of Parliament, though more often than not he succeeded in forcing his will on it. He was a supreme egotist and ruthlessly removed all who stood in his way. His reign will be forever remembered for the executions that claimed two queens, two ministers, the remarkable Sir Thomas More, and those unfortunate nobles of royal blood whom Henry perceived as potential threats to his heirs. Religious persecutions also continued during Henry's reign; in 1540, "heretics" were burned for questioning royal authority in spiritual matters. Remarkably, the king's personal popularity with the common people remained constant.

The old lion bequeathed his crown first to his only son Edward, then to his daughters Mary and Elizabeth and, finally, to the offspring of his sister Mary and her husband, the Duke of Norfolk. Not included in the succession were the descendants of Henry's older sister Margaret, the widow of James IV of Scotland. This was significant, for it affected and, in fact, cost the life of their granddaughter, Mary Stuart, who was by then married to the future Francis II of France, a match that made allies of two of England's greatest enemies.

Edward VI, a consumptive child, reigned but never governed. A council appointed by Henry VIII named his uncle, the Duke of Somerset, as Edward's Lord Protector, but a rebellion caused his execution in 1552. Power was then assumed by the Duke of Northumberland, who, anticipating the young king's early death and determined not to let the Catholic Mary succeed him, embarked on an ambitious and dangerous plan. Lady Jane Grey, grandchild of Henry VIII's younger sister, was a remote claimant to the throne. Northumberland married her to his son, and subsequently persuaded the dying king to declare both Mary and Elizabeth illegitimate. Edward VI obligingly died on July 6, 1553, but Northumberland had gravely miscalculated: England remained royal to the Tudor line and whatever support Northumberland had originally secured quickly evaporated. He paid with his life for his deadly ambition — as did Lady Jane Grey and her husband for their complicity in the plot.

Mary Tudor's reign lasted from 1553 to 1558. Slighted and humiliated for most of her life, the queen was determined to undo the English Reformation and to return the land to the faith of her Aragonese forebears. To solidify the Spanish connection, she agreed to marry the future Philip II, son of her mother's protector, Charles V. In July 1554, the wedding took place, with England's Cardinal Pole, returned from exile, officiating.

But the Reformation could no longer be undone in England. An unsuccessful revolution headed by Sir Thomas Wyatt ended all of the queen's hopes to turn back the hands of time by peaceful means. A period of brutal repression began, claiming the lives of leading Protestant churchmen, including Archbishop Cranmer, who had served Henry VIII so ably and faithfully.

They were burned as heretics and their martyrdom simply reinforced the Protestant cause.

Ultimately, Mary Tudor's rule proved to be a failure on all counts. She failed to realize that in English minds Catholicism was inseparably linked with foreign influence. The English Bible had been widely circulated during the reign of Henry VIII. Combined with the English Book of Prayers (the achievement of the martyred Cranmer), they formed powerful instruments for the Reformation. The queen's strictly political marriage was also a fiasco. There was no physical attraction between the two dour personalities and, besides, Mary was ten years older than Philip. To top off a series of misjudgments, the Spanish alliance dragged England into war with France, resulting in the loss of Calais, the last English stronghold on the continent. When the unhappy queen died on November 17, 1558, disillusioned, sick, and prematurely old at 42, England greeted the news with jubilation. She was pitilessly termed "Bloody Mary" in the Holinshed *Chronicles*, according to which she possessed "not the favor of God, nor the hearts of her subjects, nor yet the love of her husband." And yet, the frustrations of her life inspired Victor Hugo to write the play *Marie Tudor* in 1833 that in turn led to operas by Giovanni Pacini (1843) and Antonio Carlos Gomes (1879).

With England irreversibly embracing the Protestant faith, the nation turned with renewed confidence to Mary's half-sister Elizabeth in 1558. Her rule, though not peaceful in any sense, brought solid achievements to the realm and a fame to the remarkable queen that was enhanced, to a considerable degree, by the operas she inspired.

* * *

From the onset of her reign, Queen Elizabeth displayed a mastery of the art of government. Like her father and grandfather, she possessed a keen political judgment and knew how to select the ablest advisors. Though she may have resented it when even her closest intimates tried to dictate her policy, to be a close councilor to Elizabeth was nowhere nearly as life-threatening as had been the case with Wolsey and Cromwell in Henry VIII's time. Under her rule, England became Protestant by law. Mary's Catholic legislation was repealed, but a spirit of tolerance prevailed toward English Catholics as long as they did not ally themselves with foreign powers.

Catholic-Protestant enmities, however, did create a threat in nearby Scotland, where Mary Stuart openly advocated her claim to the English throne.

The claim had a solid foundation: she was the granddaughter of Henry VIII's sister Margaret—a legitimate Tudor descendant in Catholic eyes, which regarded Henry's marriage to Anne Boleyn and Elizabeth, their offspring, illegitimate. After Mary lost her royal husband, King Francis II of France, in 1560, there was nothing to hold her there, and she returned to Scotland in 1561 at the invitation of Scotland's Catholic lords. She was an impulsive and passionate woman and, unlike her royal cousin, unwise in political matters, a failing that eventually caused her ruin.

Neither impulsive nor passionate, Elizabeth never allowed her emotions to interfere with ruling the nation. She realized early on that a husband for her would create unsurmountable problems. She coolly turned down a marriage proposal (after the death of Mary Tudor) by a most unlikely suitor, Philip II, realizing that such an alliance with an ultra-Catholic ruler could not have been right for Protestant England.

Speculation concerning the peculiar love life—or lack of it—of the "Virgin Queen" has fueled the imagination of novelists and playwrights for centuries. Giovanni Federico Schmidt, a poet of the royal theaters of Naples, credited an unnamed English romance as the source for his libretto for Rossini's *Elisabetta, regina d'Inghilterra* (1815). Linked to history by tenuous threads, it concerns a romance of sorts between Elizabeth and one of her early court favorites and intimates, the Earl of Leicester.

He was the son of the Duke of Northumberland, who had led the conspiracy against Mary Tudor and paid with his life for it. The Earl of Leicester lost his wife in 1560 under mysterious circumstances, and foul play was suspected once his closeness to the queen became evident. Historians have not unearthed any evidence pointing to Leicester's being the queen's lover, but Gloriana (as her subjects came to call her) left no doubt in her own words about a more important issue: "I will have here but one mistress and no master."

In the Rossini opera, Leicester is something of a two-timer. He is secretly married to a fictitious Scottish princess, reproached by the jealous queen for his disloyalty, and pursued by a villainous "Norfolk", a political rival. (The real Duke of Norfolk was actually to be involved in an anti-Elizabethan plot in 1572, and beheaded.) The opera ends happily with the queen blessing the lovers. In the final ensemble, she proclaims:

> *Fuggi amor da questo seno*
> *Non turbar più il viver mio.*

Altri affetti non vogl'io
Che la gloria e la pietà.

(Flee, love, from this breast,
Do not disturb my life any more.
I want no other passions
Than glory and mercy.)

Nice operatic sentiments, these, but they severely oversimplify the life of this great and fascinating ruler. She had other things beside love and mercy to live for. Leicester continued to be her loyal councilor (often at odds with Lord William Cecil, the queen's chief minister), defended the Crown in battle, and died of natural causes in 1588.

When 17-year-old Mary Stuart returned to Scotland, she was, like Elizabeth, a queen without a spouse. Her Protestant subjects — followers of the sternly anti-Catholic John Knox — were hostile to her. To strengthen her claim to the English throne, knowing that she had sympathizers among the members of Catholic nobility in North England, she married her cousin Henry Stuart, Lord Darnley (also a cousin to Elizabeth) in 1565. It was an unfortunate choice, for Darnley, a dissolute weakling, was extremely unpopular. Although the marriage produced a son who was to rule over both England and Scotland, it lasted only nineteen months. When Darnley, in a jealous rage, murdered David Riccio, a court musician imported from France and Mary's special favorite, a rebellion broke out under the leadership of the Earl of Bothwell. Darnley was killed, possibly with Mary's connivance, and Mary entered into a liaison with Bothwell, her husband's murderer. The outraged populace demanded Mary's abdication as Bothwell escaped to Denmark. Leaving her infant son behind, protected by a regent, Mary made her way to England to become Elizabeth's uninvited and most certainly unwelcome guest for twenty years.

The brief but tumultuous reign of Mary Stuart is captured with reasonable operatic faithfulness in Thea Musgrave's *Mary, Queen of Scots* (1978), based on Amelia Elguera's novel *Moray*. The first act introduces one of the crucial characters of the drama, Mary's half-brother James, the Earl of Moray, who has designs on the Scottish throne. In the second act, where the composer ingeniously superimposes the unpopular "foreign" dances at Mary's court on the lusty Scottish reels to highlight native disdain against foreigners, Darnley — egged on by Moray's agents — murders Riccio. Afraid of Moray's power, Mary banishes him. In the third act, anxious to protect herself and her infant son, she turns to Bothwell, who seduces her as the price for his protection. Darnley is killed during the confrontation between the forces of Moray and Bothwell, in which the latter is defeated. (Mary is not implicated in Darnley's murder in the opera.) James forces Mary to abdicate, but he is murdered by a Scottish patriot, and the infant James VI is proclaimed King of Scotland.

In the course of history, Mary's arrival in England created enormous problems. She was, after all, in line for the English throne as long as the "Virgin Queen" remained single. Pressures on Elizabeth to reconsider her status mounted but she, remaining adamant, tamed the restless Parliament by asserting, "Do not upbraid me with miserable lack of children, for every one of you, and as many as are Englishmen, are children and kinsmen to me."

As long as Catholic Mary Stuart was alive, she represented a threat to the survival of Protestant England at a time when Spain and France were seething with anti-Protestant fervor. The threat manifested itself first in largely Catholic North England, where in 1569 the lords rebelled but failed to organize an effective striking force. During this period, Elizabeth gave secret support to the French Huguenots and, after the St. Bartholomew massacre which shook England, to the Protestant Dutch, as well.

The expanding power of Spain caused another Catholic uprising in England that resulted in a spate of executions in 1581. The assassination of William of Orange in 1584[*] proved that no Protestant ruler or pretender was safe from the punishing hand of the Counter-Reformation. Fearing an immediate invasion from Holland, Elizabeth sent Leicester with an English army to the Netherlands. The Spanish invasion did not materialize, but Philip was clearly behind a conspiracy against the Crown that centered around the Catholic Anthony Babington in 1585. It incriminated Mary Stuart, whose subsequent trial for treason became a political necessity. Urged on by Parliament, Elizabeth signed her rival's death warrant. The next day, she had a change of heart, but it was too late: Mary was executed in the great hall at Fotheringay Castle on the morning of February 8, 1587. By that time, England was at war with Spain, whose Philip II had always regarded Mary Stuart the rightful Catholic ruler of England.

The plight of Mary Stuart and the rivalry of the two queens inspired an enormous number of literary treatments — some 20,000, according to Lady

---

[*]   See page 179.

Antonia Fraser, Mary Stuart's biographer. Clearly, the most enduring among them was Schiller's 1800 play *Maria Stuart*, on which Donizetti's opera *Maria Stuarda* (1840) is rather closely based. In his customary fashion, Schiller rearranged historical facts to serve his dramatic imagination and yet, with all the liberties taken, the play's spirit radiates historical authenticity.

Following Schiller's example to further sharpen the religious, political, and temperamental contrasts between the two queens, Donizetti's opera presents them as rivals for the love of Robert, the Earl of Leicester. (Rumors about Leicester being Elizabeth's lover freely circulated in Europe, but at no time was he romantically linked with Mary.) Furthermore, Mary's lengthy 19-year captivity is radically condensed, climaxing in the dramatically exciting—but historically inaccurate—confrontation between Mary and Elizabeth. Actually, they never met face to face; once again, history proved too prosaic for Schiller. Thus, on stage, Elizabeth upbraids her rival for her scandalous past, calling her a "betrayer of the marriage bed, whose evil heart plans new crimes and deceptions." Enraged, Mary calls the queen,

> *figlia impura di Bolena, meretrice, indigna, oscena....*
> *profanato è il soglio inglese,*
> *vil bastarda, dal tuo piè...*

choice phrases hardly in need of translation.

To quote Antonia Fraser, "One's first reaction may be—how absurd, how inaccurate, but how magnificent; but on second thought, it is possible that is exactly how Mary Queen of Scots *would* have behaved if such a scene had taken place." After all, by her own Catholic lights, Elizabeth was the offspring of a union declared invalid while Catherine of Aragon was alive.

William Cecil, the opera's "villain", was indeed a steadfast advocate of Mary's execution—not so much out of cruelty but out of political pragmatism. The figure of George Talbot (Earl of Shrewsbury), who offers spiritual solace to Mary in her final moments after getting an ambiguous reply from her regarding her role in the Abington conspiracy, is on shakier grounds. The historical Talbot was a Protestant noble, not a secret Catholic priest.

This and a few other historical inaccuracies are eliminated in the English National Opera's excellent production of the Donizetti opera, using Tom Hammond's fine English translation. Expressly designed for audiences that know their history, the Talbot episode is deprived of its religious ritual. Furthermore, the first two acts are advanced to 1571, when Mary was actually held captive at Chartsworth. The third act — at Fotheringay — takes place sixteen years later, a more plausible and historically more accurate solution.

Antonia Fraser calls attention to the Scottish queen's "particular histrionic quality". Surely she was extremely histrionic in her death. Shedding the severe black garment she wore as she entered the place of execution, she refused with great dignity an offer of a last-minute conversion (accurately observed in the opera), and revealed underneath a petticoat of crimson velvet. Bardari, Donizetti's librettist, makes no reference to this historical detail, but opera producers would be unwise to ignore this supremely theatrical touch.

When the news of Mary's execution reached Elizabeth, she blamed her advisers — in her characteristic fashion — for a deed that caused the death of an anointed queen. Schiller's play captures this in chilling fashion; in opera it would be an anticlimax following the ultra-effective execution scene — thus Donizetti wisely ignores it.

* * *

Elizabeth's next crisis was a decisive confrontation with Philip II, with whom, as a result of clashes in the Netherlands and English raids on Spanish shipping, a warlike relationship had existed for years. The Royal Navy, established by Henry VIII, had grown into a substantial fleet, and bold sea captains like Sir Francis Drake had long threatened Spanish pride. Following a particularly effective and damaging raid on Cadiz in 1587, Philip assembled a formidable Armada of some 130 ships and more than 30,000 soldiers and seamen. It was commanded by the Duke of Medina Sidonia, an able administrator but a most reluctant admiral with virtually no seafaring experience. His ill-judged adventure pitted the Spanish forces against a better equipped navy, determined English defenders, and certainly superior leadership. When the Armada's attempts to link up with soldiers from the Netherlands under Duke Alexander of Parma failed, Spanish defeat was inevitable. Nearly half of the proud Armada was destroyed and England emerged from the encounter as a first-class naval power. Protestantism in England was no longer challenged and the independence of the northern provinces of the Netherlands was secured.

Philip accepted this severe blow to Spanish pride and to the cause of the Counter-Reformation with his customary stoicism. He looked for no scapegoats and restored the hapless Medina Sidonia to his former post as Governor of Cadiz. The war with England dragged on for many more years, accomplishing nothing for either nation while exhausting both treasuries.

The remaining years left to Philip were spent in preparing his son for the succession. Meticulous and gravely serious to the end, he adhered to a strict schedule for handling matters of state even though his progressively debilitating gout left him virtually crippled. On September 11, 1598, he addressed the future Philip III in this manner:

> In a very few hours I shall be covered only with a
> poor shroud and girded with a coarse rope...Death
> will place my crown on your brows...My days are
> numbered and are drawing to a close...

Two days later — days devoted to religious meditation — Spain's stern but prudent king died at the age of seventy-one. The desolation of his final days is eloquently anticipated in these words by the operatic Philip in Verdi's *Don Carlos:*[*]

> *Je dormirai dans mon manteau royal*
> *Quand aura lui pour moi l'heure dernière.*
> *Je dormirai sous les voutes de pierre*
> *Des caveaux de l'Escorial.*
>
> (I shall sleep in my royal mantle
> When the final hour has struck for me,
> I shall sleep under the stone vaults
> Of the crypts of the Escorial.)

The sun was setting for Elizabeth, too. Friends and enemies alike were dying around her: Leicester, the early favorite, had died in 1588, France's Henry III and Catherine de'Medici in 1589, Sir Francis Drake in 1596, Sir William Cecil, her faithful Minister, in 1598. Elizabeth was now 65; her England was embroiled in domestic factionalism and faced a new threat from Ireland, a Catholic land openly sympathetic to Spain. The unrest culminated in an open rebellion in 1596 with Spanish backing, led by Hugh O'Neill, Earl

---

[*]   See pages 165-171

of Tyrone. It was this Irish revolt that led to the downfall of the Earl of Essex, the last of the queen's favorites.

Robert Devereux, the Earl of Essex, was Leicester's stepson, an able soldier who proved his valor in the wars against France and Spain. Vain and ambitious, he was given absolute command of an English army in 1599 to crush the Irish rebellion. There, unable to defeat Tyrone, he concluded a peace treaty with him against the queen's orders. On returning to London, he tried but did not succeed in convincing his sovereign of the rightness of his actions. The queen was patient for a while—for her affection for a man half her age was real—but Essex overestimated his power over her. When his defiance led to an abortive revolt against the queen, she quickly resolved to "teach him better manners." In this she was readily aided by the Earl's many enemies, headed by Robert Cecil, who had succeeded his father to the office of the queen's Secretary of State. On February 15, 1601, the Earl of Essex paid with his life for his excessive ambition and foolhardy actions.

The unquestionably fascinating relationship between the aging queen and her dashingly youthful courtier captivated literary imagination almost instantly. Corneille was among the first playwrights to respond (*Le Comte d'-Essex*, 1678). The basis for Gaetano Donizetti's 57th opera, *Roberto Devereux* (1837), however, was François Ançelot's *Elisabeth d'Angleterre* (1832). Actually, Donizetti was not the first composer to deal operatically with the story. That honor fell to his contemporary, Saverio Mercadante, whose *Il Conte d'Essex* had an unsuccessful run at La Scala in 1833. (Mercadante's librettist had been the renowned Felice Romani, whose work was followed closely enough by Donizetti's Salvatore Cammarano to warrant a charge of plagiarism.)

Aside from the normal operatic procedure of condensing approximately two years into 24 hours, Donizetti's *Roberto Devereux* sacrifices historical truth to romantic contrivance. There are historical characters aplenty in the opera, but they all follow the librettist's lead. Essex's political blunders are minimized: he is victimized by the queen's jealousy, not by military failure and treasonable behavior. His infatuation with the operatic "Sara Nottingham" is fictitious. The historical Lady Nottingham was as old as Elizabeth; her husband, Charles Howard, Lord Nottingham, was the queen's loyal courtier, neither a friend nor an enemy to Essex (whereas the relationship between the two men is crucial to the opera's plot). The operatic actions of Sir Robert Cecil and Sir Walter Raleigh—Essex's comrade in arms, but no friend—call for no serious historical reservations. On the other hand, the episode of the ring—a love token that could not have saved Essex's life—is a dramatic device that Donizetti scholar William Ashbrook traced all the way back to John Webster's 1623 play *The Devil's Lawcase*. Above all, the opera misrepresents Elizabeth's character by obscuring Essex's treasonable acts, matters that the sovereign would not have overlooked for personal reasons. The opera's final scene, with Elizabeth's spectral vision and her designation of James VI as the future ruler of England, is an effective realignment of history in the service of Italian operatic conventions.

Historically far more accurate is Benjamin Britten's *Gloriana*, written for the 1953 coronation of Elizabeth II. Here the action develops over an extended period, allowing better insights into Essex's arrogant and impulsive character. It also reveals his historically documented rivalry with Sir Walter Raleigh (who followed Essex to the executioner's block within a year, though for unrelated reasons). The crucial Irish campaign takes place between Acts II and III of the Britten opera. The third-act episode when Essex suddenly enters the queen's chambers and finds her without her wig and beauty preparations is a true historical incident: it happened on September 28, 1599, two days before she ordered his arrest. In the opera, however, the queen's initial outrage dissolves into bittersweet reminiscences of their relationship.

Britten's Essex, nonetheless, is a traitor. Gloriana is the central character and the opera ends with subtle evocations of documented events of her final years. The opera was coolly received in 1953 and its composer was taken to task for not stressing the regal aspects of the queen on such a festive occasion. Since then, however, it has enjoyed several revivals.

In the early morning of March 24, 1603, Queen Elizabeth died, and with her ended the Tudor dynasty. She ruled over an England of remarkable men: Shakespeare, Bacon, Marlowe, Raleigh, Donne. Intellectual pursuits flourished, religious hysteria was tamed and, in the words of Sir Winston Churchill, "a working harmony between Sovereign, Lords, Commons, and the tradition of English monarchical government had been restored and gloriously enhanced." But much of what had been accomplished was undone as the English Crown passed to her successors.

XVIII

FLORENCE, THE MEDICI, AND
THE BIRTH OF OPERA

Euridice (Peri); *Orfeo* (Monteverdi); *Don Quixote*
(Paisiello, Salieri, Massenet, *et al.*); *The Makropoulos Affair* (Janácek)

It is ironic to note that Pope Clement VII, the august arbiter of legitimacy in the case of Henry VIII's marriage, was himself the illegitimate son of the murdered Giuliano de' Medici, brother of Lorenzo the Magnificent.* Caught in the crossfire of ambitions between three powerful kings — Charles V, Francis I, and Henry VIII — Clement nonetheless managed, by evasion and doubledealing, to influence the politics of all three empires. But he was also the head of the powerful House of Medici, and the dominance of the wealthy republic of Florence was uppermost in his mind.

The Medici were banished from Florence in 1527 following the invasion of Italy by the armies of Charles V, but Pope Clement restored them to power in 1530. He did so by disposing of his political enemies in a bloodthirsty manner that belied his name since it betrayed no evidence of clemency. He abolished the city's old constitution and established Alessandro, his grandnephew, as the ruler of Florence. Then, by marrying his young cousin Catherine to the future Henry II of France, Clement laid the foundation for a long-lasting Medici influence in that country, too. When in 1532 Alessandro de' Medici was proclaimed Duke of Florence by Charles V, all vestiges of the Florentine Republic were extinguished. Once a family of bankers, descendants of shopkeepers, the Medici were now aristocrats with powerful royal connections.

The cunning statesmanship of Pope Clement, who accomplished all this, might have been appreciated in less violent times. The fact is that he was extremely unpopular in both Rome and Florence, and his death in 1534 was

---

*   See page 129.

greeted with jubilation. Nor was Alessandro granted much time to relish his dukedom: a brutal authoritarian and an unprincipled lecher, he was murdered by his own cousin Lorenzino in 1537. His successor, appointed by the emperor—since the duchy had become hereditary—was Cosimo, a young man of eighteen who was to rule for nearly four decades. He was the first Medici to follow royal custom by placing a number after his name. Some thirty years later he was elevated to the even greater title of Grand Duke.

Unlike his Medici forebears who patronized the likes of Michelangelo (who created the famous Medici Tombs in Florence) and Raphael, Cosimo I was only moderately interested in painting and sculpture. But he compensated for this lack by encouraging music, and when the time came for him to marry (royally, of course) Eleonora of Toledo, the daughter of the Viceroy of Naples, the wedding was celebrated with great pomp and musical splendor. Antonio Landi's five-act play *Il Comodo* was the centerpiece of entertainment, with seven *intermedi* based on mythological subjects written for the play by Francesco Corteccia, maestro di cappella to the Medici court.

Music by then had been enjoying a lively tradition in Florence, and Corteccia was by no means the first composer to cultivate the relatively new form of the *intermedio*, a musical composition to be played between acts and as an epilogue to a play. Following the example of the Flemish madrigal composer Philippe Verdelot (also active in Florence at the time), he incorporated madrigals in his *intermedi*, usually commenting on the events within the play in the manner of the classical Greek choruses. As the *intermedi* grew in length, involving dialogues, duets, and even choruses, they gradually became the more important part of the performance. They also paved the way for an emerging new form that had, so far, no name.

Aside from creating a harmonious atmosphere for music, Cosimo I laid out beautiful gardens in Florence, built roads, and reformed the city's educational and administrative systems. But history still remembers him as a ruthless despot who dealt with his opponents, and with the conquered republic of Siena, with ferocious brutality. His son and successor, Francesco I (1574-1587), could also claim credit for scientific and artistic achievements (such as the enlargement of the Uffizi Gallery, built by Vasari for Cosimo I), but he, too, was a despot who nearly ruined the duchy's economy.

Few tears were shed when Francesco died (poisoning was suspected) in 1587 and was succeeded by his younger brother Ferdinando I, a man of a rather noteworthy past. He had been made a cardinal at fourteen—a less startling fact for a Medici than it would be for others—and a resident of

Rome, where he assembled a large collection of Greek and Roman statues and built the Villa Medici to house them. He restored peace and prosperity to Florence and spent lavishly on new buildings and the creation of a new and important port—Livorno—which soon attracted Huguenots from France, Catholics from England, and Jews from everywhere, all finding a haven under the new Grand Duke's tolerant administration.

Ferdinando I ceased to be a cardinal in 1589, when he married the Princess Christine of Lorraine, granddaughter of Catherine de' Medici and thus a distant cousin. It was a splendid ceremony in the Medici tradition, culminating in a performance of *La Pellegrina*, a play by Girolamo Bargagli enriched by a set of musical *intermedi*. By this time, as though responding to some law of nature, the relationship between the play and the surrounding music had become reversed: the latter, with its ambitious content and elaborate dimensions, simply overwhelmed the former. Opera, yet unnamed, was on its way.

The poets and musicians involved in the creation of the *intermedi* for the ducal wedding included such remarkable talents as the poet Ottavio Rinuccini, the madrigalist Luca Marenzio, and the composers Jacopo Peri, Giulio Caccini, and Emilio de' Cavalieri, the overall artistic director of the enterprise. Not the most talented but perhaps the most significant among them was Giovanni de' Bardi (1534-1612), Count of Vernio, a cultivated patron of the arts, whose house was a meeting place for a group of Florentine creative minds. They were commonly known as "*La Camerata*". Peri and Caccini were members of the Camerata, as were Vincenzo Galilei (father of Galileo) and Jacopo Corsi, who assumed leadership after Bardi's departure for Rome. The Camerata sought to revive the method of musical declamation used in the ancient Greek theaters. While no one then—or now—could know for certain how the ancient Greek actors projected their lines in their open-air theaters, Jacopo Peri, in his foreword to his opera *Euridice,* had interesting ideas on the subject:

> I believe that the ancient Greeks and Romans (who, according to the opinion of many, sang their tragedies throughout) used a kind of music more advanced than ordinary speech, but less than the melody of singing, thus taking the middle position between the two.

The members of the Camerata agreed on the basic principle that theatrical projection of this kind must be based on the clear understanding of the text. This could only be achieved through the avoidance of the contrapuntal writing of the madrigalist school and through strict adherence to performance by a solo voice with the simplest instrumental accompaniment. We know that a musical work called *Dafne* by Peri, using fellow Cameratan Rinuccini's text and embracing these principles, was performed in 1597 in the palace of Count Jacopo Corsi. It is also known that, with some additions and elaborations, the work was repeated the following year at the Pitti Palace for Grand Duke Ferdinando de' Medici. Unfortunately, its musical score disappeared; only Rinuccini's libretto has survived.

Peri was soon at work, however, on his next musical subject, based on the myth of Orpheus and Eurydice, again with Rinuccini as librettist. The authors called their work *dramma per musica*, a term that was soon supplanted by *opera in musica* until, decades later, it evolved into its final abbreviated form. A new century was dawning as the new genre achieved dramatic continuity in the first completed opera to be handed down to posterity. And history conspired to create a splendid setting for its inauguration in 1600 — the wedding of Henry IV of France and the Princess Maria de' Medici. It came about as a result of characteristic Medici maneuverings.

The Spanish hegemony over the Italian states had rarely been challenged during the long rule of Philip II. Italy was safe for Catholicism, and Philip was content with ruling Italian souls without territorial acquisitions or even a military presence. Cosimo Medici, who obtained his title of Grand Duke from Pope Pius V with Philip's reluctant approval, never questioned Spanish dominance, nor did his son Francesco. His grandson Ferdinando had other ideas. Under the rule of Philip III (1598-1621), a retiring man and a weak ruler, Ferdinando sensed a decline of Spanish power in Europe and attempted to reestablish good relations with France, Spain's traditional rival. Already married to a French princess himself, he backed Henry Navarre's claim to the French throne. First he helped him obtain the papal absolution needed to become Henry IV.[*] Then — after the stormy breakup of Henry's first marriage to Marguerite of Valois (which had begun so tumultuously against the bloody background of St. Bartholomew's Day in 1572)[**] — Ferdinando proceeded to promote Henry's marriage to his orphaned niece,

---

[*]   See page 179.
[**]   See page 177.

Maria de' Medici. The wedding took place on October 6, 1600, with a magnificent ceremony followed by several days of festivities attended by princes, cardinals, poets, and musicians from all over Europe. This was the background of what posterity has recognized as the first opera in history, Peri's *Euridice*. Peri himself sang the tenor role of Orpheus, and Count Corsi led the small instrumental ensemble from the harpsichord.

The Italian princely houses of Savoy, Ferrara, and Mantua had long been infuriated by the Medici political maneuverings and aspirations. Nonetheless, Francesco Gonzaga, Duke of Mantua, attended the wedding and in all likelihood Claudio Monteverdi, his court musician at the time, was part of the ducal entourage that heard *Euridice* at the festivities. Given the rivalry between the Gonzaga and Medici houses, there is little doubt, though concrete proof is lacking, that Monteverdi's *Orfeo*, with a libretto by Alessandro Striggio, came about as a result of this rivalry. Monteverdi, a greater theatrical genius than any of the Cameratans, created a more imposing spectacle and was able to endow the mythical characters of Orpheus and Eurydice with warm human qualities. His *Orfeo* was introduced with extraordinary success in 1607, and he was immediately commissioned to compose two musical works for the impending wedding of Francesco Gonzaga and Margherita di Savoia. Eventually, Monteverdi transferred his activities to Venice and there helped to launch a glorious period of operatic creativity. In Rome, too, an important school of composers cultivated the new genre, largely under the patronage of the powerful princely family of the Barberini.

Princely patronage eventually ceased to be a prerequisite for operatic performance. With the opening of the Teatro San Cassiano in Venice—the first public opera house—in 1637, the popularity of the new entertainment grew at an astonishing pace. Venice alone, a city of 125,000 people, was able to support six opera companies simultaneously, with seasons up to thirty weeks a year. And all this happened in a few short decades following the birth of opera at that splendid ducal wedding on October 6, 1600, organized by the Grand Duke Ferdinando de' Medici, whom we may gratefully remember as opera's godfather.

But the marriage Ferdinando had masterminded was not the kind that is made in heaven. Maria de' Medici was a tall and heavyset woman, rather unappealing compared to the ladies of Henry IV's court. The king, twenty years older than his Florentine bride, was a man of perpetual sexual ardor, surrounded by mistresses, and marriage did not change his mode of life. A royal offspring, the future Louis XIII, was produced by September 1601, with six more royal children to follow. But the king's various mistresses were also productive, causing the Medici ambassador to report to Florence that the Louvre resembled a brothel more than a palace. The Grand Duke Ferdinand died in 1609, deeply disappointed in his niece's failure to uphold Catherine de' Medici's high standard as Queen of France.

For all his excessive devotion to the pleasures of the flesh, Henry IV proved to be a worthy ruler. He concluded an advantageous treaty with Spain, established religious peace within France, and tried to organize a giant European league against expanding Habsburg power. That may have been a dangerous enterprise, but it was his religious tolerance that proved to be the king's undoing: on May 14, 1610, he was assassinated by François Ravaillac, a fanatical Catholic.

Maria de' Medici then became regent for her 10-year old son Louis XIII, whom she betrothed to the Spanish Infanta, Anne, daughter of Philip III. Notwithstanding her uncle Ferdinando's unfavorable judgment of her abilities, the queen dowager remained a power behind the throne of her son, while the supreme influence on Louis rested with his Minister of State, Cardinal Duke de Richelieu.

Peace between France and Spain had been secured by the dynastic union between Louis XIII and his Spanish wife. Her father, Philip III, clearly wished for lasting peace: he concluded a treaty with England in 1604, and acceded to the virtual independence of the seven northern provinces of the Netherlands in 1609. While the expulsion of the Moriscos * in that same year dealt a severe blow to Spain's economy, this was a shining period in the realm of art and literature — the age of El Greco (1547-1614), the playwright Lope de Vega (1562-1635), and the religious composer Tomás Luis de Victoria (1548-1611). Above all, Miguel de Cervantes Saavedra completed his *Don Quijote* (published in two parts, 1605 and 1615), creating an incomparable picture of the Spain of his day. This outstanding epic novel was translated into more languages than any other book save the Bible. According to the *Oxford Dictionary of Opera*, it has also inspired 83 operas in three centuries, an amazing total that includes the names of Caldara, Piccinni, Telemann, Paisiello, Salieri, Mercadante, Mendelssohn, Donizetti, Chapí, Massenet, DeKoven, Falla, Petrassi, and Halffter. This surpasses even the list of composers inspired by the Spanish author's contemporary, William Shakespeare; after all,

---

*   See also page 174.

the bard's operatic influence rests on at least twenty of his plays. (They were written during the reigns of Elizabeth I and James I, son of Mary Stuart and Lord Darnley, who was crowned on July 24, 1604.)

* * *

In Central Europe, meanwhile, the Turks were still occupying most of Hungary, keeping the armies of the Emperor Maximilian II (grandson of Charles V) engaged in a bloody stalemate neither side was able to resolve. Even more ineffective, politically, was his son, Rudolf II, whose reign (1576-1612) was marked by Catholic-Protestant friction. An avid astrologer and astronomer, Rudolf is immortalized in Janáček's opera *Vec Makropoulos (The Makropoulos Affair)*. It is a known fact that Rudolf had some alchemists at his court, for he himself dabbled in the occult arts. It was one of these court alchemists named Hyeronymus Makropoulos (according to Karel Capek's play on which the opera is based) who concocted a potion intended to give the emperor 300 more years of life. It was tried out on the alchemist's daughter first; she became ill and the alchemist was thrown into prison. But she survived to become, 300 years later, Emilia Marty, one of the most fascinating of all opera heroines. Possessor of the sensational Makropoulos secret, she was unwilling to go on living once she discovered that her soul had long since died.

Looking back at the period around 1600 when opera as we know it began, we see, then, a relatively peaceful few years, calling to mind Schopenhauer's bleak observation that "History has nothing to record save wars and revolutions: the peaceful years appear only as brief pauses or interludes, scattered here and there." *Intermedi*?

XIX

RUSSIA'S TIME OF TROUBLES

The Maid of Pskov (Rimsky-Korsakov); *The Tsar's Bride*
(Rimsky-Korsakov); *The Oprichnik* (Tchaikovsky); *Boris
Godunov* (Mussorgsky); *Dimitri* (Dvořák); *A Life for the
Tsar* (Glinka)

In 1567, Ivan IV, Tsar of Russia, presented himself as a suitor to England's
Queen Elizabeth through the mediation of the English trader-explorer Anthony Jenkinson. She, of course, had no intention of marrying him — or
anyone else — but she was also mindful of the favorable, near-monopolistic
conditions English merchants were enjoying in Russia. She therefore cour-
teously offered her domain as a possible asylum in the event that political
conditions should force the Tsar to seek it, but made no comment on the
marriage proposal.

The Tsar was thirty-seven then, and already known in England as "Ivan
the Terrible". ("Awesome" is a more accurate translation of the Russian
"Grozny", by which the sovereign was known to his own people, but judging
by his deeds, "Terrible" was not misapplied.) A grandson of Ivan III, he was
an infant when he succeeded his father and grew up in a climate of violence
and treachery, in constant fear of being murdered, the fate accorded to his
two brothers. From early childhood on, he harbored a deep hatred for the
powerful boyar families — the Glinskys, the Belskys and, in particular, the
Shuiskys, who, as descendants of Alexander Nevsky, had monarchical ambitions and treated young Ivan with contempt. In 1543, at age thirteen, Ivan
suddenly ordered the arrest of Prince Andrey Shuisky and had him executed
in the most brutal manner imaginable. This, and further acts of unspeakable
cruelty, soon established his unquestioned authority, and the powerful
boyars began to live in fear of him.

After his coronation in 1547, Ivan decided to take a wife from the highest
Russian nobility. His choice fell on Anastasia Romanovna, of the family that
was to give Russia the Romanov dynasty two generations later. A devout person of gentle character, she was treated by her husband with great devotion,

though the latter's unbridled lust for cruelty continued unabated. When a devastating fire burned much of Moscow to the ground in 1547, Ivan became terrified of what he perceived to be God's punishment. He consulted churchmen, listened to their stern pronouncements, publicly confessed his sins, and promised a new era of Christian justice. Indeed, for the next decade, with the aid of chosen counselors, the Tsar introduced several major reforms. When his armies conquered the khanates of Kazan and Astrakhan (1552-1556), adding the rich lands of the Volga basin to his empire, the young Tsar was hailed as a worthy heir to Alexander Nevsky. He may have been feared by the powerful boyars, but achieved great reverence and popularity with the people at large.

The relatively calm period came to an end with the death of Tsarina Anastasia in 1560, fatally weakened by her sixth and final childbirth. (Only two of the children, Ivan and Feodor, survived.) Feeling abandoned by God, Ivan turned from grief to a wild rage and abandoned himself to debauchery. With the death of Anastasia, he was freed of all restraining influences that had heretofore curbed his base and cruel impulses. First he banished his wise and trusted advisers, the priest Sylvester and the prince Alexei Adashev, for their alleged hostility to Anastasia, and then he ordered the arrest and prompt execution of several prominent boyars, including those who had served him faithfully and distinguished themselves in the Kazan wars.

He followed this bloodbath with the setting up of a separate state within the state, the *oprichnina*, to be ruled by Ivan and administered by the *oprichniki*, a special guard chosen by the Tsar, charged with guarding his life and destroying his enemies. Dressed in black uniforms and displaying their dreaded emblem of a broom and a dog's head, the *oprichniki*, placed above the law and encouraged by the Tsar to indulge in wanton cruelty, soon became his instruments of terror. Eventually, grown to an army of 6,000, they tortured, pillaged, and raped at will. A wave of executions also began with the death of Alexander Shuisky, one of the outstanding military leaders of the country.

In 1561, Ivan married Maria, a Circassian princess who had caught his eye, but soon tired of her. He was still married to her when he offered himself as a suitor for Queen Elizabeth's hand. When that plan failed, Ivan deluded himself into thinking that the English queen, like himself, was at the mercy of perfidious advisers. When his second Tsarina died in 1569, it was generally assumed that she was poisoned at the Tsar's order. But Ivan welcomed the opportunity to accuse and promptly destroy his royal cousin, the Prince Vladimir Andreyevich, with his entire family.

The death of his second wife was probably the final stroke that caused the Tsar to abandon all restraints and embark on an endless campaign of purges and massacres. No longer satisfied with torturing and executing individuals, he wanted to punish entire communities. In 1570, he methodically slaughtered the inhabitants of Novgorod on the false charge that they were in league with Lithuania, the land Ivan coveted but, despite several incursions, could not wrest from his arch-enemy, the Polish King Sigismund II. The number of Novgorod's victims was estimated to reach as many as 60,000. Among the few leaders who were spared was the Archbishop Pimen, who was exiled to a distant monastery. Novgorod, a city that was then next to importance only to Moscow, never recovered from the tragedy.

With Ivan's return to Moscow, the bloody purges continued, and this time even the oprichniks were not safe from Ivan's murderous rage. Alexei and Feodor Basmanov, once the Tsar's favorites, were thrown into prison. There, young Feodor was persuaded to kill his father to save his own head. Having obeyed the order, Feodor Basmanov was tried as a parricide, publicly tortured and executed.

Young Feodor Basmanov appears prominently in Tchaikovsky's fourth opera, *The Oprichnik* (1872), based on a contemporary play by Lazhechnikov. He befriends young Andrey Morozov and persuades him to join the oprichniks to avenge himself on an enemy. Andrey must take a solemn oath to renounce all his family ties in exchange for power and licentiousness that goes with the life of the dreaded group. Since he wants to marry, Andrey has a change of heart, and Basmanov suggests that the Tsar may release him from his vow. Quite the opposite happens. On the night of the wedding festivities, Andrey's mortal enemy announces that the Tsar wishes to "see" the bride — alone. When Andrey forcefully protests, he is arrested and taken to be executed in the presence of his mother. That final scene may have been inspired by Verdi's *Il trovatore*, but that kind of wanton sadistic cruelty was typical of Ivan's actions, and the opera's characters frequently comment on oprichnik terror.

Russian censorship in 1872 did not allow the Tsar to be presented on stage in person, and this had a great deal to do with keeping Rimsky-Korsakov's first opera, *The Maid of Pskov*, off the stage for more than twenty years. The action in this opera takes place in 1570, immediately following the massacre and destruction of Novgorod. Pskov was earmarked for a similar fate, but

Ivan, in whom religious mysticism and atrocious cruelty comfortably coexisted, found a spiritual experience there and spared the city.

In the opera, Ivan discovers that Olga, the adopted daughter of his host, the boyar Yuri Tokmatov, is actually his own illegitimate child, born of a youthful liaison. Olga subsequently perishes in a skirmish between the Tsar's army and a group of rebellious defenders. Her loss leaves the Tsar, who in this opera reveals an unsuspected tender streak, completely devastated.

When *The Maid of Pskov* was finally allowed to be performed in a revised form (St. Petersburg, 1895), it attracted the attention of young Feodor Chaliapin, for whom a new production of the opera was staged in the private theater of the Russian magnate Savva Mamontov. After consultation with the historian Vasily Kliuchevsky and extensive studies of the Tsar's likeness in some famous paintings and sculptures, the great basso evolved a characterization of towering authority. The Tsar appears in only three scenes. Chaliapin made his initial entry on horseback and, without uttering a word, created an impression of "formidable menace", in the words of Vladimir Stasov, an important eyewitness. He was equally impressive in his wild and overpowering grief, collapsing beside the body of the dead Olga. Rimsky-Korsakov himself later wrote that "the success of *The Maid of Pskov* was due to the great talent of Chaliapin, who created an incomparable Tsar Ivan." The surviving photographs of Chaliapin in this role lend support to all superlatives.

In 1571, Ivan decided to marry again and once more the search was on for a worthy bride. He chose Marfa Sobakina, the daughter of a prosperous merchant, who was promptly elevated to the rank of boyar. The bride died within two weeks after the wedding, on November 13, 1571. Naturally, poisoning was suspected, and a new wave of terror swept Muscovy. This particular episode inspired a play by Lev Mey and, subsequently, a quite remarkable opera, *The Tsar's Bride*, by Rimsky-Korsakov (1899).

Virtually all characters in this opera are historical personages. Ivan himself makes an appearance on horseback (Act II, Scene 3), accompanied by an oprichnik. They halt on a street near the Sobakin house, the Tsar gazes intently at Marfa, frightening her with his expression, and then silently departs. In the opera, Marfa's engagement to the young boyar Lykov is broken as a result of the Tsar's interest in her. But she is also pursued by Grigory Griaznoy, a brutal oprichnik who happens to be one of Ivan's favorites. Griaznoy's discarded mistress obtains a lethal potion from

Feodor Chaliapin as Ivan the Terrible in
The Maid of Pskov (Rimsky-Korsakov)
CREDIT: Metropolitan Opera Archives

Bomelius, the Tsar's physician. Believing it to be a love potion, Griaznoy pours it into Marfa's drink at the wedding feast. In the final scene, realizing that Marfa, the new Tsarina, is nearing death, Griaznoy confesses his guilt and Maliuta, the brutal head of the *oprichniki,* gleefully announces his death sentence.

There is dramatic license here and there in the Rimsky-Korsakov opera, but the fact is that the death of the Tsar's young bride immediately launched a wave of executions, and an opportunity for the Tsar to rid himself of perceived traitors. The real Griaznoy was indeed executed, along with Prince Gvozdev-Rostovsky (also mentioned in the opera); the poisons of Elysius Bomel (known as Bomelius) played a great part in their fate. Soon thereafter, when the Tsar tired of the entire *oprichnina* and dissolved the hated organization, the grateful people of Russia blessed Ivan for his wisdom. Grigory Maliuta was the only leader who managed to retain the Tsar's continued trust, and so did his son-in-law, Boris Godunov, a young and ambitious nobleman who began to assume an ever increasing role in Ivan's policy making. The dreaded Maliuta eventually perished in a brief war against Sweden over the territory of Livonia.

In that same action-packed year of 1572, the Polish King Sigismund II died without an heir, and Ivan eagerly proposed himself to the Polish Diet as a candidate. The Diet, however, chose Henri de Valois, *"Le Roi malgré lui,"* * who reigned briefly and nonchalantly and was subsequently deposed in 1575. His successor, Prince Stephen Bathory of Transylvania, emerged as a wise and courageous ruler who confronted Ivan in many battles without losing any ground. Far more successful were Ivan's expansions toward the East, culminating in the conquest of all of Siberia.

Ivan was fifty years old in 1580, in failing health, but still unwavering in his suspicions and ready to destroy all who, in his view, aspired to power. After several short-lived marriages, some without church sanction and most ending with his wives' demise under dubious circumstances, he married for the seventh and last time in 1580, concomitantly with marrying his second son Feodor to Irina, the sister of Boris Godunov.

Ivan, the first-born prince, was the mirror image of his father: intelligent, literate, lecherous, and cruel. To the immense joy of his father, the young Tsarevich often joined him to witness tortures and executions, among them

---

*   See page 178.

the horrendous end of the poisoner Bomelius, who was roasted alive. But even the son and heir could not be safe from the Tsar's murderous rage. While engaged in a renewed war with Poland that was not going well for Russia at the time, the Tsarevich dared to express a view contrary to his father's. Enraged, Ivan leaped from his seat and struck his son with his long spear, mortally wounding him. On November 19, 1581, the Tsarevich died. His father, mad in grief as he had been in all his behavior, uttered cries like an animal during the funeral service, praying for God's mercy. But, as he saw no immediate signs of divine retribution, Ivan gradually returned to his old ways.

On November 19, 1583, his wife Maria Nagaya presented Ivan with a newborn son, Dimitri. Thereafter the monarch's health sank rapidly. Doctors, astrologers, and sorcerers were consulted, but the decline was irreversible. Feeling the end near, Ivan appointed a council of Regents for his older son, Feodor, a young man of 26, feeble in mind and body and not considered able to rule. The five-man council included Prince Ivan Shuisky, Prince Yuriev, the Tsarevich's uncle, and Boris Godunov, his brother-in-law. Ivan's obsession of being surrounded by conspirators whom he blamed for all his bloody deeds continued to the day he died, March 18, 1584. He was buried in a monk's robe beside the son whom he had killed in a murderous rage. The people of Russia, whom he had terrorized for forty years, mourned him as God's anointed representative, and were fearful of the nation's future now that the awesome Ivan was no more.

To eliminate possible disputes about the legitimate succession, the Regents exiled the infant Dimitri, born of Ivan's last marriage, together with his mother, to the small town of Uglich. There, the young Tsarevich perished under suspicious circumstances in 1591, seven years later. That tragic incident provided the inspiration for *Boris Godunov* — both the play by Alexander Pushkin (1823) and the opera by Modest Mussorgsky (1869).

Ivan had never considered his second son Feodor Tsar material, nor did the young man show any leadership abilities once he reluctantly assumed his royal position. He was all too happy to cede the responsibilities of government to his strong-minded wife Irina and to her brother, Boris Godunov. The latter quickly asserted his power over the Princes Mstislavsky and Shuisky, the most influential boyars, who regarded Boris as an upstart. Once solidified as the *de facto* ruler, Boris proved to be wise and relatively moderate in both his domestic and foreign policies. He continued maintaining friendly relations with England, promoted trade with other Western nations, repulsed

Tatar incursions that threatened the welfare of newly acquired Siberia, and maintained peace with his dangerous neighbors, Poland and Sweden. He even tried to improve the lot of the peasantry by curbing the excesses of the autocratic big landowners.

In 1598, the placid Feodor died and with him the 600-year old Varangian dynasty of Rurik * came to an end. There was no one to immediately challenge the position of Boris Godunov, and the Patriarch of Moscow, who owed his position to Boris, offered him the crown. Boris declined, shrewdly suggesting that this was a matter for the *Zemsky Sobor* (National Assembly) to decide. When the Assembly, rumored to be strongly influenced by Boris's agents, ruled in his favor, he accepted and was immediately crowned. He began his rule by imprisoning and exiling the members of the Romanov family, relatives of Tsar Ivan's first and most beloved wife, Anastasia, who might have claimed succession. (Ivan would have opted for more radical measures.)

Just the same, Boris had an uneasy time governing. Not having inherited the throne in what the masses regarded as a legitimate manner, he was not accepted as God's representative by them the way they had accepted the murderous Ivan or his weakling son Feodor. The boyars never ceased to plot against him and, to make matters even worse, a failed harvest in 1601 caused famine throughout the nation. With the plague closely following the deadly famine, people perished by the thousands and blamed Boris for their misfortunes. The issue of the allegedly murdered Tsarevich resurfaced and rumors began to circulate that another child had been buried in his stead.

It is true history that resounds in the Tsar's agonizing monologue in the second act of Mussorgsky's opera:

> God condemns me and sends rebellion,
> plots and intrigues, conspiracies in Poland.
> Death, disease, and
> villainy surround me;
> pestilence and famine have ravaged my kingdom.
> Impoverished, destitute, Russia groans.
> And all who suffer this vengeance of heaven
> believe in their hearts I am guilty.
> They lay the blame on me for their sorrows,
> the name of Tsar Boris rouses their hatred.

---

* See page 118.

In 1603, a young man claiming to be the legitimate Tsarevich Dimitri emerged in Poland. He was subsequently identified by church authorities as Grigory Otrepiev, an unfrocked monk and runaway serf of the Romanovs. The Pretender found a friendly reception in Poland, where he was permitted to organize a band of warriors for a campaign against Godunov. His infatuation with Marina Mniszek, the ambitious daughter of an adventurous nobleman, eventually led to their marriage, thus solidifying the Pretender's ties with Poland.

While the romanticized Polish Scene in Mussorgsky's *Boris Godunov* is not historically accurate in all points, the operatic character of the Jesuit Rangoni (a creation of Mussorgsky, for he does not appear in Pushkin's play) symbolizes the strong Catholic support for the Pretender's cause. He embraced Roman Catholicism in 1604 and, in a document dated April 24 of that year, assured the Pope that, once established on the throne, he would enforce Catholicism in Russia.

Tacitly supported by the Polish king Sigismund III (Stephen Bathory's successor), the Pretender set out from Kiev leading a motley army of some four thousand troops. Masses of disgruntled Russians bolstered his strength as more and more people of every social class chose to accept the Pretender as Tsar Ivan's legitimate heir. In April 1605, Boris Godunov suddenly died. His young son Feodor was crowned, but ruled for only six weeks. The boyars quickly abandoned the Godunovs, murdered young Feodor and his mother and, led by the turncoat Vasily Shuisky—whose deceitful character is faithfully portrayed in the opera—quickly cast their lot with the Pretender. On June 20, 1605, the false Dimitri triumphantly entered Moscow.

The next episode in Russian history is movingly foretold in the plaint of the Simpleton that ends Mussorgsky's opera:

> Darkness nears....the darkest night
> Sorrow, sorrow on earth;
> Weep, weep, Russian folk,
> Poor starving people!

The false Dimitri's rule did not last long. It failed to lighten the burden of the peasantry and disappointed the boyars, who wanted their ancient privileges restored. The Russian churchmen were alarmed by Dimitri's Polish entourage, who behaved rowdily and showed indifference to Russian customs. The raucous way in which Dimitri's wedding to Marina Mniszek was celebrated in the spring of 1606 caused general outrage and served as the final blow to Muscovite patience. On May 17, the Pretender was murdered by the boyars, who had his body burned and his ashes fired by cannon in the direction of Poland. Marina was banished and, though she was later involved in various intrigues and adventures, she ceased to be influential in Tsarist politics.

The Pretender's brief and tumultuous rule is romantically treated in Antonin Dvořák's fifth opera, *Dimitri* (1882). Its plot centers on a love affair between Dimitri and Xenia, Boris Godunov's daughter, who was indeed spared when her mother and brother were slaughtered. The opera presents a dramatically effective conflict between Xenia and Marina, but their rivalry ends when Xenia, holding Dimitri responsible for the downfall of the Godunovs, enters a convent. Shuisky is the villain in Dvořák's opera, as well. It is he who personally kills Dimitri — and that is not too far removed from historical fact.

History, however, recognizes Vasily Ivanovich Shuisky as Russia's next Tsar (1606-1610). Unpopular from the outset, he ruled under chaotic conditions, fighting rebellious masses and contending with yet another false Pretender with strong Polish support. Eventually, Shuisky was deposed and forced to take monastic vows by his fellow boyars. A group of them, headed by Feodor Romanov (who had assumed the monastic name *"Filaret"* when Boris Godunov made him Patriarch of Russia), sought a Polish alliance for the sake of internal stability, but without success. It was actually the Church that provided the needed leadership, uniting various Russian and Cossack forces to repel the Polish invaders, who had already taken several Russian towns, left undefended by internal chaos. By October 1612, Russia's leaders were united enough to elect a new Tsar. As usual, there were several candidates until finally the choice fell on 16-year old Mikhail Romanov, son of Filaret. Since the Romanovs were related to the fondly remembered Anastasia, Ivan the Terrible's first wife, there was a link to the ancient Rurik dynasty, and thus young Mikhail was a popular choice with the masses.

Glinka's opera *A Life for the Tsar* deals with the events of 1612. In the village of Domnin, the people react with great jubilation to the election of the new Tsar. Meantime the Polish nobles, angered that their own Prince Vladislav was denied the Russian throne, reveal the historical fact that the new Tsar's father, Filaret Romanov, is in Polish captivity, and resolve to capture the son, as well. We also learn that, at the time of his election, young Mikhail and his mother were at a convent some two-hundred miles from Moscow—another historical fact.

In the third act of the opera, a band of Polish soldiers sets out to find the young Tsar and force Ivan Susanin, a peasant from Domnin and a patriot, to be their guide through the forest. He leads them deep into the woods where they are hopelessly lost. Susanin thus heroically sacrifices his "life for the Tsar" and dies a martyr's death. The opera ends with the Tsar's coronation and the celebration in Moscow's Red Square. In his book *The Tsardom of Moscow 1547-1682*, Part I, Professor George Vernadsky of Yale University cites documentary evidence that a land grant was issued by Tsar Mikhail in 1619 to Susanin's son-in-law, Bogdan Sobinin (the tenor hero of the Glinka opera), thus lending historical confirmation to the operatic Susanin's heroism.

When young Mikhail was crowned in 1613, his father, Filaret, was still in Polish captivity. Eventually, a truce with Poland facilitated his release, and it was the father who wielded the power from behind the young Tsar's throne. Enduring peace with Poland was not to come, but Mikhail's reign lasted for thirty-two years, and the continuity of the Romanov dynasty was ensured for the next three centuries.

XX

THE THIRTY YEARS' WAR

Friedenstag (Richard Strauss); *Der Freischütz* (Weber); *The Devils of Loudun* (Penderecki); *Cyrano de Bergerac* (Alfano/Damrosch); *La muette de Portici* (Auber); *Salvator Rosa* (Gomes); *I Puritani* (Bellini)

The first half of the seventeenth century witnessed vast changes in the political landscape of continental Europe. The decline of Spain as a political and military power continued while France rose to a position of dominance as a result of the sagacity and ruthlessness of the all-powerful Cardinal Richelieu, mighty minister to the ineffectual King Louis XIII. The Habsburg empire, already weakened by the independent actions of Germany's Protestant princes and involved in a struggle for survival, proved inadequate in political strength and economic resources to counter Richelieu's stratagems. The conflagration known as the Thirty Years' War, which devastated much of Europe, dealt a deadly blow to Habsburg power — a circumstance Richelieu did much to bring about.

The patchwork of European territories which, as Voltaire was to observe a century later, was neither holy nor Roman and hardly an empire, still carried that outdated misnomer in the seventeenth century, with a Habsburg ruler as its traditional head. The election of the Emperor rested with seven electors: three Catholic prelates, three Protestant German princes, and the King of Bohemia, usually a Habsburg prince and, of course, a Catholic. This established structure was suddenly overturned when the prosperous and strongly nationalistic land of Bohemia rejected the Habsburg choice, Ferdinand of Styria, as their king. On May 23, 1618, rebellious crowds in Prague took violent action: they hurled Ferdinand's deputies out of the window of the royal castle of Hradcany. That the deputies miraculously survived did not alter the Bohemian declaration of independence from Habsburg rule. Their choice was the Protestant Elector Frederick of the Rhineland Palatinate, the son-in-law of England's King James I.

The master plan behind all this, envisaged by Frederick's chancellor

Christian von Anhalt, was to gain a Protestant majority among the Electors and thus assure a Protestant emperor. Unfortunately, there was no real military alliance of Protestant rulers to back up Anhalt's grand design. During the next eight years of savage fighting against the powerful Habsburg armies led by Albrecht von Wallenstein and Count Johan Tilly, the largely mercenary Protestant forces and their Danish allies were destroyed. Frederick escaped to Holland, Ferdinand (who had become Emperor in the interim) took back his Czech crown, executed the leaders of the Bohemian rebellion, and distributed their confiscated lands among his Habsburg supporters. Wallenstein, named governor of Prague, was rewarded with enormous estates, including an entire province, and elevated to dukedom. Although Bohemia was subdued, the war did not end; Ferdinand was determined now to subjugate the Protestant German lands as well. In 1629, he promulgated his Edict of Restitution, which outlawed all Protestant denominations except Lutheranism and introduced a land reform that threatened German property owners with economic ruin.

Ferdinand's implacable drive to extend Habsburg power awakened the rest of Europe to the growth of the Habsburg menace. It was a threat that united Protestant as well as Catholic nations, for it was at this juncture (1630) that France's all-powerful Cardinal Richelieu entered the picture. A new and most devastating phase of the Thirty Years' War began. Richelieu had helped to arrange a truce between warring Poland and Sweden, thus freeing the Swedish army, the best fighting force of all Europe, to enter the war—a Protestant army, to be sure, but richly subsidized by Cardinal Richelieu's France.

Heading that army was Gustavus Adolphus, a brave warrior and leader of unparalleled gifts. He was by no means Richelieu's pawn, for he entered the fray pursuing Baltic territorial claims of his own. But he did make dramatic advances, increasing the strength of his army by attracting thousands of German Protestants and inspiring his troops by his own valor in battle. Throughout 1631, Swedish and Habsburg armies were engaged in bloody confrontations, with unspeakable atrocities committed on both sides. The worst was probably the siege of Magdeburg, a city that was taken by Tilly's Habsburg army on May 20 after holding out for six months. Tilly was unable to check the murderous rage of his victorious troops, which destroyed not only the entire defending garrison, but also half of the city's 36,000 inhabitants. As described in a contemporary account:

> The great and splendid city that had stood like
> a fair princess in the land was now... given over to the
> flames, and thousands of innocent men, women, and
> children, in the midst of a horrible din of heartrend-
> ing shrieks and cries, were tortured and put to death
> in so cruel and shameful a manner that no words would
> suffice to describe, nor tears to bewail it.

This traumatic event is mentioned in Weber's opera *Der Freischütz* (1821), set in Bohemia, shortly after the Thirty Years' War. In contrast to conventional productions with fairy-tale bucolic settings, recent stagings in Germany and England are historically faithful and reveal a bleak and ruined landscape. When the evil Caspar, a huntsman in league with the Devil, sings his lusty Drinking Song in Act I, he casually remarks, between stanzas, that as a young man he served in Tilly's army and was present "*beim Magdeburger Tanz*" (at the Dance of Magdeburg) — a horror that would release hidden demons in anyone.

Tilly, already seventy-one at the siege of Magdeburg, died a year later, but his name passed into history forever associated with that event. As the historian C. V. Wedgwood, author of *The Thirty Years War*, observes, "Years later, imperialist soldiers crying for quarter would be met with the answer 'Magdeburg Quarter' as they were shot down."

On the morning of November 16, 1632, the imperial army led by Wallenstein (whom the Emperor had dismissed as a potential rival but now recalled as a last resort to save imperial fortunes) confronted the near-invincible army of Sweden outside the town of Lützen. The battle raged all day and, though it ended with a victory for the Swedish army, it claimed the life of the valiant Gustavus Adolphus, the one unifying force in the Protestant cause. While the Emperor was forced to annul the Edict of Restitution in 1635, the war, far from over, simply entered a new phase. With Germany as its main zone of devastation, the armies of Catholic France and Protestant Sweden faced the soldiers of Habsburg Spain and Austria — a fighting force deprived of its best leader when Wallenstein was murdered by his own conspiring officers, probably with the Emperor's encouragement. When Ferdinand himself died of natural causes in 1637, only one of the mighty players in the deadly game that produced the Thirty Years' War was left alive — Cardinal Richelieu of France.

This remarkable man had become a bishop through his family's connections at twenty-one, but his rise thereafter was the result of his own astute political judgment and unquestioned abilities. He became Louis XIII's prime minister at thirty-nine in 1624, suppressed the Huguenot opposition but did not deny them their religious freedom. A strong France was his primary aim and, recognizing the Huguenots' strength, he made his peace with them, nominated their leaders to high office, and obtained their support against the Habsburgs. This brought France into direct conflict with Spain, notwithstanding the dynastic bond between the two countries: the Queen of France, Anne of Austria, was the sister of the Spanish King Philip IV (1621-1665). (He is immortalized in countless Velasquez paintings, a great womanizer and tireless begetter of children—thirty-two of whom were illegitimate.) When a group of pro-Spanish aristocrats, opposed to Richelieu's stand, entered into secret negotiations with Spain, they paid with their lives for their audacity. Richelieu, already mortally ill in 1641, was still in absolute control.

Although an advocate of diplomatic solutions, Richelieu could be ruthless, as evidenced by the gruesome episode of Urban Grandier in the town of Loudun in 1634. Grandier was a charismatic priest opposed to the government's centralizing tendencies. This brought him into conflict with the royal commissioner, Labardemont. When instances of hysterical behavior were noted among the nuns in Grandier's vicarage, the priest was brought to trial on the grounds of association with the devil. Persisting to the end in his innocence, despite a mass of damaging evidence, Grandier was brutally tortured and burnt alive. The grisly story is related in Aldous Huxley's novel *The Devils of Loudun* which, in turn, forms the basis of Krzystof Penderecki's opera of the same title. In the opera, with the composer as librettist, no opportunity for visual, emotional, and musical shocks in telling this grisly tale is left unexplored.

Another episode during the French-Spanish hostilities is worth noting for its literary and musical association. It was the siege of Arras in 1640, where the historical Cyrano de Bergerac was wounded, as related in Edmond Rostand's celebrated play. Cyrano was a gifted political writer and dabbler in the sciences at a time when great literary minds (Descartes, Corneille, Molière) flourished in France. His writings (in which Cyrano predicted not only a journey to the moon but also the discovery of a sound-reproducing device like the phonograph) were published by his friend Le Bret. Le Bret is a character in the Rostand play *Cyrano de Bergerac* as well as the two operas based on it—one by Walter Damrosch (1913), the other by Franco Alfano

(1936). Both operas are faithful to the play, but the play is highly Romanticized history.

Despite the grim episode depicted in *The Devils of Loudun*, Richelieu is remembered as a champion of religious tolerance. He was also a connoisseur of music and a lover of all the arts. In his triumphant foreign policies, he freed France, as well as Italy, of Spanish domination and strengthened the Netherlands and Germany at the expense of Habsburg power. None other than his Spanish counterpart, the Count of Olivares, called him "the ablest minister that Christendom has possessed these last thousand years." When he died on December 4, 1642 at the age of fifty-seven, he left a strong France in the hands of a weak ruler, Louis XIII, who had been content to let Richelieu run the country in his name. Louis followed his great minister five months later, leaving behind a five-year old heir who was to become the *"roi soleil"*, Louis XIV, under the tutelage of Richelieu's own designated successor, Cardinal Mazarin (*né* Giulio Mazarini).

With the main characters of the Thirty Years' War in their graves, it was time to end the war itself. All the exhausted participants yearned for peace, but the obstacles were endless and, with the war still dragging on, its changing fortunes constantly altered bargaining positions. When, after four years of frustrating negotiations, the Treaty of Westphalia was signed in 1648, it failed to solve such essential problems as religious freedom and local autonomy. Still, the independence of Switzerland and Holland was finally established, and Sweden and France both acquired certain German lands. The central administration of the Habsburg Empire was further weakened by the recognized independence of German princes, but the kingdom of Bohemia remained a hereditary Habsburg property.

Richard Strauss's opera *Friedenstag* (1938) takes place on the last day of the Thirty Years War, October 24, 1648. The idea for the opera came from the novelist Stefan Zweig, who, inspired by Velasquez's painting *The Surrender of Breda* (a 1625 episode in the Dutch-Spanish wars), wanted to create a powerful antimilitarist statement at the time of Hitler's expansionism. The rising tide of Nazi power forced Strauss to choose another librettist, Joseph Gregor, to carry out Zweig's vision, and the opera itself was eventually suppressed. In the action, the Catholic commandant of a besieged city, who describes himself as a veteran of Magdeburg, is determined to fight to the death rather than surrender his post. But then word comes that the treaty has been signed. Catholics and Protestants join their voices in greeting "the rebirth of friendship" as the chorus intones Gregor's Schiller-like phrases:

Die uns erschüttern, die uns noch blenden
Zeichen sind es, die niemals enden!
Brücken, die wir zu beschreiten nicht wagen,
Leicht werden sie die Zukunft ertragen....

What moves us and still blinds us
Is only an illusion without end!
Bridges that we dare not cross:
The future will deal with them...

In 1633, the French artist Jacques Callot, who observed much of the devastation first hand, completed a series of etchings called the *Miseries and Misfortunes of War*. For graphic detail of war's horrors and waste, the collection rivals Goya's shocking pictorial account of the Napoleonic Wars. For thirty years, millions throughout Europe perished and suffered for reasons few understood in what C.V. Wedgwood termed "the outstanding example in European history of meaningless conflict." Devastated Germany was the greatest loser, for the Peace of Westphalia offered no shield against the breakdown of social order and the disintegration of its society.

* * *

In 1647, while the negotiators at Münster and Osnabrück were still hammering out the finer points of the Westphalian Treaty, the population of Naples rose in revolt against the Spanish governor, who had imposed a special tax on the sale of fruit. The rebellion was organized by a fisherman named Tommaso Aniello, popularly known as Masaniello. A hundred thousand inhabitants marched on the palace of the viceroy and forced him to withdraw the tax. Masaniello then seized power for several days, but allowed that power to go to his head. He was killed by his own people, reportedly on orders from Spain, and the revolt died away. But Masaniello became a subject of legend, the embodiment of the fearless popular hero in the face of tyranny. His short-lived revolution inspired two operas: Auber's *La muette de Portici* (1828) and Gomes's *Salvator Rosa* (1874).

Both operas focus on the brief span of the Neapolitan revolt (July 7 to 16, 1647, as specified in the libretto of the Gomes opera), and both are rich in tumultuous incident. Antonio Ghislanzoni, Gomes's librettist, places the Baroque painter Salvator Rosa (1615-1673) into the thick of the action as a

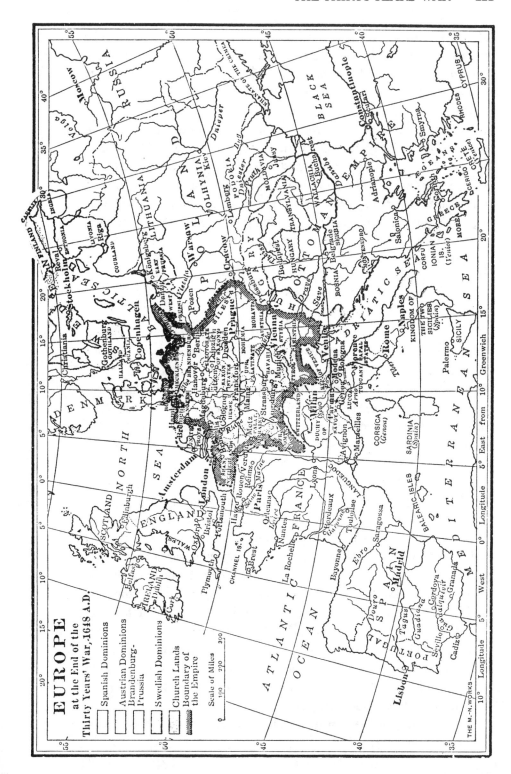

EUROPE
at the End of the
Thirty Years' War, 1648 A.D.

Spanish Dominions

Austrian Dominions

Brandenburg-
Prussia

Swedish Dominions

Church Lands

Boundary of
the Empire

Scale of Miles
0   100   200   300

THE M. N. WORKS

Masaniello partisan. In the libretto of *La muette de Portici* (co-authored by Eugène Scribe and Germain Delavigne) Masaniello's mute sister Fenella, danced by a ballerina, throws herself into the abyss just as Vesuvius erupts in time for the final curtain. (Masaniello's death occurs off-stage in both operas.)

These excesses aside, *La muette de Portici* exacted its own importance in the currents of history. During a performance at the Théâtre Royal de la Monnaie in Brussels on August 25, 1830, the stirringly patriotic duet *"Amour sacré de la patrie"* received a prolonged ovation. At the end of the performance, a crowd formed, took to the streets and invaded some public buildings. This was the beginning of a revolution that led to Belgium's independence from Holland, to which it had been annexed after the fall of Napoleon.

* * *

Spain came out of the Thirty Years' War greatly impoverished, lacking the economic resources to counter Richelieu's masterly moves against Habsburg interests. Richelieu also saw to it that the beleaguered rule of Philip IV would be further weakened by keeping the hopes of an independent Catalán republic alive. Having lost his wife and first-born son, Philip married again, following the Habsburg family tradition by choosing an Austrian niece. The marriage produced the desired heir, the future Charles II, whose legacy was an empire in disarray.

Although politically weakened and economically impoverished, Spain enjoyed a golden period of arts and letters during the reign of Philip IV. It was the age of Velasquez, Zurbaran, and Murillo and, among the playwrights, Shakespeare's two great Spanish contemporaries, Lope de Vega and Calderon de la Barca. Not on their literary level but more important to opera was Gabriel Tellez, a monk who assumed the literary pseudonym of Tirso de Molina (1584-1648), traveled throughout the Iberian peninsula and the West Indies, and wrote a large number of plays. The most important of these was *El Burlador de Sevilla*, which was printed in 1630 and staged in Barcelona that year. While he probably used legends circulating in Spain long before, it was this literary monk who bequeathed to posterity the adventures of the sacrilegious libertine Don Juan Tenorio and his ultimate destruction by the *"Convidado de Piedra"* (Stone Guest).

The popularity of Tirso's play was enormous. Several imitations of transitory literary fame followed almost immediately. In 1655 in Paris, Molière created his *Le Festin de Pierre*; in 1736, Italy's Carlo Goldoni came out with his *Don Giovanni Tenorio, ossia Il Dissoluto*. The latter play, and probably the earlier ones as well, could hardly escape the attention of the Italian librettists Giovanni Bertati and Lorenzo da Ponte, who began working on operas for Giuseppe Gazzaniga and Wolfgang Amadeus Mozart almost simultaneously around 1787. That the Gazzaniga-Bertati opera on the same theme (*Don Giovanni Tenorio, ossia Il Convitato di Pietra*) appeared earlier than the Mozart-Da Ponte work is evident from Da Ponte's generous borrowings from it. Nevertheless, it was Mozart's *Don Giovanni* that brought Tirso de Molina's fascinating character immortality.

* * *

With the Reformation already an accomplished fact by the end of Queen Elizabeth's reign, the factors that brought about the Thirty Years' War had no direct effect on England. Nevertheless, the country did not escape a great deal of unrest. James I (1603-1625) was forced to dissolve Parliament three times because of that body's opposition to his kind of royal absolutism. The first wave of Puritan settlers arrived in America during this period: Virginia was settled in 1607, Plymouth in 1620. But amidst all the political turmoil, the arts flourished, as they did in Spain—these decades produced the best Shakespeare plays, the poems of Ben Jonson and John Donne, and the King James Bible.

The relationship between the Crown and Parliament grew even worse under Charles I (1625-1649), aggravated by a costly and unsuccessful war against Spain. For eleven years, the king governed without Parliament; when it was summoned again in 1640, it violently opposed the king over vital religious and military issues. On July 12, 1642, Parliament voted to raise its own army, an action that produced a civil war between the "Roundheads" (Puritans and Parliamentarians) and the "Cavaliers" (royalists). At first no substantial gains were made by either side, but with the emergence of the Puritan leader Oliver Cromwell the tide turned. The royalist armies were soundly beaten in several battles; the king was forced to surrender to the Scottish army for his own safety, but it turned him over to Parliament in January, 1647. After an unsuccessful effort to reestablish his authority with Scottish help, the king's fate was sealed. Tried before a high court for treason and for being the enemy of the people, he was beheaded on January 30, 1649.

The action of Bellini's *I Puritani* (1835) begins at this point, as the chorus of *"guerrieri di Cromwell"* sings an anthem of praise celebrating their victory over the Stuarts. The Puritans are holding a mysterious highborn lady captive, with orders to deliver her to Parliament. She is, as she reveals to Sir Arthur Talbot, a knight with royalist sympathies, Henrietta Maria, *"figlia a Enrico, a Carlo sposa"*, daughter of Henry IV of France and widow of the executed Charles I. (These historical nuances are usually obscured amidst *bel canto* fireworks.) The gallant Arthur (Arturo) spirits her away, endangering his own life as a traitor to Cromwell's cause and inflicting instant dementia on Elvira, his operatic bride. He is captured in Act III, threatened with death, but is dramatically pardoned by order of Parliament. The lovers are happily reunited as the chorus celebrates England's freedom, voicing *"A Cromwello eterna, eterna gloria!"*

For the next eleven years, England was without a king. As continental Europe was facing the dire consequences of the Thirty Years' War, England was governed by the iron hand of Oliver Cromwell.

XXI

FRENCH SPLENDOR AND
ENGLISH RESTORATION

Lully; Purcell; *Lucia di Lammermoor* (Donizetti); *The Prince of Homburg* (Henze); *La Damnation de Faust* (Berlioz)

Rising from the ashes of the Thirty Years War, the nations of Europe were groping for a new age of stability. In Germany, the Holy Roman Empire was becoming more shadow than substance and Habsburg influence waned with the growing independence of the local princes. In England, Cromwell's policies did not survive the "Lord Protector"'s capable rule and the country returned to monarchy after his death in 1658. France, enjoying the fruits of economic power secured by Richelieu and his successor Mazarin, continued with absolutism as the surest way to sustain internal peace and prosperity. The reign of Louis XIV, who ruled longer (1643-1715) than any monarch in history, proved to be a period of unparalleled artistic and intellectual achievement.

As he stated in the famous line attributed to him — "*L'état, c'est moi*" — Louis was indeed the embodiment of the state itself. With the aid of able administrators chosen for their gifts rather than their aristocratic heritage who owed him absolute loyalty, he established a smoothly functioning central government based on economic solvency and strict army discipline. The former was assured by the shrewd economic policies of his minister Jean-Baptiste Colbert, while the latter was enforced by the newly created office of the Inspector General, headed by a man whose very name today stands for disciplinarian firmness — a certain Martinet.

But these are not the reasons why the second half of the seventeenth century is often recalled as "The Age of Louis XIV". It was in the fields of the arts, philosophy, and science that the period made its greatest contributions to civilization. The spectacular palace of Versailles may have been built for the king's own glorification and as a testament to his enormous vanity — but it nonetheless became the center of European culture through his lavish patronage of the arts. That patronage embraced annual allowances to Molière (1622-1673) and Racine (1639-1699) and made it possible for Lully (1632-1687) to create the first important French operas.

The king's first exposure to opera probably occurred in 1660 when he married Maria Teresa, the daughter of Philip IV of Spain, a political union brought about by Cardinal Mazarin, Louis's all-powerful prime minister, who actually governed the nation until his death. A full-length opera, *Celos aun del aire matan* (Jealousy, even unfounded, can kill) by Juan Hidalgo, with libretto by Calderon, was composed for the royal wedding.

By then, however, opera was not entirely new in France; the Italian-born Mazarin had done a great deal to introduce the art form by inviting Italian composers and performers to Paris. Lully himself was a native of Florence, but he was brought to France as a child and became entirely French in his cultural outlook. Except for the rudiments of music, he was largely self-taught, and attracted the young king's attention early on with his brilliant violin playing. He later made up for the gaps in his formal musical education with private lessons by various court musicians, and began composing a prodigious number of ballets for the court. Along with his talents went an insatiable ambition; exploiting the king's favor, he obtained a royal monopoly in 1672 to produce operas at the Académie de Musique (a privilege the king transferred to him from the Abbé Perrin, the founder of that institution). From that time until his death in 1687, Lully ruled the operatic life of France. In addition to his ballets, he wrote incidental music to a large number of plays by Molière and others and, above all, over a dozen operas to the texts of Philippe Quinault, usually on heroic and mythological subjects (*Thésée*, *Phaëton*, *Roland*, *Armide et Renaud*, *Acis et Galatée*, etc.). Lully's dramatic gifts and his theatrical imagination were not equalled by his compositional skills, but his prodigious creativity made him a vital presence in the establishment of French national opera. On March 27, 1687, while conducting his own *Te Deum*, celebrating his king's recovery from a severe attack of gall stones, Lully struck his own foot with the walking stick he used as a baton. Under the treatment of an incompetent doctor, gangrene developed and it cost Lully his life.

An account of the relation of opera to the brilliant age of Louis XIV would not be complete without at least a partial list of works later composers derived from the major French dramatists of the seventeenth century. Molière's *Les Précieuses Ridicules* was set by Galuppi (1752) and Lattuada (1929); *L'Amour Médecin*, by Wolf-Ferrari (1913); *Le Médecin malgré lui*, by

Gounod (1858); *M. de Porceaugnac,* by Franchetti (1897) and Martin (1963); and *Le Bourgeois Gentilhomme* was the primary inspiration for Richard Strauss's *Ariadne auf Naxos* (1912).

Among the tragedies of Corneille, *Le Cid* inspired Cornelius (1865) and Massenet (1885); *Horace,* Cimarosa (1796) and Mercadante (1846); *Polyeucte,* Donizetti (1838) and Gounod (1878). And the severe classical dramas of Racine were the source of *Andromaque* by Grétry (1780) and Rossini's *Ermione* (1814); of *Mithridate* by Graun (1750) and Mozart (1770); of *Iphigénie en Aulide* by Graun (1748) and Gluck (1774), and of *Athalie* by Handel (1720). This list, incidentally, is incomplete, and contains only the best-known composers.

In strange contrast with the abundance of the operatic subjects that originated during that splendid age stands the surprising paucity of operas written *about* the period. There is no list here, merely an unlikely pair of stage works: Hindemith's *Cardillac* (1926), a grim philosophical tale of greed and murder, and Planquette's *Les Cloches de Corneville* (1877), a charming operetta with an amiable though commonplace plot involving family treasures, mistaken identities, and a haunted castle. Both take place in 17th-century France, but could have just as easily occurred in other places and other centuries.

While the arts and literature flourished, Louis XIV's ambitions to enlarge France involved him in several wars against Holland and, eventually, against the Habsburg Emperor and his ally, the Elector of Brandenburg. One of these battles (Fehrbellin, 1675) serves as the background to a German classic play, *The Prince of Homburg* by Heinrich von Kleist (1811), which inspired Hans Werner Henze's opera (1960) of the same name. The play's Prince, a sensitive, dreamy sort, makes a wrong decision during the battle and is court-martialed. Although he is offered a dignified way out, his sense of honor does not allow him to seek a pardon, but his gallantry so impresses the Elector that he tears up the Prince's death sentence.

These events take place at a crucial point in German history. The Electorate of Brandenburg, an important part of what was then still the Holy Roman Empire, had been governed by the Hohenzollern House since 1417. A succession of able princes contributed to its growth until the devastation of the Thirty Years War. Frederick William, the noble Elector in Kleist's play and Henze's opera, rightfully earned the "Great Elector" appellation he received from his contemporaries: he repopulated some of his devastated lands, added new territories, established vital economic reforms, and suc-

cessfully fought off the Swedish forces that threatened Brandenburg's
domination of the Protestant German states. When he died in 1688, he left
a duchy on the verge of becoming a kingdom — which it became in 1701 when
Emperor Leopold I granted the "Great Elector" 's son Frederick the title of
"King of Prussia". Thereafter the Hohenzollern House continued to rule
Prussia through the years of Bismarck (when Germany became unified), until
the end of World War I.

* * *

While French policies elevated that nation's prestige throughout the Continent, England, focusing on internal affairs, succeeded in avoiding the
dangers of civil war and laid the groundwork for its emergence as a world
power. The efficient but unpopular rule of Cromwell had been undermined
by rebellious royalists, Scottish and Irish insurgents, and by the general dissatisfaction over costly wars against Holland and Spain. When the "Lord
Protector" died on September 3, 1658, the only acceptable political solution
was to recall the son of the executed king, the throne's legitimate claimant.
In 1660, Charles II was welcomed in London with flowery parades and, as
historian Lacey Baldwin Smith observes, "The skeletons of war, rebellion,
and regicide were firmly and securely shut into the closet of forgetfulness."

After living in French exile for fifteen years, Charles II was more French
than English in his taste and policies. His new Parliament, loyal to the king
but unwilling to grant him a "divine right" succession, maintained its control
over the purse strings of the government. In a widespread social reaction to
Cromwellian austerity, there was a revival of games, dancing, music, and
theater. Morals loosened, with Charles himself showing the way with a succession of mistresses, aristocratic and otherwise (as exemplified by the
popular Nell Gwynn, "the Protestant whore").

While musical plays of every kind had been discouraged under Cromwell's
reign, Charles II, full of admiration for the lavish spectacles at the Court of
Louis XIV, tried (unsuccessfully) to create a Royal Academy of Music and
even imported Italian musicians to that end. A series of semi-operas were
created in this period, most notably *Venus and Adonis* by John Blow (with
librettist unknown), in which Mary Davies, one of the king's mistresses, sang
Venus, and their daughter, Lady Mary Tudor, appeared as Cupid. Blow and
his younger contemporary, the short-lived Henry Purcell (c1659-1695), were

the principal figures in the slow and halting development of English opera that reached an early peak with Purcell's *Dido and Aeneas* in 1689.

Back in 1670, while England was party to a triple alliance with Holland and Sweden, intending to keep the ambitions of Louis XIV in check, Charles circumvented Parliament and signed a secret treaty with France that guaranteed him a stipend of 200,000 pounds a year. He also secretly committed himself to join the Church of Rome at a convenient future time. For a while, he did nothing about the conversion, but his brother James, the Duke of York and next in line to the throne, openly professed his belief in Roman Catholicism.

This, of course, caused great apprehension in Protestant England, eased somewhat by the marriage of Mary, James's oldest daughter and heir, to the Protestant William of Orange in 1677. But a false charge of a Catholic conspiracy, called the "Popish plot", soon inflamed all England and began a series of Catholic persecutions that sent many innocent men to their death. Although the anti-Catholic fury eventually abated, Charles's popularity was undermined by the barrenness of his queen and by his insistence that his Catholic brother James be his successor. That succession became a fact when Charles died on February 6, 1685, but England could not long countenance a Catholic king: a bloodless revolt ended James's reign and sent him into exile in 1688. His daughter Mary was invited by Parliament to rule with her husband, who was crowned William III and reigned jointly with his wife until her death in 1694, and alone thereafter until 1702.

We encounter the names of William and Mary in the first act of Donizetti's *Lucia di Lammermoor* when Enrico Ashton informs his sister Lucia that only a politically advantageous marriage could restore his waning fortunes. Donizetti's librettist, Salvatore Cammarano, shows his faulty knowledge of English history when he presents "Guglielmo" and "Maria" as political adversaries. Quite apart from the fact that the opposite was true, the entire issue was totally irrelevant in 1669, when the tragic events in Lammermoor Castle supposedly took place, long before William and Mary's reign.

It was on August 24, 1669, that Miss Janet Dalrymple, daughter of James Dalrymple, Lord of Stair, married David Dunbar of Wigtonshire. Her previous engagement to Lord Rutherford, not meeting with her parents' approval, was broken and Rutherford left Scotland never to return. After the wedding feast, piercing shrieks were heard from the nuptial chamber. The bridegroom was found severely wounded, his bride in a distraught state, incoherent and apparently insane. She died on September 12. Dunbar recovered from his wounds, married again, and died after falling from his horse in 1682.

These were the facts as set forth in exhaustive detail by Sir Walter Scott in the introduction to his lengthy novel *The Bride of Lammermoor* (1819) that incorporates several legends surrounding the true story, with the names of the principals changed. Despite the length and ponderousness of Scott's narrative, composers literally pounced on the gloomy tale. *Le nozze di Lammermoor* by Michele Enrico Carafa appeared in 1829, followed by Ivor Friedrich Bredal's *Bruden fra Lammermoor* in 1832, with Danish libretto by Hans Christian Andersen, and Alberto Mazzucato's *La Fidanzata di Lammermoor* in 1834. All three were soon consigned to cobwebs with the arrival of Donizetti's opera in 1835.

His *Lucia di Lammermoor* reduces the novel's thirty characters to seven, dispensing with everything that would impede theatrical effectiveness. Neither the heroine's father — in actuality the Lord of Stair, a distinguished figure in modern Scottish law — nor her conniving mother appear. Lucia Ashton (Dalrymple) faces her ordeal under pressure from her operatic brother, Enrico. (The historical brother, Sir John Dalrymple, was also a prominent jurist and politician, later raised to earldom.) Present, of course, are both the rejected bridegroom, Edgardo Ravenswood (Rutherford) and his rival Arturo Bucklaw (Dunbar), as well as enough members of the Ashton retinue to make up an operatic Sextet.

* * *

Coinciding with these gloomy events in Scotland in the shadow of the English Restoration, a major change realigned the power structure in central Europe. The Ottoman Turks, who were still occupying Hungary and Transylvania since their invasions in the 16th century, embarked on a major offensive with Vienna as their goal. In 1683, after a long and brutal siege, they were decisively repulsed by a powerful army led by Prince Eugene of Savoy, with substantial help from various German princes and the Polish King Jan Sobieski. Although Hungary was thus freed from the Turks, one yoke was exchanged for another; Habsburg supremacy was ruthlessly enforced, and portions of the country that were devastated by the Turkish wars were resettled with German and Serb immigrants, whose arrival laid the seeds for ethnic unrest in later centuries.

Rebellious Hungarians organized under the leadership of the Transylvanian Prince Rákóczy*, Francis (Ferenc) II. The Prince had hoped for outside involvement to help his cause, but much of Europe then was caught up in the War of the Spanish Succession, occasioned by the death of the last of the Spanish Habsburgs, Carlos II. (His brother-in-law, Louis XIV, was one of the claimants.) Left to his own devices and vastly outnumbered, Prince Rákóczy surrendered his forlorn and depleted armies in 1711, and Hungary came under absolute Habsburg rule until 1867.

In his exile, Rákóczy went to Paris, where he was warmly greeted by the Sun King and his court. Special festivities with a *"Cotillon Hongrois"* were organized for his amusement. He received generous sums from the royal treasury for his own expenses and for helping Hungarian exiles. But the Peace of Utrecht (1713), where the issue of the Spanish succession was settled, removed all of Rákóczy's hopes for French involvement in his struggle. He ended his days in Turkish exile, surrounded by a circle of loyal officers, in 1735.

Toward the end of his Paris stay, Rákóczy had rented a house for his officers (Malaquais No. 9), known as *"Hôtel de Transylvanie"*. Eventually, without the Prince's knowledge, it was turned into a gambling house, an establishment repeatedly mentioned in Abbé Prévost's novel *Histoire du Chevalier Des Grieux et de Manon Lescaut*. The arrest of the lovers takes place in this colorful locale in the fourth act of Massenet's *Manon*. (The opera's action is placed into 1721.)

Some of the most beautiful Hungarian historical folk songs, recalling lost battles and lamenting the bitter fate of the exiles, relate to Rákóczy's doomed struggle. One of them, a marching tune, served as a basis for Franz Liszt's youthful piano arrangement of the "Rákóczy March". This, in turn, led to Berlioz's brilliantly orchestrated version that appears in his semi-opera *La Damnation de Faust* (the first part of which the composer moved to a Hungarian locale). When Berlioz introduced the March in the Hungarian capital in 1846, according to his *Memoirs* "the room was shaken by the most unheard-of cries and stampings; the concentrated fury of all this burning audience exploded in accents that made me shiver with terror.... It was a lucky thing for me that I had placed (the piece) at the end of the concert, for anything played afterwards would have been entirely lost." In Hungary, where

---

*   Also spelled "Rákóczi".

Rákóczy remains a national hero to this date, that march still evokes a stirring response.

The Peace of Utrecht that dashed Rákóczy's hopes in 1713 worked out to the advantage of Louis XIV, whose armies had suffered severe losses in encounters with the Austrian Prince Eugene of Savoy and the English Duke of Marlborough. The Spanish Succession was settled with placing Philip V, a Bourbon prince, on the throne of Spain. France was still a major power when its *grand monarque* died in 1715.

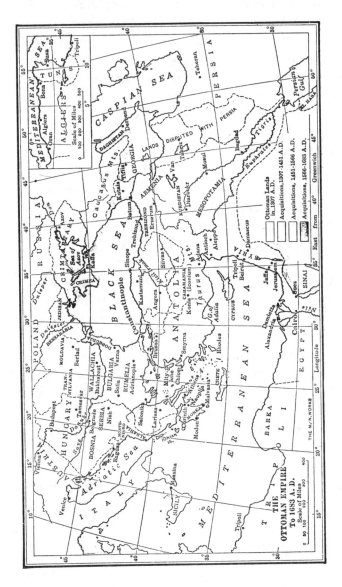

XXII

PETER THE GREAT—AND THE
GREAT NORTHERN WAR

Khovanschina (Mussorgsky); *Zar und Zimmermann*
(Lortzing); *Mazeppa* (Tchaikovsky); *Der Bettelstudent*
(Millöcker); *Der Zarewitsch* (Lehár); *Un giorno di regno*
(Verdi)

What historians call The Age of Enlightenment—with science prevailing over religion, rational thought over blind faith—began in the early years of the eighteenth century. But wars continued to plague Europe and, while the Peace of Utrecht temporarily settled matters in the West, the ambitions of three powerful rulers clashed in the North. All three were remarkable men: Tsar Peter I of Russia, who ruled from 1682 to 1725, the Elector of Saxony, Augustus II (1694-1733), and King Charles XII of Sweden (1697-1718).

Peter was the third Romanov ruler of Russia, son of Alexis and grandson of Mikhail,[*] who had started the dynasty in 1613. The only son from his father's second marriage, Peter was only four years old when Alexis died in 1676. Both his older brothers were ill or incompetent or both. When Feodor, the oldest, died in 1682, the boyars elected the older half-brother Ivan to rule jointly with Peter, both under the regency of their ambitious older sister Sophia. Already then, at ten years of age, young Peter witnessed unspeakable cruelties when the Streltsi, soldiers of the Moscow garrison, exterminated Peter's maternal relatives, probably on Sophia's orders. He grew up harboring an unforgiving hatred for the Streltsi and suffering from convulsions that could have been the result of that early trauma.

Sophia, a strong and able woman, governed her unruly country reasonably well with the aid of her lover and principal minister, Prince Vasily Golitsyn. The Prince, a well-educated man and an admirer of French culture, was open to reforms, and was not without partisans. But Russia was torn by a

---

[*]   See page 214.

severe religious conflict between the official Orthodox Church, supported by the Romanovs, and the Old Believers (Raskolniki), who resisted church reforms and refused to pay taxes to a government they identified with the Antichrist. Thus it was a chaotic Russia that Sophia governed for seven years (1682-1689) while Peter grew to adolescence in the Moscow suburb of Preobrazhenskoe, living with his mother, the ex-Tsarina Natalia. Popular dissatisfaction with an unsuccessful campaign against the Turks by Golitsyn provided the opportunity for the ambitious young Tsar to make his move. On October 16, 1689, he entered Moscow, dispatched Sophia into exile, and assumed supreme power. His complacent half-brother Ivan retired from public life without challenging Peter's authority; he died seven years later.

Mussorgsky's epic opera *Khovanschina* (1886 posth.) deals with the seven turbulent years of Sophia's regency with considerable historical accuracy. The first act takes place immediately following the 1682 massacre, with the Streltsi openly boasting of their exploits. Later action introduces us to the fierce and ambitious Prince Ivan Khovansky, the commander of the Streltsi, ostensibly serving Sophia, but secretly plotting to seize the throne for his own son Andrei. Khovansky is sympathetic to the cause of the Old Believers, under the leadership of the charismatic Dosifei (not an actually historical character).

The second act of *Khovanschina* offers the confrontation of the "three Princes": the still powerful Khovansky, the sophisticated Golitsyn, who senses his impending loss of power, and Dosifei (whom the opera identifies as the former Prince Mishetsky to place him on an equal footing with the others), who vainly urges them to make peace and return to the old doctrine. Also present is the shady boyar Shaklovity, who brings ominous news of Peter's assumption of power and the Tsar's knowledge of the Khovansky plot—the "Khovanschina," a coinage attributed to Peter himself. Word soon comes that Peter's own army has attacked the Streltsi.

In the third act, Khovansky is stabbed to death by Shaklovity, a vivid theatrical stroke at variance with history, for the real Ivan Khovansky was executed publicly on Sophia's orders. The real Shaklovity later met a similar end, but it was Peter who ordered the boyar's execution for having been a confidant of Sophia. The act ends as the Streltsi, prepared to be executed *en masse* in St. Basil's Square, are pardoned in a gesture of magnanimity. History tells us, however, that Tsar Peter, remembering the dread that the ill-disciplined horde had inflicted upon him in his childhood, was not that magnanimous. Some nine years later, with his power consolidated, he had the en-

Peter I ("the Great") of Russia
CREDIT: Culver Pictures Inc.

tire regiment of Streltsi exterminated. They were hanged or beheaded, following a series of unspeakable tortures, and the Streltsi disappeared from the pages of Russian history.

Mussorgsky's *Khovanschina* ends as the Old Believers, led by Dosifei, choose self-immolation instead of the certain death awaiting them at the hand of Peter's soldiers. This is based on a historical event: following the death of a leader named Avvakum who was burned at the stake, 20,000 Old Believers sought martyrdom in flames rather than surrendering to reformed Orthodoxy.

Peter, who had gained unchallenged power in his early youth, sometimes showed more interest in learning than in governing. He had great plans for Russia and surrounded himself with foreign advisors—primarily two of his favorite generals, the Scot Patric Gordon and the Swiss François Lefort—in his eager effort to learn about Western ways. Among other things, he was determined to reorganize his army, to build a navy, and eventually to provide Russia with a sea outlet on the Baltic, an area ruled by Sweden and Poland.

In 1697, this farsighted monarch embarked on an unprecedented step. He organized a "Great Embassy" composed of himself and a group of Russian nobles to visit Europe and learn its secrets. By traveling incognito, it was Peter's intention to move freely and to ask questions without a great deal of ceremonial inhibitions. He assumed the guise of a noncommissioned officer named "Peter Michailov." Such a guise, however, was rather difficult for a man who stood nearly seven feet tall, was commanding in appearance, possessed of nearly superhuman strength, and afflicted with a clearly noticeable facial twitch.

Passing through Swedish-held Livonia (Latvia), the "Great Embassy" moved on to Königsberg, where Frederick, the Elector of Brandenburg, gave them a royal reception. Here Peter went hunting with the Elector, concluded a treaty of friendship, and studied artillery and fortifications with the Brandenburg officers. Later, on meeting the widowed Electress of Hanover, Sophia, and her daughter Sophia Charlotte (the future grandmother of Frederick the Great), he impressed both ladies despite his awkwardness and rough manners. As the Electress later described him: "He is a prince at once very good and very bad; his character is exactly that of his country. If he had received a better education, he would be an exceptional man, for he has great qualities and unlimited natural intelligence."

After presenting his hosts with lavish gifts, Peter and his Great Embassy sailed down the Rhine into Holland, a tiny state of two million people, fiercely heroic in defense of their independence and the envy of Europe for their diligence, efficiency, and prosperity. Holland's success rested on its remarkable commerce and shipping; Zaandam, as Peter soon learned, was the center of Dutch ship-building at the time, and it was this town the young Tsar was determined to explore. He spent seven days in Zaandam working in the shipyards, dressed in the simple garb of a working man, mixing with the people and sharing meals with them. He would have stayed longer had his incognito not been uncovered; throngs surrounded him wherever he went despite specific orders from the town's Burgomaster forbidding the townspeople to trouble "distinguished persons who wish to remain unknown."

Such an idyllic episode in the fearsome ruler's life was ripe with theatrical possibilities. A play by Mélesville-Merle-de Boirie (1818) served as a source for Donizetti's 1827 opera buffa *Il Borgomastro di Saardam*, which, after some initial success, vanished from the stages after 1840. Far more successful was *Zar und Zimmermann* (1837), with libretto and music by Gustav Albert Lortzing, to this day considered an extremely popular light opera in all German-speaking lands. In both operas, the beleaguered Burgomaster is given comic opportunities. Both present Peter in the best possible light; in Lortzing, the Tsar's historical alias is used to further romantic purposes: there is a "Peter Michailov", working side-by-side with the disguised Peter in the shipyards, and he, too, benefits from the Tsar's generosity.

Utilizing the experience gained in Zaandam, Peter joined his "embassy" in Amsterdam and began working in earnest, along with some of his officers, in the shipyards of the Dutch East India Company. He labored there for four months, answering to the name "Carpenter Peter", living the life of a common workman, sometimes even cooking his own meals. In his free time, he studied geometry, anatomy, botany, and architecture. His thirst for knowledge was indeed insatiable — he even learned to pull teeth, to the horror of his entourage.

State matters, however, were not neglected. Peter made a royal visit to William of Orange (England's William III and Holland's head of state), a correctly courteous affair not marked by any warmth between two men totally dissimilar in outlook and personality. But William placed a royal yacht at his guest's disposal to take him to England for a short visit on January 7, 1698.

During his four months in England, Peter's inquiring mind absorbed Protestant religious doctrines freely dispensed by high church officials. He visited Westminster Abbey, Windsor Castle, Hampton Court, and the Tower of London, where the axe that had severed the head of Charles I fifty years earlier was carefully kept from view.

Leaving England with great admiration for most things English, Peter departed to Amsterdam to rejoin other members of his Embassy. The entire group left on May 15, 1698 for Vienna via Dresden and Prague. In Vienna the Tsar was lavishly entertained, but his diplomatic efforts to draw the Emperor Leopold I into a war against Turkey failed. With Vienna recently liberated from a Turkish siege,* peace on that front seemed more desirable to the Habsburg monarch. It was in Vienna that Peter received word about a revolt of the Streltsi, and he ended his visit abruptly on July 19 to return to Russia via Poland.

---

* See page 230.

By 1700 Peter's rule over Russia was unchallenged. With the Streltsi exterminated, he had his once powerful and conniving stepsister Sophia confined to a convent, where she died a few years later. The Tsar knew that his power had to rest on a standing army and was determined to build one through conscription. He also laid the foundation of the Russian navy. Powerful sea and land forces were necessary since Peter had joined on November 22, 1699 a coalition with the rulers of Denmark and Poland against Sweden for the control of the Baltic.

Poland's August II was a king after Peter's own heart. He had succeeded the heroic and powerful Jan III Sobieski, the conqueror of the Turks, by a voice vote. (Monarchy in Poland was not hereditary; kings were chosen from various contending noble houses. On the death of Sobieski, no fewer than 18 candidates presented themselves.) August II — actually the Elector Frederick Augustus of Saxony — outspent all his rivals and became King of Poland in 1697, an honor for which he embraced Catholicism. A dynamic man, and something of an athlete, he was known as "Augustus the Strong" and, according to legend, the father of 354 illegitimate children.

The new allies, Peter I and Augustus II, were powerful men and great warriors but they severely underestimated their Swedish antagonist. Charles XII, a fearless general, reacted to hostile actions against him by daringly attacking Denmark and forcing the Danish king into a humiliating peace treaty, thus removing Denmark from the anti-Swedish union. This was followed by the battle of Narva (November 20, 1700), where a Swedish army defeated a much larger Russian force, causing an unexpected blow to Peter's ambitious plans.

A campaign through Poland followed, where Charles allied himself with the Polish nobles who had opposed Augustus. Taking advantage of a divided country, Charles deposed Augustus and, with the aid of anti-Saxon nobles, proclaimed Stanislas Leszczynski to be King of Poland on July 12, 1704.

This is the historical background to Carl Millöcker's operetta *Der Bettelstudent* (1882). The romantic and fictitious plot ends with the "liberation" of Crakow and the departure of the Saxon "occupiers," grossly simplifying the issues into patriotic confrontations between Poles and Saxons, ignoring the fact that Poland at the time was deeply divided, that the new King Stanislas by no means enjoyed universal popularity, and that he himself had been established as a result of foreign (Swedish) pressure.

Thus by 1704, the intrepid Charles XII had successfully removed Denmark and Poland from the coalition against Sweden, but Peter, his principal enemy, was gathering strength. The "Great Northern War" was entering a new and devastating phase when Charles committed a fatal error, one made by several other leaders in history too—invading Russian territory. He received encouragement in this venture from Ivan Mazeppa, hetman (leader) of the Ukrainian Cossacks, a subject of the Tsar but disloyal to him and anxious to win independence for Ukraine.

On this occasion Mazeppa, a survivor of many previous crises—he had been an ally of Sophia and Golitsyn but was able to cast his lot with Peter at the opportune time—chose the wrong side. He overestimated the strength of the Swedish army, whose reckless advance into Russia was soon slowed down by Peter's "scorched earth" policy. Moreover, fearful of the Tsar's power, most of Mazeppa's own Cossacks abandoned him by the time the Hetman could join forces with a Swedish army decimated by illness and starvation.

It was at Poltava, near Kharkov in Ukraine in a decisive battle on May 11, 1709, that the vastly outnumbered Swedish army was forced to surrender. Charles and Mazeppa escaped into Turkey, where the Hetman soon died, while Charles tried in vain to enlist the Sultan in a campaign against Russia.

Peter's triumph at Poltava, recalled as one of the great victories in Russian history, inspired a great epic, Pushkin's *Poltava* (1828). In that heroic poem Pushkin combined stirring battle scenes with a merciless portrait of Mazeppa, whom he characterized as "a man of ambition, steeped in perfidy and crime." Hardly anything of Pushkin's panoramic vision was retained in Tchaikovsky's opera *Mazeppa* (1883), despite the fact that the opera's libretto (by Viktor Burenin, as revised by the composer) contains many of Pushkin's original lines. Peter the Great does not even appear in the opera, and the great battle is represented mainly by a stormy orchestral interlude.

Tchaikovsky's *Mazeppa* deals with the fierce Cossack's tragic real-life involvement with Maria, the young daughter of the wealthy Kochubey. Though Mazeppa, at this point of the action, is a man in his sixties, Maria truly loves him and when her father refuses to marry her to Mazeppa, she willingly allows herself to be abducted. To avenge his humiliation, Kochubey denounces Mazeppa's treasonable Swedish negotiations to Peter the Great. The Tsar, however, refuses to believe the accusation and delivers Kochubey to his enemy Mazeppa, who has him tortured and executed. Meanwhile, Mazeppa's treason is discovered, and he must escape. The last scene shows the abandoned Maria, maddened by guilt, singing a lullaby recalling her happy childhood.

It is obvious that Tchaikovsky's concern was with human emotions, not the national issues motivating the participants in the Great Northern War, not even the cause of Ukrainian independence championed by Mazeppa, an issue that was decisively settled by the devastating defeat of Charles XII at Poltava. Other far-reaching consequences of that battle caused Leszczynski to renounce the Polish throne, which was again occupied by Augustus II with Peter's blessing. Finally, along with Ukraine, Peter also appropriated the Baltic principalities.

Meanwhile, Sweden's Charles XII, tragically frustrated but unbowed, made desperate attempts to create new alliances against Russia. His constant agitations exhausted the Sultan's hospitality and in 1714 he was expelled from Turkey. Unable to contemplate a peaceful existence, Charles invaded Norway hoping to win more land before returning to Sweden, the country he had been ruling from abroad ever since 1700, when he had started out on his reckless foreign adventures. It was not to be: on December 12, 1718, the life of that restless king ended at thirty-seven when he was struck down by a Norwegian bullet. There was no one left to wage war any more, least of all in Sweden: in the treaty of Nystad (August 30, 1721), Russia obtained Livonia, Estonia, and part of Finland. Thus, the Great Northern War ended with Sweden's humiliation, Poland's economic ruin and political dependence on Russia, and Russia's emergence as a great power.

Victorious as his campaigns had been, Peter the Great's internal reforms were even more far-reaching. In his tireless efforts to modernize his country, the Tsar revitalized its industries, reorganized its antiquated educational system and encouraged hundreds of young Russians to study abroad. He also built the magnificent new city of St. Petersburg, and assumed full control over the Holy Synod, an institution he established to replace the old ecclesiastical system of the Patriarchy.

Peter married twice. His first wife, Eudoxia, ended up in a nunnery after presenting Peter with a son, Alexis. In 1712, the Tsar was married again, to Catherine, a strong woman of peasant origin, with whom he lived happily. His relationship with the Tsarevich Alexis was a tense one, for the young man took no interest in his father's reforms, and opposed him at many turns. At one point (1716), Alexis even left Russia to escape his father's control. He was intercepted, brought back to Russia, and arrested, while those accused of helping him escape were tortured and executed. Alexis himself died in prison, after repeated "questioning," which meant repeated blows by the knout.

Alexis's brief and futile attempts to escape his father's clutches gave Franz Lehár's librettists the idea for the operetta *Der Zarewitsch* (1927). Its escapist, sentimental treatment, totally fictitious, provided Lehár with opportunities to write melting melodies, particularly for the tenor hero originally portrayed by the peerless Richard Tauber. Not even the slightest hint at the dark tragedy of the true Alexis was allowed to becloud the operetta's bittersweet romance.

Peter the Great's stormy and violent life ended on January 28, 1725, in his fifty-third year. He died of a bladder and intestinal infection and probably uremia, brought about by a lifetime of excessive drinking. History remembers him as a great patriot but remains undecided in its attempt to balance his brilliant and innovative accomplishments with his brutal and tyrannical side. In the words of his outstanding biographer Robert K. Massie: "How does one judge the endless roll of the ocean or the mighty power of the whirlwind?"

* * *

Among the nations involved in the Great Northern War, Poland suffered more than any other, a victim of "Swedish terror, Russian deceit, and Saxon intrigue," according to a British historian. The "Saxon intrigue," of course, refers to Augustus II, the great opportunist who ruled more successfully as Elector of Saxony than he did as the beleaguered King of Poland. By then his ducal capital of Dresden was established as one of Europe's musical centers, with several orchestras and lively ballet and operatic performances. Augustus himself was a lover of opera, and his court theater was a home of many celebrated Italian singers and musicians. In 1730, Johann Adolf Hasse, one of Europe's most eminent composers, and husband of the famous prima donna Faustina Bordoni, was named court Kapellmeister, an event that was followed by the premiere of Hasse's opera *Cleofide* (1731) under lavish circumstances. (It is possible that this opera, in which the generosity of Alexander the Great is celebrated, was intended as an allegory to Hasse's new ducal patron.)

Dresden continued to flourish when the durable Augustus died in 1733, but more trials awaited Poland. Stanislas Leszczynski, who had in the meantime become the father-in-law of France's Louis XV, attempted to regain the throne with French support and with the endorsement of several Polish families. He traveled to Warsaw incognito, leaving a French aristocrat named

Beaufleur to impersonate him in Paris in order to hide his trip from his enemies. But he encountered too much opposition in Poland; a Russian army entered the country and established Augustus III, son of the Saxon Elector, as the King of Poland. Giving up his long-held dream of ruling the country, Leszczynski returned to France to end his days there as Duke of Lorraine and Bar.

His escapade in disguise inspired the play *Le faux Stanislas* by Alexandre Vincent Pineu-Duval, which was introduced in Paris in 1808. Ten years later, Felice Romani adapted it for an operatic libretto, *Il finto Stanislao*, for the Bohemian composer Adalbert Gyrowetz. It failed to succeed, and Romani was free to offer his libretto to Giuseppe Verdi twenty years later, to become *Un giorno di regno* (Kingdom for a Day). It was Verdi's second opera (1840), a half-successful effort in a comic vein for which Verdi was not yet ready at that point in his career.

The historical Stanislas does not appear in the opera. His alter-ego Belfiore (Beaufleur) is the central figure, something like an aristocratic Figaro, keeping things constantly in motion. In the opera's finale, he joyfully announces that his days of parading as a king are over because

> *Finalmente in Varsavia è giunto Stanislao.*
> *S'è dichiarata in suo favor la Dieta...*
>
> (Stanislas has finally arrived in Warsaw.
> The Diet has decided in his favor...)

This was the historical truth insofar as it went. The joyful ending of *Un giorno di regno* gives no hint of the clouds that were gathering over Poland in 1733, foreshadowing the loss of the country's independence, and the tragedy of repeated partitions. Full sovereignty for Poland came only in 1918, at the end of World War I.

XXIII

HANDEL'S LONDON — VOLTAIRE'S PARIS

Handel; *The Beggar's Opera* (Gay-Pepusch); *Martha*
(Flotow); *The Rake's Progress* (Stravinsky); Rameau;
Manon (Massenet); *Manon Lescaut* (Auber / Puccini);
Adriana Lecouvreur (Ciléa)

After the Great Northern War, during which both England and France had enjoyed relative stability, the two nations developed in different directions. In England, technological and industrial advances and profitable colonial expansion went side by side with increasing parliamentary power over a weakening monarchy. By contrast, in France the power of the monarchy and of the privileged classes continued unchecked — despite such enlightened thinkers as Voltaire, Rousseau, and Montesquieu, who propagated their revolutionary theories.

In England, following the death of the unpopular William of Orange, Queen Anne ascended the throne in 1702 under an Act of Parliament. She was the younger daughter of James II, driven from power for his Catholicism.[*] The age of "good Queen Anne" brought about the political union of England and Scotland in 1707 under the name of Great Britain. According to Winston Churchill, it was "one of the greatest reigns in English history... rendered glorious by Marlborough's victories and guidance." (That this statement comes from the most illustrious heir of John Churchill, the first Duke of Marlborough, should in no way diminish its historical validity.) Though not free of political strife, it was a peaceful period, its pace set by the tranquility of the court, where Sarah, the Duchess of Marlborough, acted as the Queen's closest advisor. A formidable lady, the Duchess would have hardly tolerated the antics of such a flighty person as the fictitious Lady Harriet Durham, supposedly Maid of Honor to Queen Anne in Flotow's *Martha* (1847), who is so bored with the monotony of court life that she assumes the disguise of a commoner and lands in a series of embarrassing adventures.

---

[*]   See page 229.

The age of Queen Anne was also the age of Sir Isaac Newton and Sir Christopher Wren, and of literary giants like Alexander Pope, Daniel Defoe, and Jonathan Swift. It furthermore brought to the English shores a remarkable Saxon by the name of Georg Friedrich Händel, who was to leave an indelible mark on English musical taste and operatic life.

A prodigiously gifted musician, Händel had been an organist in his native Halle when he moved to Hamburg in 1703, age eighteen, for better advancement. Three years later he left for Italy, where he spent three valuable years absorbing Italian musical culture and associating with the leading Italian musicians of the period. It was the cultivated and music-loving Electress Sophia who invited the young man to become court conductor in Hanover in 1710, but after a very brief stay, he decided to move on to London, where he was to gain eternal glory—while losing only the umlauts from his name.

It is quite remarkable that Handel, who spoke no English in those days, was able to persuade the administration of the Haymarket Theatre—possibly with the aid of certain influential patrons—to mount his first opera composed for the English stage in 1710. That opera, *Rinaldo*, was a complete triumph and made Handel an operatic celebrity overnight. Still under contract to the Hanover court, he had to return there for a brief stay, but soon managed to extricate himself from his obligations to the Elector without much difficulty.

In 1713, England garnered a great political triumph with the Treaty of Utrecht, which ended the costly War of the Spanish Succession. France was forced to recognize the Protestant succession of English kings and the fact that the crowns of France and Spain could not be united. The treaty also ceded Gibraltar to England, providing that maritime nation with a substantial strategic advantage. There was every reason for the festivity celebrated by Handel's *Utrecht Te Deum* that was performed at St. Paul's Cathedral on July 7, 1713. There is no record of a royal commission for it, nor is it likely that the Queen, in ill health and, at best, a lukewarm musical enthusiast, attended the event. She did settle an annual pension of 200 pounds on her dutiful ceremonial composer (Handel had expeditiously composed a Birthday Ode in her honor earlier that year).

Queen Anne died on August 1, 1714. Since none of her seventeen children from her marriage to Prince George of Denmark survived into adulthood, Parliament, intent on excluding James II's Catholic descendants from succession, had designated Sophia, granddaughter of James I and wife of the Elector of Hanover, as Anne's successor. Since she was already deceased at the time of Anne's death, it was her son George Ludwig who was proclaimed King George I of England. He was the first of England's Hanoverian monarchs, a good-natured, dullish man whose knowledge of English was no better than that of Handel, his erstwhile court conductor.

The English did not take their new king easily to their heart, and the fact that he arrived with not one but two mistresses in his entourage did not help matters. George I was a poor successor to Queen Anne altogether. Abortive attempts on behalf of the Stuart Pretender, "James III" of Scotland, and the financial spectulations and subsequent ruin of the South Sea Company provided a restless counterpoint to his rule and he continued to preoccupy himself with Hanover affairs, leaving the administration of England in the hands of his ministers. The ablest of these, Sir Robert Walpole, took office in 1721 as England's first true "Prime Minister".

Meanwhile, Handel's fortunes continued to rise. In July 1717, as the King journeyed by barge on the Thames from Whitehall to Chelsea, he was entertained by repeated performances of Handel's *Water Music*. A string of new operas from Handel's pen (*Radamisto, Floridante, Ottone, Giulio Cesare,* and *Rodelinda*) brought a new vital spirit into England's musical life between 1720 and 1725, spiked by an element of rivalry with fellow composer Giovanni Bononcini (whose stock also rose during this London heyday of Italian opera) and the antics of temperamental Italian singers.

On one of his frequent visits to Hanover in the summer of 1727, George I died, unlamented by his British subjects, and particularly so by his son, the Prince of Wales, with whom he had been on the worst of terms. Handel wrote four coronation anthems for the succession of George II, including the famous *Zadok the Priest*. By then he was a naturalized British subject, "Composer of the Court" with a generous income of 600 pounds a year. He enjoyed the good will of the king, and even more that of the highly cultivated Queen Caroline, at whose court Newton, Pope, Chesterfield, and other great minds of England were cordially welcomed. So was Voltaire during his English stay, who remembered her as "an amiable philosopher seated on the throne." Her royal husband, too, loved Caroline dearly, his several mistresses notwithstanding.

Handel needed the support of the court, for the Royal Academy of Music, which he had founded in 1720 with the support of aristocratic backers, had fallen on difficult days. After eight years of cultivating Italian opera (487 performances in all, 245 of which featured Handel's operas) it went out of business, its ruin precipitated by the public's growing impatience with "foreign" texts, by the scandalous behavior of its performers and their avid admirers, and, most of all, by the radical change in public taste.

That change was symbolized by the sensational success of John Gay's *The Beggar's Opera*, introduced at the Theatre Royal, Lincoln's Inn Fields, on January 29, 1728. Far removed from the artificialities of Italian Baroque operas, this was a play about recognizably common — actually, *quite* common — characters, with racy and pungent dialogue interspersed with a generous number of short and hard-hitting songs. Gay and his clever orchestrator John Pepusch mercilessly satirized the florid ornamentations of the Italian operatic style and showed no less mercy in pillorying the decline of morality and the widespread corruption rampant in that period of English history. Peachum's opening song sets the tone:

> Through all the Employments of Life
> Each Neighbour abuses his Brother,
> Trull and Rogue they call Husband and Wife,
> All Professions be-rogue on another.
> The Priest calls the Lawyer a Cheat,
> The Lawyer be-knaves the Divine,
> And the Statesman, because he's so great,
> Thinks his Trade as Honest as mine.

The Beggar's Opera mirrored the debasement of morals in English society according to the 18th-century historian Sir John Hawkins:

> ...the rights of property, and the obligations of the law that
> guards it, are disputed on principle; young men, apprentices,
> clerks in public offices, and others, disdaining the arts of
> honest industry, and captivated with the charms of idleness
> and criminal pleasures, now betake themselves to the road, af-
> fect politeness in the very act of robbery, and in the end be-
> come victims to the justice of their country.

William Hogarth (1697-1764) provided vivid illustrations to *The Beggar's Opera*. A sought-after artist who disdained portraying elegant clients in their finery captured English life as he saw it: in realistic, often sordid, images. In 1731, he created a series of prints called *A Harlot's Progress* in which he depicted the step-by-step degradation and destruction of a country girl. The British public eagerly bought this account of its self-condemnation, encouraging Hogarth to create the *Harlot's* parallel in *A Rake's Progress* (1733).

Here the story of a young man is related as he squanders his inheritance, gives in to drinking and wenching, marries for money but gambles away his new fortune; he is jailed and eventually ends up in "Bedlam," the famous hospital for the insane.

Igor Stravinsky discovered the Hogarth prints in 1947. Taken in particular with the horror of the Bedlam scene, he approached W. H. Auden, and the latter, in partnership with Chester Kallman, eventually provided the libretto for Stravinsky's *The Rake's Progress* (1951). They gave Hogarth's youth the name of Tom Rakewell, and created the characters of Nick Shadow and Anne Truelove to accompany the hero through his travails and, in a Faustian sense, fight for his soul. There are other characters in the opera that the librettists created to enliven the drama, but several scenes are clearly inspired by Hogarth's prints.

In 1745, Hogarth returned once again to his chosen form of a morality tale by way of engravings. That was *Marriage à la Mode*, a cruel display of greed, moral corruption, and total decadence in highborn circles. The fourth of the six scenes in the series, depicting a morning reception as the lady of the house is having her hair dressed, provided Hugo von Hofmannsthal with the inspiration for the Marschallin's levée scene in the first act of Richard Strauss's *Der Rosenkavalier*.

The Beggar's Opera scored a huge success as an exceptionally skillful and thoroughly English form of entertainment. It was hailed by, among others, Pope, Swift, and Dr. Johnson; it may have hastened the fall of the powerful prime minister, Sir Robert Walpole, and certainly forced the temporarily stymied but remarkably resilient Handel into a new musical challenge, the creation of the English oratorio.

The direct cause of Walpole's fall, however, was England's involvement in a war with Spain over the activities of the South Sea Company, whose directors pursued trade with the New World far beyond the limits imposed by the Treaty of Utrecht. There were hostile acts on both sides and, while Walpole would have favored a negotiated settlement, growing anti-Spanish sentiment in England and the agitation of the opposition forced his hand. On October 19, 1739, war was declared.

Detached from the martial atmosphere, Handel was turning out a string of large-scale oratorios (*Alexander's Feast, Saul, Israel in Egypt*) during the years of turmoil and was creating his *Ode to St. Cecilia's Day* when the war broke out, but the public responded to another tune: "*Rule Britannia*", (Ode in Honour of Great Britain), written by James Thomson with music by

Thomas Arne. As England was drawing herself into a war with consequences extending far beyond Spanish and American trade, Sir Robert Walpole, whose cautionary policies had kept the country out of war for two decades, was forced to resign.

* * *

In France, the long reign of Louis XIV, so magnificent in cultural and artistic achievements, ultimately brought a string of humiliating military defeats and an exhausted treasury. Nor did the country's political system become enlightened or liberalized after the Sun King's seven decades of despotic rule. The new king, Louis XV, was only five years old in 1715. For the next eight years, France was ruled by a regent, the Duke of Orléans, nephew of the dead king, a bright and able man, but tolerant of the widespread corruption around him and dissolute in his own personal life.

During the Regency, the government was in the hands of two able ministers, Dubois and Fleury, while the reorganization of the country's ruined finances was accomplished by the Scottish enterpreneur John Law, the comptroller general. With his radical reforms encouraged by the court, Law stabilized the currency, organized a state bank, expanded trade, and founded the Mississippi Company, a large colonial enterprise that financed the production of tobacco and coffee in Louisiana. Quick fortunes were made in wild speculation but, ultimately, the inevitable decline set in. When the hoped-for large-scale emigration did not materialize, prisoners and prostitutes were deported to Louisiana—the fate of Manon and her impulsive lover Des Grieux in Prévost's contemporary (1731) novel and in the operas of Auber (1856) and Puccini (1893). In Massenet's *Manon* (1884), death claims Manon on the road to the embarcation point of Le Havre.

Massenet's librettists, Meilhac and Gille, place the opera's action into 1721, and even allow Guillot a disrespectful reference to *"le Régent"* and *"sa Maitresse"* in the scene at the gambling house (Act IV, Scene 1).

In the operatic character of Guillot de Morfontaine, a lecherous nobleman wealthy enough to hire the entire operatic corps de ballet to impress a woman, Massenet created a symbol of decadence rampant in the Paris of the period, with the Regent himself providing the most prominent example for debauchery. Eventually Law's Banque Royale fell victim to the excessive greed of the Regent and other speculators. Law himself left France with his family, and disappeared into obscurity. As for the Duke of Orléans, whose

Voltaire (F. M. Arouet)
CREDIT: Culver Pictures Inc.

eight-year Regency gave France a period of internal peace and substantial liberalization of education and culture, he died on December 2, 1723 at the age of only forty-nine, a few months after Louis XV assumed the throne.

But Louis was only thirteen at the time, and entirely content to leave the country's administration in the hands of Louis Henri, Duc de Bourbon, and later to his longtime tutor, the able and ambitious Bishop André de Fleury, who was made both Cardinal and Prime Minister in 1726. By then, the child king was married to Marie Leszczynska, the daughter of Stanislas, the unsuccessful pretender to the Polish throne, now comfortably ensconced as the Duke of Lorraine. Marie, seven years older than her royal husband, bore him ten children and, like other queens of the period, calmly witnessed a long procession of mistresses, the legendary Madame de Pompadour — elegant, vivacious, and a true lover of the arts — occupying a prominent place among them.

The leading intellectual figure during the long 59-year rule of Louis XV was François Marie Arouet de Voltaire (1694-1778). Brilliant from the out-set, he gained early recognition for his wit and literary excellence, as well as two brief periods of incarceration at the Bastille for his anti-religion and anti-establishment views. He spent nearly three years in England (1726-1729), admiring the freedom and practicality of English society before returning to immerse himself in France's cultural life, to which he contributed prodigiously.

Music continued to flourish in France during the Regency and the reign of Louis XV, but not at the splendid level it had attained during the era of Lully and the Sun King. Jean-Philippe Rameau (1683-1764), the leading composer of the period, excelled as an organist and musical theoretician, but failed to attract interest in his early operatic attempts. When he set music to Voltaire's drama *Samson* in 1727, the production was forbidden on the grounds that Biblical subjects were not to be treated in opera. The tide turned in Rameau's favor later with his very successful spectacular operas *Hippolyte et Aricie* (1733), *Les Indes galantes* (1735), and *Castor et Pollux* (1737).

Drama, on the other hand, had enjoyed a golden period of unbroken success since Molière's time. Actors were very popular and were welcome in aristocratic salons despite the fact that the entire profession was under excommunication by the Church, which denied them burial in consecrated ground.

No theatrical personality shone brighter in those years than Adrienne Lecouvreur (1692-1730), a born actress who made a name for herself in her early youth, lived through several tumultuous liaisons and made her debut at the Comédie Française on March 27, 1717 in Crébillon's *Electre*. Applauding her, among others, was Voltaire, already a fervent admirer and, possibly, a great deal more than that.

What Voltaire admired about Lecouvreur was her nearly revolutionary directness of communication, a style the contemporary *Mercure de France* summed up this way:

> To her belongs the glory of having introduced simple, noble, and natural declamation and of banishing cant.

Her roles encompassed many leading characters in the dramas of Racine, Corneille, Voltaire (*Hérode et Mariamne*) and their lesser contemporaries, sharing the spotlight on occasion with Mme. Duclos (Marie-Anne de Chateauneuf), her principal rival.

A crucial and ultimately tragic turn in this celebrated tragedienne's life occurred in 1721 when she succumbed to the undoubtedly considerable charms of Maurice de Saxe, a gallant soldier apparently irresistible to women but rather flexible in his morals and untamed in his ambition.

Maurice was the legitimized natural son of Augustus II, King of Poland and Elector of Saxony, and the Countess Maria-Aurora von Königsmark of Sweden. Enthusiastically embracing a military career, he fought in several campaigns commanding his father's regiments, and arrived in Paris as a celebrated hero in 1720. He was twenty-four, four years younger than Adrienne, and consumed with ambition to become the Duke of Courland, a part of today's Latvia, then under the suzerainty of Augustus II, King of Poland, his father. Despite Russian opposition, Maurice persisted, with his father's secret approval, in pursuing his ambition. To maintain his armies, which had been engaged in skirmishes with Russian troops under the leadership of Maurice's rival, Prince Menshikov, heavy financial support was needed—and much of it came from the devoted Adrienne Lecouvreur. She pawned her diamonds and silverware for the cause, believing that Maurice would marry her, especially after 1727 when he finally had to give up all hopes of obtaining the throne of Courland.

Adrienne's reward for her sacrifice was gross ingratitude. Her vainglorious lover betrayed her with the promiscuous Duchesse de Bouillon, leading to a triangle of jealousy, intrigue and violence. This is at the core of the play *Adrienne Lecouvreur* by Scribe and Legouvé, once a triumphant vehicle for such tragediennes as Rachel and Sarah Bernhardt, and the basis for Francesco Ciléa's opera *Adriana Lecouvreur* (1902).

The opera records the tumultuous last weeks of Adrienne's life in the year 1730. It is full of well-observed historical and theatrical detail, populated by such members of the Comédie Française as the Messrs. Poisson and Quinault, and Mlles. Jouvenot and Dangeville, all fellow artists of Lecouvreur. There are shades of Voltaire in the operatic character of the devoted stage manager Michonnet, full of admiration for Adrienne's art and smitten with her person. Not slavishly bound by history, the opera's libretto (by Arturo Colautti) nevertheless mixes in historical ingredients with scholarly ease. When, in the opera's third act, Adriana confronts the Duchess (Princess in the opera) by quoting a passionate monologue from Racine's *Phèdre*, which suggests the great tension between the rivals, that scene is based on historical fact: on November 10, 1729, she actually delivered that monologue

Renata Tebaldi and Franco Corelli as Adriana and Maurizio in
Adriana Lecouvreur (Ciléa)
CREDIT: Opera News

on the stage of the Comédie Française, with the Duchess—and all the Paris cognoscenti—in the audience.

Though the opera presents Maurice de Saxe (Maurizio) in a fairly sympathetic light, it is not blind to his vanity. When he describes a military confrontation with "*il ruso Mencikoff*" at Mittau (Courland's capital), he is not above comparing his own heroism with that of Sweden's much-feared and admired Charles XII.

Lecouvreur's theatrical death by poisoned flowers grew out of various rumors surrounding the Lecouvreur-Bouillon rivalry. The real Adrienne had symptoms of dysentery several years before her illness turned fatal in 1730. On March 15, 1730, she appeared for the last time as Jocaste in Voltaire's *Oedipe*. She died five days later, with her doctor, Maurice de Saxe, and Voltaire (represented by the loyal Michonnet in the opera) at her bedside. The autopsy confirmed death by natural causes. The Archbishop of Paris refused religious burial, and the body of that great actress was promptly interred in an unmarked spot on the bank of the Seine. She was mourned by her colleagues, and many influential friends and admirers protested her final indignity. In a long poetic eulogy Voltaire wrote:

> They deprive of burial her who in Greece would have altars. I have seen them adoring her, crowding about her; hardly is she dead when she becomes a criminal! She charmed the world, and you punish her! No, those banks will never henceforth be profane; they hold your ashes, and this sad tomb will be for us a new temple, honored by our chants, and consecrated by your shades.

Maurice de Saxe continued his exploits on the battlefield and in the boudoir for many more years, ending his life as Maréchal de France in 1750, a life in which Adrienne Lecouvreur was a mere episode. Voltaire's sharp intellect and tireless pen continued to stir French society with his political writings extolling the rights and liberties of English citizens as examples to follow and his plays where he habitually challenged traditional Christian values. Those plays have since fallen into obscurity, buried by changing times and fashions, but in the nineteenth century they still inspired operas by Rossini (*Tancrède, Mahomet, Sémiramis*), Bellini (*Zaira*), and Verdi (*Alzire*). Invariably, though, Voltaire's provocative thoughts and poetic eloquence were tamed and devitalized by the streamlining requirements of operatic discipline.

Verdi's *Alzira* (1845), dealing with a relatively "modern" (16th century—unlike Voltaire's customary mythological or medieval preoccupations) subject, is perhaps worth special consideration. In a story where Spanish conquerors confront the Incas of Peru, Voltaire cannot hide his sympathies for Zamore, the "noble savage" accused of murdering the conquering Spanish governor. But what may have shocked the Paris audience when the play was introduced in 1736 lost all its disturbing pungency in the opera's libretto a century later. "In the hands of Cammarano," as Julian Budden observed, "the sting of skepticism is removed and the play's intellectual content reduced to a minimum. Religion and politics, the two *raisons d'être* of the drama, are scarcely mentioned."

The symbol of the "noble savage", a human being untainted by civilization—whose advent 18th-century thinkers no longer accepted as an unmixed blessing—had been a recurrent literary figure ever since Daniel Defoe's pathbreaking novel *Robinson Crusoe* (1719). (Such an unspoiled creature is the central character in Haydn's 1779 opera *L'isola disabitata*.) Jean-Jacques Rousseau, Voltaire's contemporary and philosophical antagonist, admired Defoe and went even beyond him in his advocacy of "return to nature". Not Voltaire, who readily embraced civilization for all its shortcomings: "This profane time is just for my ways. I love luxury, even a soft life, all the pleasures, the arts in their variety, cleanliness, taste, and ornaments."

In 1736, Voltaire began corresponding with an admirer, young Prince Frederick of Prussia, later to become Frederick the Great, the most enlightened and cultivated ruler of the age. When Frederick became King in 1740, he repeatedly invited Voltaire to join him in his Potsdam court. After brief visits during the next decade, during which their correspondence continued, Voltaire accepted the King's invitation and briefly set up residence in Potsdam in 1750. He was a wealthy man by then who had managed his financial affairs wisely. Opera contributed to all this, for it was Voltaire who had provided the librettos to Rameau's *Le Temple de la gloire* (1745), a thinly disguised tribute to King Louis XV, and *La Princesse de Navarre* (1747). Thanks to the benevolence of the King's principal mistress, the legendary Madame de Pompadour, Voltaire, the erstwhile prisoner of the Bastille, was now in favor at court. Not only was he admitted (rather belatedly) to the Academy, on May 9, 1746, but he was also appointed *gentilhomme ordinaire de la chambre*, with special court privileges.

XXIV

FREDERICK THE GREAT AND
MARIA THERESA

Graun; Gluck; Haydn; *La forza del destino* (Verdi); *Der Rosenkavalier* (Richard Strauss); *Candide* (Bernstein)

It was Voltaire who first dubbed Frederick II, King of Prussia, "Frederick the Great." The mutual attraction of these two men was unavoidable. Voltaire had never met a monarch like Frederick: a brilliant intellectual, a lover of the arts, a philospher, a gifted writer and musician. Things had been different, of course, before he ascended the throne, when Frederick had to keep his artistic inclinations in check — even his passion for the flute — because his martinet father, Frederick William I, considered music a useless pastime. It all changed in 1740 when Frederick became King of Prussia: Johann Joachim Quantz, his longtime flute teacher, was appointed court composer, a position he held until his death in 1773. Quantz wrote 300 flute concertos for his kingly pupil who, state matters notwithstanding, practiced daily. Carl Philip Emanuel Bach was cembalist at the same court. In 1747, Frederick invited Johann Sebastian himself to visit his Potsdam court and it was there that he composed his *Musical Offering* on melodic ideas suggested by that remarkable king.

But it was not all music in Potsdam. Frederick was an ambitious ruler, and his ambition centered on establishing Prussia as a major European power. From his efficient disciplinarian father, he inherited a rich treasury and a well-trained army. Opportunity beckoned in 1740 when the Habsburg Emperor Charles VI died without leaving a male heir. His daughter, Maria Theresa, inherited the Habsburg dominions: Austria, Hungary, Bohemia, the Austrian Netherlands and the Italian duchies of Tuscany and Lombardy, but her right to succeed her father as Emperor was challenged by the Elector of Bavaria, Charles Albert, with the support of France, a traditional Habsburg enemy. Taking advantage of Austria's evident weakness, Frederick invaded the fertile land of Silesia, one of the richest Habsburg possessions. Beleagured by the Prussians in the North, while Spanish troops were to reclaim Habsburg territory in Italy, Maria Theresa's able generals nonetheless held their own for a while. As the war dragged on on many fronts, France fought the Austrian troops in the Netherlands under the supreme leadership of the aging Maurice de Saxe, [*] while Spanish forces and their French allies captured Parma and Milan.

The War of the Austrian Succession [**] forms the background of two wildly different operas, Richard Strauss's *Der Rosenkavalier* and Giuseppe Verdi's *La forza del destino*. In the first act of *Der Rosenkavalier*, Baron Ochs identifies his would-be father-in-law, Herr von Faninal, as a man who has recently been "raised by Her Majesty to the nobility. He has supplied the army in the Netherlands." A few minutes earlier in the action, surprised by the approaching Ochs in the Marschallin's boudoir, Octavian, with youthful bravado, makes a gallant gesture and declares "I am no Neapolitan general: where I stand, I stand"—an allusion to a clash between Austrian and Neapolitan troops in 1744 where the latter retreated rather hastily. And the first scene of *La forza del destino's* third act places Don Alvaro and Don Carlo di Vargas, two mortal enemies (both under assumed names), in an army camp near Velletri, south of Rome. Both wear the uniforms of the Royal Spanish Grenadiers. The date of the battle near Velletri was August 11, 1744, involving an Austrian army led by Prince Lobkowitz and a Spanish army under Duke Philip, son of Philip V of Spain and younger brother of Carlos III, the Bourbon King of Naples and the Two Sicilies. It was a bloody encounter that ended with the withdrawal of the Spanish forces.

Carlos III eventually was to rule Spain, but as King of Naples he had already carved his name into operatic annals by commissioning the construction of the famous Teatro San Carlo of Naples. It opened with great pomp on November 4, 1737, the feast day of the saint after whom the king—and the opera house—was named: San Carlo. (Carlos was married to Maria Amalia of Saxony, daughter of the Saxon king Augustus III. An English envoy called them the world's ugliest couple.)

---

[*]   See page 251.

[**]   The cause of the hostilities is spelled out in a most unlikely setting. In the second act of the Johann Strauss operetta *Der Zigeunerbaron (The Gypsy Baron)*, the recruiting officer Homonay announces: "Our fatherland is in need! Bavaria, Italy, France and Spain would dispute our Queen's rights in Spain. Take up your arms and move against Spain for our Queen Maria Theresa!"

Carlos inherited his love of the arts from his mother, Isabel Farnese, a strong-willed and highly unpopular queen. She loved music, however, and it was to her credit that the famous castrato Carlo Farinelli was invited to the Spanish court. Eventually, the melancholy and eccentric King Philip V also came under Farinelli's spell, whose duties required him to spend every day with the king from midnight until 5:00 a.m.—hours the king set aside for music and conversation. Philip would ask for the same Italian arias time after time. (Henry Pleasants, in his book *The Great Singers*, has identified four of the king's special favorites: two from Hasse's *Artaserse* and one each from operas by Ariosti and Giacomelli, all with elaborate ornamentations provided by Farinelli.)

Philip's eccentricities eventually turned into evident insanity that, among other things, caused him to disdain shaving and other manifestations of cleanliness. He died on July 9, 1746—while the War of the Austrian Succession was still in progress—to be succeeded by his oldest son, Fernando VI. Music flourished in the new king's court, as well. Farinelli was retained, Domenico Scarlatti was engaged as court music master, and the best singers of Italy were imported for the court's delectation.

Not to be outdone by Spain, Frederick the Great cultivated opera on an even larger scale. His appreciation of Italian opera had begun when he discovered Hasse's *Cleofide* in his youth. In the very year he became King of Prussia (1740), he appointed Karl Heinrich Graun (1704-1759), next to Hasse the most important creator of Italian operas on German soil, as his court composer. The establishment of the Berlin Opera House followed two years later; its architect was also charged with building Frederick's magnificent palace "Sans Souci" near Potsdam, completed in 1747. Nor was the role of that remarkable monarch limited to merely *enjoying* opera; when in 1755 the prolific Graun undertook the writing of an opera on a comparatively modern subject, the conquest of Mexico, the libretto for his *Montezuma* was provided by Frederick himself—in French, a language he preferred to all others, translated into Italian by a court poet.

The War of the Austrian Succession ended with the peace treaty of Aix-la-Chapelle on October 18, 1748. Frederick kept Silesia, while the Habsburgs retained most of their original inheritance and, as a further concession, Maria Theresa's husband, Francis of Lorraine, was recognized as the "Holy Roman Emperor," a title—as Voltaire aptly observed—by then a misnomer on all three counts. In England, which suffered relatively little, the peace was celebrated with a great display of fireworks, for which Handel's *Music for the*

Royal Fireworks was commissioned. The aging composer carried on unstintingly, despite progressive blindness, creating several dramatic oratorios as well as his glorious *Messiah*. He died in London on April 14, 1759, and was laid to rest at Westminster Abbey.

After eight years of peace, the unresolved enmities erupted again in 1756 in the so-called Seven Years' War, which soon took on global dimensions. Maria Theresa's crafty chancellor, Prince Kaunitz, created an alliance against Frederick between France, Austria, and Russia (ruled then by Tsarina Elizabeth, the daughter of Peter the Great). Spain resumed her hostilities with England and, in faraway North America, border disputes created a war between French and English forces. After initial setbacks, the tide again turned in Frederick's favor: Russia's Elizabeth, his sworn enemy, died and her successor, Peter III, an admirer of Frederick, withdrew the Russian armies. The young Tsar was soon assassinated by his own officers; his successor, Catherine II (later to be known as Catherine the Great, 1762-1796), continued a neutral policy for Russia. The Seven Years' War ended with Frederick making small concessions but retaining Silesia, and England expanding her possessions at the expense of France and Spain. To counterbalance the loss of Silesia, Maria Theresa took part in the first partition of Poland, a cynical act that gained important territories for the Habsburg Empire, Russia, and Prussia while appropriating the resources of an independent nation. England's Horace Walpole termed the three participating powers "the most impudent association of robbers that ever existed."

Frederick's longtime antagonist Maria Theresa radiated the personality of a benevolent maternal figure, but she ruled with a strong hand at the head of an efficient bureaucracy. Vienna's many beautiful baroque and rococo buildings survive as impressive monuments to her rule. The Empress appreciated opera without quite sharing the passion her father, Charles VI, had displayed for it. (It was the late Emperor who had established the Neapolitan Pietro Metastasio, né Trapassi, at the Viennese court. Metastasio became the most prolific librettist of the age, whose eloquent dramas were eagerly set to music by the best operatic minds of Western Europe.)

While the two major wars during Maria Theresa's reign curtailed lavish court entertainment in Vienna, the resourceful Count Giacomo Durazzo, the director of the imperial theatres, managed to maintain them at an impressive level. He had at his disposal the considerable talents of Christoph Willibald Gluck (1714-1787), a resident of Vienna since 1748, though he traveled freely to Rome and Naples to supervise productions of his operas. The war

Maria Theresa
CREDIT: Opera News

Frederick the Great (after a drawing by H. Ramberg)
CREDIT: Culver Pictures Inc.

was not yet over when Vienna saw the original production of Gluck's *Orfeo ed Euridice* with text by Raniero Calzabigi. It was coldly received in 1762, nor was more Viennese warmth generated to greet *Alceste*, another masterly Gluck opera, five years later. In 1770, following yet another unfriendly reception accorded his *Paride ed Elena*, Gluck left Vienna for France, never to return.

Opera during Maria Theresa's reign bloomed not in Vienna but at the country estates of the Princes Eszterházy, where Haydn was established as court musician in 1761. In the magnificent estate of Eszterháza, modelled on Versailles, Haydn conducted the orchestra, created music in many forms, and presided over operatic productions, including his own operas, that eventually would dwarf every other type of music making.

Court life in Paris, meanwhile, was a picture of decadence as the aging Louis XV allowed his administration to be influenced by a series of mistresses. Several military failures were balanced by the high level of French literature. Voltaire, whose intellectual affinity to Frederick the Great never blossomed into true friendship, returned to France in 1753. In 1759, while the Seven Years' War was still raging, he published his *Candide,* a wicked satire dealing with religious presumptions, priestly abuses, political corruption, and the destructiveness of wars. Though severely condensed, some of the savage wit and cynicism of Voltaire's unwieldy work is captured by Richard Wilbur and various other authors who shaped the libretto of Leonard Bernstein's opera/operetta/musical *Candide* (1956), a work that has been brought to stage in various incarnations.

Voltaire died in 1778 after spending most of his energies during his final decade in attacking organized Christianity. Frederick the Great, with whom Voltaire continued to maintain an intellectually stimulating correspondence, followed him in 1786. A hardworking ruler who demanded nothing less from his subjects, he had raised Prussia to the rank and prestige of a major power without passing on his enlightened views to his people. By then, his antagonist Maria Theresa was also dead, leaving the imperial throne to her son Joseph II (1780-1790), in whom enlightened thoughts and absolutist inclinations uneasily coexisted.

And yet the world was changing in ways that went far beyond the imagination of these rulers. Louis XV died in 1774, and was succeeded by a grandson who would never reach old age. In England, the long rule of George III (1760-1820) may have begun auspiciously with a favorable conclusion of the Seven Years' War in which France consented to losing territories in North America and Canada. But the cooperation of the colonial settlers in that war was half-hearted: they were people accustomed to freedom and unwilling to share Old-World burdens. The taxation imposed by the British Parliament was violently opposed and various absolutist actions by the British government of George III fueled a popular hatred that led to the Boston Massacre of 1770. The independence of the American colonies was soon to follow.

XXV

TOWARD THE REVOLUTION

Mozart; Goethe; Schiller; *Luisa Miller* (Verdi); *I Masnadieri* (Verdi); *Werther* (Massenet); Beaumarchais; *Mignon* (Thomas); *Il barbiere di Siviglia* (Paisiello / Rossini); *Le nozze di Figaro* (Mozart)

In many ways, the Empress Maria Theresa was far from the ideal of an enlightened monarch that Frederick the Great personified. Her devout Catholicism made her intolerant of other faiths; she hated Freemasonry and viewed the dangerous and revolutionary currents drifting in from England and France with apprehension. At the same time, she stood on high moral principles, and her concern for her subjects' welfare was genuine. On the other hand little was done to ease the lot of the peasantry for fear of intruding on the rights of the nobility, a pillar of the empire in times of war.

In the old tradition of the Habsburg rulers, Maria Theresa eagerly pursued the broadening of dynastic power. She bore her husband sixteen children and, though many died prematurely, the survivors flourished. Their first-born son, as Emperor Joseph II, shared imperial power with her after 1765, upon the death of her consort, Francis I. The second son, Leopold, was made Grand Duke of Tuscany, and his younger brother Ferdinand became Governor of Lombardy—Italian territories then still part of the Empire. Their daughter Marie Antoinette married France's Louis XVI; another daughter, Maria Carolina, became Queen of Naples. Neither inherited their mother's practical good sense and strong moral principles.

From spring to fall, the imperial court stayed at Schönbrunn, a sumptuous palace surrounded by splendid gardens, built on the Versailles model, not fully completed until 1780, the year of the Empress's death. Hugo von Hofmannsthal's masterly libretto of *Der Rosenkavalier* faithfully suggests the luxurious life of Vienna's nobility; it gives no hint of high intellectual activities for, in fact, there were hardly any. Newspapers were censored, challenging ideas were discouraged, literature—in sharp contrast to what was going on in various German centers at the same time—was insignificant.

There was, however, music. On January 10, 1768, Leopold Mozart and his two gifted children, Wolfgang and Nannerl, were graciously received by the Empress, but no imperial gestures were extended toward their employment, nor were they given further encouragement. During the summer of that year, his twelfth, Wolfgang Amadeus Mozart completed his first two operas: *La finta semplice* and *Bastien und Bastienne*. Court intrigues by Gluck and other entrenched members of Vienna's musical establishment prevented the performance of the former. (It was staged in Salzburg in early 1769). The young composer was more fortunate with *Bastien und Bastienne*, a pastoral one-acter with a subject derived from Rousseau's *Le devin du village* (1752), which was performed — according to several Mozart biographers — at the garden theater of Dr. Franz Anton Mesmer, the scientist who was to become famous for his theory of healing through magnetism.

Mozart's next encounter with the imperial house was no more fortunate. He composed, on a royal commission, the festive "serenata" *Ascanio in Alba* for the wedding of the Archduke Ferdinand of Lombardy and the Princess of Modena in 1771. Maria Theresa regaled him with a gold watch bearing her portrait. However, when her son the Archduke approached her with an idea of employing that talented youngster as a musician at his ducal court, the Empress advised him (in a letter dated December 12, 1771) "not to burden yourself with useless people, and not to give such people permission to represent themselves as belonging in your service. It gives one's service a bad name when such people run about like beggars; he has, besides, a large family."

After *Ascanio in Alba*, Mozart wrote one more opera for Italy, *Lucio Silla*,[*] commissioned by the Regio Ducal Teatro of Milan and introduced at that theater on the second day after Christmas 1772. Four years later, the Ducal Teatro was burned down. Responding to the traditional love of the Milanese for the theater and, in particular, for opera, the Archduke Ferdinand, with the gracious encouragement of his imperial mother, resolved to build a new theater, even larger and more beautiful than the old one. That new theater, later to become known universally as "Teatro alla Scala", opened on August 3, 1778, with *Europa riconosciuta*, a new opera by the still young Antonio Salieri, later to become Mozart's bitter rival in Vienna.

During the last decade of her reign, Maria Theresa viewed the politics of

---

[*]   See page 11.

her son and co-emperor Joseph II with grave concern. Unlike his devout
mother, Joseph was attracted to the ideas of Voltaire, and even sought the
friendship of his mother's arch-enemy, Frederick the Great, whom he visited
on repeated occasions in 1769 and 1770. He visited France, too, and, watching that country's growing disorder, urged his sister Marie Antoinette to
abandon her frivolous ways.

When the Empress died in 1780, Joseph quickly went about to put some
of his liberal ideas into action. Capital punishment was abolished, divorces
were made legal, the ban over Masonic lodges was removed, and church control over the nation's social life was generally weakened. This brought about
a revision of censorship laws, with a significant increase in academic
freedom.

Joseph was a firm believer in German national theater and looked kindly upon the flourishing of the form of *singspiel,* with its combination of drama,
speech, and popular tunes. And when Mozart raised the singspiel to an unprecedented level with his *Die Entführung aus dem Serail* in 1782, he finally
achieved his first really great success in Vienna.

The Turkish element so entertainingly handled in *Die Entführung* had
been a familiar phenomenon on the Austrian stage ever since Vienna's
liberation from the Turkish siege in 1683.* A few years later, when Joseph —
as a result of his alliance with Russia — was reluctantly drawn into a war with
Turkey, Mozart's engaging singspiel suddenly gained contemporary
relevance. That war (1788-89) turned out a disaster for Austria, one of the
final blows the well-meaning but hapless Emperor was to suffer.

Joseph II had attempted too much in too short a time. Austria was not
ready for his reforms: the clergy was antagonistic, the nobles distrusted him,
and all classes suffered from heavy taxation. Within the empire, there was
unrest, particularly from the Hungarians, whose long traditions the Emperor
wilfully slighted when he refused to be crowned King of Hungary. In rapidly declining health, Joseph died unlamented on February 20, 1790, after re-
scinding virtually all of his reforms save the abolition of serfdom.

* * *

During the years when Frederick the Great built Prussia into a significant

---

*   See page 230.

political and military power, the rest of Germany consisted of a loose federation of states, headed by various kings, dukes, and princes, all exercising considerable independence yet formally accepting the "Holy Roman" Emperor in Vienna as their titular superior. Some of these rulers emulated the example of Frederick and governed their lands with various degrees of tolerance; others were petty tyrants who paid little heed to the ferments of the enlightenment and the unquenchable desire of peoples to reorganize society.

The duchy of Saxe-Weimar stood in those years as a beacon of culture, a center of intellectual and literary revival for all of Germany. The movement began under the rule of the Dowager Duchess Anna Amalie (1758-1775), a niece of Frederick the Great, and gained new impetus with the ascension of her son Karl August. He began his reign by inviting Johann Wolfgang von Goethe to join other literary greats like Christoph Wieland (1733-1813) in a remarkable gathering of intellectuals that turned Weimar into the "Athens of Germany."

Goethe (1749-1832) was born in Frankfurt-am-Main, a "free city" traditionally designated as a seat for the coronation of the Holy Roman emperors. At age fifteen, he attended the coronation of Joseph II and, as his autobiography attests, by then he had developed a strong attraction toward the "eternal feminine" that inspired much of his poetry. Wherever he went (the universities of Leipzig and Strasbourg), he managed to fall passionately in love. The object of his infatuation in 1771 was Friederike Brion, daughter of the town pastor at Sesenheim, near Strasbourg, whom he abandoned upon obtaining his doctorate at law. Their romance forms the plot — in a somewhat modified fashion that places the poet in a more favorable light — of the Franz Lehár operetta *Friederike* (1928).

In 1772, as a young lawyer, Goethe spent some time in Wetzlar, where he fell in love with Charlotte Buff, the fiancée of Goethe's friend, a local notary named Georg Christian Kestner. When Charlotte finally married Kestner, her decision deeply wounded the poet. A few months later, he learned that a fellow lawyer and poet named Karl Wilhelm Jerusalem had shot himself (with a pistol borrowed from Kestner) over a similarly unrequited love for another man's wife. Partaking of all these ingredients, the plot of *Werther* began to take shape in Goethe's mind. His novel (in epistolary form), *Die Leiden des jungen Werther* (1744), in which several true life episodes were faithfully enough captured to cause embarrassment to the real Charlotte and Kestner, swept through Europe, was embraced by all lovers and, unfortunately, actually caused a wave of suicides. Surprisingly, it was a French composer, Jules Massenet, who fashioned a successful opera out of this out-standing example of the German *Sturm und Drang,* one of the first manifes-tations of German literary rebirth.

The libretto of Massenet's *Werther* (1892) faithfully follows the novel, al-lowing for such harmless liberties as turning Kestner into "Albert". Only the end of the novel—where the dying Werther is discovered by his servant who then runs to fetch the doctor—was considered too prosaic for operatic pur-poses. Massenet's soaring love music, followed by the painful juxtaposition of carefree singing by children with Werther's pathetic death, provide the kind of musical invention that has enabled the opera to outlive the imper-manent fame of a once sensational novel.

In 1775, Goethe, basking in the success of his novel on the heels of his stor-my earlier play *Götz von Berlichingen,* * accepted the invitation of his ducal admirer, Karl August of Saxe-Weimar. He moved to Weimar, a city teeming with stimulating intellectual activity. Twelve years later, he was joined there by Friedrich Schiller, the other literary giant of the new Germany.

Aside from being the principal ornament to the court, Goethe held several administrative posts in the duke's cabinet. In a relatively brief time, he be-came involved in an intense love affair with a married woman several years his senior, and his literary inspiration burned with perhaps an even greater intensity. "*Erlkönig*" was but one of the great lyric poems written during his early Weimar years, as were the dramas *Egmont, Iphigenie auf Tauris,* and *Torquato Tasso,* all with significant musical associations. Eventually, though, he grew impatient with court life. Working on his novel *Wilhelm Meister,* and taking a cue from the famous song of longing he wrote for Mignon, one of the novel's characters, "*Kennst du das Land wo die Zitronen blühn...*", he was yearning for the sunny Italian skies. His generous duke consented to a leave of absence for Goethe and, since the amorous knot that bound him to Weimar was also loosening by then, the poet's Italian journey (1786-88) proved desirable in many ways.

Wilhelm Meisters Lehrjahre is a sprawling novel of several episodes, popu-lated by many characters Wilhelm encounters as he sets out on his journey in search of wisdom and knowledge. From the novel's vast panorama, Ambroise Thomas cannily plucked the touching waif Mignon to build an opera around her in 1866. She dies a poignant death in the novel; in the

---

*   See page 153.

opera—which dispenses with most of Wilhelm's adventures and most of the characters that inhabit the novel—she is happily reunited with her long-lost father and finds her love for Wilhelm reciprocated as the orchestra intones the theme of her principal aria. That aria, *"Connais tu le pays"*, is the French equivalent of the Goethe lyric *"Kennst du das Land wo die Zitronen blühn"*, lovingly set by Schubert, Schumann, Wolf, and other composers in German lands. In its transformation from novel to opera, Goethe's creation took on a thoroughly French character.

Unlike Goethe's enlightened Duke Karl August of Weimar, Duke Karl Eugen of Württemberg, the duchy where Friedrich Schiller was born in 1759, was a tyricannical ruler. Schiller's father was a surgeon in the duke's regiment and, on parental advice but without enthusiasm, young Friedrich followed the same path. An avid reader, under the influence of Rousseau, Klopstock, and the young Goethe, he wrote his first play, *Die Räuber (The Robbers)*. It was an angry play, full of bitterness against society—a prime example of *Sturm und Drang* along with Goethe's *Götz von Berlichingen* —and it was so astonishingly successful that Duke Karl Eugen forbade his regimental surgeon to write any more plays.

Die Räuber was a play written by a very angry young man. In later life, Schiller became embarrassed by it, but Verdi's friend and librettist Andrea Maffei, who fashioned the libretto of *I Masnadieri* based on *Die Räuber* in 1847, wrote that "I cannot think of any other literary work which would lend itself so well to musical treatment."

In his play, Schiller created fictional characters along Shakespearean lines. As Julian Budden observes: "Karl Moor is half Hamlet, half Coriolanus; Franz is descended from Iago, Maximilian from Lear." But these characters all inhabit Schiller's actual 18th-century world. When the evil younger brother Franz (Francesco in the opera) begins his sinister plotting to disinherit the first-born son Karl (Carlo), he deceitfully spreads the news of his death at the Battle of Prague in the Seven Years' War (May-June 1757). Driven to the life of an outlaw, Carlo leads his fellow bandits in a revolutionary cry against a corrupt world that can be changed only by violence. Maffei's words echo Schiller's outrage at the actions of the contemporary local tyrant, the Duke of Württemberg. A furious play, *Die Räuber* is somewhat preposterous, too, in its piled-up violence—which somehow behooves an Italian opera like *I Masnadieri* more—but both play and opera have managed to hold the stage to this day, albeit with frequent modifications in the former.

Unable to continue in Württemberg, Schiller left his position and escaped to Mannheim. During a briefly penurious period that followed, he wrote another violent and stormy play, *Kabale und Liebe*, the source of inspiration for another Verdi opera, *Luisa Miller*. Here, again, Schiller lashed out against tyranny.

The true villain in both play and opera is a ruler who never appears on stage and is referred to only as "the sovereign" or the "Duke". It is clearly modeled on Karl Eugen, and the city where the action takes place was probably meant to be Stuttgart, the capital of the duchy. The characters of Count Walter, who wields the sovereign's authority, and of his sinister councilor Wurm, are based on personalities known to Schiller; only the innocent young lovers Louise and Ferdinand (Luisa and Rodolfo in the opera) and Louise's father are fictional. Schiller's play is revolutionary in the sense that it focuses on the conflict between social classes — an issue that held a strong appeal to Verdi. Count Walter represents an aristocracy that is beyond redemption. His goodnatured son is drawn toward the honesty of the bourgeois Miller family and is destroyed by a system that does not allow defection. The hated Wurm — an appropriate name in Schiller's scheme — represents bourgeoisie corrupted by aristocracy.

Schiller wrote his *Kabale und Liebe* in 1784; its action — and that of Verdi's *Luisa Miller* — is imbued with the spirit of a Europe on the brink of a social revolution. With that spirit burning in him, Schiller completed his play *Don Carlos*, about another tyrant, Philip II of Spain, and a fictitious hero, the Marquis of Posa, the eloquent spokesman of Schiller's own revolutionary sentiments.[*] When the play was finished in 1787, the poet moved to the welcoming, enlightened world of Weimar.

Karl Eugen, the tyrannical duke Schiller escaped from, continued to rule on the basis of severe taxation and intimidation until 1793. He was one of several German princes who sold thousands of young men to England to be used as cannon fodder against the American Revolutionary Army.

England was ruled by George III, the first Hanoverian king to be born in that country, whose long reign (1760-1820) witnessed the American and French revolutions and the Napoleonic wars. In 1778, France recognized the United States of America and joined its war against England; the following year Spain, allied to France, laid siege to Gibraltar. Hostilities soon spread to the Netherlands and the Baltic region. In the face of all these disasters,

---

[*]   See pages 165-169.

the English people and a growing majority of Parliament desired peace. Although the King would have preferred to continue, Parliament prevailed and in a series of peace treaties effected in Paris and Versailles, the independence of the American colonies was recognized (1782-83).

* * *

After 1774, France was ruled by the well-meaning but weak-spirited Louis XVI. Attempts were made to abolish the remnants of serfdom and to correct the most flagrant abuses of an inequitable tax system, but class distinctions continued and the third estate (the middle class and the peasantry, more than four fifths of the population) continued to suffer. Widespread corruption, abuses in high places — aggravated by the extravagance and haughty behavior of the unpopular Austrian Queen, Marie Antoinette — fueled a growing resentment against France's bankrupt system of bureaucracy. Nor did the success of the American Revolution escape notice.

An active part in the success of that Revolution had been played by a remarkable factotum — scientist, inventor, businessman, musician, playwright, and sometimes diplomat — named Pierre-Augustin Caron. Watchmaking was the field in which he first made his name, and he counted Louis XV and Madame Pompadour among his satisfied customers. In 1756, he married a prosperous widow with a large property, and added the name of her estate, Beaumarchais, to his own. In 1761, determined to get ahead in the world, Pierre bought the rights to a public office, which automatically made him an *écuyer*, the lowest degree of French nobility.

Family matters caused Beaumarchais to travel to Spain in 1764 where, with his remarkable gift for making friends in high places, he spent an adventuresome year and soaked up enough lasting impressions to write a delightful comedy called *Le barbier de Séville*. It is about a clever factotum of a barber and has a cast of entertaining characters, including an aging doctor (Bartholo) with a fascination for young females, a character based on the author's own father, the ever-philandering André Caron. For a decade, the play remained in manuscript; when it finally reached the Comédie Française in 1775, its success placed Beaumarchais into the forefront of the French playwrights of his age.

Even in its modified form — for Beaumarchais had thought it wise to tone down the sharply anti-aristocratic language of the original draft — *Le barbier de Séville* was a daring play for the period, but, of course, its action plays out

Beaumarchais (P. A. Caron)
CREDIT: Opera News

in the Spain of Carlos III and not in the France of Louis XV and XVI. In any case, while Giovanni Paisiello's *Il barbiere di Siviglia* — the first of several 18th-century operas based on that remarkable play — first performed at the court of Catherine the Great in 1782, abounds in richly comic situations, Giuseppe Petrosellini's libretto is a far cry from Beaumarchais's daring sallies against the aristocracy. The same is true, of course, of Cesare Sterbini's libretto for Rossini's opera with the same title (1816). What both operas have in common is the vital, ebullient personality of Figaro, whose impudent, mocking nature and resilient ability to master just about any situation strikes us as a thinly disguised self-portrait of Beaumarchais himself.

Beaumarchais, however, was no revolutionary. Having already served Louis XV as a confidential agent charged with the mission of preventing the circulation of an embarrassing pamphlet against Mme. du Barry, he accepted an assignment in 1775 from the Comte de Vergennes, foreign minister to the new king, Louis XVI, to investigate the growing conflict between England and its American colonies. Rightly assessing the situation, Beaumarchais recommended that France be involved in the conflict through extending aid to America and thereby weakening England. One of Beaumarchais's reports sounded a tone of genuine emotion:

> The Americans, resolved to suffer anything rather than yield, and filled with that enthusiasm for liberty which has so often made the little Corsican nation so dangerous to the Genoese, have 38,000 effective men under the walls of Boston.... I say, Sire, that such a nation must be invincible.

Louis XVI was reluctant to support revolutionary activity against another monarchy, but Beaumarchais's enthusiasm had Vergennes's total sympathy and by May 1776, war supplies began to be shipped to America, in secret, channeled through a company Beaumarchais founded for that purpose — Roderigue Hortalez & Cie. He invested large sums of his own money, but millions of livres were supplied by the French Treasury, through the offices of the Spanish ambassador — for Spain, too, had shown interest in curbing English power — and by several private investors who believed in the success of the enterprise.

Shortly after America's Declaration of Independence — which elicited a most enthusiastic reaction from Beaumarchais — Silas Deane, America's secret agent in France, reported back that he could not have completed his mission without "the generous, indefatigable and spirited exertions of Monsieur Beaumarchais, to whom the United States are, on every account, greatly indebted." When the Revolutionary War ended, Silas Deane unsuccessfully urged Congress to reimburse Beaumarchais. Neither he nor Beaumarchais lived to see the day when, in 1835, Congress recognized the rightness of the claim and paid 800,000 livres to Beaumarchais's heirs.

Elated by America's triumph and by the important role he had played in it, Beaumarchais gave himself the literary challenge to write a continuation of his *Le barbier de Séville* in which Figaro — his creation and somewhat of an alter-ego — would appear as a more mature and more fully developed character.

Le mariage de Figaro turned out to be a very different play from its predecessor, a play written by a man disillusioned by the society around him. In Figaro's long soliloquy in Act IV, he unleashes a violent outburst against the ineptitude of aristocrats, the looseness of morals, the cruelties of useless wars, and the intrusion of censorship on free speech. Here is a portion from it:

> Nobility, fortune, rank, position! How proud they make a man feel! What have *you* done to deserve such advantages? Put yourself to the trouble of being born — nothing more! For the rest — a very ordinary man! Whereas I, lost among the obscure crowd, have had to deploy more knowledge, more calculation and skill merely to survive than has sufficed to rule all the provinces of Spain for a century!

This is the central theme of the play: a struggle of wits, but for big stakes, between Figaro and his master, Count Almaviva, rightly perceived in the France of the 1780s as the symbol of the struggle between commoners and aristocrats. Count Almaviva stands as a not-quite-the-worst embodiment of the aristocracy Figaro-Beaumarchais despises; his wife — the former Rosine of *Le barbier* — is an idealized image of the eternally feminine; Figaro's fiancée Suzanne, according to the Beaumarchais biographers, is a counterpart of the author's sharp-witted sister Julie. Chérubin represents a nostalgic image of the author's own adolescence. Bartholo, older and less obnoxious than in the earlier play, again modeled after André Caron, is here properly recognized as Figaro-Beaumarchais's own father.

Le mariage de Figaro was accepted by the Comédie Française in 1781 but, when it was submitted for royal approval, Louis XVI, shocked by the outspokenness of the Act IV soliloquy, forbade its staging. By then, due to the ministrations of the author, the play had been widely read by people of importance and attracted the support of many courtiers, as well as Queen Marie Antoinette and her entourage. Finally, after a private performance in September 1783 at the palace of the Comte de Vaudreuil, the king relented. He ordered Beaumarchais to alter a few insignificant but face-saving passages, and *Le mariage* received its first presentation on April 27, 1784. In a masterstroke of public relations, and fending off whatever actions his enemies might have taken — and he did have enemies — Beaumarchais announced that all proceeds of the play would go to a newly founded hospital for nursing mothers. Convinced at last that Beaumarchais, the playwright, was a glory to France, Louis XVI authorized a staging of *Le barbier* — not *Le mariage* — at the royal palace of Trianon, near Versailles. Le Comte d'Artois, the king's brother, took the part of Almaviva, and Marie Antoinette, once a pupil and patroness of Gluck, appeared as Rosine.

While these events were taking place in France, Paisiello's opera *Il barbiere di Siviglia*, successfully launched in St. Petersburg, began its journey through the European capitals, and reached Vienna in 1784. Mozart and his librettist-partner Lorenzo da Ponte, an enterprising adventurer rather in the Beaumarchais mold, seized the idea of creating an operatic sequel to Paisiello's work. *Figaros Hochzeit*, the German translation of *Le mariage*, was widely circulated, but under the reign of Joseph II what was allowed to be read was not automatically allowed to be seen on stage. Aware of censorship restrictions and anxious to please aristocratic and bourgeois audiences alike, Da Ponte shaped his operatic libretto accordingly.

What he and Mozart placed before the public at Vienna's Burgtheater on May 1, 1786, almost exactly two years after the French court presentation of the Beaumarchais play, is a timeless human comedy, unlike the play, which is inextricably linked with pre-Revolutionary France. The struggle of wits between Figaro and his master still motivates the action, but Figaro's fourth-act aria, *"Aprite un po' quegli occhi,"* focuses only on jealous anger, devoid of the revolutionary rhetoric of Beaumarchais's provocative lines.

Actually, Beaumarchais, like his idol Voltaire, was a revolutionary only in the unfettered ideas of his imagination — he rejected the kind of violence that would lead to chaos. Nonetheless, Napoleon came to describe *Le mariage de Figaro* as "the Revolution already in action." As for Mozart's *Le nozze di Figaro*, let us defer to Johannes Brahms: "Every number in *Figaro* is for me a marvel; I simply cannot understand how anyone could create anything so perfect."

XXVI

CATHERINE II AND OTHER GREATS

The Queen of Spades (Tchaikovsky); *Le Postillon de Lonjumeau* (Adam); *Capriccio* (Richard Strauss); *Mozart
and Salieri* (Rimsky-Korsakov)

There is a fancy dress ball in the second act of Tchaikovsky's *The Queen of
Spades* (1890), set in St. Petersburg during the reign of Catherine the Great.
Central to the episode, with its French-influenced *rococo* spirit characteris-
tic of Russian society in the 1770s, is a pastoral intermezzo called *The Faith-
ful Shepherdess*, where three principal singers exchange gallantries to music
composed in a Mozartian spirit. The scene ends with the grand entry of
Catherine herself, accompanied by the French ambassador and assorted
princes as the chorus of guests, amid bows and curtsies, sings "*Slavsya sim
Yekaterina, Slavsya nezhnaya k nam mat! Vivat! vivat! vivat!*" ("Long live
Catherine, long live our gentle mother! Long life to her!")

The opera's libretto, written by Modeste Tchaikovsky with the partial assistance of the composer himself, is based on a short story by Pushkin, but
its spirit is far removed from its literary source. Pushkin's tale is set in the
author's own period, in the 1820s, more than a generation past the operatic
setting. Unlike the Tchaikovsky brothers, who intensely involved themselves
in the troubled lives of their characters – the obsessive gambler Herman and
the trusting Lisa, who becomes the victim of that obsession – Pushkin views
their relationship with a dispassionate detachment; he is an observer at a
philosophical distance from the strange doings of society. In contrast with
the brevity of the novel, the opera delves deeper into the main characters.
For example, the aged Countess, on retiring for the night, recalls her youth
at the glamorous French court of Louis XV, where she was known as the
"Moscovite Venus" ("*Veneroyu Moskovskoi*" – Pushkin's phrase). There she
moved in the highest circles: "Le Duc d'Orléans, le Duc d'Ayen, Duc de Coigny, La Comtesse d'Estrades, La Duchesse de Brancas...Madame Pompadour...even the King himself..." as she recalls in a faint voice before lulling
herself to sleep with the French aria "*Je crains de lui parler la nuit*" that

Catherine II of Russia
CREDIT: Culver Pictures Inc.

Tchaikovsky borrowed from André Grétry's opera *Richard Coeur-de-Lion* (a slightly anachronistic touch, for this 1784 opera came too late to be identifed with the Countess's youth).

Tchaikovsky endured more than his share of criticism from his contemporaries for having dared to depart in many telling details from Pushkin's classic, but it was those very departures that lent Pushkin's slender and sardonic tale the Romantic quality needed for an opera. Actually, those carping critics should have *praised* Tchaikovsky for paying a lavish tribute to the fabled Empress, who, aside from turning Russia into a major European power, enriched her nation's cultural — and, certainly, musical — life.

Catherine was not a native Russian, nor was she called Catherine at birth. She was born Princess Sophia Augusta Frederica of the House of Anhalt-Zerbst, a minor principality in central Germany. It was Frederick the Great — who had his own political agenda — who recommended this obscure princess as a proper mate for the future Tsar of Russia. The recommendation was made to the daughter of Peter the Great, the Empress Elizabeth Petrovna, who, being childless, chose her sister's son as her successor—a feeble and unbalanced youth.

It was not a marriage made in heaven. The young princess, educated by outstanding tutors, was brought up with an appreciation of French culture that she cultivated for the rest of her life. She was sixteen when she married the future Peter III in 1745, assumed the name Yekaterina, accepted the Orthodox faith, and began her Russification. The marriage was "blessed" with two children of dubious paternity. On Tsarina Elizabeth's death, Peter III became Tsar of Russia on January 5, 1762. Dissolute, ill-tempered, and unpopular, he ruled for only six months. A coup d'état deposed him and he died under mysterious circumstances, probably killed by officers loyal to Catherine, who thereafter ruled Russia for more than three decades.

Her reign (1762-1796) transplanted French culture into Russia in ways clearly mirrored in Tchaikovsky's *The Queen of Spades*. The use of the French language, which the Empress spoke fluently, was encouraged, and the imperial palaces and those of the Russian aristocrats soon began to reflect the courtly manners—and decadent morals—of Versailles and the French chateaux.

Music became a fashionable pastime in Russia, by then far from a musical wasteland, though only liturgical music enjoyed a wide audience. Ballet and Italian opera had been introduced through visiting Italian troupes as far back as 1732, and had enjoyed much appreciation during Elizabeth's reign. But it was under Catherine—by her own admission a person of no musical talent whatever—that the importation of celebrated composers and singers assumed a large scale and Italian opera became the center of the Russian musical world.

Baldassare Galuppi (1706-1785) was the first famous Italian composer at the Russian court. He came in 1766, stayed for two years and was followed by Tommaso Traetta (1729-1779), who spent six years (1768-1774) in St. Petersburg. Both men wrote new works for the Russian court in addition to staging previously introduced operas. Then came the celebrated Giovanni Paisiello (1740-1816), renowned master of the *opera buffa*. During an eight-year stay, he composed several new operas, capping his activity with *Il barbiere di Siviglia* (1782), a comic masterpiece that remained one of the most popular operas of Europe until Rossini's work by the same title eclipsed it more than thirty years later.

Paisiello returned to Naples to face stormy political times there. He was followed at St. Petersburg by the Italian composer who endured 18 Russian winters, more than any predecessor: Giuseppe Sarti (1729-1802). Of his several operas , two were written to Russian texts, the last (*The Early Reign of Oleg*, 1790) to a libretto by the Empress herself. The Spanish composer Vicente Martin y Soler (1754-1806) came to St. Petersburg in 1788 under Sarti's directorship to supervise the local production of his opera *Una cosa rara* following its Vienna premiere. It was given in a Russian translation, itself a "*cosa rara*" in those days. Martin stayed on for several more years and, after a period spent in London, returned to Russia in 1796. He died in St. Petersburg ten years later.

It was a curious stroke of history that placed Sarti and Martin in Russia at the same time. Both were respectable composers in their own right, and yet true immortality came to them only through Mozart's decision to quote from their operas (*Fra i due litiganti* and *Una cosa rara*) in the banquet scene of *Don Giovanni* (1787). They were still in Russia on December 5, 1791, when Mozart died.

The death of an impecunious musician without impressive credentials at the Viennese court was not likely to cause immediate reverberations in the high circles of St. Petersburg. But the rumor mills of Vienna soon began to circulate the legend that Mozart was poisoned by his envious rival, the court composer Antonio Salieri. Curiously, it was in Russia that this unsubstantiated myth surrounding Mozart's death gained literary respectability. And it was due to Alexander Pushkin, the great poet and playwright and an essential factor in Russian opera.

In 1830, five years after Salieri's death, Pushkin wrote three short plays dealing with the psychological causes of three of the original sins: greed, envy, and lust. Taking the legend of Mozart's poisoning quite seriously in his two-character play *Mozart and Salieri*, Pushkin created an insightful study of the conflict between genius and mediocrity. He packed a wealth of accurate historical detail into Salieri's opening monologue:

> I was happy, and enjoyed in peace
> My labors, my success, my fame — no less
> The labors and successes of my friends,
> My fellow workers in the art divine.
> No! Never did I know the sting of envy,
> Oh, never! — neither when Piccini triumphed
> In capturing the ears of the skittish Paris,
> Nor the first time there broke upon my sense

Iphigenia's opening harmonies.....
But now — myself I say it — now
I do know envy! Yes, Salieri envies,
Deeply in anguish envies. O ye Heavens!
Where, where is justice, when the sacred gift,
When deathless genius comes not to reward
Perfervid love and utter self-denial,
And toils and strivings, and beseeching prayers,
But puts her halo round a lack-wit's skull,
A frivolous idler's brow?... O Mozart, Mozart!

In the play, Mozart unsuspectingly drinks Salieri's poisoned refreshment, after casually assuring the older man (whom he seriously regards as his equal) that villainy and genius cannot be combined in the same person. As Mozart, feeling ill, departs, Salieri begins to torment himself: "Was he really right? Am I no genius?"

Rimsky-Korsakov turned Pushkin's *Mozart and Salieri* into a one-act opera in 1898 without any alteration of Pushkin's text. The resulting style of melodic recitative, though far from unique in Russian opera, failed to please the public and, to this day, the work is rarely given. The reaction of Feodor Chaliapin, the first Salieri, however, is worth noting: "It is works like these that bring new life and meaning into opera...I remain convinced that this is a new form of art which successfully unites music with psychological drama."

* * *

Sarti was still Catherine's principal court composer during the three-year (1788-1791) visit of Domenico Cimarosa, who wrote two operas and a number of festive cantatas for the Russian court before departing. On his homeward journey, he reached Vienna in early 1792, shortly after Mozart's death. Preceded by his fame and Russian successes, he was instantly rewarded by an imperial commission for a new opera. That turned out to be *Il matrimonio segreto*, the only opera in history to have its first and second performances fall on the same evening, February 7, 1792. Emperor Leopold II was so pleased with the first that he commanded an encore, after treating the composer and the entire cast to supper. He needed to relax: the news from France about the imprisonment of his sister, Marie Antoinette, and her husband, Louis XVI, were alarming. Leopold died barely three weeks later; he was spared the knowledge of the royal couple's tragic end, but Cimarosa's

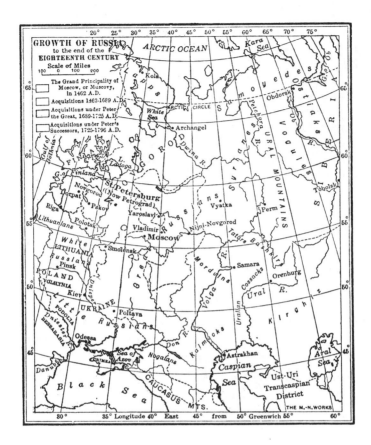

hopes of parlaying instant success into a lasting Viennese court position died
with him. He returned to Naples and eventual imprisonment for his political
views.

In the Russia Cimarosa left behind, Italian musical culture continued to
flourish, but native composers also began to assert themselves. Two of them,
Evstigney Fomin (1761-1800) and Vasily Paskevich (c. 1742-1797) enjoyed
the rare honor of having Catherine the Great as their librettist-collaborator.

The literary activities of this remarkable woman were not limited to opera
librettos. She wrote poems, memoirs, the extensive *Notes on Russian History*,
and corresponded with the greatest French *philosophes* of her time: Voltaire,
Diderot, and Grimm. They were all impressed by the brilliance of her mind
and by her ability to sustain discourse on the level of equals. Learning that
Denis Diderot was in straightened financial circumstances, Catherine had
her French emissary purchase the philosopher's library for a substantial sum,

but requested him to remain its "custodian" at a salary of a thousand livres per year for life. These friendships, however, did not interfere with her politics, which remained focused on Russian interests that were frequently at cross purposes with those of France.

This, then, was the world of Catherine's Russia with its French *rococo* currents that Tchaikovsky artfully wove into the fabric of *The Queen of Spades*. But, though the Empress may have approached (though hardly matched) the sexual appetites of France's Louis XV, it is not likely that the intellectual, fair-minded and eminently practical Catherine felt anything but contempt for the thoroughly immoral reign of her French contemporary, with its luxurious entertainments, lavish opera-ballets, splendid hunts, and *"liaisons dangereuses"*.

Opera, naturally, flourished under Louis XV. The Académie Nationale de Musique et Danse, which began with Lully under the Sun King, continued with performances at the Palais Royal until 1763. When that theater was destroyed by fire, it was quickly rebuilt and continued until its second destruction in 1781. The opera ballets of Jean-Philippe Rameau (1683-1764) and his imitators set the pace. Here the nobility often participated by donning pastoral costumes and singing the parts assigned to shepherds and shepherdesses much in the manner of Lisa, Polina, and Tomsky in *The Queen of Spades*. This was music rich in ornamentation but relatively poor in substance and original ideas, thus setting the stage for the evolution of a fresh antidote, the *opéra comique*. Its surge was heralded by an outstanding Italian example, Pergolesi's *La serva padrona*, staged by the *Bouffons Italiens* in 1752. Jean-Jacques Rousseau, who always regarded French music inferior to Italian, quickly created his *Devin du village* on that model and, with its enthusiastic reception, paved the way for a whole range of entertaining light operas by André Danican Philidor (1726-1795), Pierre Alexandre Monsigny (1729-1817), and Belgian-born André Grétry (1742-1813), whose popularity with audiences continued past the dissolute reign of Louis XV well into the years of his ill-fated successor. It was the air from Grétry's 1784 opera *Richard Coeur-de-Lion* that Tchaikovsky borrowed for the Countess in *The Queen of Spades*.

Two generations after the actual events, Adolphe Adam's opéra comique *Le Postillon de Lonjumeau* (1836) captured the operatic milieu of France in the 1770s. The title character is Chapelou, the village postman who is gifted with a phenomenal natural voice. Passing through Lonjumeau one day, on a journey decreed by his Majesty Louis XV, the Marquis de Corcy—director of the court opera—is forced to stop because his carriage has overturned. While musing about the traditional headaches of opera impresarios—such as the difficulty of finding a tenor for Rameau's *Castor et Pollux*—he overhears Chapelou's carefree singing and finds to his astonishment that the young man possesses an effortless high D. After introducing himself (*"Je suis intendant des menus plaisirs de sa majesté Louis Le Quinzième"*), he persuades the nonplussed Chapelou that his voice is worth a fortune and will eventually make him an operatic star. Dazed by prospects of fame and fortune, the young man abandons his home and his new bride to embark on a career. He gets his deserved comeuppance in the Second Act, in which further references are made to contemporaneous operatic performers such as Joseph Legros (1730-1793), a leading tenor in Gluck's operas.

Gluck's arrival in Paris in 1770 soon divided the music-loving French public into two violently opposed factions: the reform-minded followers of Gluck and the partisans of Niccolò Piccinni of Naples, who upheld the traditions of Italian opera. What began as a debate over artistic principles eventually degenerated into senseless excess, involving rude attacks, even duels. By 1781, however, the tempest had subsided. Gluck, the presumed "victor", grew tired of it all and returned to Vienna, where he died in 1787. Piccinni, virtually forgotten, died in Passy, France, in 1800.

That famous debate which divided operatic enthusiasts is elegantly reflected in Richard Strauss's last opera, *Capriccio* (1942). Set in the Paris of 1775, it has for its characters the lovely Countess Madelaine, her debonair brother, the composer Flamand, and the poet Olivier. They converse with great sophistication about the intricate relationship between words and music in opera and the relative virtues of Gluck's reforms and Italian traditions. The cast is completed by the practical stage director La Roche (in whom Strauss and librettist Clemens Krauss envisioned an 18th-century Max Reinhardt) and the glamorous actress Clairon, modeled on Mlle. Hyppolite, an 18th-century member of the Comédie Française. The literate but extremely wordy libretto (the opera is called "a conversation piece for music in one act") incorporates, without attribution, Charles de Saint-Evremond's 17th-century definition of opera as "a bizarre affair made up of poetry and music, in which the poet and the musician, each equally obstructed by the other, give themselves no end of trouble to produce a wretched book." Throughout, the conversation flows on an elevated plane, with informed references to Voltaire, Rameau, and Gluck.

It was the Age of Enlightenment, the age that challenged religion and showed concern for the lower classes — an age of ferment. While its currents did not erupt into revolutionary action until the closing decade of the eighteenth century, several countries began experiencing political unrest. Russia's Catherine, an avid reader of Voltaire and Montesquieu, appointed a commission to study the emancipation of the serfs. Her enlightened instincts, however, were soon stifled by the powerful nobles on whom imperial power depended, and who were unwilling to accept diminished control of their lands and laborers. A rebellion nonetheless erupted in 1772, led by a charismatic Cossack named Emelyan Pugachev, who organized an outlaw army powerful enough to march on Moscow. Eventually his forces had to yield to a superior army; Pugachev was captured and executed. Pushkin immortalized this episode in Russian history, with considerable sympathy toward the rebels, in his 1836 short novel *The Captain's Daughter*.

In foreign matters, too, Catherine the Great displayed a strong hand. In her aim to control the Black Sea, she found herself in a protracted war with Turkey that ended with a most advantageous treaty in 1774, ceding sufficient Turkish territory to Russia to open the Black Sea and the Bosporus to Russian shipping. The successful conclusion of that war, on the other hand, upset Austrian ideals about the balance of power. Frederick the Great, a mastermind from the sidelines, came up with the solution, with defenseless Poland as the victim. The resulting partition of Poland allowed Russia certain territorial gains unobjectionable to Austria, with the latter — and Frederick's Prussia — participating in the spoils. Poland, ruled at that time (1764-1795) by Stanislaw Poniatowski, Catherine's erstwhile lover, lost about one-third of her territory and about one-half of her population. Subsequent partitions in 1793 and 1795 led to the abolishment of Polish independence. It took more than a century, at the end of World War I, for Poland to reemerge as an independent nation.

Pugachev's rebellion left its impact on Catherine, and the news coming from the France she so admired terrified her. Like Austria's Joseph II, whom she had met personally in 1781, the Empress had no fondness for idle aristocracy, but she viewed the growing French encroachment on royal privileges with alarm. In 1789, the year the National Assembly was formed and the Bastille stormed, Catherine authorized a ban on the writings of her once idolized Voltaire. She broke all relations with France in 1793 when the royal pair was guillotined. Death came to her not soon thereafter, on November 17, 1796, of a ruptured artery in the brain. In the estimate of the English historian G.P. Gooch, "she was the only woman ruler who has surpassed England's

Elizabeth in ability, and equaled her in the enduring significance of her work."

XXVII

THE FRENCH REVOLUTION

Andrea Chénier (Giordano); *Dialogues des Carmelites*
(Poulenc); *Thérèse* (Massenet); *Lodoïska* (Cherubini);
Tarare (Salieri); *Dantons Tod* (von Einem)

Political agitation against the established regimes of Europe was widespread during the last two decades of the eighteenth century. France was only one of the countries facing political unrest, but nowhere did political and economic crises erupt with the drama, violence, and far-reaching effect than it did in the French Revolution of 1789.

Reasons for the Revolution were ample. France was a country ineptly administered by a government mired in a deficit it could not control; excessive taxation placed undue burdens on the peasantry, and the nobility carried on with sometimes insufferable arrogance. The bitterness of the lower classes was shared by the urban bourgeoisie—a middle class increasingly familiar with the writings of Rousseau and other writers of the Enlightenment that attacked inequality and dared to challenge the theretofore inviolable institutions of Church and Monarchy. Representatives of the "Third Estate"— lawyers, writers, municipal employees, merchants, who belonged neither to the clergy nor to the nobility—demanded equal voice in running the country. Even the king, the well-meaning Louis XVI, agreed in principle that reforms were needed and that France should be ruled by some form of constitutional monarchy. In June 1789, largely moved by a pamphlet called "What is the Third Estate?" by the Abbé Siéyès, representatives of this group established the Constituent Assembly with the purpose of drafting a written constitution. Honoré Riqueti de Mirabeau, a nobleman from Provence, distinguished himself as the Assembly's principal spokesman.

Conditions in the country, however, remained chaotic. There were widespread food shortages, and troop concentrations in and near Paris fueled rumors of repressive action against the people. On July 14, 1789, the Bastille, an old fortress-prison, was stormed by a mob that easily overpowered its defenders and freed the fort's relatively few inmates. Several officials held

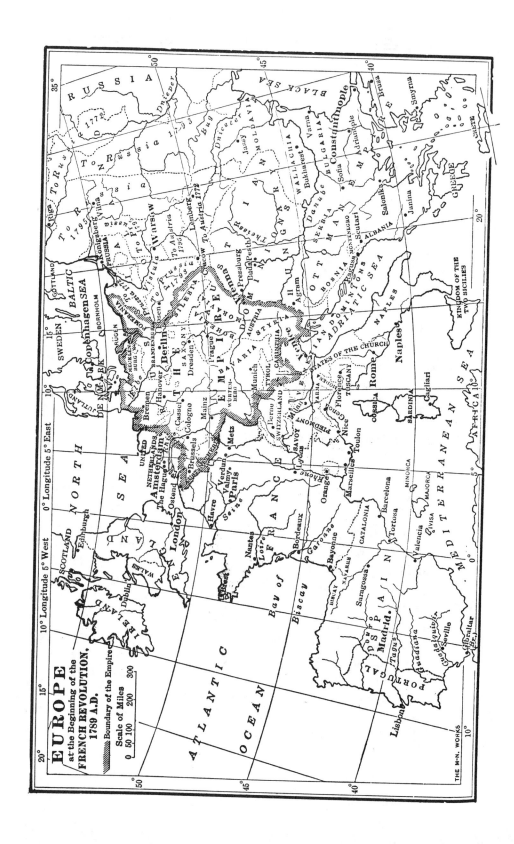

EUROPE
at the Beginning of the
FRENCH REVOLUTION,
1789 A.D.

Boundary of the Empire

Scale of Miles
0 50 100 200 300

THE M·N· WORKS

responsible for the food shortages were murdered, and insurrection quickly spread to various regions of France. To restore order, a National Guard
was formed under the command of the Marquis de Lafayette, whose earlier
American experience had not prepared him for this kind of mob violence.
The fall of the Bastille, in itself, was of small import, but it was to become a
symbol of the Revolution. The tricolor, combining blue and red, the colors
of Paris, with white, the color of France, was another. People sensed the
beginning of a new era, which was indeed the case, but it was also the beginning of tragic things to come. Several aristocrats, including the Count of Artois, the king's brother, left the country. On August 27, the "Declaration of
the Rights of Man", a bill of rights based on English and American principles,
was enacted. A few weeks later, on October 6, an armed band of
revolutionaries forced the royal pair to leave Versailles and settle in the
Tuileries Palace. With royal veto powers curtailed, the king became a virtual
hostage of the Constituent Assembly.

Beaumarchais, that cautious revolutionary whose *Le mariage de Figaro*
had sounded the first warning signal for the *ancien régime,* watched the rising
flames at the storming of the Bastille from his window on the Faubourg Saint-
Antoine with a mixture of satisfaction and alarm. Long an admirer of the
American Revolution, he had hoped that France, too, would see the emergence of an era where freedom and equal justice would prevail. But the sight
of wild mobs carrying the heads of aristocrats on bloody spikes repelled and
frightened him. Not long before, on June 8, 1787, an opera of his—*Tarare*,
with music by Antonio Salieri, a court composer in Vienna—was launched
in Paris with great success. In many ways, it could be regarded as a revolutionary work, but in Beaumarchais's civilized and philosophical manner.
Tarare is an honest, talented commoner living in an imaginary oriental
kingdom ruled by a despot named Atar. Surmounting enormous obstacles,
not the least of which is the stupidity of the king, Tarare nevertheless triumphs and reaches the pinnacle of honor and fame through his own merit.
The opera's naive philosophy embodied the hopes of reasonable Frenchmen
that a bright new era was dawning. When, after the bloody fall of 1789, a relative calm set in, the management of the Opéra decided to revive *Tarare*. The
ever-enterprising Beaumarchais made a few quick changes to assure the
work's political correctness. This new version, introduced on August 3, 1790,
ended with Tarare crowned king and enjoying roughly the same powers—
and limitations—that the Constituent Assembly granted Louis XVI.

Writing contemporaneously, Beaumarchais and Salieri had to resort to a safe oriental allegory, but the ominous events of 1789 were faithfully recorded in two later operas — *Dialogues des Carmelites* (1957) by Francis Poulenc and *Andrea Chénier* (1896) by Umberto Giordano. In the first scene of the Poulenc opera (which is a nearly verbatim setting of a play by Georges Bernanos) the Chevalier de la Force tells his father, the Marquis, about a demonstration by an angry mob before their palace, surrounding and threatening the carriage of his sister, Blanche. Frightened by the experience, Blanche decides to retire from such a cruel world and seek peace in a convent. Several weeks later (in the opera's second scene), Blanche is admitted to the Carmelite Convent in Compiègne by a mortally ill Mother Superior. Before dying in the opera's first act, the Mother Superior is tormented by a vision of their convent being desecrated. Bernanos, whose play was an adaptation of a German novel based on the memoirs of a sole survivor, places the events in April-May, 1789.

During this period the eminent French poet André Chénier, following in his father's footsteps, served his country in the diplomatic service. Born in Constantinople in 1762, where his father served at the time, he absorbed a profound love of Hellenic culture through the influence of his Greek-born mother. After spending much of his adolescence traveling and enriching his own lyric poetry with translations from the classics, he spent the years 1787 to 1789 as secretary at the French Embassy in London. Meanwhile, his younger brother Marie-Joseph, a talented poet in his own right, achieved some fame with his revolutionary writings, particularly with the play *Charles IX*.

On his return from abroad in the summer of 1790, André Chénier, in sympathy with the aims of the Revolution from his early youth, instantly committed his pen to the cause, but his belief in individual liberty rejected the extreme manifestations he came to witness.

While Luigi Illica's libretto to Giordano's *Andrea Chénier* is largely fictional, the text is rich in carefully observed period detail. When the gossipy Abbé arrives at the Coigny Estate in Act I and makes a casual reference to the Third Estate, followed by the mention of Necker, the unpopular finance minister, he evokes a derisive reaction from the aristocratic guests. Later they are outraged by Chénier's famous *Improvviso* aria, which gives poetic expression, very much in character, to his ardent patriotism, as well as his sympathy for the downtrodden. The sudden intrusion of the mob — interrupting the courtly dances typical of the *ancien régime* — is also more than an inspired theatrical touch, and the Countess's observation that their rebellious servant,

Carlo Gérard, was a man "ruined by all that reading" (*"L'ha rovinato il leg-gere"*) conjures up the spirit of Rousseau.

The real André Chénier, for all his fiery writings, remained a man of reason and a believer in the rights of the individual. As the various extremist clubs vied with one another in demagoguery, they became targets of Chénier's angry polemics. In his odes, which he called *Iambes*, remaining true to his classic learning, he attacked Marat, Desmoulins, even Robespierre – the emerging leader of the powerful Jacobins – and cast his lot with the Feuillants, a dissident group formed on July 15, 1791. With Talleyrand, Siéyès, and Lafayette among its members, this group was dedicated to constitutional government and to the saving of the monarchy.

André Chénier was, unquestionably, France's greatest poet in 1791. Who was the greatest composer? There were several who could have claimed that distinction and opera, particularly, could provide a natural outlet for the revolutionary fervor that held the country in its grip. In fact, operatic activities proved an extension of giant open-air pageants in celebration of holidays and patriotic events resounding with the stirring strains of the new revolutionary anthem *La Marseillaise* by soldier-composer Rouget de Lisle (1760-1836) and many others like it. There were two opera houses, the Théâtre Favart and the Théâtre Feydeau, eagerly awaiting new creations by French composers, old and new, all seemingly galvanized by the general excitement: Grétry, Gossec, Dalayrac, LeSueur and, above all, that thoroughly Gallicized Italian, Luigi Cherubini (1760-1842). Whether the omnipresent revolutionary zeal was induced by genuine enthusiasm or dictated by fear, these operas often turned into monster events with giant orchestras and massed choruses.

Of the many operas enjoying momentary success on their way to (probably deserved) oblivion, two rate honorable mention. One of them was *Guillaume Tell* by Grétry, intoduced on April 9, 1791, the year before Rossini was born and thirteen years before Schiller wrote his classic play. Essentially a composer of opéra comique, Grétry lacked the dramatic power needed for the massed scenes of Swiss revolutionary action, but he did produce a number of passionate and exciting episodes to enlist the sympathy of revolutionary Paris. More significant in every respect was *Lodoïska* by Luigi Cherubini, which was introduced at the Théâtre Feydeau on July 18, 1791, just about the time when André Chénier decided to cast his lot with the Feuillants.

Lodoïska was an early example of the so-called "rescue operas" in which heroes and heroines in dire predicament are dramatically saved through some benevolent turn of fate. The opera takes place in Poland, a country cruelly divided by several major European powers.[*] France took no part in that shameful action and, understandably, the French public evidenced great sympathy for Poland's plight. To abbreviate *Lodoïska*'s rather complicated plot, the eponymous heroine is rescued by her lover Floreski from captivity by Floreski's political enemy, the sinister Baron Dourlinski. The resemblance between this and the most celebrated of all "rescue operas", Beethoven's *Fidelio*, is obvious if we regard the principal characters: Lodoïska (Leonore), Floreski (Florestan), and Dourlinski (Pizarro), though in Cherubini's opera there is also a comic character, Floreski's servant Varbel, who is a clear descendant of Mozart's Leporello. It should be added, at the risk of anticipating historical chronology, that these stock "rescue" characters did not pass directly from Cherubini to Beethoven. We meet them in Pierre Gaveaux's *Lenore ou l'amour conjugal* (1798) and in Ferdinando Paër's *Leonora* (1804), both operas set in Spain. There is, however, a substantial difference between these works. In all likelihood, Cherubini set his *Lodoïska* to a fictional libretto, while Gaveaux based his opera on a libretto by J.N. Bouilly, eyewitness to an actual event in Tours during the Reign of Terror. In turning his experience into an opera libretto, Bouilly thought it wise to transfer the story to 16th-century Spain for fear of antagonizing the French authorities.

During those tense and fearful times, the amiable plots of the early *opéra comique* gave way to stories where political agitation, inflamed passions, and persecutions became paramount. But in these "rescue operas" (as Winton Dean observed in his essay *Opera under the French Revolution*) "crude political propaganda [has been] replaced by a glorification of the human spirit, especially when fired by some ennobling ideal. This was the wider message of the Revolution that inspired the whole Romantic age." *Lodoïska*, probably the best example of this ideal, was given two hundred times in 1791, an unprecedented event in the history of opera.

In the midst of these theatrical events—specifically between the premieres of Grétry's *Guillaume Tell* and Cherubini's *Lodoïska*—on June 20, 1791, seeing his hopes for a constitutional monarchy fatally endangered, Louis XVI decided to leave the country to seek help from abroad. The royal pair was apprehended at Varennes, near the eastern border, and returned to Paris, now prisoners of the Revolution. A new constitution was signed by

*   See page 258.

the king—who had no other options—and a new Legislative Assembly was convoked on October 1 with the participation of various parties: constitutionalists, royalists, Jacobins, and Girondists—a new group so named because several of its leaders came from the region of the Gironde. The new Assembly was faced with a political crisis: France's position was threatened by a coalition between the new Habsburg Emperor Leopold II (Marie Antoinette's brother) and the King of Prussia, both concerned with the plight of Louis XVI and responsive to the stirring of a growing number of French émigrés.

It was in this period that the unfortunate André Chénier chose to deliver a number of fiery attacks on the Jacobins, predicting that their activities, if unchecked, would bring about the destruction of France's legitimate government. (The poet's crucial activities during the years 1792-93 are not chronicled in Giordano's opera.) A further unfortunate twist was that André's attacks were publicly refuted by his younger brother Marie-Joseph Chénier, a committed Jacobin. Undeterred, on April 15, in the *Journal de Paris,* André Chénier delivered a sardonic attack on Robespierre, singling out the Jacobin leader by name.

Five days later, France's Legislative Assembly declared war on Austria, now ruled by Leopold's son, Francis II. It began with several French defeats, for the French army, having lost many of its officers to emigration, was inadequately led. In an ill-advised move, the Austrians issued a manifesto on August 3 ordering Paris "to submit at once and without delay to the King"—to the discredited king and to his Austrian wife whom the people, incensed by constant revolutionary agitation, deeply distrusted.

The Austrian manifesto produced violent results. Demonstrations erupted on August 10. Boosted by volunteers from Marseilles who brought with them the fiery new song that was already becoming the emblem of the Revolution, the mob attacked the Tuileries and, after bitter fighting with the Swiss Guards—with over a thousand casualties on each side—took the king prisoner. Robespierre immediately called for his dethronement, signaling the end of the French monarchy and the beginning of what history came to call the "Reign of Terror". As anti-royalist demonstrations turned into riots accompanied by atrocities, the Legislative Assembly lost its ability to govern and power was passed to the Paris Commune and to the Jacobin Club. Lafayette, discredited at home for his moderate views, was captured by the Austrians, who—along with their Prussian allies—took several important French towns, while the French revolutionary armies under Charles

Dumouriez managed to score at least one morale-lifting victory at Valmy on September 20.

In Paris, a prominent lawyer named Georges Jacques Danton became Minister of Justice, but he was either unable or unwilling to prevent a series of massacres that cost the lives of some 2000 people—politicians, priests, aristocrats, or plain citizens accused of anti-revolutionary attitudes—all brutally claimed by mob justice. André Chénier, progressively distressed by the directions the Revolution had taken, spent these months hiding in the country. The offices of the *Journal de Paris* were sacked; the names of André Chénier and his fellow poet Roucher appeared on the list of proscribed persons, marked for execution.

A singularly outrageous event during these "September massacres" occurred at the Carmelite Convent of Compiègne, where several bishops and dozens of priests were butchered along with a number of officials of the old régime who had sought escape there from the atrocities of Paris. La Force, a nearby prison, was the site of many such horrors including—according to historian Simon Schama—the killing of dozens of adolescent boys between the ages of twelve and eighteen.

Interestingly enough, the principal character in Georges Bernanos's play on which Francis Poulenc's opera *Dialogues des Carmelites* (1957) is based is named Blanche La Force. Exultant in her faith and fearful of outside dangers, Blanche—a fictitious character—seeks refuge at the Carmelite Convent. In the fourth scene of the opera's Second Act, two businesslike *"commissionaires"* enter and inform the Prioress that, by order of the Legislative Assembly, the Carmelite Order is dissolved and all nuns are to evacuate the premises by October 1 (1792). When the Prioress expresses her outrage, one of the commissionaires replies, "I have no choice but to howl with the wolves." The opera then telescopes the tragic fate of its participants. In Act III, the frightened Blanche escapes from the convent. She finds her father's estate in ruins and learns that he has been guillotined. During her absence from the convent, all the Carmelite nuns have been arrested (with the exception of Mother Marie, the sole survivor) and, in the third scene of the act in the Conciergerie, a death sentence is pronounced on all of them for "openly seditious" activities and "treacherous plots". In the final scene, joined by the returning Blanche, they all go to their death singing, initially, the *Salve Regina,* with the chorus going weaker with each deadly crush of the blade. Blanche briefly adds her own voice to the words of *"Veni Creator"* until she, too, is silenced. The dramatic effect is overwhelming. Like Giordano's

Andrea Chénier, the Poulenc opera embraces the entire span of the Revolution. The execution of the Carmelite nuns — an historical fact — took place on July 17, 1794, a few days before the fall of Robespierre and the end of the Terror.

The massacres of September 1792 caused a sharp division among the various revolutionary groups. The Girondins, who abhorred anarchy, deplored them, while Robespierre and the Jacobins regarded them as necessary steps for the Revolution to purge itself from its enemies. The same division separated the groups over the fate of the captive Louis XVI. Robespierre and Saint-Just contended that a trial itself was unnecessary: to be a king was crime enough. Their position was strengthened when an iron chest was found containing proof of the king's communications with the Austrians. In any case, the king was brought before the National Convention (convoked on September 22, 1792, simultaneously with the declaration of the French Republic). The Convention acted swiftly, and the hapless king's death sentence was carried out on January 21, 1793. Of the Convention's 721 members, 683 found him guilty, but only 361, the exact majority, asked for the death penalty, among them the Duc d'Orléans, a royal relative also known as "Philippe Égalité" for his republican sympathies. The fateful decision forever separated the "regicides" from the minority, whose members thereafter bore the burden of suspicion. None lived more dangerously than the aging lawyer Malesherbes, who had undertaken the king's defense. (He paid for it with his life a year later.) Surviving documents have proved that André Chénier had assisted Malesherbes in the defense and, still a believer in constitutional monarchy, even published several articles favorable to the king.

The fearful times of 1792 and 1793 are reflected in *La Caverne*, a gruesome opera by Jean-François LeSueur, which was introduced on February 23, 1793, with tremendous success and given a hundred times all over France in a little over a year. An opera written in a calmer age, Massenet's *Thérèse* (1907), faithfully captures the bloody events of this period. The first act is set in October 1792, during the early days of the Austrian War, with the Girondins still in a position of power. André Thorel and his wife Thérèse offer shelter to the exiled Marquis Armand de Clerval, Thérèse's erstwhile lover and André's childhood friend. They do this despite their clear political differences and despite André's lingering jealousy. The second act takes place eight months later. During that period, the king has been executed, the war has taken an unfavorable turn, and the Girondists have become involved in a deadly struggle for survival. Risking his own life, the noble-hearted André manages to help his aristocratic friend escape by way of a safe-conduct intended for himself. When André is arrested and is carried away toward imprisonment and certain death, the desperate Thérèse defiantly cries out, *"Vive le roi!"*, thereby sealing her own fate as the curtain falls. (This fictitious but historically faithful episode may have been inspired by the fate of the prominent Girondist leader Camille Desmoulins and his wife Lucile, who were united in death in April 1794.)[*]

Weighty events indeed occurred during the eight-month period that separates the first and second acts of Massenet's *Thérèse*. Reacting to the execution of Louis XVI, England, Holland, and Spain formed a coalition against France. After a series of military reverses in March 1793, the French General Dumouriez surrendered to the Austrians, taking along several high officials, among them the Duc de Chartres, son of Philippe Égalité. A few weeks later, dictatorial powers were concentrated on the newly formed Committees of General Security and Public Safety. Robespierre, heading the most uncompromising wing of the Jacobins (called "The Mountain" because its members sat on top rows) gained ever rising importance. Along with these newly formed Committees, a Revolutionary Tribunal was established, charged with the persecution of suspects. A new and powerful pressure group arose: the *"sans-culottes"*, citizens of the lower classes, who were hardest hit by France's economic woes caused by the war. Demanding equal rights with the more privileged classes, they forced the Convention to order the arrest of 29 of its own Girondist members.

In the second act of Giordano's *Andrea Chénier*, set in June 1794, a crowd gathers near the Pérronnet Bridge and enthusiastically calls out the names of the revolutionary heroes conveniently parading before it: "Robespierre, Barère, Collot d'Herbois, Saint-Just... David... Barras... Fouché." The *sans-culotte* Mathieu lights a lamp on a monument to Marat and sings the revolutionary song *"Carmagnole"*, while Chénier has his brief meeting with Madelaine de Coigny. He fights and wounds his operatic rival Gérard and manages to escape while the crowd shouts "Death to the Girondins!"

Librettist Illica offers here an ingenious combination of historical fact and inventive fiction. The various leaders hailed by the crowd were all powerful individuals, to varying degrees responsible for the horrors, and David was

---

[*]   See page 296.

the famous painter whose works captured many highlights of the Revolution for posterity. Whether they ever marched in the same procession is debatable and, in any case, Illica's chronology was faulty. By June 1794, the real André Chénier was a captive at St. Lazare prison after being arrested on March 7 during a random search. While the arrest itself may have been accidental, Chénier had already placed himself in deadly danger with his poems and political pamphlets. In one of his *Iambes*, he celebrated the valor of Charlotte Corday, killer of the rabid demagogue Marat, and more than once invoked the names of Robespierre and Danton with biting irony. Before his arrest, Chénier could still witness — albeit from his hiding place — the execution of Marie Antoinette on October 16, 1793, also that of the "regicide" Philippe Égalité and dozens of Girondist leaders. He could also derive a patriot's satisfaction from the victory of the French forces over the British at Toulon (December 15, 1793), a battle in which a young artillery officer named Napoleon Bonaparte first distinguished himself.

In the spring of 1794, soon after Chénier's capture, Robespierre, heading the Committee of Public Safety, proceeded to crush his rivals for power, one by one. After the destruction of the Girondins, his first victims were the followers of Hébert, an inflammatory orator of the Marat stripe, who attacked even Robespierre for not carrying out the aims of the Revolution vigorously enough. He and his fellow "ultras", as they were called, were guillotined on March 24. Next to fall was Georges Danton (April 6, 1794), a spellbinding speaker, unlike Robespierre, who wrote well but spoke without charisma. In the early months of the Terror, Danton — somewhat opportunistically — had allied himself with Robespierre to hasten the downfall of the Gironde. But eventually he grew tired and disgusted with the endless massacres and, allied with Camille Desmoulins (a former schoolmate of Robespierre), advocated a moderate course, wishing for the killings to stop and the good work of the Revolution to begin. Robespierre, however, would not tolerate any break in the revolutionary ranks. Besides, Danton's resounding voice and fiery rhetoric aroused his jealousy.

Danton's final days are compellingly captured in *Dantons Tod*, a play by Georg Büchner, written in 1835, a mere 41 years after the event, on which Gottfried von Einem's 1947 opera is based. Faithful to the play's outline but heavily condensing its action, the opera shows Danton as a believer in the immutability of history, a philosophy the tragically short-lived Büchner (1813-1837) himself adhered to. His Danton is a passive figure swept along by the currents of history. Deeply disillusioned by the bloodthirsty excesses of the Revolution, he looks forward stoically to death's inevitability. Büchner portrays the two leaders of the Revolution in long monologues that are unavoidably curtailed in the opera. For Robespierre, a cool, incorruptible, and uncompromising intellectual, Terror represents the "arm" of the Revolution, while Virtue is its strength. The two are inseparable. Without Terror, Virtue is powerless; all excesses are justified as long as Terror's swords are wielded by "heroes who fight for freedom." To Danton, Robespierre seems "disgustingly virtuous.... I'd be ashamed to walk around between heaven and earth for thirty years with that moral expression on my face and only for the miserable pleasure of finding others worse than myself" (Act I Scene 6). It is after this scene — considerably shortened in von Einem's opera, that Robespierre and his faithful ally Saint-Just decide that Danton must die.

So much for Büchner's remarkable play and its respectful operatic condensation by Gottfried von Einem. The real Danton went to his death on April 6, 1794 after vigorously but vainly defending his cause before the Revolutionary Tribunal, the institution whose principal architect he had been. He was accompanied to the guillotine by Camille Desmoulins and Hérault de Sechelles. Both the play and the opera end with Lucile Desmoulins's desperately suicidal cry *"Vive le roi,"* possibly a true historical gesture that clearly left its mark on Massenet's *Thérèse.* [*]

Soon after disposing of his greatest rival, Robespierre put through the Convention an edict permitting the worship of an impersonal Supreme Being, who was then honored by a three-day-long *Fête de l'Etre Suprème* (June 6-7-8) in the Tuileries. An interesting by-product of this edict was a document signed by all the important composers of the day — Gossec, Méhul, Berton, Cherubini, and Dalayrac — in which they offered their services, pointing out the importance of music to the people. It is a miracle that all these composers managed to survive. Less fortunate was the famous scientist Antoine Lavoisier, who was arrested in his laboratory and executed on May 8, 1794. Another sequel to the three-day *Fête* in June was the solemn chanting of a "Hymn to the Eternal Being" by Marie-Joseph Chénier (composed, in all likelihood, by a committee of professors) by twenty-four hundred singers to the accompaniment of a huge orchestra with cannons. Grétry was heard to remark that the occasion seemed like a reenactment of the demolition of the Bastille.

---

[*]   See page 294.

Marie-Joseph Chénier, still a Jacobin with a strong instinct for survival, enjoyed recognition but not enough influence to help his brother, André, who was writing some of his most enduring poetry in his prison cell. There he met Aimée de Coigny, arrested with her current lover, Le Comte de Montrond. She was to be immortalized as the fictional "Maddalena" in Giordano's opera, linked to the poet in a touching romance that was mere operatic invention. Just the same, *La Jeune Captive*, perhaps Chénier's most celebrated poem, was inspired by the real Aimée.

On June 10, the Revolutionary Tribunal was granted the power to deliver sentences without examining evidence. This, of course, resulted in a substantial increase in executions — more than 300 within a month, including the sixteen Carmelite nuns guillotined on July 17 at the Place du Trône.* Thus empowered, the Tribunal was asked to consider a totally unfounded "prison plot conspiracy" involving eighty prisoners at Saint Lazare. Following a general act of accusation drawn up by the notorious prosecutor Fouquier-Tinville, on the afternoon of July 23 two enormous tumbrils transferred twenty-five of the accused prisoners to the Conciergerie for the first trial. Only one of them, a young Duchess, was spared. Unbeknown to André Chénier, who was scheduled for the next deadly ride, his father Louis and his brother Marie-Joseph desperately tried to obtain his release. Whether as a result of the prevailing chaotic conditions or the work of André's enemies, these efforts failed. On his last night of imprisonment, after watching the two tumbrils roll away, he sat down to write his last poem. "*Comme un dernier rayon, comme un dernier zéphyre,*" reads the opening line as the poet contemplates the last ray of the sun and the last gentle breeze at the end of a beautiful day, while he sounds his lyre at the foot of the scaffold, awaiting his turn. This is the poem Luigi Illica skilfully condensed and transmuted into the operatic Andrea's poetic farewell to life, the aria "*Come un bel dì di maggio.*"

On the afternoon of July 24, André Chénier, his poet friend Joseph Roucher, and twenty-four other prisoners mounted the waiting tumbrils and were taken to the Conciergerie, with jeering multitudes following them on their fateful journey. There, the greatest French poet of his time spent his last night on earth. His "trial", as well as that of the other defendants, was a mechanical affair conducted with cold efficiency by Fouquier-Tinville. Sweeping accusations — complicity in the alleged "prison plot", unfounded

---

*   See page 293.

Placido Domingo as *Andrea Chénier* (Giordano)
CREDIT: Winnie Klotz/The Metropolitan Opera

linkage with the disgraced General Dumouriez—were presented and verified by corrupt witnesses. The public booed, cheered, applauded in an atmosphere fairly accurately captured in the third act of Giordano's opera. It is doubtful that the real Chénier was allowed the kind of eloquent self-defense and passionate assertion of patriotism Illica granted his operatic namesake in the aria "*Sì, fui soldato*". Nor was there a Carlo Gérard to voice his profound disillusion with the way the ideals of the Revolution had turned into senseless bloodbaths and to take up the poet's cause in a brief, impassioned confrontation with the unbending Fouquier-Tinville.

André Chénier, Roucher, and twenty-five men and women were executed shortly after four o'clock on Friday, July 25 at the Place du Trône, now called Place de la Nation. His father and brother learned of his death only the next day when the list of the victims was made public. His body was thrown into a common grave containing the remains of 1199 men and 197 women, all of whom perished between June 14 and July 27, 1794. Aimée de Coigny was not among them. Released from prison, presumably through bribery, she later remarried, lived a full life linked to various lovers, and died in 1821 at the age of fifty-one. André Chénier may have been one of the few men in her life with whom acquaintance did not grow into a liaison.

Aside from Joseph Roucher—fellow poet and martyr—the opera *Andrea Chénier* features only one historical personality: the prosecutor Fouquier-Tinville, who appears briefly and performs like an automaton in the service of his masters. He served the Revolution with a dispassionate efficiency exhibited in modern times by the likes of Adolf Eichmann. When his turn came to be guillotined in May 1795, he died protesting his innocence: he was merely obeying orders, doing his duty. And what about Gérard, the opera's noble "villain"? History offers no examples of domestic servants becoming leaders of the Revolution. These were lawyers, politicians, scholars, actors—even aristocrats. Yet there was certainly a great deal of Danton's character in this complex operatic figure: ambitious for power yet disillusioned by the bloody role he was forced to play. "*Ho mutato padrone,*" he exclaims in the third act... "I am now an obedient servant of violent passion! Worse, I kill and tremble and as I kill, I weep."

Had Chénier survived three more days, he would have escaped the guillotine. A palace revolution within the Convention brought the accusation of tyranny against Robespierre. His enemies, forming a solid block, declared him an outlaw and arrested him on July 27 in a stormy session during which Robespierre either attempted suicide or was shot in the jaw by a zealous opponent. The following day Robespierre and more than a dozen of his closest allies, Saint-Just included, were executed. The untamed monster devoured the last of its own children, and the Reign of Terror was over. Shortly thereafter, the Convention abolished the Revolutionary Tribunal and closed the Jacobin Club.

On September 11, 1794, Marie-Joseph Chénier's tragedy *Timoléon* was introduced at the Comédie Française with incidental music by Méhul, and Cherubini's new opera *Élisa* was unveiled at the Théâtre Feydeau on December 13. Life went on for the citizens of Paris, but chaotic conditions prevailed everywhere, with a harsh winter and starvation in some of the towns. Nor did the bloodshed stop: brutal reckoning claimed the lives of those implicated in previous terrorist activities and Jacobin associations, including the unlamented Fouquier-Tinville (May 8, 1795).

Some of the émigrés returned amidst talk of re-establishing the monarchy, but this was short-lived; France was to remain a republic. Relative normalcy eventually returned. The cult of the "Supreme Being" was abolished and people could practice their religion. Even elaborate fashions were allowed without the anti-aristocratic prejudices earlier attached to them. Miraculously, the French army was able to sustain itself in these trying times against its enemies, thus contributing to the endurance of the republican spirit.

The form of government that was to guide the French Republic for the next four years was the Directory. Under the new Constitution of 1795, legislation was divided between two chambers: the Council of the Elders (250 members) and the Council of the 500. This latter body drew up a list of names out of which the former chose the five directors to govern the five divisions of the newly constituted government. All five original "directors" — Paul Barras and Lazare Carnot, among them — had voted for the execution of Louis XVI.

On the military front, peace treaties were signed with Prussia, Holland, and Spain, but the war against Austria and England continued. Most of the fighting took place on Italian soil, with victories by Napoleon Bonaparte finally securing the Peace of Campo Formio in October 1797. Two years later, on November 19, 1799, the Directory yielded central authority to the rule of the three Consuls: Jean Cambaceres, Charles Lebrun, and General Bonaparte.

XXVIII

MASKED BALLS AND MUTINIES

Le bal masqué (Auber); *Il Reggente* (Mercadante); *Un ballo in maschera* (Verdi); *Billy Budd* (Britten)

The bloody events of Paris had wide repercussions all over Europe and caused real alarm among its crowned heads. Even such an enlightened ruler as Russia's Catherine the Great turned to repressive measures by increasing censorship and imprisoning or exiling free-thinking speakers and writers. Also, conveniently equating patriotic Polish revolutionaries with "Jacobins", she ordered military action that eventually resulted in the second partition of Poland (1793).* Another monarch, setting aside the egalitarian principles he had upheld in his youth, urged a royalist crusade against France. But his plans did not get very far: he was assassinated on March 16, 1792.

That monarch was Gustavus III of Sweden, a gifted, complex, and controversial man. From his somewhat eccentric and rather despotic German-born mother—Queen Louisa Ulrika, sister of Frederick the Great—Gustavus inherited a love of the arts and patronage of artistic endeavor. She had founded the Drottningholm Court Theater outside Stockholm in 1754. Destroyed by fire, it was rebuilt and enlarged ten years later and exists to this day in a remarkable state of preservation, its original stage machinery virtually intact. As a young prince, Gustavus developed a fondness for the theater. During a brief visit to Paris in 1771, he impressed Rousseau with his intelligence. It was there that he received news of his father's death.

Crowned King at age 25, Gustavus pursued his artistic inclinations by writing plays and even acting in some of them. He also designed scenery and supervised productions in the tiny Drottningholm Theater. More importantly, he founded the Swedish Academy and the first Royal Opera House, which opened on January 18, 1773 with the premiere of *Thetis och Pelée* by the Italian composer Francesco Uttini, who had been engaged earlier as court

---

*   See page 283.

Gustavus III of Sweden
CREDIT: Opera News

musician by Queen Louisa Ulrika. That, incidentally, was the first opera written in the Swedish language. Thus operatic life began in Stockholm, with Gluck's *Orfeo ed Euridice, Iphigénie en Aulide*, and *Alceste* soon following. This, in turn, led to the building of a new and larger opera house on the site of today's imposing structure, which opened on September 30, 1782 with Johann Gottlieb Naumann's *Cora och Alonzo*. The next decade witnessed a virtual golden age for Swedish music, with new productions of operas by Gluck, Naumann, and Joseph Martin Kraus (1756-1792), the German-born successor of Uttini at the court.·

But, as music prospered, the country found itself in financial distress and political turmoil. For all his sympathies with French enlightenment, Gustavus turned against the Revolution after the capture of Louis XVI. He did continue to entertain the vision of social equality but, in so doing, he antagonized the nobles. Convinced that the king was leading the country to ruin, a group of conspirators — among them the Counts Ribbing and Horn — decided to overthrow him. One of the conspirators, Captain Ankarström, harboring a personal grievance, carried the plan a fatal step further and shot Gustavus at a masked ball on March 16, 1792. The scene was the Royal Opera House, the very house the king had founded. The bullet — a combination of lead and carpet tacks — struck Gustavus below the heart; death came to him, after much suffering, only twelve days later. Ankarström was executed in a savage manner after a public flogging, by decapitation, his body quartered. Ribbing and Horn were sent to permanent exile.

Regicides were not common in Europe, and the fate of King Gustavus — to be followed within less than a year by the execution of Louis XVI — deeply affected the ruling houses of Austria, England, and Spain. It took several decades before such matters could be presented to the public in the theater, and it was not surprising that the ever-prolific Eugène Scribe led the way. For Scribe, however, the bare historical facts of the Stockholm event would not do. Disregarding the Swedish king's well-known indifference to the female sex, he invented a love affair between the king and the fictitious Amélie, Madame Ankarström, and made the husband the king's secretary and confidant. The page Oscar, who adores the king and hardly ever leaves his side, was an invention inspired partly by operatic convention (Mozart's Cherubino, perhaps) and partly by Scribe's honoring the historical Gustavus's sexual inclinations. It was Daniel François Auber who first turned the Scribe play into an opera in 1833 (*Gustave III ou Le bal masqué*) after Rossini had turned it down. It received a glittering production, with a particularly dazzling staging of the masked ball, but the critics rightfully pointed out that Auber, whose real strength lay in the field of the *opéra comique*, was out of his element in tackling such a serious historical subject. Nonetheless, *Gustave III* did achieve a total of 169 performances, although those after 1834 were subjected to severe cuts. The *Gazette des théâtres* predicted that historians would look back with great favor on the masked ball scene, but this prediction turned out to be over-optimistic. An interesting detail in Scribe's play, properly highlighting the historical Gustavus's interest in theatrical matters, was the scene where the king addresses the artists—Hamlet-like—who are about to entertain the ball guests. Two survivors of the fatal Stockholm event were still alive at the time of the Auber premiere: Madame Ankarström, who strenuously and understandably objected to the operatic representation of her relationship with the king, and the exiled Count Ribbing, who, by then a resident of Paris, actually acted as Scribe's consultant on such historical details as the playwright chose to retain. Long absent from the operatic repertoire (but one never knows when it may reappear—stranger things have happened...), *Gustave III* is aptly summarized by Julian Budden as "a rather uninteresting museum piece, though one from which Verdi did not scorn to learn."

But before Verdi came Saverio Mercadante and his *Il Reggente*, produced in Turin in 1843. Unlike France's relatively tolerant Louis Philippe, the King of Sardinia did not allow the representation of a regicide on stage. Thus Mercadante's librettist, Salvatore Cammarano, was forced to move the action to 16th-century Scotland, turning Gustavus into the regent Murray and the conspirators into adherents of the imprisoned Mary Stuart. *Il Reggente* was a sombre tragedy without the enlivening light and sardonic touches of Scribe and Auber—elements Verdi was wise enough to retain later.

In 1857, given the lukewarm reception accorded to Mercadante's opera, Verdi did not hesitate to tackle Scribe's plot again, assigning the adaptation to Antonio Somma. Their projected opera, originally titled *Una vendetta in domino*, was intended for the Teatro San Carlo of Naples, next to La Scala Italy's most prestigious theater, but Verdi could not countenance the alterations demanded by the Neapolitan censors. Thus it was in Rome, at the Teatro Apollo, where *Un ballo in maschera* was finally introduced on February 17, 1859. By that time, however, Scribe's original Swedish setting was virtually forgotten. Budden and other Verdi scholars faithfully chronicle the various censor-friendly versions Verdi and Somma had considered—one set in 12th-century Pomerania, another in 14th-century Florence—before settling on the opera's final title with the action set in faraway and semi-exotic Boston. The names of some of the principal characters — Riccardo, Renato, Samuel, and Tom — became unconvincingly "Americanized", Amelia and Oscar were carried over from Scribe, while the sooth-saying Madame Arvidson became Ulrica — with a conscious nod, perhaps, to the historical Gustavus's mother, Queen Louisa Ulrika. Most opera houses nowadays prefer the original Swedish setting, specifically including the Royal Opera of Stockholm, where a recent production attempted to emphasize the king's homosexuality in gesture and action. Verdi's music, particularly the intense love duet with Amelia in the second act, militates against such efforts; this is an instance where searching for historical truth is pointless. On the other hand, producers need not ignore history in allowing Gustavus/Riccardo to die from a pistol shot — Verdi's original hero was stabbed only because the Roman censors would not allow firearms on stage.

* * *

The ruler of the Kingdom of Naples in Verdi's time was Ferdinand II, the grandson of Ferdinand I (1759-1825) who reigned during the tumultuous period of the French Revolution and its aftermath. Still a child when he inherited the throne from his father, Charles III (the founder of the Teatro San Carlo),[*] he married Maria Carolina, one of Maria Theresa's many daughters, in 1768. The king was seventeen then, the new queen 19 months younger. Ferdinand was a native of Naples, a true creature of that fun-loving city: rough in manners, a rather irresponsible lad, fond of hunting and other manly sports. "Ugly, but not absolutely repulsive," was the way his brother-in-law, the visiting Joseph II, described him. Opera did not rank high among his concerns, but the San Carlo flourished: Charles Burney, the music historian who visited Naples as the guest of Sir William Hamilton, the British Ambassador, witnessed performances of Jomelli's *Demoofonte* and Paisiello's *Le trame per amore*.

It has been suggested that the plot of Mozart's *Così fan tutte*, which takes place in Naples, was based on an actual incident as related by the Emperor Joseph to Lorenzo da Ponte. Although definite proof of this is lacking, we can easily imagine that the sophisticated cynicism and moral ambiguities of

---

[*]   See page 256.

that Mozart opera stemmed from the Emperor's impressions in that sunlit, pleasure-loving, and carefree city. Nor is it surprising that the same city in the same period should serve as the background to Rossini's *Il Turco in Italia*, with its flirtatious heroine Fiorilla, her henpecked elderly husband Geronio and gallant "attendant" Narciso. It was a licentious society indeed that Joseph encountered during his brief visit, one in which husbands who claimed exclusive rights to their wives were considered unreasonable. The king had his mistresses and soon Queen Maria Carolina herself was linked in rumors to General Sir John Acton, an expatriate Englishman and minister at the Court.

Goethe quickly fell under the city's intoxicating spell. "Naples is a paradise," he wrote in 1787; "in it every one lives in a sort of intoxicated self-forgetfulness... here one can do nothing but live. You forget about yourself and the world; and to me it is a strange feeling to go about with people who think of nothing but enjoying themselves." Goethe was not impervious to the beauty of Emma Hart, a young British woman with whom Sir William Hamilton consoled himself after his wife died in 1782. "She is an Englishwoman about twenty years old," observed the great poet. "One beholds there, in perfection, in movement, in ravishing variety, all that the greatest artists have rejoiced to be able to produce." In 1791, Emma Hart, a lady of a somewhat checkered past, finally became Lady Hamilton at twenty-six, when Sir William was 61 years old.

It was on this fairly loose and relatively carefree Neapolitan world that the news of the French Revolution descended. The royal pair sought an alliance with England; hence the Hamiltons were favored guests at Court, where Sir John Acton as Prime Minister wielded great power, and the queen honored the beautiful Emma with her friendship. The assassination of King Gustavus of Sweden in March 1792 greatly alarmed Maria Carolina, coming as it did within days of the untimely death of her brother, the Emperor Leopold of Austria. The queen abhorred the French, but Naples was no military power and nothing would have been gained by interrupting the flourishing trade between France and the Neapolitan Kingdom—personal desires notwithstanding. But the situation continued to worsen with the execution of Louis XVI (January 21, 1793). It was deathly fear for the fate of her sister Marie Antoinette that moved the queen to write to Marchese di Gallo, her Austrian emissary, that "I should like this infamous nation to be cut to pieces, annihilated, dishonored, reduced to nothing for at least fifty years." Nonetheless, the Revolution did not lack sympathizers among the intellectuals and lower classes in Naples, soon to be known as "Jacobins". A widespread conspiracy was discovered in 1793 and its leaders were executed.

On September 11, 1793, the *HMS Agamemnon*, commanded by Captain Horatio Nelson, sailed into Naples harbor on a diplomatic mission. His task was to insure the support of King Ferdinand in British operations against the French in the Mediterranean. Specifically, reinforcements were needed for the Port of Toulon, which had been seized by the British some weeks before. Nelson's reception, accompanied by a spectacular eruption of Vesuvius, could hardly have been warmer. As he presented his credentials, the beautiful Emma Hamilton acted as interpreter. Their initial meeting, however, was brief. The captain returned to sea and new battles. It so happened that Toulon remained only briefly in British hands; it was soon reoccupied by the French forces under Napoleon Bonaparte.

The fortunes of war continued to favor the French, while the execution of Marie Antoinette on October 16, 1793, plunged her bereaved sister Maria Carolina into deepest despair. But she was helpless in her fury. In July 1795, Spain (now ruled by Charles IV, Ferdinand's younger brother) concluded a separate peace with France, enabling Bonaparte to begin his Italian conquest. By October, Ferdinand himself was obliged to sign a peace treaty with the conqueror, leaving Naples "nominally neutral but never in our feelings," as Maria Carolina wrote to Emma Hamilton.

Meanwhile, Captain Nelson secured the important Corsican forts of Bastia and Calvi—victories that managed to counter-balance several allied losses to the French on land. At the siege of Calvi, on July 12, 1794, Nelson was wounded in his right eye, an injury that contributed to his loss of sight some years later. His fleet carried out a successful police action in the Mediterranean during these months, with Leghorn as a frequent stop for repair and supplies. It was in that seaport where Nelson also found comfort in his loneliness in the friendly arms of a local opera singer named Adelaide Correglia. More significant was his promotion to Commodore in early 1796, at which time he assumed command of a 74-gun ship, the *Captain*. By that time, with Spain joining England's enemies, the position of the British fleet in the Mediterranean was endangered enough for Nelson to abandon Corsica, the scene of his earlier triumphs. In a bold attack on five Spanish ships, he fought alongside his men with great courage—a heroic act that brought Nelson a promotion to Rear Admiral.

Nelson's personal popularity, however, could not hide the fact that the British Navy was suffering from problems of morale. Sailors had to put up with appalling conditions at wages that had not risen for a century. They demanded more humane conditions, fully aware of more liberal attitudes prevailing in America, and conscious of even more radical changes in France and the insurrectional trends in nearby Ireland. Mutiny first broke out at Spithead, an anchorage for the British Navy near the Isle of Wight in the English Channel near Portsmouth. This event was of moderate impact, referred to by a naval historian as "the first sitdown strike." The strikers demanded and won a slight increase in pay and a guarantee of receiving their pay in full, without the interference of illegal "brokers". Thanks to the intervention of the elderly and highly respected Admiral Lord Howe, discipline was soon restored. Far more serious was the mutiny at the Nore, another naval base, which broke out a month later and which was referred to in naval annals as "the Great Mutiny". This involved violence, pilfering of merchant vessels, and seditious talk. As described by Herman Melville in his novel *Billy Budd, Sailor:* "Reasonable discontent growing out of practical grievances in the fleet had been ignited into irrational combustion as by live cinders blown across the Channel from France in flames." This mutiny had to be suppressed by the execution of the organizers. Admiral Nelson was not directly involved in these actions, but his views on such activities were quite rigid: a firm royalist, to him mutineers were comparable to the French regicides.

In March 1798, after a brief stay in London and Bath, the Admiral set to sea again on board of *HMS Vanguard*, his new 74-gun flagship. He held strategic conferences with other ships under his command, the captains of *Culloden, Theseus, Minotaur, Goliath, Swiftsure, Audacious, Bellerophon, Majestic*, and *Leander*. They were eager to engage the French fleet, looking for a decisive victory. What was the location on those crucial days of *HMS Bellipotent*?

Well, that ship, commanded by Edward Fairfax Vere, was firmly anchored in the Melville novel, the source of Benjamin Britten's opera *Billy Budd*, with libretto by E.M. Forster and Eric Crozier. In the opera, *Bellipotent* was rechristened *HMS Indomitable*, with its principals, the stalwart and tortured Captain, the handsome and ill-fated Billy, and the monstrously evil Claggart left intact, along with the other colorfully etched officers and crew members carried over from the novel.

Billy Budd, the novel's and opera's hero, is a man of incorruptible honesty and a natural peacemaker who brings out the best in his restless and weary shipmates. To Claggart, however — that innately evil 18th-century Iago — he represents a dangerous antipode, a menace that must be destroyed. Falsely accused by Claggart of mutinous activity, Billy lashes out in mute fury and kills his accuser with a single blow. Captain Vere, the only witness, is convinced that Claggart has lied, and he knows that Billy is immensely popular with his shipmates. But he is powerfully reminded of the mutinies at Spithead and the Nore; the danger of such events recurring is an ever-present nightmare to naval commanders. Thus Captain Vere is obliged to enforce discipline even if it takes the deadly toll of human sacrifice. Nor is the example of France ever far from the Captain's mind. Earlier in the opera, recalling the mutiny at the Nore, the Captain exclaims: "Revolution, sedition, the Jacobins, the infamous spirit of France... France who has killed her king and denied her God, France the tyrant who wears the cap of liberty, France who pretends to love mankind and is at war with the world, France the eternal enemy of righteousness. That was the Nore. Ay, we must be vigilant. We must be on our guard."

In the Melville novel, Captain Vere is killed in a naval battle soon after Billy Budd's execution; in the opera, he survives to reminisce as a guilt-ridden old man in the Epilogue.

* * *

In July 1798, after several conferences with his captains, Nelson came to the conclusion that his best chance to engage the French fleet in action lay in Egyptian waters. In a letter dispatched to the Hamiltons in Naples he wrote: "We must have a victory. We shall sail with the first breeze and be assured I will return either crowned with laurel, or covered with cypress."

XXIX

NAPOLEON

Tosca (Puccini); Cherubini; Paisiello; Spontini; *Goya*
(Menotti); *Madame Sans-Gêne* (Giordano); *Germania*
(Franchetti); *War and Peace* (Prokofiev); *L'Aiglon*
(Honegger and Ibert)

As Nelson's fleet was speeding toward a decisive confrontation with the French in the summer of 1798, revolutionary fever held continental Europe in its grip. Inspired by the accomplishments of the French Directory, a number of small republics sprang up, each arising from forces within its own territory, each aiming to overthrow the Old Order. The "Batavian" Republic, recognized by France, neutralized anti-French sentiments in Holland and even posed a certain threat to Britain; its "Helvetian" counterpart organized a series of uprisings in Switzerland under French protection. Italy—still a composite of various duchies and republics and the Papal States, framed by the Kingdom of Sardinia in the north and the Kingdom of Naples in the south—was severely affected. The "Cisalpine" Republic challenged the Austrian rule over Milan, while the "Ligurian" Republic replaced the ancient and aristocratic republic of Genoa, once the domain of the Fieschi and Simone Boccanegra. In early 1798, responding to a street riot that caused the death of a French general, French troops were sent in to occupy Rome, and the short-lived Roman Republic was established.

After these relatively easy successes, General Bonaparte, a rising military leader but not yet a Consul, obtained the consent of the Directory to embark on a Mediterranean campaign. Its purpose was the conquest of Malta and Egypt, setting the stage for the invasion and eventual conquest of England. Malta was overcome without much fighting and in early June, 1798—by now with Sir Horatio Nelson's superior fleet in hot pursuit—the exhausted French troops occupied Alexandria, as well. Defeating an army of determined but undisciplined Mamelukes (mercenaries), the French forces took Cairo on July 24. The report of his lightning victories in such a faraway land, coupling the name of Bonaparate with the image of the ancient pyramids, produced an enormous impact all over Europe.

One week later, however, on August 1st, Admiral Nelson's fleet discovered the French anchored at Abukir Bay, and ordered an immediate attack. Within a few hours of fierce fighting, the "Battle of the Nile" was over with a decisive English victory: eleven of the participating thirteen French battleships were captured or destroyed, with 1700 men killed, including one admiral and three captains, 1500 wounded and 3000 taken prisoner. The French army, cut off from its home base, remained marooned in a hostile land. It took more than a year for Bonaparte to elude the British blockade and make his way back to Paris, leaving his troops, under General Kléber, to the mercy of diseases and enemy attacks not only by the natives but also by the Turkish army, since the French invasion had brought the Sultan into the war.

In the fall of 1798, the victorious Nelson — who received a baronetcy from his grateful government in recognition of his triumph — was lavishly treated in Naples by the King and Queen and the hospitable Hamiltons. However, in his report to his superior, the Earl St. Vincent, he expressed his desire to return to sea, for he found Naples "a country of fiddlers and poets, of whores and scoundrels." Meanwhile, since Nelson shared the concerns of King Ferdinand and his French-hating Queen about Rome's republican experiment,[*] he had no difficulty in persuading his royal hosts that the time was opportune for a Neapolitan army to march on Rome, which it did on November 22nd. The latter's occupation of the Eternal City was brief, however, and was soon put to an end by the French general Championnet. Nor did the French counterattack stop there. In January 1799, a French force, supported by Cisalpine Italians, occupied the city of Naples. The King and Queen, accompanied by the Hamiltons and protected by Nelson, escaped to Palermo, the southern capital of the Neapolitan kingdom. It was in Palermo that the haughty admiral and the beautiful Emma Hamilton went beyond mutual admiration to become lovers, while the city of Naples fell under the rule of the newly established Neapolitan ("Parthenopian") Republic.

As he was hurriedly embarking to Sicily, the King expected Domenico Cimarosa, his *maestro di cappella,* to follow him. But Cimarosa, who harbored republican sentiments, was of a different mind (and, later, he would

---

*   See preceding page.

pay dearly for his decision). His place at court was taken by Gasparo Spontini (1774-1851), a younger man on his way up, who subsequently composed three operas in Palermo.

In volatile Naples, life for the new republic was uneasy. The poor and uneducated rural population—the *lazzaroni*—looked at the activities of the local "Jacobins", mainly members of the educated upper classes, with skepticism. While hardly anyone wished for the return of the Bourbons, the leaders of the revolution had neither the know-how nor the resources to alleviate the misery of the masses. Sensing the Republic's vulnerability, when French troops were withdrawn to be deployed elsewhere, an insurgent army arose under the leadership of Cardinal Fabrizio Ruffo, and put an end to the Neapolitan Republic after only six months of existence.

Ruffo promised to spare the lives of the opposition leaders if they surrendered. But the King and Queen in Palermo's safe haven were determined to show no mercy, and they were encouraged by Admiral Nelson, a committed monarchist and enemy of all revolutionary action. He had the leader of the revolution, Admiral Francesco Caracciolo, hanged, followed by the execution of more than a hundred republican figures, priests and women among them. The Bourbon vendetta also claimed the unfortunate Cimarosa among its victims: barely escaping the death penalty, he was thrown into prison and died, a broken man, two years later.

French forces suffered defeat all over Italy in late 1799. With the sole exception of Liguria, all of the short-lived republics—Naples, Milan, Rome—vanished. When the aged Pope Pius VI died, as a prisoner of France, the cardinals held their conclave in Venice—conditions in Rome were too chaotic. After a long delay, they ironically chose as his successor, to rule as Pius VII, the liberal Cardinal Chiaromonti, the former Archbishop of Imola, known for republican sentiments. These were the conditions awaiting Bonaparte when he finally returned to Paris after the Egyptian adventure. His daring and flamboyance were exactly what France needed to reverse its fortunes. When the Directory was overthrown, the General became one of the three consuls; a month later he was named First Consul at age thirty.

The year 1800, with Rome in turmoil, provides the background to Sardou's bulky five-act play *La Tosca,* on which Puccini's lean and action-packed *Tosca* is based. (The opera was introduced in Rome in 1900, exactly a century after the historical events.) While the play is full of fascinating and accurately observed historical detail, its operatic condensation leaves many questions unanswered, though given the work's fast action and unceasing momentum, audiences are rarely likely to raise them. When, for instance, the hunted and bedraggled Angelotti is recognized by Cavaradossi early in Act I, the painter exclaims: "Angelotti, consul of the doomed Roman Republic!" This line is delivered in fast, barely decipherable sixteenth notes, its meaning totally lost on audiences unfamiliar with this particular phase of Italian history.

Both Cavaradossi and Angelotti are creations of Sardou, but neither was produced out of thin air. Cavaradossi embodies the young patriotic intellectual, held to be a "*Volterriano*", a follower of Voltaire, precisely the type persecuted by the oppressive government of King Ferdinand of Naples. Angelotti was modeled on two historical characters. One of them was a man named Ange*lucci,* consul of the short-lived Roman Republic, who was not killed for political activities but died a natural death several years later. The other was the ill-fated naval officer Francesco Caracciolo, who, prior to his execution by Admiral Nelson, was actually found hiding in a well, like Angelotti in the second act of *Tosca.*

There is no doubt that during the Neapolitan occupation of Rome in 1800, someone like Sardou's Scarpia was in charge of political security, though that person may not have been as theatrically fascinating. His office was logically the Palazzo Farnese — a Bourbon property by inheritance. But, despite references to the Queen (Maria Carolina) in the opera's second act, the fact is that in the summer of 1800 the Queen was in the port city of Leghorn on her way to Vienna to solicit aid against Bonaparte. There is, however, an appropriate historical touch in the Sacristan's jubilant, if mistaken, announcement of Napoleon's defeat at Marengo by the Austrian army under General Mélas (Act I). History indeed tells us that Mélas was so sure of his victory that he sent out a number of dispatches to that effect. But the tide unexpectedly turned in the afternoon of the battle when Louis Desaix, one of Napoleon's best generals, launched a daring counterattack that caught the Austrians by surprise and turned defeat into victory. Desaix fell in the battle and was solemnly eulogized by Napoleon, who nonetheless later credited his own strategic genius for the victory at Marengo. In the opera, of course, the French victory is duly reported to Scarpia during Cavaradossi's torture, and the painter's jubilant "*Vittoria!*" outburst, hailing the defeat of tyranny, seals his doom.

The battle of Marengo (June 15, 1800), a crucial event, assured the survival of the new order in Western Europe. The revived Batavian Republic eventually became the Kingdom of Holland, and the reborn Cisalpine

Republic later led to the foundation of the Kingdom of Italy. Naples remained a kingdom, but Ferdinand and Maria Carolina continued in exile, their throne occupied by Napoleon's brother Joseph and, later, by his brother-in-law Joachim Murat.

But these developments were still in the future on June 18, 1800 when Bonaparte celebrated the Marengo victory with a festive *Te Deum* at the cathedral of Milan. On July 14, there was a jubilant celebration of Bastille Day in Paris, with the participation of contralto Giuseppina Grassini of La Scala Milan, with whom Napoleon carried on a not too secret affair. This involvement, however, was discreetly kept from Josephine Beauharnais, his wife of four years. It was, in any case, of short duration. Napoleon was not a man for long romantic attachments, but he did eventually provide La Grassini with means for luxurious living.

Since February 19, 1800, the First Consul had established his residence in the former royal palace of the Tuileries and within a few months he managed to transform the triumvirate of the Consuls into a virtual dictatorship. On Christmas Eve, 1800, as he was driven to the Opéra to hear Haydn's oratorio *The Creation,* a bomb exploded near his carriage, killing several members of his escort. Several newspapers were suppressed as a result, and Fouché, the minister of police, was entrusted with extraordinary powers of censorship. Fouché was just one of the extremely able men Napoleon chose for his administration, creating a system that still survives in certain essential features. On May 19, 1802, the day he created the Legion of Honor (the composer Méhul being one of the first recipients), with a plebiscite hugely in his favor, Bonaparte was made First Consul for life – a king in all but name.

A short-term truce with England, arranged at Amiens in March 1802, came to an end when Great Britain declared war on May 18, 1803 and revived its support of the French royalists. An anti-Bonaparte coup among high French officers was uncovered by Fouché in early 1804, and the young Duc d'Enghien was accused of being one of its organizers. Although his innocence was soon established, Enghien was summarily court-martialled and shot – an act that horrified Europe and was to haunt Napoleon for the rest of his life. Nonetheless, the Senate on May 18 confirmed a proposal to declare Napoleon emperor and to make his office hereditary. The plebiscite that followed was a mere formality: Napoleon was duly crowned on December 2nd, 1804 by a somewhat unhappy Pius VII – a splendid event captured in a large-scale painting by David (which, however, contains several historical inaccuracies).

Napoleon's rule was, in the main, good for opera. He enjoyed the light comic operas of Grétry, but never warmed to the more ambitious works of Cherubini and Méhul. Actually, his Corsican blood drew him naturally toward the Italian operas of Zingarelli, Paër and, in particular, of Paisiello, whom he appointed *Maître de Chapelle* in 1802. As such, it was to Paisiello that the honor fell to compose a *Mass* and *Te Deum* for the Emperor's coronation. That distinction notwithstanding, Paisiello was neither happy nor appreciated in Paris and returned the following year to Naples, with Jean-François Le Sueur succeeding him at court. Paisiello continued to enjoy the favor of Naples's Bonapartist kings but, after Napoleon's fall, King Ferdinand deprived him of his pensions. Thus Paisiello, once a favored composer of two mighty rulers, Catherine the Great and Napoleon, died sick and destitute in 1816.

With England, Russia, and Austria joined in a coalition against him, in late August 1805 Napoleon ordered his Grand Army to advance, and entered Vienna on November 13. Beethoven's *Fidelio* was in its final rehearsals, but the composer's princely patrons and other aristocrats fled the city. Only a small and dispirited audience, including several French officers, attended opening night at the Theater an der Wien a week later. After one more performance, *Fidelio* was temporarily dropped. A private concert was given at Schönbrunn on December 14 with Cherubini conducting excerpts from Italian operas. An eyewitness described Napoleon's behavior at the concert as dour and unappreciative.

There was good reason for his glumness: on October 21st the combined French and Spanish fleet was overwhelmingly defeated at Trafalgar by Nelson's battleships. The Admiral sustained a mortal wound, but died only after his great victory was certain. Although Napoleon did not fully acknowledge the finality of his loss, there could be no further talk of invading England, and France thereafter ceased to be a threat to English shipping.

On land, however, the French army remained invincible. On December 2, 1805, near the Moravian village of Austerlitz, Napoleon scored perhaps the most brilliant victory of his campaign over a combined Austrian-Prussian army. Under the humiliating peace treaty of Pressburg that followed, Austria lost large Italian territories and the German lands were completely reorganized. Once again, the Bourbons were expelled from Naples, and it gave Napoleon special joy to single out the disgrace of "that criminal woman" (Maria Carolina). Napoleon's brothers and sisters were married into European dynasties and became kings, duchesses, and princes. Brother

Joseph Bonaparte became King of Naples, to be eventually succeeded by brother-in-law Joachim Murat when Joseph was given the thankless honor of becoming King of Spain. (The unlamented Maria Carolina did not live to witness Napoleon's downfall; she died in Vienna in 1814.)

The victory at Austerlitz was soon followed by an equal triumph at Jena (October 1806) and another peace treaty that humiliated Russia. Warsaw was next to fall — Napoleon had encouraged the Poles to provide troops for his army in exchange for his promised support in their independence struggle. A Russian counterattack at Eylau (February 1807) resulted in a nominal French victory, with catastrophic losses on both sides. Hostilities ceased with the Treaty of Tilsit, with humiliating consequences for Prussia as a new Kingdom of Westphalia was created under Napoleon's youngest brother, Jerome. The new Grand Duchy of Warsaw under the King of Saxony failed to satisfy Polish dreams of independence. (An 18-year-old Polish beauty named Marie Walewska had previously offered her own personal contribution to the patriotic cause. The son who was born of her brief romance with Napoleon grew up as Count Walewski.)

At the end of 1807 Napoleon's power was at its zenith, soon to be sacrificed to his insatiable ambition. Determined to draw Spain into his organized blockade of English trade, he forced the abdication of Charles IV of Spain in favor of Joseph Bonaparte. Though Charles and his singularly unappealing wife Maria Luisa, to say nothing of their corrupt minister Manuel Godoy (the queen's lover), were unpopular, the Spanish people refused to accept French rule. They rose to involve the French army in an endless warfare that introduced the word "guerrilla" into the international vocabulary. Instances of unbounded savagery followed on both sides, and the determined resistance to the reign of his well-intentioned brother Joseph forced Napoleon to keep Madrid occupied and a substantial army mired in Spain.

Francisco Goya, the great Spanish painter, left to posterity merciless portraits of the porcine King Charles IV, his coarsely repulsive queen and their no less unattractive son, the future Ferdinand VII. He also created a series of etchings called *The Disasters of War,* a graphic documentation of the unspeakable horrors of guerrilla warfare. When, years later, British troops under Wellington finally succeeded in pushing the French army out of Spain, Ferdinand was established on the throne and Goya retired to the country. He eventually settled in France, where he died in 1828.

The bloody Spanish war is but a distant echo in Gian Carlo Menotti's last opera, *Goya* (1986). Taking considerable liberties in his own libretto (though not exceeding those taken by Verdi and Puccini in theirs), Menotti highlights the romantic episodes in the painter's early life and the serenity of his final years. The unsavory royal couple and Manuel Godoy do appear in a not too sympathetic light, but the opera's main focus is the struggle that creative artists must face in a corrupt and oppressive environment—a problem that must have also confronted the real Goya.

During the frustrating Spanish campaign, another Italian composer came into French operatic limelight: Gasparo Spontini. He had arrived in Paris, after a brief stay in the Sicilian court, in 1803, [*] and soon managed to find favor with the Empress Josephine, to whom he dedicated his one-act opera *Milton* (1804). His cantata *L'eccelsa gara,* performed on February 8, 1806, to celebrate Napoleon's victory at Austerlitz, also seemed like an excellent career move leading to the brilliant success of his *La Vestale* (1807), with its massed choruses and inflated pageantry something of a milestone in the history of French grand opera. Napoleon himself took personal interest in Spontini's next opera, *Fernand Cortez,* believing that its heroic portrayal of a conqueror might influence public opinion in favor of his Spanish campaign. Indeed, in the opera's libretto by Étienne Jouy there are no cruelties recorded against the Mexicans; Cortez and his officers are unfailingly chivalrous. No wonder that Napoleon took keen interest in this opera, which was introduced on November 28, 1809.

By then, however, signs of crumbling in Napoleon's empire were manifest. Ever since Trafalgar, he was frustrated by England's naval superiority, and the blockade, the so-called "Continental System", was not working. In Holland, he was even forced to dethrone his own brother Louis, who defied the Emperor by continuing trade with the British.

Although in 1809 virtually all of Europe was either under French rule or allied with Napoleon, Austria—a reluctant ally at best—was ready to mobilize against him, encouraged by the Spanish uprising. This caused Napoleon to take Vienna again on May 13, 1809. Among the many frightened citizens of the Imperial City was 77-year-old Joseph Haydn. Although Napoleon posted an honor guard to safeguard his house, the great composer died three weeks later. The French and Austrian armies clashed at Wagram (near Vienna) on July 6th with huge casualties on both sides. In the peace treaty that

---

[*]   See page 312.

followed (Schönbrunn, October 14) Austria had to accept new territorial losses and faced a dramatic new development.

Napoleon knew that his was a life in constant danger and he was increasingly concerned about dying without a legitimate heir. Since Josephine Beauharnais, his complacent wife, was barren, marriage to Marie Louise, the daughter of his arch-enemy, the Emperor Francis II, made eminent sense — at least to Prince Metternich, whose creative mind promoted it. On January 12 the Metropolitan Archbishop of Paris pronounced Napoleon's marriage to Josephine annulled — an unpopular act with the general public. Three months later, on April 1, 1811, without the consent of Pope Pius VII, Napoleon married Marie Louise. Ferdinando Paër, *maître de chappelle* since 1807, duly composed a wedding march for the occasion. The bride was nineteen.

1811 is the year when most of the action of Umberto Giordano's opera *Madame Sans-Gêne* takes place, though its first act, set in the stormy revolutionary year of 1792, already introduces us to all its principal characters. They are all very young: Catherine Hubscher, a washerwoman from Alsace, her lover, Sergeant Lefebvre, and the Austrian Count Neipperg, whom these two save from the fury of a revolutionary mob. A Corsican lieutenant named Bonaparte is mentioned among Catherine's customers. Nineteen years later (1811), Napoleon is emperor and Lefebvre, now one of his marshals and Duke of Danzig besides, is married to Catherine. She is known as *"Madame Sans-Gêne"* ("Madame of No Constraint") because of her outspokenness and inability to embrace the courtly demeanor demanded by her new station. Aware of this, Napoleon urges Lefebvre to divorce her and orders Catherine to appear before him in person. In that private audience, Catherine reminds the emperor of her blameless revolutionary past, of her patriotism and, to jog his memory, even presents him with an unpaid laundry bill from his lieutenant days. She also manages to relieve Napoleon's mind of his jealous thoughts concerning Count Neipperg — who is now an aide to Marie Louise and, apparently, pays too much attention to her. Completely disarmed, Napoleon orders Lefebvre to cherish his wife for the treasure that she is.

Virtually all the characters in the opera are historical personalities. In addition to the principals, brief appearances are made by Fouché, the minister of police, and Napoleon's two sisters, Queen Carolina — wife of King Joachim Murat of Naples — and Princess Elisa of Parma. Even Roustam, the Emperor's Egyptian valet, is historical. And history recognizes Count Neipperg as Marie Louise's eventual lover and, after Napoleon's death, future husband. The incidents are fictitious but the play—by *La Tosca*'s Victorien Sardou and E. Moreau—on which Giordano's opera (with libretto by Renato Simone of *Turandot* fame) is based handles its ingredients brilliantly.

In 1811, the years of *Madame Sans-Gêne*'s action, Marie Louise bore Napoleon a son, Napoleon François Joseph, who was named King of Rome. Now most of Europe belonged to Napoleon and only Great Britain and Russia separated the emperor from his dream of world domination. France, in the interim, had been turned into a virtual police state. Napoleon dismissed Fouché, whom he suspected of having become excessively power-hungry, and replaced him with General Savary, who carried out his harsh duties with a less independent mind. Confident in his military strength, bolstered by large numbers of Polish, German, and Austrian conscripts, Napoleon invaded Russia on June 23, 1812, using as a pretext Tsar Alexander's unwillingness to seal Russian ports to British shipping. In deciding on that fateful step, Napoleon may have been right in supposing the Russian army inferior to his, but he underestimated the vastness of the territory he was about to invade, and severely underestimated the tenacity of the Russian people. Their conscripts (mainly serfs) may have resented their oppressed status, but they were fiercely loyal to their tsar and believed, as their priests kept insisting, that the invaders were in the service of the Antichrist.

Again, as in Spain, Napoleon was unprepared to fight the kind of war in which Moscow was left to burn and in which the retreating Russian army drew the French invaders a thousand miles from home—with increasingly less food and exposed to relentless cold. As the Comte Philippe de Ségur wrote later: "It was no longer a war of kings that we were fighting, but a class war, a religious war, a national war—all sorts of war rolled into one."

Tolstoy's monumental novel *War and Peace* deals with the Napoleonic War on a panoramic scale. When in 1941 Sergei Prokofiev undertook the task of turning Tolstoy's epic into an opera, Russia was again being invaded by a foreign army and the nationalistic element in the novel became pointedly relevant. Hitler now became the new Napoleon, and Stalin combined the images of both Tsar Alexander I and Field Marshal Kutuzov. The opera abounds in stirring patriotic choruses. In Scene 8, on the eve of the battle of Borodino (August 15, 1812), the chorus sings:

> When our father Kutuzov called the people together
> To beat the French, the people rose in a mighty force.

A determined Napoleon (portrait by Paul Delaroche)
CREDIT: Culver Pictures Inc.

> He who comes against Russia with the sword
> Will not escape alive.

Napoleon himself appears in the opera's ninth scene, directing the battle and planning the occupation of Moscow in the company of his marshals Berthier and Caulaincourt. He receives word of great casualties and commits his reserves to battle. At the end of the scene, in a brooding monologue, he asks: "I am the same person, much more experienced than before. So why doesn't the awesome sweep of my hand bring us victory?"

Technically, Napoleon was the victor at Borodino, but victory came at the cost of staggering losses. A horrendous sight of 50,000 corpses of men and horses awaited the emperor when he visited the battle site, also some 20,000 wounded, screaming for help. On August 27th (Scene 10 in the Prokofiev

A determined Napoleon: Pasquale Amato
in *Madame Sans-Gêne* (Giordano)
CREDIT: Metropolitan Opera Archives

opera), Kutuzov gives his orders to evacuate Moscow. Within a few days, the city was — as the Tolstoy original has it — "deserted as a dying, queenless hive is deserted." When Napoleon entered Moscow on September 14, he found most of it destroyed by fire, with exhausted French and straggling Russian soldiers pillaging and looting unchecked.

Knowing that the condensation of more than a thousand pages of the Tolstoy novel would be an impossible task, Prokofiev followed the examples of Mussorgsky and Tchaikovsky by constructing his opera in a number of representative scenes (eleven at first, later expanded to thirteen), on the assumption that Russian audiences would be familiar with the literary source. Accordingly, Scene 11 of the operatic *War and Peace* depicts the burning, chaotic Moscow, while Scene 12 touchingly illustrates the delirium of Tolstoy's hero, Andrey Bolkonsky, dying of his wounds. In the final chorus of the opera (Scene 13), the people sing: "We have smashed the enemy. Glory to our holy Mother Country, glory to our army, hurrah for Field Marshal Kutuzov!"

What started out as an invading force of more than half a million was reduced to a demoralized and disintegrated army of fifty thousand. Napoleon gave the order to retreat and returned to Paris in early December. The tenuous alliance of powers bound to him at the peak of his military strength was now crumbling. Prussia was first to defect, joined by Count Bernadotte, once a marshal of France and now about to become King of Sweden. Austria's wily Metternich advanced a peace proposal requiring Napoleon to make serious territorial concessions; when it was rejected — as Metternich no doubt expected it would be — he persuaded Emperor Francis to declare war on his son-in-law (August 12, 1813). With all his enemies now closing in on him, a decisive battle took place at Leipzig (October 14-19), where the French army was crushed. Merciless climate and extended supply lines were no longer responsible — this time, Napoleon was defeated by a combined German-Russian-Swedish army, well led and joined in a patriotic spirit of national liberation. Alberto Franchetti's opera *Germania* (1902) deals with the nationalist movement that gripped German lands in the wake of the Napoleonic wars.

And now that mighty empire, created by invasions, terror, and forced alliances, was tottering. The Coalition armies led by Blücher and Schwarzenberg were pushing forward on French soil, while Bernadotte and his Swedish forces were bearing down on the north. Spain, where so much had been lost already, was now lost for good. Paris capitulated on March 30th, forcing

Napoleon's abdication the following day. On April 6th, the Senate voted to return Louis XVIII—brother of the executed king—to the French throne, a process facilitated by Talleyrand's behind-the-scenes maneuvering. The defeated emperor was taken to the island of Elba with a small retinue of loyal officers. His wife and son, the infant "King of Rome", were not allowed to join him. On that tiny island he maintained a miniature imperial court and received the visit of his mother, Letizia (Madame Mère) and his sister Pauline—also, briefly, of Marie Walewska and *her* son. Meantime, in Paris, republicans and royalists alike hailed the cessation of hostilities. On July 5th, 1814, in faraway America, Thomas Jefferson wrote to John Adams: "The ruthless destroyer of ten millions of the human race... the great oppressor of the world... how miserably, how meanly has he closed his inflated career! What a sample of the bathos will his history present!"

In September, Napoleon's former enemies convened in Vienna to lay the foundation of a new world order. The Tsar of Russia came, as did the King of Prussia, and major statesmen like Castlereagh and Talleyrand. Meetings followed meetings in the midst of glittering balls, parades, and receptions and such distractions as the repeated performances of Beethoven's noisy orchestral piece *Wellington's Victory* (Vienna had known it since 1813). *Fidelio,* shaped by its composer into its final form, was now received with enthusiasm.

At the conferences Talleyrand effectively argued on behalf of a new and non-threatening France, but the fate of Poland and Saxony were still unsettled when, in March 1815, the Congress was stunned by the news of Napoleon's landing in France and marching on Paris. Then the Congress of Vienna hastily adjourned after deciding to leave Poland under Russian domination and to create a confederate Germany, comprising all the states other than Prussia and Saxony.

When Napoleon left Elba, he boldly gambled on the unpopularity of Louis XVIII and the loyalty of his officers. He was right on both counts, but the French populace, exhausted by the wars, received him with apathy, and the army he was able to raise was no match for the combined allied forces. The end of the famous "Hundred Days" came with the battle of Waterloo in Belgium (June 15-18, 1815). Four days later Napoleon abdicated for the second and last time. Rather than surrendering to Louis XVIII, he chose to put himself under the protection of Great Britain in the hope that he would be allowed to sail for America. That was not to be. The British government considered him an outlaw—there was even talk in high places of executing him.

Finally St. Helena, a remote rocky island in the south Atlantic, was chosen

for the exiled ruler. There he spent the remaining six years of his life, surrounded by a small staff, in meditation, and in justifying his tumultuous life
and exploits. He died on May 5th, 1821 of what the official post mortem
report diagnosed as a "cancerous ulcer of the stomach."

The kind of complex man Napoleon Bonaparte was had to be the stuff of
legends. If Thomas Jefferson regarded him as a "moral monster", Goethe,
another contemporary, admired his stride "like a demigod from victory to
victory... in a permanent state of enlightenment, which is why his fate was
more brilliant than the world has ever seen or is likely to see after him." His
companion at St. Helena, Comte de Las Cases, who published his *Mémorial
de Ste. Hélène* in 1823, quotes Napoleon as saying "The memory I leave behind consists of facts that mere words cannot destroy." He also exclaimed
once: "What a romance my life had been!"

Spoken like an operatic character.

CODA

Henri Beyle was an officer in Napoleon's army, who took part in the Russian
campaign of 1812, observed its horrors at a close range, and shared the
humiliation of the bitter retreat. He was already making his way in the literary
world under the pen name Stendhal when his *Vie de Rossini* appeared in
1824. Rossini was only thirty-two that year, but he was already the rage of
Italy, and Stendhal's enthusiastic praise of his music and fascinating—if not
always accurate—portrayal of his life did much to start the young composer
on his world-wide fame. It is appropriate in this context to cite the opening
paragraph of *The Life of Rossini,* as translated by Richard N. Coe:

> Napoleon is dead, but a new conqueror has already shown him-
> self to the world; and from Moscow to Naples, from London to
> Vienna, from Paris to Calcutta, his name is constantly on every
> tongue. The fame of this hero knows no bounds save those of
> civilisation itself; and he is not yet thirty-two! The task which I
> have set myself is to trace the paths and circumstances which
> have carried him at so early an age to such a throne of glory.

While this may read like Romantic exaggeration (and we can well doubt
the Calcutta assertion), according to a later and more reliable biographer,

Giuseppe Radiciotti, at least twenty-three of Rossini's operas were being performed worldwide in 1823. In Vienna he caused a rage that deflected attention from Beethoven and Schubert, and he was by far the most popular composer in Russia, Spain, Portugal, and South America. By 1824 — when he settled in Paris — all of his operas had been staged in Italy. All that remained of his operatic creativity was a pasticcio (*Il Viaggio a Reims*), two French operas refashioned from Italian originals (*Le Siège de Corinthe* and *Moïse*), and his last operas, *Le Comte Ory* (1828) and *Guillaume Tell* (1829).

Between the years 1815 and 1822, Rossini's operatic activity centered on Naples. King Ferdinand, who emerged from his Palermo exile after Napoleon's fall, paid personal homage to him at the premiere of *Zelmira,* his last opera composed for Naples, on February 16, 1822. With three important theaters introducing new operas regularly and with works by Paisiello, Cimarosa, Zingarelli, Paër, and Mayr on the boards, Naples was justly regarded then as the musical capital of Italy. It continued to be ruled by the Bourbons until the unification of Italy nearly forty years later.

In France, Gasparo Spontini, who had greatly enjoyed Napoleon's favor, showed amazing powers of resilience by celebrating the restoration of Louis XVIII, as well, with a hastily composed festive opera — *Pélage, ou Le Roi de la Paix* — which apparently sank without a trace. But he soon found himself out of favor and went on to tempting positions in Germany. Méhul died in 1817; Cherubini, who never found his way into Napoleon's affection, found more sympathy under the Bourbon rule. In his august position as director of the Paris Conservatory of Music he exerted great influence but gained few friends with his austere personality.

In 1840, under the reign of Louis-Philippe, the cult of Bonapartism reached new heights in France. Napoleon's remains were brought back from St. Helena to be reburied in the Invalides. Twenty years later, his nephew, Napoleon III, created a mighty monument for him, a granite sarcophagus surrounded by twelve figures representing the emperor's greatest victories.

In 1940, the remains of the ill-fated King of Rome were laid to rest nearby. Napoleon's only legitimate son, sometimes referred to as Napoleon II, separated from his father at the age of three and rarely visited by his mother, Marie Louise, was brought up under Metternich's personal care. He was given the title of Duke of Reichstadt; a German tutor attended to his education, and every effort was made to separate him from a French identity. But he was a studious youngster who learned a great deal from books and grew up with a deep admiration for his father, bordering on hero worship. Consumptive since childhood, he caught pneumonia at a military parade and died on July 22, 1832. His grandfather, the Emperor Francis, who was truly fond of him, ruefully remarked: "His death was a misfortune for nobody except myself." He lived only twenty-one years. Edmond Rostand's 1900 play *L'Aiglon* chronicled the last two years of the unfortunate youth's life; in 1937, Arthur Honegger and Jacques Ibert turned that play into an opera that was introduced in Monte Carlo the same year.

History Through the Opera Glass ends here, rather dramatically, with the fall of Napoleon and its immediate aftermath. Great historical events continued to shake up the world—the war between Greece and Turkey (1822-1829), the Paris Revolution of 1830, the whole wave of European revolutions in 1848-1849—but these historical events prompted relatively minor operatic reverberations. In fact, 19th-century creators of opera increasingly moved away from historical subjects in their growing concern with human ambitions, conflicts, and emotions in naturalistic settings. Bizet's *Carmen* (1875) provided the decisive turning point: historical backgrounds thereafter mattered little, psychology and sociology became the ruling elements.

New paths were charted such as the *verismo* movement which grew out of naturalism. *Verismo* was not limited to Italy, though its most prominent representatives—Mascagni's *Cavalleria rusticana* (1890) and Leoncavallo's *Pagliacci* (1892)—are profoundly Italian products. Both operas deal with life among the common people of southern Italy, and with events that could have been taken from contemporary newspapers, which indeed was the case with *Pagliacci*.

Nineteenth-century Paris served as a background to several important operas, but it mattered little whether France was a monarchy or a republic in the story of Puccini's *La Bohème* (1896), Giordano's *Fedora* (1898), or Charpentier's *Louise* (1900). Social distinctions and inequities became important, far more so than they had been in operas set in pre-Napoleonic times. Richard Strauss's *Arabella* (1933), Alban Berg's *Lulu* (1937), and Benjamin Britten's *Death in Venice* (1973) probe into the darker undercurrents of European society, while the oppressive aura of Tsarist Russia speaks to us from the tragic pages of Janácek's *Kat'a Kabanova* (1921) and *From the House of the Dead* (1930), and from Shostakovich's *Lady Macbeth of Mzensk* (1934).

Nineteenth-century America is reflected in such divergent operas as Puccini's *La Fanciulla del West* (1910, northern California in the late 1840s), Douglas Moore's *The Ballad of Baby Doe* (1958, Colorado in the 1880s), and Marc Blitzstein's *Regina* (1949, Alabama around 1900)—but, again, specific historical events and their protagonists are seldom encountered.

There is no telling where modern operas may take us. Surely we must allow a certain amount of time to elapse before contemporary events can be approached from a "historical" perspective at all. And yet there is strong operatic material in the tragedy of the anti-Nazi martyr Dietrich Bonhoeffer, or in the life of Martin Luther King. And, some day, a future Wagner may create a modern Ring based on the Kennedy family archives. On the other hand, John Adams has already followed Leoncavallo's example in creating *Nixon in China* and *The Death of Klinghoffer* from contemporary headline events, and Anthony Davis has forged an opera out of *The Life and Times of Malcolm X,* to say nothing of Ezra Laderman's *Marilyn.*

Technological innovations that are changing our everyday lives may well redefine the operas of the future — their form, their content, and their manner of presentation. "Historical" operas in the traditional sense may then become an outdated concept. Historical accuracy has already been taken rather lightly by certain modern producers who have re-imagined *Carmen* in the context of the Spanish Civil War, or placed *Tosca* in Mussolini's Italy. Far more outlandish examples are chronicled by Henry Pleasants in his book *Opera in Crisis* (Thames and Hudson, 1989). There, citing a litany of modern excesses, Mr. Pleasants has diagnosed a phenomenon called "produceritis" as one of the "plagues" of contemporary opera.

But things may change. I am reminded of George Bernard Shaw's dictum that "the novelties of one generation are only the resuscitated fashions of the generation before last." Meanwhile it is history itself, of course — history as it actually happened — that remains the eternal teacher. The nearly 200 operas discussed in this volume, most of whose subjects fall within the symmetrical borders of the rise of Caesar and the fall of Napoleon, give us a perspective on our past as enlightening — not to say entertaining — as it is unique.

HISTORICAL FRAGMENTS FROM THE OPERA GLASS
DID YOU KNOW THAT...

In 1372, a Castilian fleet commanded by Ambrosio Boccanegra (nephew of Simone) defeated an English convoy bringing reinforcements to Aquitaine — signaling Castile's siding with France in the Hundred Years' War.

* * *

The Genoese patrician family of Fiesco (Fieschi) befriended the Colombos before Cristoforo was born. A member of that family, Bartolomeo Fieschi, joined Columbus on his last voyage (1502) and captained the vessel *Vizcaina.*

* * *

Cardinal Ippolito d'Este, who built the famous Villa d'Este at Tivoli near Rome, where Franz Liszt lived and composed, was the son of Lucrezia Borgia.

* * *

The notorious Borgia family orginated in Spain and their name was Borja. A direct descendant, born on Christmas Eve 1887, was Lucrecia Borja Gonzalez de Riancho, better known as the celebrated soprano Lucrezia Bori.

* * *

One of Benvenuto Cellini's patrons was Cardinal Marco Cornaro, brother of Caterina Cornaro, the heroine of Donizetti's opera by that name.

* * *

When Pope Pius IV appointed a commission of eight cardinals to study the reform of church music in 1562, one of the members of the commission, delegated by Philip II of Spain, was a Count Luna, a descendant of Count di Luna of *Il trovatore* fame.

* * *

The Spanish domination of the Low Countries in the sixteenth century is emphasized in Wagner's *Der fliegende Holländer,* where Wagner's directions, frequently ignored by modern producers, call for the Dutchman to come ashore in Spanish attire.

* * *

When, in Verdi's *La forza del destino,* Carlo de Vargas promises the "order of Calatrava" to the disguised Don Alvaro, who had saved his life, he refers to the oldest and most distinguished military decoration in Spain. It goes back to the twelfth century, when it was first awarded to the heroic defenders of the village of that name by King Sancho III in 1158 and approved by Pope Alexander III in 1164.

* * *

Isabella (Elizabeth) Farnese (1692-1766) married Philip V of Spain in 1714. She secured Parma and Piacenza for her son Philip, who founded the line Bourbon-Parma. The Palazzo Farnese in Rome, scene of *Tosca*'s second act, was the property of the family's descendant, Ferdinand of Naples, at war with France. Ironically, the French government later acquired the palace, and it is now the French Embassy.

* * *

Wieland's poetic drama *Oberon,* before being turned into an opera by Carl Maria von Weber, was translated into English by John Quincy Adams while he was United States Ambassador to Prussia in 1797-1801.

* * *

Catherine the Great had many lovers, whom she treated with great generosity. One of them, in a long line of favorites (Orlov, Poniatowski,

Potemkin, Lanskoi, Mamonov, etc.) was Ivan Rimsky-Korsakov, who enjoyed presumably exclusive rights to the imperial boudoir from 1778 to 1780. He was an ancestor of composer Nikolai Rimsky-Korsakov.

* * *

Mozart's one-acter *Der Schauspieldirektor* and Salieri's *Prima la musica e poi le parole* were introduced at the imperial palace of Schönbrunn on February 7, 1786. In addition to the Emperor Joseph II, the invited celebrities included Prince Stanislas Poniatowski, nephew of the King of Poland and one of Catherine the Great's lovers.

* * *

Contralto Giuseppina Grassini (1773-1850) became Napoleon's lover on June 4, 1800. They carried on a brief relationship in Paris. Strictly neutral in politics, after Napoleon's fall she became the mistress, first of Viscount Castlereagh, the British Secretary of War, then the Duke of Wellington, during her London engagement. She retired in 1823 with a comfortable fortune, and died on January 2, 1850, still a beautiful woman, in her 77th year.

* * *

When Napoleon occupied Warsaw in 1806, the upheaval endangered the livelihood of Ernst Theodore (later E. T. A.) Hoffmann. He was then an obscure jurist who dabbled in music and poetry. He moved to Bamberg to direct an opera company and later made his fame as an essayist and teller of bizarre tales. Offenbach's *Les Contes d'Hoffmann* made him even more famous.

* * *

When Giuseppe Verdi was born on October 9, 1813. the tiny village of Le Roncole in the province of Parma was temporarily under French occupation. The infant's name, accordingly, was entered in the municipal register as "Joseph Fortunin François Verdi".

* * *

Opera composers, themselves, are featured sometimes in the operas of other composers—for example Lully in *Les trois ages de l'opéra* by Grétry (1778) and *Lully et Quinault* by Isouard (1812); Alexander Stradella in *Il cantore di Venezia* by Marchi (1835) and *Alessandro Stradella* by Flotow (1844); Mozart in *Szenen aus Mozarts Leben* by Lortzing (1832) and *Mozart and Salieri* by Rimsky-Korsakov (1898); Cimarosa in Isouard's 1808 opera appropriately titled *Cimarosa*. Non-operatic composers who have been similarly musical-ized include the subjects of *Palestrina* by Pfitzner (1918); *Taverner* by Davies (1972); *Friedemann Bach* by Graener (1931); and *Chopin* by Orefice (1901).

SELECTED BIBLIOGRAPHY

Abraham, Gerald (ed.), *The Age of Beethoven.* New York: Oxford University Press, 1982.

Acton, Harold, *The Bourbons of Naples.* New York: St. Martin's Press, 1956.

Altamira, Rafael, *A History of Spain,* transl. by Muna Lee. New York: D. Van Nostrand Co., 1949.

Ashbrook, William, *Donizetti.* London: Cassell & Company, Ltd., 1965.

Asztalos, Miklós, *Rákóczi Ferenc és kora.* Budapest: Dante, 1934.

Bain, R. Nisbet, *Slavonic Europe.* New York: Cambridge University Press, 1908.

Bainton, Roland H., *The Age of Reformation.* New York: D. Van Nostrand Co., 1956.

Baker, Frank Granville, "Gustav Unmasked". *Opera News,* December 6, 1975.

Barzini, Luigi, *The Italians.* New York: Atheneum Publishers, 1964.

Benedetti, Jean, *Gilles de Rais.* New York: Stein & Day, 1972.

Bergamini, John D., *The Spanish Bourbons.* New York: G. P. Putnam, 1974.

Berlioz, Hector, *Memoirs of Hector Berlioz,* ed. by Ernest Newman; transl. by R. & E. Holmes. New York: Alfred A. Knopf, Inc., 1932.

Billings, Malcolm, *The Cross and the Crescent.* New York: Sterling Publishing Co., Inc., 1987.

Bowle, John, *Henry VIII.* Boston: Little, Brown & Co., 1964.

Brion, Marcel, *The Medici,* transl. by G. & H. Cremonesi. New York: Crown Publishers, Inc., 1969.

Büchner, Georg, *Complete Plays and Prose,* transl. by C. R. Mueller. New York: Hill & Wang, 1963.

Budden, Julian, *The Operas of Verdi,* Vols. I-III. New York: Oxford University Press, 1973, 1979, 1981.

Buehr, Wendy (ed.), *The Horizon History of Russia.* New York: American Heritage Publishing Co., 1970.

Chaliapin, Feodor, *An Autobiography,* as told to Maxim Gorky, transl. by N. Froud & J. Hanley. New York: Stein & Day, 1967.

Cellini, Benvenuto, *Autobiography,* transl. by John Addington Symonds. New York: Random House (The Modern Library).

Chamberlin, E. R., *The Fall of the House of Borgia*. New York: The Dial Press, 1974.

Churchill, Winston S., *A History of the English Speaking Peoples*. New York: Dodd, Mead & Co., 1956-1962.

Cleugh, James, *The Medici*. New York: Doubleday & Co., Inc., 1975.

Collis, Maurice, *Cortes and Montezuma*. New York: Harcourt, Brace & Co., 1954.

Cooper, Martin, *Opéra Comique*. New York: Chanticleer Press, 1949.

Coslow, Jules, *Ivan the Terrible*. New York: Hill & Wang, 1961.

Cotterill, H. B., *Medieval Italy*. New York: F. A. Stokes Co., n.d.

Dean, Winton, *Essays on Opera*. Oxford: Clarendon Press, 1990.

Dent, Edward J., *The Rise of Romantic Opera*. New York: Cambridge University Press, 1976.

Dmytryshin, Basil, *Medieval Russia*, 2nd Ed. Hinsdale IL: The Dryden Press, 1970.

Durant, Will & Ariel, *The Story of Civilization*, Vols. 3-11. New York: Simon & Schuster, 1944-1975.

Duruy, Victor, *A History of France*, 4th Ed. New York: Thomas Y. Crowell Co., 1929.

Erskine of Marr, The Hon. R., *MacBeth*. Inverness: Robert Carruthers & Sons, 1930.

Finley, M.I.; Smith, D. M.; & Duggan, C., *A History of Sicily*. New York: Viking Penguin Inc., 1986.

Federn, Carl, *Dante and His Time*. New York: Haskell House Publishers Ltd., 1974.

Florinsky, Michael T., *Russia*. New York: The Macmillan Co., 1953 (2 vols).

Fuchs, Viktor, "The Other *Ballo*". *Opera News*, March 17. 1962.

Geiger, Eugen, *Der Meistergesang des Hans Sachs*. Bern: Francke Verlag, 1956.

Gooch, G. P., *Frederick the Great*. New York: Dorset Press, 1990.

Gordon, C. D., *The Age of Attila*. Ann Arbor: The University of Michigan Press, 1960.

Grant, Michael, *The Twelve Caesars*. London: Weidenfeld & Nicholson, 1975.

Grout, Donald J., with Williams, H. W., *A Short History of Opera*. New York: Columbia University Press, 1988.

Hadas, Moses, *A History of Rome*. New York: Doubleday Anchor Books, 1956.

Hallam, Elizabeth (ed.), *The Plantagenet Chronicles*. New York: Weiden-feld & Nicholson, 1986.

Hilsenbeck, Dr. Fritz, *Nürnberger Gestalten aus neun Jahrhunderten*. Nürnberg: Verlag Karl Ulrich & Co., 1950.

Hoover, Kathleen, "In the Beginning". *Opera News,* April 29, 1961.

Jamison, E. M., & others, *Italy—Medieval and Modern*. London: Oxford University Press, 1917.

Kehl, Anton, *"Grünewald" Forschungen* (Doctoral Thesis). Erlangen-Nürnberg, 1964.

Kirchner, Walter, *A History of Russia,* 3rd Ed. New York: Barnes & Noble, Inc., 1963.

Kleine-Ahlbrandt, Laird, "The Real Poet". *Opera News,* February 5, 1966.

Krehbiel, Henry E., *A Second Book of Operas*. New York: The Macmillan Co., 1917.

Lang, Paul Henry, *Music in Western Civilization*. New York: W. W. Norton & Co., Inc., 1941.

Langer, William L. (ed.), *An Encyclopedia of World History*. Boston: Houghton Mifflin Co., 1940, 1948.

Ledesma, Francisco Navarro, *Cervantes, The Man and Genius,* transl. by D. & G. Blis. New York: Charterhouse, 1976.

Lemaitre, Georges, *Beaumarchais*. London, 1728; New York: Alfred A. Knopf, Inc., 1949.

Leonard, Richard Anthony, *A History of Russian Music*. New York: The Macmillan Co., 1957.

Lenfant, Jacques, *The History of the Council of Constance.*

Loewenberg, Alfred, *Annals of Opera 1597-1940,* 3rd Edition Rev. Totowa NJ: Rowman & Littlefield, 1978.

Markham, Felix, *Napoleon*. New York: Penguin Books USA, Inc., 1963.

Márki, Dr. Sándor, *Rákóczi Ferenc Élete*. Budapest: Szent István Társulat, 1925.

Massie, Robert K., *Peter the Great, His Life and World*. New York: Alfred A. Knopf, Inc., 1980.

Milton, Joyce & Davidson, Caroline, *One Family, Two Empires*. Rizzoli Editore, HBJ Press, 1980.

Mitchison, Rosalind, *A History of Scotland*. London: Methuen & Co., Ltd., 1970.

Morrison, Samuel Eliot, *Admiral of the Sea—A Life of Christopher Columbus*. Boston: Little, Brown & Co., 1942.

Mowat, R. B., *Europe, 1715-1815*. New York: Longmans, Green & Co., 1929.

Muir, Dorothy, *A History of Milan under the Visconti*. London: Methuen & Co., Ltd., 1924.

Newman, Ernest, *The Wagner Operas*. New York: Alfred A. Knopf, Inc. 1949.

Novak, Maximilian, *Defoe and the Nature of Man*. New York: Oxford University Press, 1963.

Okey, Thomas, *Venice and Its Story*. New York: E. P. Dutton & Co., Inc., 1930.

Orselli, C.; Rescigno, E.; & Garavaglia, R., *Nascita dell'Opera*. Milan: Gruppo Editoriale Fabbri, 1983.

Osborne, Charles, *The Complete Operas of Verdi*. New York: Alfred A. Knopf, 1970.

Palmer, R. R., *The World of the French Revolution*. New York: Harper & Row, 1971.

Passage, Charles E., *Friedrich Schiller*. New York: Frederick Ungar Publishing Co., Inc., 1975.

Pendle, Karin, *Eugène Scribe and French Opera of the 19th Century*. Ann Arbor MI: UMI Research Press, 1979.

Pernoud, Régine, *Joan of Arc,* transl. by Edward Hyams. New York: Stein & Day, 1966.

Petrie, Sir Charles, *Philip II of Spain*. London: Eyre & Spottiswoode, 1963.

Pierson, Peter O.M., "The Tragedy of Philip II". *Opera News,* February 24, 1979.

Plumb, J. H., *The Horizon Book of the Renaissance*. New York: American Heritage Publishing Co., 1961.

Pocock, Tom, *Horatio Nelson*. New York: Alfred A. Knopf, Inc., 1988.

Respighi, Elsa, *Ottorino Respighi*. Milan: G. Ricordi & Co., 1954.

Richtman, Jack, *Adrienne Lecouvreur, the Actress and the Age*. Englewood Cliffs NJ: Prentice Hall, Inc., 1971.

Rosenthal, Harold & Warrack, John, *The Concise Oxford Dictionary of Opera,* 2nd Edition. Oxford: Oxford University Press, 1979.

Ross, J. B. & McLaughlin, M. M. (eds.), *The Portable Medieval Reader*. New York: The Viking Press, 1949.

Ruggiers, Paul G., *Florence in the Age of Dante*. Norman OK: University of Oklahoma Press, 1964.

Runciman, Steven, *The Sicilian Vespers*. New York: Cambridge University Press, 1958.

Sadie, Stanley (ed.), *The New Grove Dictionary of Opera,* mng. ed. Christina Bashford. New York: Grove's Dictionaries of Music Inc., 1992 (4 vols).

Sanderlin, George, *Eastward to India*. New York: Harper & Row, 1965.

Scarfe, Francis, *André Chénier, His Life and Work*. Oxford: Oxford at the Clarendon Press, 1965.

Schaffran, Emmerich, *Geschichte der Longobarden*. Leipzig: Hase & Koehler, 1938.

Schama, Simon, *Citizens—A Chronicle of the French Revolution*. New York: Alfred A. Knopf, 1989.

Schmidgall, Gary, *Literature as Opera*. New York: Oxford University Press, 1977.

Schweitzer, Frederick M., *A History of the Jews Since the First Century A.D.* New York: The Macmillan Co., 1971.

Shulman, Laurie C., *Music Criticism of the Paris Opera in the 1830s*. Ann Arbor MI: UMI Research Press, 1985.

Sinor, Denes, *History of Hungary*. New York: Frederick A. Praeger, 1959.

Smith, Lacey Baldwin, *Elizabeth Tudor, Portrait of a Queen*. Boston: Little, Brown & Co., 1975.

_____, *This Realm of England*. Boston: D. C. Heath & Co., 1966.

Smith, Patrick J., *The Tenth Muse (A Historical Study of the Opera Libretto)*. New York: Alfred A. Knopf, 1970.

Smith, Rhea Marsh, *Spain—A Modern History*. Ann Arbor: The University of Michigan Press, 1965.

Suetonius, *The Twelve Caesars,* transl. by Robert Graves. New York: Penguin Books, 1979.

Stendhal, *The Life of Rossini,* 2nd Ed., transl. by Richard N. Coe. London: John Calder Ltd., 1985.

Tasso, Torquato, *Jerusalem Delivered,* transl. & ed. by Ralph Nash. Detroit: Wayne State University Press, 1987.

Tenbrock, Robert-Hermann, *A History of Germany*. Munich: Max Huber Verlag, 1968.

Teubner, Curt, *Die Edgarsage*. Halle: E. Karras GMBH, 1915.

Thompson, J. M., *Napoleon Bonaparte*. London: Basil Blackwell, Ltd., 1952, 1988.

Tuchman, Barbara W., *A Distant Mirror— The Calamitous 14th Century.* New York: Ballantine Books, 1978.

Vernadsky, George, *The Tsardom of Moscow, Part I.* New Haven: Yale University Press, 1969.

Walshe, M. O'C., *Medieval German Literature.* Cambridge MA: Harvard University Press, 1962.

Wandruszka, Adam, *The House of Hapsburg,* transl. by C. & H. Epstein. New York: Doubleday & Co., 1964.

Ward, Kaari, *Jesus and His Times.* Pleasantville NY: The Readers Digest Association, Inc., 1987.

Wedgwood, C. V., *Richelieu and the French Monarchy.* New York: The Macmillan Publishing Co., 1962.

_____, *The Thirty Years War.* New York: Methuen & Co., 1981.

Weigall, Arthur, *Nero, the Singing Emperor of Rome.* New York: G. P. Putnam & Sons, 1930.

Weinstock, Herbert, *Rossini: A Biography.* New York: Alfred A. Knopf, 1968.

Wilkins, Ernest Hatch, *A History of Italian Literature.* Cambridge MA: Harvard University Press, 1954.

Young, Alexander, *A Short History of Belgium and Holland.* London: T. Fisher Unwin Ltd., 1915.

Zülch, W. K., *Der historische Grünewald.* Munich: F. Bruckmann Verlag, 1938.

CHRONOLOGY

Including representative operas on historical subjects.[*]

Prepared by THOMAS P. LEWIS

BC/BCE

3000-51 **Period of Egyptian pharaohs.** c.1375-1358: **Akhnaten.** 116: Ptolemy Lathyrus (Ptolemy IX Soter ["Savior"] II), joint ruler with his mother Cleopatra III[**] deposed by her in favor of his younger brother Ptolemy X Alexander. **81: Cleopatra Berenice** daughter of Ptolemy Lathyrus succeeds to her father's throne; she may have married her cousin Alexander (Ptolemy XI "Auletes" or "the Piper" Alexander II) by order of Roman dictator Sulla.

¶*Akhnaten* (Glass, 1984)

¶*Berenice, regina d'Egitto* (Perti, 1709; D. Scarlatti, 1718; Araia, 1734; Handel, 1737 — on Cleopatra Berenice). For related "Berenice" operas SEE ALSO 280 BC and 1-337 AD (emperor Titus) entries, below.

¶*Tolomeo et Alessandro, ovvero La corona disprezzata* (D. Scarlatti, 1711), *Tolomeo re d'Egitto* (Handel, 1728; Porpora, c.1730)

¶OTHER: *Aida* (Verdi, 1871 — "in the time of the pharaohs")

1400-500 **Biblical times.** 1270: **Exodus of the Hebrews** from Egypt (traditional date). 586-539: **Captivity of the Hebrews** in Babylonia.

¶*Daniel* (Schürmann, 1701)

¶*Die wohl und beständig liebende Michal, oder Der siegende und fliehende David* (J.W. Franck, 1679), *David et Jonathan* (Charpentier, 1688), *Le roi David* (Mermet, 1846; Honegger, 1921), *David* (Milhaud, 1954). SEE ALSO SAUL, below.

¶*Joseph en Egypte* (Méhul, 1807), *Josef och hans bröder* (*Joseph and His Brothers*) (Rosenberg, 1948 opera-oratorio), *Joseph and the Amazing Technicolor Dreamcoat* (Lloyd Webber, 1968 musical show)

¶*Joshua* (Knecht, 1764)

¶*Judith und Holofernes* (M. Hebenstreit, 1849), *Judith* (Fusz, 1814; E. Naumann, 1858; A.F. Doppler, 1870; Ettinger, 1921; Honegger, 1926; E. Goosens, 1929; N. Berg, 1935), *Giuditta* (Raimondi, 1827; Levi, 1844; A. Peri, 1860; Gnecchi, 1953), *Yudif* (Serov, 1863; Chishko, 1923). See also L. Kozeluch, 1799; Silveri, 1885; Falchi, 1887. SEE ALSO: *Holofernes* (Reznicek, 1923)

¶*Moses oder Der Auszug aus Ägypten* (Süssmayr, 1792), *Mosè in Egitto* (Rossini, 1818), *Moses* (Seyfried, 1813; A. Rubinstein, 1891), *Mosé* (G. Orefice, 1905), *Moses und Aron* (Schönberg, 1954)

¶*Der gestürtzte und wieder erhöhte Nebucadnezar, König zu Babylon* (Keiser, 1704), *Nabucco* (Verdi, 1842). See also Ariosti, 1706

¶?*Der Fall des grossen Richters in Israel, Simson, oder Die abgekühlte Liebesrache der*

---

*   ? = uncertain identification.

**   Great-grandmother of Caesar's Cleopatra (Ptolemy XI, following, was to become the latter's father).

Deborah (Graupner, 1709), *Samson* (Rameau, 1727; Müller, 1808; Duprez, 1857; Szokolay, 1973), *Sansone* (F. Basili, 1824; C. Conti, before 1831), *Samson* (Raff, 1875), *Samson et Dalila* (Saint-Saëns, 1877), *Shamshoun wa Dalilah (Samson and Delilah)* (Husni, 1922). See also Tucek, 1803; Mercadante, 1831; Champein, early 19th cent. SEE ALSO: *The Warrior* (Rogers, 1944 musical show on Samson)
¶*Saul, König in Israel* (Seyfried, 1810), *Saul* (Vaccai, 1829; Ceccherini, 1843; Buzzi, 1843; Speranza, 1844; Contilli, 1941), *Saul og David (Saul and David)* (Nielsen, 1901),
¶*Semiramis boscareccia* (Manfredi, 1593—the original "Semiramis" possibly the historical figure Sammuramat, wife of the Assyrian king Shamshi-Adad V, 824-810 BC; other versions place Semiramis as early as 3rd millenium BC and as e.g. Queen of Babylon, 8th cent BC), *La Semiramide in India* (Sacrati, 1640), *La Semiramide* (Cesti, 1667; P.A. Ziani, 1670), *Semiramis* (Strungk, 1681; Husni, Kamil al-Khol'i & Riyad al-Sunbati, 1930), *Semiramis, oder Die allererste regierende Königin* (J.W. Franck, 1683), *Semiramide* (A. Scarlatti, 1701; Pollarolo, 1714; Vivaldi, 1732; K.H. Graun, 1754; Sarti, 1762; Bernasconi, 1765; Rossini, 1823), *Semiramide regina dell'Assiria* (Porpora, 1724), *Semiramide in Ascalona* (Caldara, 1725), *Semiramide riconosciuta (Semiramis recognized)* (Vinci, 1729; Porpora, 1729, 1739; Giacomelli, 1730; Leo, 1730; Porta, 1733; Aliprandi, 1740; Jommelli, 1741, 1753, 1762; Lampugnani, 1741; Hasse, 1744; Terradellas, 1746; Gluck, 1748; Galuppi, 1749; Perez, 1757; Giuseppe de Majo, 1751; G. Scarlatti, 1751; Rutini, 1752; Cocchi, 1753; Brusa, 1756; Fischietti, 1759; Manfredini, 1760; Sarti, 1762; Sacchini, 1764; Bernasconi, 1765; Myslivecek, 1765; Traetta, 1765; Bertoni, 1767; Guglielmi, 1776; Salieri, 1782; Schacht, ?; Meyerbeer, 1819), *Il finto Nino, overo La semiramide riconosciuta* (Araia, 1737), *La morte di Semiramide* (Portugal, 1801), *Sémiramis* (Catel, 1802), *Semirâma* (Respighi, 1910). SEE ALSO: *La regina creduta re* (G. Bononcini, 1706). See also Aldrovandini, 1701; Destouches, 1718; Paisiello, 1773; Mortellari, 1784; Gyrowetz, 1791; Borghi, 1791; Cimarosa, 1799; Nicolini, early 19th cent.; Garcia, 1828
¶?*Salomon* (Schürmann, 1701), *Die über die Liebe triumphirende Weisheit, oder Salomon* (Keiser, 1703), *Sad Salomona (The Judgment of Solomon)* (Elsner, 1806), *Solomons Urteil* (P. Ritter, 1808). SEE ALSO: *La Reine de Saba* (Gounod, 1862), *Die Königin von Saba* (Goldmark, 1875), *Sulamith* (Klenau, 1913—on the Song of Solomon)
¶OTHER: *Die Makkabäer (The Maccabees)* (A. Rubinstein, 1875), *Esther* (Strungk, 1680; Weisgall, 1993), *Dèbora e Jaéle (Deborah and Jael)* (Pizzetti, 1922), ?*Esther* (Meyerowitz, 1957)

1220-1210   Trojan War (traditional date). Basis of the *Iliad, Odyssey* and *Aeneid.* 1184: legendary arrival of Aeneas in Italy.
Les Troyens (Berlioz, 1858), *King Priam* (Tippett, 1962)

753   Rome founded (traditional date). 715-672: **Numa Pompilius,** fabled 2nd king of Rome. 672-642: period of **Tullus Hostillius,** 3rd king of Rome, during whose reign the legendary Horatius (or three Horatii brothers) and Curiatus (or three Curiatii brothers) battled on behalf of warring Rome and neighboring town of Alba Longa respectively.
¶*Der fromme und friedfertige König der Römer Numa Pompilius* (Conradi, 1691)
¶*Orazio (Horatius)* (Tosi, 1688), *Orazio e Curiazo* (Bertoni, 1746), *Les Horaces* (Salieri, 1786), *Gli Orazi ed i Curiazi* (Zingarelli, 1795; Cimarosa, 1796), *Gli Orazi e i Curiazi* (Portugal, 1798), *Orazi e Curiazi* (Mercadante, 1846)

606 **Destruction of Nineveh.** End of the Assyrian Empire, which had long dominated the Near East.

?568-?488 Gautama Buddha.

?551-478 Confucius.

550-336 Classical world from Cyrus to Alexander. ?559-530: **Cyrus the Great,** founder of the Persian Empire;[*] ?540-489: **Miltiades,** Athenian general—defeated Persians at Battle of Marathon (490). 529-522: **Cambyses II** ruler of Persia. 525-459: **Themistocles,** Athenian statesman and general. 521-486: **Darius I** (b.558?), general in army of Cambyses II, becomes ruler of Persia. ?495-429: **Pericles,** Athenian statesman, orator and general. 485-465: **Xerxes I "the Great",** son of Darius I, ruler of Persia. 480: Xerxes invades Greece; battles of Themopylae, Salamis. 479: Persians defeated at Plateau, Mycale. 465-424: **Artaxerxes I** succeeds his father Xerxes I. 450?-404: **Alcibiades,** Athenian general, protége of Socrates, exiled and assassinated. 435?: death of **Phydias** (b.c. 500), Greek sculptor. 420?: **Timon** citizen of Athens—proverbial misanthrope said to have allowed only Alcibiades as his friend. 424-405: **Darius II,** king of Persia—divides empire into 20 provinces (satrapies). 399: death of **Socrates** (b. 470). 359-336: **Philip II** (b. 382) King of Macedonia.

¶*Alcibiade* (M.A. Ziani, 1689), *Alcibiades* (Capranica, 1746)
¶*Artaserse, ovvero L'ormondo costante* (Grossi, 1669), *Artaserse* (Sandoni, 1709; Ariosti, 1724; Vinci, 1730; ?Chiocchetti, 1730; Hasse, 1730; Zamparelli, 1731; Bambini, 1733; Bioni, 1733; Boschi & Hasse, 1734; Paganelli, 1737; F. Poncini Zilioli, 1737; Schiassi, 1737; Araia, 1738; Brivio, 1738; Ferrandini, 1739; Adolfati, 1741; Arena, 1741; Chiarini, 1741; Gluck, 1741; Graun, 1743; Scalabrini, 1743; Duni, 1744; Terradellas, 1744; Abos, 1746; Bernasconi, 1746; V. Ciampi, 1747; Maggiore, 1747; G. Scarlatti, 1747; Carcani, 1748; Perez, 1748; Smith, 1748; Galuppi, 1749, 1751; Jommelli, 1749, 1756; Lampugnani, 1749; Mele, 1749; G. Bollano, 1750; Pampani, 1750; Dal Barba, 1751; Pescetti, 1751; Fischietti, 1754; Cocchi, 1755; O. Mei, 1755; Peretti, 1755; Gasparini, 1756; Pampani, 1756; ?G. Quagliattini, 1757; Scolari, 1757; J.C. Bach, 1760; Sarti, 1760; Arne, 1762; Majo,

---

[*] Peris—later Persia—was the name given by the Greeks to a region of southern Iran. Its people had migrated there from Russia or central Asia before the 600s; were ruled by the Assyrians, and then the Medes, until the 500s. In 550 Cyrus overthrew the Median king, Astyages; defeated the latter's brother-in-law, Croesus, at Sardis c.546. He conquered Babylon in 539, freeing the Jews from Babylonia captivity c. 536. By the time of his death in battle (530), Cyrus had conquered the whole of Asia Minor, Babylonia, Syria and Palestine, and made Persia the world's leading nation. His son Cambyses II conquered Egypt four years later.

1762; Piccinni, 1762; Fiorillo, 1765; Sertori, 1765; Ponzo, 1766; Boroni, 1767; Sacchini, 1768; Paisiello, 1771; Vento, 1771; Manfredini, 1772; Myslivecek, 1774; Borghi, 1775; Bertoni, 1776, 1779, 1788?; Guglielmi, 1777; Re, 1777; Caruso, 1780; Rust, 1781; Ullinger, 1781; Zannetti, 1782; Alessandri, 1783; Cimarosa, 1784; Schacht, 1785; Bianchi, 1787; Anfossi, 1788; Tarchi, 1788; Andreozzi, 1789; Zingarelli, 1789; ?Parenti, 1780s; Ceracchini, 1795; G. Nicolini, 1795; Portugal, 1806), *Artaserse Longimano* (Pampani, 1737), *Artaserse re di Persia* (Isouard, 1794). SEE ALSO: *Dal er ser el hijo al padre* (Corradini, 1736), *The Regicide* (Lucas, 1840) ¶*Der hochmüthige, gestürtzte und wieder erhabene Croesus (The proud, overthrown and again exalted Croesus)* (R. Keiser, 1678), *Croesus* (Förtsch, 1684)

¶?*Ciro* (Cavalli & Provenzale, 1654; F.B. Conti, 1715), *Siroe re di Persia (Cyrus King of Persia)* (Vinci, 1726; Porta, 1726; Porpora, 1727; Sarro, 1727; Vivaldi, 1727; Handel, 1728; Fiorè, 1729; Bioni, 1732; Hasse, 1733; Latilla, 1740; Perez, 1740; G. Scarlatti, 1742; Manna, 1743; Scalabrini, 1744; Mazzoni, 1746; Wagenseil, 1748; Cocchi,1750; Conforto, 1752; Uttini, 1752; Galuppi, 1754; Lampugnani, 1755; Errichelli, 1758; Piccinni, 1759; Raupach, 1760; G.B. Cedronio,?1760; Boroni, 1764; Guglielmi, 1764; Tozzi, 1767; Traetta, 1767; Franchi, 1770; Borghi, 1771; Sarti, 1779; Beltrami, 1783; Ubaldi, 1810), *Ciro riconosciuto (Cyrus recognized)* — Astyages king of Media yields his throne to Cyrus (Araia, 1731; Caldara, 1736; Rindaldo di Capua, 1737; Leo, 1739; Chiarini, 1743; Jommelli, 1744, 1747, 1749, G. Meneghetti, 1758; Galuppi, 1745; Smith, 1745; Verocai, 1746; Duni, 1748; Hasse, 1751; Fiorillo, 1753; Sarti, 1754; G. Meneghetti, 1758; Cocchi, 1759; Galuppi, 1759; Piccinni, 1759; Petrucci, 1765; Puppi, 1765; Mango, 1767; P. Persicchini, 1779; Tarchi, 1796; Capotorti, 1805; Mosel, 1818), *Cyrus in Persien* (Seyfried, 1803), *Ciro in Babilonia, ossia La caduta di Baldassare (Cyrus in Babylon, or the Fall of Belshazzar)* (Rossini, 1812), *Ciro in Babilonia* (Raimondi, 1820)

¶*L'incoronazione di Dario* (Freschi, 1684; Perti, 1686; Aldrovandini, 1705; Vivaldi, 1717), *Dario* (Ariosti, 1725; G. Scarlatti, 1741; Galuppi, 1751), *La disfatta di Dario* (Cafaro, 1756; G. Giordani, 1789). SEE ALSO: ?*Palmira, regina di Persia* (Salieri, 1795 — incl. "King Darius of Persia")

¶*Miltiade à Marathon* (Lemoyne, 1793)

¶*Pericle re di Tiro* (Cottrau, c.1915), *Pericles* (Hovhaness, 1975). SEE ALSO: *Americles* (Leslee, 1983 — after Shakespeare drama)

¶*Filippo, re della Grecia* (Pollarolo, 1706), *Filippo Re di Macedonia* (Vivaldi & G. Boneveni, 1721)

¶*Die schöne Galatea* (Suppé, 1865 — features sculptor Phydias)

¶*La patienza (pazienza) di Socrate con due moglie* (Draghi, 1680; Caldara & Reutter, 1731; Almeida, 1733), *Der geduldige Sokrates* (Telemann, 1721)

¶*Temistocle in Persia* (Draghi, 1681), *Il Temistocle* (Chelleri, 1721; Orlandini, 1737), *Temistocle* (M.A. Ziani, 1701; Porpora, 1718, 1743; Caldara, 1736; Chinzer, 1737; Latilla, 1737; Orlandini, 1737; Ristori, 1738; Poncini Zilioli, 1739; Bernasconi, 1740; Maggiori, 1743; Costantini, 1744; Finazzi, 1746; Jommelli, 1757, 1765; Manna, 1761; Durán, 1762; Schwanenberger, 1762; Uhde, 1762; Monza, 1766; J.C. Bach, 1772; G. Brunetti, 1776; Ullinger, 1777; Beltrami, 1780; Pacini, 1823), *Thémistocle* (Philidor, 1787)

¶*Timon of Athens* (Purcell, 1694 masque; J. Tunick, 1971; S. Oliver, 1991), *Timon* (K. Nürnberg, 1985). ?See also Leopold I (1696)

¶*Xerse* (Cavalli, 1654; G.B. Bononcini, 1694), *Xerxes in Abydus* (Förtsch, 1689), ?*L'incoronazione di Serse* (Tosi, 1690), *Serse* (Handel, 1738), *Il ritorno di Serse* (Portugal, 1797; Zingarelli, 1809)

¶ALSO: *Marathon–Salamis* (Carrer, 1886)

510   **Roman Republic established** (traditional date). 498: Republic
          formed after death of Lucius **Tarquinius** Superbus (Tarquin the
          Proud — Etruscan prince and last king of Rome, 534-510), killed
          at Lake Regillus; according to legend his son Tarquinius Sextus
          in 509 ravished **Lucretia** (wife of the Roman consul Tarquinius
          Collatinus) who, dishonored, commits suicide. 509: consulship of
          Lucius Junius **Brutus** — nephew and enemy of Tarquin the Proud
          and "Founder of the Roman Republic".[*] 493: Gaius Marcius
          (**Coriolanus**), Roman general, conquers town of Corioli;
          banished from Rome 491. c.324: **Lucius Papirius Cursor** leads
          war against the Samnites. Also: **Titus Manlius**, Roman consul in-
          volved in hostilities against rebellious Latins.

          ¶*Il Coriolano* (Cavalli, 1669; Graun, 1749; Niccolini, 1808), *Caio Marzio Coriolano*
          (Perti, 1683; Caldara, 1717; Ariosti, 1723; N. Conti, 1734), *Marzio Coriolano* (Pol-
          larolo, 1698), *Coriolano, o L'assedio di Roma* (G. Nicolini, 1808), *Coriolanus*
          (Baeyens, 1941; Cikker, 1974), *Koriolan* (Sulek, 1958)
          ¶*Lucio Papirio Dittatore* (Caldara, 1719; Giacomelli, 1729)
          ¶*Il Giunio Bruto* (Tosi, 1686; Cimarosa, 1781 — on Roman consul Lucius Junius
          Brutus who opposed Tarquin the Proud and the Etruscans), *Giunio Bruto, overo
          La caduta dei Tarquinii* (A. Scarlatti, Cesarini & Caldara, 1711), ?*Bruto* (G.
          Nicolini, early 19th cent.). SEE ALSO: *Mutio Scevola* (Cavalli, 1665), *Muzio
          Scevola* (Monari, 1692; G. Bononcini, 1695; Amadei, Bononcini & Handel, 1721 —
          brave exploits of Mucius Scaevola as King Lars Porsena of Etruria attempts to
          restore the expelled Tarquinius Superbus to the Roman throne). SEE ALSO:
          Die kleinmühtige Selbst-Mörderin Lucretia, oder Die Staats-Thorheit des Brutus
          (Keiser, 1705 - fate of Lucretia Collatinus), ?*Der romanische Lucretia* (Schweit-
          zelsperger, 1714), *Lucretia* (Marschner, 1826), *Lucrezia* (Respighi, c.1936), *The
          Rape of Lucretia* (Britten, 1946)
          ¶*Tito Manlio* (Pollarolo, 1696; Giannettini, 1701; Ariosti, 1717; Vivaldi, 1719;
          Vivaldi, Boni & Giorgi, 1720; Manna, 1742; Jommelli, 1743; Abos, 1751; Latilla,
          1755; Cocchi, 1761; P.A. Guglielmi, 1763; Borghi, 1780; G. Giordani, 1784; Tar-
          chi, 1791)

336-323   Period of **Alexander the Great** (b. 356), succeeds Philip (326),
          begins Persian campaign(334), defeats Darius at Issus (333), con-
          quers Tyre and Jerusalem (332), defeats Darius at Gaugamela
          (331), occupies Babylon, Susa and Persepolis (330), invades India
          (327), extends empire to Indus river (326), dies at Babylon (323).

          ?*Alessandro vincitor di se Stesso* (A. Cesti, 1651; Cavalli, 1651), *La magnanimità
          d'Alesandro* (A. Cesti, 1662), *Alessandro Magno in Sidone* (M.A. Ziani, 1679),
          Alexander in Sidon (Förtsch, 1688), *Talestri innamorata d'Alessandro Magno*
          (Sabadini, 1693; Pollarolo, 1697), *La superbia d'Alessandro* (Steffani, 1698), *Ales-
          sandro il grande* (Chelleri, 1708), *Alessandro in Sidone* (F.B. Conti, 1721; G. Bonon-
          cini, 1737), *Alessandro* (Handel, 1726), *Alessandro nell'Indie (Alexander in India)*

---

[*]   Note: the last kings of Rome were succeeded by the Roman consuls Lucius Junius
      Brutus and Tarquinius Collatinus.

(Vinci, 1729; Predieri, 1731; Mancini, 1732; Pescetti, 1732; Bioni, 1733; Luccini, 1734; Schiassi, 1734; Galuppi, 1738, 1754, 1755; Corselli, 1738; Brivio, 1742; Sarro, 1743; Uttini, 1743; Jommelli, 1744, 1760; D. Perez, 1744, 1758; Chiarini, 1745; Pelegrini, 1746; Abos, 1747; Wagenseil, 1748; Scalabrini, 1749; Scolari, 1749; Rutini, 1750; Fiorillo, 1752; Latilla, 1753; G. Scarlatti, 1753; Araia, 1755; Piccinni, 1758, 1774; Holzbauer, 1759; Cocchi, 1761; Dal Barba, 1761; Sarti, 1761, 1787; J.C. Bach, 1762; Traetta, 1762; G. Brunetti, 1763; Sacchini, 1763; Fischietti, 1764; Sciroli, 1764; Majo, 1766; Gatit, 1768; J.G. Naumann, 1768; Bertoni, 1769; J. Kozeluch, 1769; ?Felici, 1771; Anfossi, 1772; Paisiello, 1773; Corri, 1774; Monza, 1775; Rust, 1775; Marascalchi, 1778; Mortellari, 1778; Vincenti, 1778; A. Calegari, 1779; Cimarosa, 1781; Cherubini, 1784; Bianchi, 1785; V. Chiavacci, 1785; Caruso, 1787; Tarchi, 1788; Gulgielmi, 1789; Gnecco, 1800; Pacini, 1824), *Alessandro e Poro* (Graun, 1744), ?*Alexander* (Teyber, 1801), *Alexander in Indien* (Ritter, 1811), *Il trionfo di Alessandro Magno il Macedone* (Andreozzi, 1815). SEE ALSO: *Poro, re dell'Indie* (Handel, 1731; Porpora, 1731; Galuppi, 1738; Gluck, 1744), *Cleofide* (Hasse, 1731; Agricola, 1754)

323-240 Post-Alexandrian **Egypt and Syria**. 323: at death of Alexander his empire is partitioned among his generals, with a new Egyptian dynasty lasting from **Ptolemy I Soter** ("Savior"), one of his generals, until the death of Cleopatra in 30 BC. 290: Berenice I, wife of Ptolemy I, has city of Berenice built on Red Sea. Meanwhile **Seleucus I (358-280) King of Syria** founds city of Antioch (named for his father) as capital city of Seleucia, on the Tigris river.[*] 285: Ptolemy I Soter abdicates, is succeeded by **Ptolemy II Philadelphus** (d.246). 280: assassination of Seleucus I, who is succeeded by son **Antiochus I Soter (324-261)**. 262: Antiochus I succeeded by **Antiochus II (Theos)** on Seleucid (north Syrian) throne. 249: Antiochus II divorces wife **Laodice** and marries **Berenice II**, daughter of Ptolemy II of Egypt. 246: Laodice murders Antiochus II and Berenice; **Ptolemy III** of Egypt (note: his own wife is named Berenice III) sets out to avenge his sister and embarks on a career of conquest in Seleucid empire (now under Seleucus II). This is **Third Syrian (Laodicean) War (246-241)**. Ptolemy III weakens most of Seleucid empire, reaches borders of India before retiring to Eygpt.
¶*Laodicea e Berenice* (Perti, 1694; A. Scarlatti, 1701); *Berenice in Siria* (Carafa, 1818). For other "Berenice" operas see 3000-51 BC and AD 1-337 entries.
¶*La pace fra Tolomeo e Seleuco* (Pollarolo, 1691; Sabadini, 1691)

264-146 Period of **Punic Wars** between Rome and Carthage. 264-241: **First Punic War** for control over Sicily. 255: capture by the Carthaginians of Roman general **Marcus Attilius Regulus** (also consul in 267, 256; d.c. 250). 218-201: **Second Punic War — Hannibal**

---

[*] Marks end of history of Babylon — the Babylonians now re-established in new city of Seleucia.

crosses the Alps into Italy. 206: Roman General Publius Cornelius Scipius Africanus (**Scipio Africanus the Elder,** 233-183)
defeats the Carthaginians in Spain. 202: Scipio Africanus the
Elder defeats Hannibal at Zama, leaving Rome without a rival in
the western Mediterranean. 149-146: **Third Punic War** — Romans
under **Scipio Africanus the Younger** (185-129) destroy Carthage.
Other events: Demetrius Soter, Seleucid king (162-150), seized
throne of Syria; exiled his son **Demetrius II ("Nicator")** to escape
the onslaught of **Alexander Balas,** usurper of the Syrian throne.
The young Demetrius II subsequently overthrew Balas and
regained his royal position.

¶*Annibale in Capua* (P.A. Ziani, 1661; Salieri, 1801, Farinelli, 1810), *Hannibal* (J.W.
Franck, 1681), *Scipio und Hannibal* (Strungk, 1698), *Hannibal in Capua*
(Schürmann, 1726), *Annibale* (Sabadini, 1706; Porpora, 1731; Giacomelli, 1731),
Annibale in Torino (Zingarelli, 1792; L. Ricci, 1830), *Annibale in Bitinia* (G.
Nicolini)

¶*Demetrio* (C. Pallavicino, 1666), *Demetrio tiranno* (Sabadini, 1694), *Demetrio* —
popular Metastasio libretto which also includes Alexander Balas and his
daught Cleonice, who eventually marries Demetrius II ((Caldara, 1731; Bioni,
1732; Giai, 1732; Hasse, 1732, 1737, 1740; Leo, 1732; Pescetti, 1732; Schiassi,
1732; Mele, 1736; Giacomelli, 1737; D. Perez, 1741; Carcani, 1742; Caroli, 1742;
Lampugnani, 1744; A. Duni, ?1746; Wagenseil, 1746; Galuppi, 1748; D. Naseli,
1748; Jommelli, 1749; Pulli, 1749; Piazza, 1750; Gibelli, 1751; Pallavicini, 1751; G.
Scarlatti, 1752; Fiorillo, 1753; Cherubini, 1755; Ferrandini, 1756 or 1758; S. Peril-
lo, 1758; Insanguine, 1759; Ponzo, 1759; Eberlin, 1760; Galuppi, 1761; Sala, 1762;
Perez, 1766; Pampani, 1768; Monza, 1769; Piccinni, 1769; Paisiello, 1771, 1779;
Bernasconi, 1772; Guglielmi, 1772; Myslivecek, 1773, 1779; Bianchi, 1774;
Bachschmidt, 1777; G. Giordani, 1779; Gresnick, 1786; Tarchi, 1787; Mayr, 1824;
A. Gandini, 1828), *Demetrio e Polibio (Demetrius and Polybius)* (Rossini, 1812 — on
the kings of Syria and Parthia). SEE ALSO: *Chi tal nasce tal vive, ovvero L'Ales-
sandro Bala* (P.A Ziani, 1678), *Cleonice, regina di Siria* (Saldoni, 1840), *Cleonice*
(Gluck, 1742)

¶*Attilio Regolo* (Pagliardi, 1693; Hasse, 1750; Jommelli, 1753; Monza & Beltrami,
1780), *Marco Attilio Regolo* (Rampini, 1713; A. Scarlatti, 1719)

¶*Scipio africano* (Cavalli, 1664; Bianchi, 1787), *Der grossmüthige Scipio* (Krieger,
1690), *Scipione preservatore di Roma* (Draghi, 1690), *La conquista delle Spagne di
Scipione Africano il giovane* (A.M. Bononcini, 1707), *Scipione nelle Spagne* (A. Scar-
latti, 1714; Caldara, 1722; Albinoni, 1724; Ferrandini, 1732; Arrigoni, 1739; Leo,
1740; Galuppi, 1746; Bertoni, 1768), *Publio Cornelio Scipione* (Pollarollo, 1712;
Vinci, 1722), *Scipione* (Handel, 1726; Araia, 1745; Sarti, 1778; G. Giordani, 1788),
Scipio in Cartagine nuova (Giacomelli, 1728), *Scipio Africanus* (Graun, 1732), *Scipio
Africano il maggiore* (Caldara, 1735), *Il sogno di Scipione (The Dream of Scipio)*
(Predieri, 1735; Nichelmann, 1744; ?Sciroli, 1752; Llussa, 1753; Sarti, 1755;
Hasse, 1758; Cinque, 1750s; Bonno, 1763; Mango, 1764; Uttini, 1764; Santos,
1768; Mozart, 1772), *Scipione in Cartagine* (Galuppi, 1742; Sacchini, 1770; Farinel-
li, 1815; Mercadante, 1820), *Der Traum des Scipio* (Porta, 1744), *La clemenza di
Scipione* (J.C. Bach, 1778), *Scipio vor Karthago* (Knecht, 1789), *Il trionfo di Scipione
in Cartagine* (G.M. Curcio, 1795). SEE ALSO: *Il trionfo della costanza* (Bernasconi,
1765)

¶ALSO: *La Sofonisba (Siface)(Sophonisba, or Syphax)* (Gluck, 1744 — Carthaginian
heroine poisons herself rather than be taken by Scipione to Rome as prisoner

of war—see also Caldara, 1708; Traetta, 1761; Portugal, 1803), ?*La caduta della nuova Cartagine* (Farinelli, 1803)

214   Great Wall of China begun.

146-44   Roman consolidation and expansion; period of **Julius Caesar** (102-44). ?155-86: **Gaius Marius,** Roman consul in 107, 104-100, 86; popular leader and principal architect of Roman army. 153-121: **Gaius Gracchus,** elected tribune 123. ?c.140-84: Lucius Cornelius **Cinna,** Roman consul in 87, 86, 85, 84. 138-78: Lucius Cornelius **Sulla** (d. 78), Roman consul 88, 80; in 87-86 defeats **Mithridates VI of Pontus** and takes Athens; dictator of Rome 82-79. 106-48: **Pompey** (Gnaeus Pompeius Magnus), member of First Triumvirate, rival of Caesar. 95-46: **Cato the Younger.** 73: Mithridates VI renews war against Rome and is defeated by Roman general **Lucullus;** 63, is defeated by Pompey and commits suicide. 73-71: revolt of slaves and gladiators under **Spartacus.** 70-19: **Virgil,** Latin poet. 58-50: Conquest of Gaul, invasion of Britain by Caesar—opened up much of western Europe to Greco-Roman domination. 51-31: **Cleopatra VII,** last queen of Egypt. 43: British under **Caractacus** defeated at Medway. 31: battle of Actium—ending civil war between **Mark Antony** and Octavian (Caesar Augustus, 27 BC/BCE-14 AD/CE), leaving the latter supreme in the Roman state.

¶*Carattaco* (J.C. Bach, 1767), *Caractacus* (Arne, 1776; ?, 1827; MacFarren, c.1834, inc)

¶*Catone Uticense* (Pollarolo, 1701), *Die Liebe gegen das Vaterland, oder Der sterbende Cato* (Keiser, 1711). *Il Catone in Utica* (Vinci, 1728; Leo, 1729; Hasse, 1731; Marchi, 1733; Torri, 1736; Vivaldi, 1737; Duni, 1740; Rinaldo di Capua, 1740; Graun, 1744; Scalabrini, 1744; Latilla, 1747; Ferrandini, 1753; Höpken, 1753; Jommelli, 1754; G. Ballabene, 1755; V. Ciampi, 1756; Poncini Zilioli, 1756; J.C. Bach, 1761; Gassmann, 1761; Majo, 1762; Piccinni, 1770; Ottani, 1777; F. Antonelli Torres, 1784; Andreozzi, 1786; Nasolini, 1789; Paisiello, 1789; Winter, 1791), *Cato* (Verocai, 1743)

¶*Il Cesare amante* (A. Cesti, 1651), *Giulio Cesare in Egitto* (Sartorio, 1676; Handel, 1724; G.M. Curci, 1796), *Giulio Cesare trionfante* (Freschi, 1682), *Il ritorno di Giulio Cesare vincitore della Mauritania* (G.B. Bononcini, 1704), *Der durch den Fall des grossen Pompejus erhöhete Julius Caesar* (Keiser, 1710), *Giulio Cesare nell'Egitto* (Pollarolo, 1713), *Cesare in Egitto* (Giacomelli, 1735; Jommelli, 1751; Sarti, 1763; G. Pacini, 1821), *Cesare e Cleopatra* (Graun, 1742), *Giulio Cesare* (D. Perez, 1762; Consorti, 1923; Malipiero, 1936), *La morte di Cesare* (Bianchi, 1788; Zingarelli, 1790), *La morte di Giulio Cesare* (Andreozzi, 1789), *Giulio Cesare nelle Gallie* (G. Nicolini, 1816), *La gioventù di Cesare* (Pavesi, 1817), *Julio César* (García Robles, 1880), *Julius Cäsar* (Carl, c.1880), *Die Ermordung Cäsars* (Klebe, 1959), *Julius Caesar* (Seyfried, 1811; A. Schmitz, 1978; Rasmussen, 1983), *Julio César* (Garcia Robles, 1880). See also Novi, 1703; Robuschi, 1790. SEE ALSO: ?*Calfurnia (Calphurnia)* (Heinicken, 1713; G. Bononcini, 1724—?on Caesar's 3rd wife Calpurnia), *Brutus* (J.C.F. Bach, 1774); also operas featuring Cleopatra incl. *La Cleopatra* (A. Cesti, 1654; Cimarosa, 1789), *La morte di Cleopatra* (Nasolini, 1791; Bianchi, 1801), *Cleopatra* (Anfossi, 1779; L. Rossi, 1876; Morales, 1891; Enna,

1894), *Gli amori di Cleopatra* (Cagnoni, c.1870), *Une nuit de Cléopâtre (A Night with Cleopatra)* (Massé, 1885), *Cléopâtre* (F. Pedrell, 1878; Massenet, 1914), *Kleopatra* (Švara, 1937) — also versions by Canazzi, 1653; Cousser, 1691; G. Scarlatti, 1760; Danzi, 1779; Weigl, 1807; Paer, 1808; Combi, 1842; Freudenthal, 1874; Freudenberg, 1882; Benoît, 1889; Hadley, 1920; P.H. Allen, 1921; O. Strauss, 1923; Brand, c.1930; La Rosa Parodi, 1938. SEE ALSO MARK ANTONY, below.
¶*Cinna* (Graun, 1748), *Il Cinna* (Portugal, 1793)
¶*Caio Gracco (Gaius Gracchus)* (G. Bononcini, 1710; Leo, 1720)
¶*Die Verurteilung des Lukullus (The Condemnation of Lucullus)* (Dessau, 1951)
¶*Marc'Antonio* (Pollarolo, 1692), *Die unglücksselige Cleopatra, Königin von Egypten* (Mattheson, 1704), *Antonius und Cleopatra* (Kaffka, 1779), *Cleopatra* (Sacchi, 1877), *Antonius und Kleopatra* (Wittgenstien, 1883; van Durme, 1959), *Antony i Kleopatra* (Yuferov, 1900), *Antony and Cleopatra* (Ardin, 1919; Gruenberg, 1961; Barber, 1966), *Antoine et Cléopâtre* (Rabaud, 1917; Bondeville, 1974), *Cetiri scene iz Sekspira (Four Scenes from Shakespeare)* (Logar, 1936), *Antonio e Cleopatra* (Malipiero, 1938), *Kleopatra* (Glonti, 1981), *Alpha et Omega* (Nürnberg, 1985). See also Sayn-Wittgenstein-Berleburg "Antony and Cleopatra" setting, 1883. For other "Cleopatra" settings SEE ALSO JULIUS CAESAR, above.
¶*Caio (Cajo) Mario* (Bioni, 1722; Jommelli, 1746; G. Scarlatti, 1755; Piccinni, ?1757; Galuppi, 1764; Scolari, 1765; Anfossi, 1770; C. Monza, 1777; Cimarosa, 1780; Bertoni, 1781; F. Bianchi, 1784; G. Giordani, 1789)
¶*Mitridate in Sebastia* (Aldrovandini, 1701), *Il Mitridate eupatore* (A. Scarlatti, 1707), *Mitridate* (Bioni, 1722; Caldara, 1728; Giai, 1730; Porpora, 1730, 1736; Terradellas, 1746; Araia, 1747; Sacchini, 1781; Tadolini, 1827), *Mitridate re di Ponto, vincitor de se stesso* (Capelli, 1723), *Mitridate, re di Ponto* (Graun, 1750; Q. Gasparini, 1767; Mozart, 1770; Tarchi, 1785), *Mitridate a Sinope* (Sarti, 1779), *La morte di Mitridate* (Nasolini, 1796; Zingarelli, 1797; Portugal, 1806). See also Aliprandi, 1738; Scheinpflug, 1754; Tarschi, 1785
¶*Pompeo Magno* (Cavalli, 1666; A. Scarlatti, 1683; Perti, 1691), *Pompeo Magno in Cilicia* (Freschi, 1681), ?*Pompeo continente* (Sabadini, 1690), *Pompeo in Armenia* (G. Scarlatti, 1744; Sarti, 1752)
¶*Spartaco* (Porsile, 1726; Platania, 1891)
¶*Silla* (Freschi, 1683), *Silla dittatore* (Vinci, 1723), *Lucio Silla* (Mozart, 1772; Anfossi, 1774; J.C. Bach, 1775; Mortellari, 1779)
¶OTHER: *Arminio* (Steffani, 1707; Handel, 1737; Hasse, 1745 — German prince brings about death of Roman general; based on Tacitus), *Norma* (Bellini, 1831 — the Romans in Britain)

4   **Birth of Jesus Christ** (traditional date). **Herod the Great** succeeded by **Herod Antipas**. Period of **John the Baptist**.
Hérodiade (Massenet, 1881 — Roman wife of Herod Antipas), *Christus* (A. Rubinstein, 1895), *Salome* (R. Strauss, 1905 — daughter of Herodias; also features Herod Antipas, John the Baptist), *Salomé* (Mariotte, 1908), ?*Jésus* (Villa-Lobos, 1918), *Tragedyja albo Rzecz o Janie i Herodzie (Tragedy or A Piece on John and Herod)* (Twardowski, 1964), *Pilate* (Hovhaness, 1966), *Jesus Christ, Superstar* (Lloyd Webber, 1972 musical show)

AD/CE

1-337   **Roman emperors from Caesar Augustus (Octavian) to Constantine the Great. 43** BC/BCE-?17 AD/CE: (Publius Ovidius Naso),

Roman poet. 27 BC/BCE-14 AD/CE: **Caesar Augustus** (founder of the imperial Roman government) succeeded by **Tiberius** (14-37). 5-40: **Cymbeline**, king of the Catuvellauni, recognized by Rome as "Rex Brittonum". 37-41: Gaius **Caligula** (b. 12) assassinated by Praetorian Guard. 47-120: **Plutarch**, Greek historian. 54: Claudius poisoned, **Nero** (54-68) becomes emperor of Rome. 69-79: **Vespasian** (Titus Flavius Sabinus Vespasianus, b. 9) — succeeded by his son **Titus** (also named Titus Flavius Sabinus Vespasianus, 79-81; b. 39?). 79: eruption of Vesuvius and destruction of **Pompeii**. 70: Jerusalem captured and destroyed by the Romans. 98-116: **Trajan,** under whom Roman Empire reaches its greatest geographical extent. 117-138: **Hadrian** (b. 76), legate of Syria; 122, visits Britain and begins construction of wall and fortifications between northern England and Scotland. 161-180: **Marcus Aurelius** (b. 121) co-emperor with **Lucius Verus** (161-169; b. 130). 193-211: **Septimius Severus**. 222-235: **Alexander Severus** (b.c. 209). 249-251: **Decius** — persecution of Christians. c.251: death of **St. Christopher**, the "carrier of Christ", at Lycia. 259: marytrdom of Saint **Polyeuctus**, Roman army officer of Greek parentage stationed in Armenia, converted to Christianity. 253-260: **Valerian**. 270-275: **Aurelian** *"restitutor orbis"*. 284-305: **Diocletian**. 306-337: **Constantine I "the Great"** (Flavius Valerius Aurelius Constantinus, b. ?280) — adopts Christianity 312.

¶*Alessandro Severo* (Lotti, 1716; Mancini, 1718; Chelleri, 1718; Sarro, 1719; Orlandini, 1723; Giacomelli, 1732; Bioni, 1733; Handel, 1738; Bernasconi, 1738; Sacchini, 1763)

¶*Ottaviano Cesare Augusto* (Legrenzi, 1682) ?*La clemenza d'Augusto* (de Luca, Pollaroli & G. Bononcini, 1697), ?*Der durch Grossmught und Gnade siegende Augustus* (Keiser, 1722), *Ottaviano in Sicilia* (Poissl, 1812)

¶*Aureliano* (C. Pallavicino, 1666), *Aureliano in Palmira* (Rossini, 1813)

¶*Caligula delirante* (Pagliardi, 1672), ?*Caligola* (Braga, 1873)

¶*Claudio Cesare* (Boretti, 1672), *Die verdammte Staat-Sucht, oder Der verführte Claudius* (Keiser, 1703), *Claudio ed Agrippina* (Schürmann & other[s]?, 1717). SEE ALSO: *Messalina* (C. Pallavicino, 1679 — third wife of Claudius, before 41; their children were Octavia, later married to Nero, and Brittanicus [Claudius Tiberius Caesar]), *Agrippina* — wife of Claudius, mother of Nero (Strungk, 1699; Porpora, 1708; Handel, 1709)

¶*La Légende de St. Christophe* (D'Indy, 1920 *drame sacré*)

¶?*Il Costantino pio* (Pollarolo, 1710), *Il Costantino* (Gasparini, 1711; Caldara, Lotti & Fux, 1716). SEE ALSO: *Massimiano* (Orlandini, 1731)

¶*Cimbelino* (van Westerhout, 1887), *Cymbeline* (Eggen, 1951; Arrieu, 1963). SEE ALSO: *Imogène, ou La gageure indiscrète* (Kreutzer, 1796), *Imogen* (Sobolewski, 1832), *Dinah* (Missa, 1894)

¶*Diocleziano* (C. Pallavicino, 1674), *Diocletianus* (J.W. Franck, 1682), *The Prophetess, or The History of Dioclesian* (Purcell, 1690)

¶*Adriano in Siria (Hadrian in Siria)* (Caldara, 1732; Giacomelli, 1733; Pergolesi, 1734; Sandoni, 1734; Broschi, 1735; Duni, 1735; Veracini, 1735; Ferrandini, 1737; Hasse, ?1737; Nebra, 1737; Porta, 1737; Ristori, 1739; Galuppi, 1740, 1758; Giai,

1740; Lampugnani, 1740; Giaino, 1741; ?Logroscino, 1742; Abos, 1746; Graun, 1746; Latilla, 1747; V. Ciampi, 1748; Scalabrini, 1749; Pampani, 1750; Adolfati, 1751; Hasse, 1752; Perez, 1752; G. Scarlatti, 1752; Valentini, 1753; Conforto, 1754; Scolari, 1754; Bernasconi, 1755; Brusa, 1757; Uttini, 1757; Rinaldo di Capua, 1758; Borghi, 1759; Mazzoni, 1760; Colla, 1762; Schwanenberger, 1762; M. Wimmer, 1764; J.C. Bach, 1765; Guglielmi, 1765; Mango, 1768; Holzbauer, c.1768; Majo, 1769; Monza, 1769; Tozzi, 1770; Sacchini, 1771; Insanquine, 1773; Monti, 1775; Myslivecek, 1776; Anfossi, 1777; Sarti, 1778; Alessandri, 1779; Rust, 1781; Cherubini,1782; Nasolini, 1789; Méhul, 1791; Mayr, 1798; ?V. Migliorucci, 1811; P. Airoldi, 1821; Mirecki, ?1826; Mercadante, 1828). SEE ALSO: ?*Die getreue Emirena* (Verocai, 1745), ?*Farnaspe* (Pescetti, 1750)

¶*Lucio Vero*—on Lucius Verus in Ephesus and Volugeses King of the Parthians[*] (Pollarolo, 1700; Albinoni, 1713; F. Gasparini, 1719; Torri, 1720; Sarro, 1722; Ciampi, 1726; Bioni, 1727; Ariosti, 1727; Araia, 1735; Manna, 1745; Jommelli, 1754; Perez, 1754; Bertoni, 1757; Sacchini, 1764; Traetta, 1774), *Lucius Verus, oder Die siegende Treue* (Keiser, 1728). SEE ALSO: *Vologeso* (Sala, 1737; Galuppi, 1748; Sarti, 1754; Bertoni, 1759; Jommelli, 1766; Colla, 1770; Sacchini, 1772; P.A. Guglielmi, 1775; Masi, 1776; Rust, 1778; Martín y Soler, 1783), *Vologeso re de'Parti* (Di Capua, 1739; Pulli, 1741; Rutini, 1775; Brunetti, 1789)

¶*Marco Aurelio* (Steffani, 1681)

¶*Nero* (Strungk, 1693; Meder, 1695; A. Rubinstein, 1876), *Nero (Die durch Blut und Mord erlangete Liebe)* (Handel, 1705), *Nerone fatto Cesare* (Perti, 1693; A. Scarlatti, 1695; Vivaldi, 1715; Orlandini, 1721), *Nerone* (C. Pallavicino, 1679; Orlandini, 1721; Duni, 1735; Boito, 1924; Mascagni, 1935), *La morte di Nerone* (Tarchi, 1792). SEE ALSO: *L'incoronazione di Poppea* (Monteverdi, 1642), *Il ripudio d'Ottavia* (Pollarolo, 1699), *Die römische Unruhe, oder die edelmühtige Octavia (The Roman Unrest, or The Noble-Spirited Octavia)* (Keiser, 1705—Nero decides to do away with his wife Octavia), *Brittanico* (Graun, 1751—on Brittanicus [Claudius Tiberius Germanicus, c. 41-55], his step-mother Agrippina, Nero), *Quo Vadis* (Chapi y Lorente, 1901 *zarzuela*; Nougués, 1909), *Misteriya apostola Pavla (The Mystery of St. Paul)* (Karetnikov, 1987—opera-oratorio on confrontation of Nero and St. Paul). SEE ALSO CLAUDIUS, above.

¶*Ovide en exil* (Hérold, 1818)

¶*Plutarque* (Solié, 1802 opéra-comique)

¶*Der im Christentum biss in den Tod beständige Märtyrer Polyeuct* (Förtsch, 1688), *Poliuto* (Donizetti, 1838), *Polyeucte* (Gounod, 1878)

¶*I due cesari (The Two Caesars)* (Legrenzi, 1683—on Bassianus Caracalla & Geta, the sons of Emperor Septimius Severus)

¶*La prosperità d'Elio Sejano* (Sartorio, 1666) & *La caduta d'Elio Sejano* (Sartorio, 1667—both operas featuring Tiberius), *L'Esule di Roma, ossia Il proscritto (The Exile from Rome, or The Proscribed Man)* (Donizetti, 1828—in the Rome of Tiberius: returned exile is sentenced to death in the Circus Maximus)

¶*Il Tito* (Cesti, 1664), *La clemenza di Tito*—on the second Titus Flavius Sabinus Vespasianus & Rome c.80 (Caldara, 1734; ?Chiocchetti, 1735; Leo, 1735; E. Peli, 1736; Marchi, 1737; Veracini, 1737; Arena, 1738; Wagenseil, 1746; Camerloher, 1747; Corradini, Corselli & Mele, 1747; Graun, 1748; Pampani, 1748; D. Perez, 1749; Correia, c.1750; Gluck, 1752; Adolfati, 1753; Jommelli, 1753, 1765; Valentini, 1753; Mazzoni, 1755; V. Ciampi, 1757; C. Cristiani, 1757; Holzbauer, 1757;

---

[*]   SEE ALSO historical Vologeses I (c.51-80) King of Parthia, who belongs to period of emperor Vespasian and not to that of Lucius Verus.

G. Scarlatti, 1757; A. Caputi, ?1750s; Cocchi, 1760; Galuppi, 1760; Franchi, 1766; Plantania, 1766; Bernasconi, 1768; Anfossi, 1769; J.G. Naumann, 1769; Sarti, 1771; Myslivecek, 1773; Bachschmidt, 1776; Beltrami, 1779; Apell, ?1787; Santos, ?1780s; Mozart, 1791; G. Nicolini, 1797; Otani, 1798; Del Fante, 1803), *Tito Vespasiano ovvero La clemenza di Tito* (Hasse, 1735), ?*Titus* (Salomon, 1774). SEE ALSO operas in which Berenice Queen of Judaea is in love with the Emperor Titus (an historical relationship), in which character of Berenice is sometimes conflated with the Alexandrian queen of three centuries earlier (see 3000-51 BC, Egypt of the pharaohs): *Berenice vendicativa* (Freschi, 1680), *Le gare di politica e d'amore (The War Between Politics and Love)* (Ruggieri, 1711), *Tito e Berenice* (Caldara, 1714; Nasolini, 1793), *Berenice* (?Bronner, 1702; Orlandini, 1725; Araia, 1730; Ferrandini, 1730; Galuppi, 1741; Perez, 1762; Fischietti, 1764; I. Platania, 1771; Rust, 1785), *Berenice in Roma* (P. Raimondi, 1824), *Bérénice* (Magnard, 1911). ALSO on Vespasian (father or son): *Vespasiano* — on Titus' father? (C. Pallavicino, 1678; Sabadini, 1689; Ariosti, 1724), *Vespasianus* (J.W. Franck, 1681), *Il Vespasiano* (Sarro, 1707). SEE ALSO: *Sabinus* (Gossec, 1773 — Gauls resist the Romans near end of reign of the elder Vespasian), *Giulio Sabino (Julius Sabinus)* (Sarti, 1781), *L'Ultimo giorno di Pompei (The Last Day of Pompeii)* (G. Pacini, 1825), *Le dernier jour de Pompéi* (Joncières, 1869), *La danseuse de Pompéi* (Nouguès, 1912 — opera-ballet on destruction of Pompeii), *Vesuvio* (Alfano, 1950 radio opera)
¶*Der die Vestung seibenbürghisch-Weissenburg eroberde und über die Dacier triumphirende Kayser Trajanus* (Keiser, 1717), *Le retour de Trajan, ou Rome triomphante* (Bochsa, 1805), *Le triomphe de Trajan* (Persuis & Lesueur, 1807)
¶*Valerianus romanum imperator* (Biber, 1684)
¶Vespasian: see TITUS above.

325   **Council of Nicaea** convened by Constantine, framed the Nicene Creed. 330: Constantinople (New Rome) built on the site of village of Byzantium (now Istanbul) — made capital of the Roman Empire. 4th cent: **St. Catherine**.
Thaïs (Massenet, 1894 — Council of Nicaea), *Historia o sw. Katarzynie (The History of St. Catherine)* (Twardowski, 1985)

361-363   **Julian** (Flavius Claudius Julianus, 331-363), Roman Emperor, opponent of Christianity — attempted to reintroduce paganism.
?*Julian the Apostate Caesar* (Saminsky, 1938)

450   **Attila (d. 453) crossed the Rhine** and laid waste the Gallic provinces. . Defeated at battle of Chalons (451) by **Aetius** — chief minister of Emperor **Valentinian III** (b. 419), who became virtual ruler of Western Roman Empire; destroyed Adriatic city of Aquileia in 452. 470: the Huns withdraw from Europe.
¶*Attila* (P.A. Ziani, 1672; Farinelli, 1806; Generali, 1807; Verdi, 1846), *Attile* (J.W. Franck, 1682), *Attila in Aquileja, ossia il trionfo de re dei Franchi* (Mosca, 1818), *Attila in Aquileja* (Persiani, 1827). SEE ALSO: *Ildegonde di Borgogna* (Malipiero, 1847)
¶*Ezio (Aetius)* (Auletta, 1728; Porpora, 1728; Hasse, 1730; ?Predieri, 1730; Broschi, 1731; Handel, 1732; Lampugnani, 1737; Jommelli, 1741, 1748, 1758, 1771; Sarro, 1741; ?Contini, 1742; G. Scarlatti, 1744; Pescetti, 1747; Bernasconi, 1749; Bonno, 1749; Gluck, 1750, 1763; D. Perez, 1751; Ferradini, 1752; Conforto, 1754; Traetta, ?1754; Graun, 1755; Galuppi, 1756; Latilla, 1758; Gassmann, 1761;

Schwanenberger, 1763; Rutini, 1763; J.C. Bach, 1764; Alessandri, 1767; Bertoni, 1767; ?Majo, 1769; Guglielmi, 1770; Sacchini, 1771; Gazzaniga, 1772; Myslivecek, 1775; Mortellari, 1777; Anfossi, 1778; Bachschmidt, 1780; Levis, 1782; Calvi, 1784; Gabriele Prota, 1784; Pio, 1785; Tarchi, 1789; Mercadante, 1827)
¶OTHER: *Ricimero re dei Goti (Ricimer, King of the Goths)* (Jommelli, 1740 — Ricimero the barbarian chieftain captures & enslaves the daughter of the emperor Valentinian III, with whom he is in love — based on narratives of Procopius and Paulus Diaconus)

476   **Deposition of Romulus Augustulus.** Extinction of the line of Roman emperors in the West.

496   **Clovis adopted Catholic Christianity.** Paved the way for intimate relations between the Franks and the Papacy.

518-565 **Late Roman Emperors (Eastern)** 518-527: **Justin.** 527-565 **Justinian I**, under whose reign the Byzantine world begins to assume its own distinct form.
¶*Bélisaire* (H.-M. Berton & Philidor, 1796 — on Roman general wronged at court of Justinian, his triumph over Bulgars in 559), *Belisario* (Donizetti, 1836). See also Saint-Lubini, c.1827; ?Maurer, 1830.
¶*Giustino (Justin)* (Legrenzi, 1683; A. Scarlatti, 1694; Handel, 1711; Vivaldi, 1724)

622   **The Hegira (Flight) of Mohammed from Mecca to Medina.** Marks the beginning of the Mohammedan era.

660s-700s **Lombard kingdom consolidates power over northern Italy.** 675: Lombard kings rule in Farentum (Apulia). 712: height of Lombard kingdom in northern Italy — King Liutprand (d. 744). (SEE ALSO 1095, below.)
Rodelinda (Handel, 1725 — Lombard queen threatened by usurper)

711   Battle of **Guadalete**: Moslems defeat the Visigoths in Spain.
Rodrigo (Vincer se stesso è la maggior vittoria) (Rodrigo; Conquering Oneself is the Greater Victory) (Handel, 1707 — Seville c. 710, featuring historical Rodrigo [d. 711] Duke of Baetica & last of the Visigothic kings), *Don Rodrigo* (Ginastera, 1964 — on period of Moslem rule in Spain from Guadalete to restoration of Christian rule after the conquest of Granada in 1492)

732   **Battle of Tours.** Victory of the Franks under Charles Martel stemmed the further advance of the Moslems into western Europe.
Genoveva (Schumann, 1848; N. Berg, 1945 — on battle of Tours). SEE ALSO: *Geneviève de Brabant* (Offenbach, 1859 — parody operetta)

800   **Charlemagne crowned Emperor of the Romans.** Founding of Carolingian dynasty, formation of Holy Roman Empire; his friend **Harun al Rashid** caliph of Bagdad (786-809) sends emissary to Charlemagne's court. 778: battle at **Roncesvalles.** NOTE: The epic poems *Orlando innamorato* by Matteo Goardo (1487) and *Orlando furioso* by Lodovico Ariosto (1510) inspired count-

less operas about the hero Roland (Orlando) and his loyalty to
Charlemagne, but include mostly fictional elements. Some of
these titles (having to do with Orlando, Angelica and Medoro)
are listed below. Not listed are the operas about Alcina, Ruggiero
and Bradamante; Ginevra and Ariodante; Olimpia; and some
other episodes.

¶*Carlo il grande* (D. Gabrielli, 1688), ?*Der tapffere Kayser Carolus Magnus und dessen erste Gemahlin Hermingardis* (Conradi, 1692), *Karol Wielki i Witykind (Charlemagne and Wittekind)* (Elsner, 1807), ?*Carlo Magno (Vitikingo)* (G. Nicolini, 1813), ?*Indiana i Charlemagne* (Damse, 1843)

¶*Abu Hassan* (Weber, 1811—featuring Harun al Rashid)

¶*Roland* (Lully, 1685; I. von Beecke, c.1770; Piccinni, 1778; Lindpaintner, 19th cent.), *Orlando generoso* (Steffani, 1691), *La fortunata sventura di Medoro, o La pazzia d'Orlando* (G. Griffini, 1697), *Orlando, overo La gelosa pazzia* (D. Scarlatti, 1711; *Orlando furioso* (Ristori, 1713; Vivaldi, 1714; Schürmann, 1722; Bioni, 1724; O. Pollarolo, 1725; A. Loffredo, 1831), *Orlando* (Vivaldi, 1727; Handel, 1733; J.J. Schneider, 1848), *Angelica ed Orlando* (Latilla, 1735), *Il nuovo Orlando* (Piccinni, 1764), *Le pazzie di Orlando* (P.A. Guglielmi, 1771), *I furori di Orlando* (J. Touchemoulin, 1777), *Orlando paladino* (Haydn, 1782), *Angelica e Medoro, ossia Orlando* (G. Nicolini, 1810), *Roland à Roncevaux* (Mermet, 1864), *Roland furieux* (L.C. Desormes, 187?). SEE ALSO: *Esclarmonde* (Massenet, 1889—Roland "conte de Blois", in Byzantium)

c.870   Period of **Premysl** founder of Prague and Premyslid dynasty and of
legendary prophetic Bohemian princess **Libuše**. (SEE ALSO 1306,
below.)

Praga nascente da Libussa e Primislao (anon. c.1730), *Libussa* (K. Kreutzer, 1822), *Libušin Snatek (The Marriage of Libusa)* (Skroup, 1850), *Libuše* (Smetana, 1881). See also J.F. Sartorio, 1764. SEE ALSO: *Šárka* (Janacek, 1887-1925; Fibich, 1897—on Premysl)

871-899   **Alfred the Great** (b. 849)—period of wars between Vikings,
Saxons and Danes. 973: King **Edgar** (957-975) crowned at Bath.

¶*Alfred* (Arne, 1740—masque containing "Rule Brittania"), *Alfredo il grande* (Mayr, 1818; Donizetti, 1823), ?*Alfred* (P. Ritter, 1820; White, 1981), *Alfred der Grosse, König von England* (Schmidt, 1830), *Alfred der Grosse* (Flotow, c.1835), *König Alfred* (Raff, 1851). See also Wolfram, 1826; Reuling, 1840; Bechtel, 1880; Gatty, 1930

¶*The King's Henchman* (Taylor, 1927—on King Edgar). SEE ALSO: ?*Le roi Edgard* (Lassen, 1855)

¶ALSO: *Gwendoline* (Chabrier, 1886—background of war between Saxons and Danes)

879-1015   Rulers of **Kiev**. 879: deaths of Rurik of Novgorod, who
founded the dynasty that ruled over the people of Rus for eight
centuries, and of his follower **Askold**. Rurik succeeded (and Askold killed) by **Oleg "the Wise"** (879-912) who established Kiev as
the center of his domain. Oleg succeeded as Prince of Kiev by
Igor (912-945); succeeded in turn by **Sviatoslav** (945-972). 980-
1015: **St. Vladimir I the Great (b. 955)** grand duke of Kiev; also

prince of Novgorod from 970. 988: **Christianity introduced into Russia.** Henceforth, the Russian Slavs came under the influence of the Greek Church and Byzantine civilization.

Nachal' noye upravleniye Olega (The Early Reign of Oleg) (Sarti, Pashkevich & Canobbio, 1790), *Wladimir, Fürst von Novgorod* (Bierey, 1807), *Askol'dova mogila (Askold's Tomb)* (Verstovsky, 1835 – 10th-century Kiev during reign of Oleg). SEE ALSO: *Sadko* (Rimsky-Korsakov, 1898 – fantasy touching on the glories of 11th-century Kiev and Novgorod)

896   Magyars led by Árpád (son of **Álmos**) cross the Carpathian mountains into present-day Hungary. 933: German king "**Henry the Fowler**" conducts defense against them in Germany.

Álmos (Mosonyi, 1862), *Lohengrin* (Wagner, 1850 – featuring King Henry)

973   Death of **Otto (Otho) I** founder of Holy Roman Empire of the German Nation (936-973); succeeded by **Otto (Otho) II** (973-983).

Teofane (Theophano) (Lotti, 1719 – on wedding of Ottono II to Byzantine princess Teofane), *Ottone* (Pollarollo, 1694), *Ottone, re di Germania* (Handel, 1719 – on Otho I, Otho II, Teofane)

982   **Greenland discovered by the Northmen.**

986-987   **Louis V King of France,** grandson of Charlemagne – end of Carolingian dynasty.

Ugo conte di Parigi (Hugo, Count of Paris) (Donizetti, 1832 – on loyalty of Hugues Capet to Louis V), *Luigi V, re di Francia* (Mazzucato, 1843)

1016-1035   **Danish King Canute rules England in relative peace;** 1028, conquers Norway. On his death kingdom divided among three sons Harold (England), Sweyn (Norway), Hardicanute (Denmark). 1040: Duncan of Scotland murdered by **Macbeth**, who becomes king. 1054: Macbeth defeated by Malcolm and Siward of Northumbria, at Dunsinane.

Macbeth (Johnson & Locke?, ?1673; Leveridge, 1702; Chélard, 1827; Piccinni, 1829; Verdi, 1847; Taubert, 1857; Bloch, 1910; Collingwood, 1934; Gatty, c.1947; Halpern, 1965; Koppel, 1970), *Makbet* (Gedike, 1947), *Murdering Macbeth* (Calabrese & Calabrese, 1960 comic operetta). See also Daffner, 1930. SEE ALSO: *Biorn* (L. Rossi, 1877 – on Macbeth, set in Norway), *Ein schottische Tragödie* (Fries, c.1965), *Hexenskat, oder Der Streik der Hexen* (Koblenz, 1984), *Nightshriek* (Ward, 1986 rock musical)

c.1043-1099   **Rodrigo Diaz de Vivar ("El Cid").**

Il Cid (Stuck, 1715; Leo, 1727; Sacchini, 1769; G. Pacini, 1853; Gouvy, 1863; Pizzetti, 1903), *Il gran Cid* (Gasparini, 1717; Piccinni, 1766; Bianchi, 1773; Paisiello, 1775; Rosetti, 1780), *Il gran Cidde Rodrigo* (Franchi, 1769), *Chimène ou Le Cid* (Sacchini, 1783), *Il Cid delle Spagne* (Farinelli, 1802), *Rodrigo und Chimene (Rodrigo et Zimène)* (Aiblinger, 1821), *Le Caïd* (A. Thomas, 1849), *Der Cid* (Cornelius, 1862, Wagenaar, 1916), *Le Cid* (Massenet, 1885), *Rodrigue et Chimène* (Debussy, 1892 – inc). See also Roesler, 1780; Savi, 1834; Neeb, 1857; Boehme, 1887. SEE ALSO: *Die Rächer* (Schindelmeisser, 1846)

c.1050   **Oldrich, 11th-century Czech prince.**
Oldrich a Bozena (Skroup, 1823)

1066   **Battle of Hastings.** Resulted in Norman conquest of England.
Garol'd (Harold) (Nápravník, 1886 — Canute's son Harold defeated by William the Conqueror)

1095   **Council of Clermont.** Beginning of **First Crusade** (1096-1099).
NOTE: Epic poem *Gerusalemme librata* by Torquato Tasso (1544-1595) centers on Crusades but includes mostly fictional elements; its story of Rinaldo and Armida furnished themes for more than 50 operas. (SEE ALSO 1575, below.)
Armida (B. Ferrari, 1639; Bertoni, 1746; Graun, 1751; Sarti, Gatti, 1755; 1759; Traetta, 1761; G. Scarlatti, 1767; Anfossi, 1770; Salieri, 1771; Sacchini, 1772; J.G. Naumann, 1773; Mysliveczeck, 1779; Haydn, 1783; Zingarelli, 1786; Alessandri, 1794; Bianchi, 1802; Rossini, 1817; Zajc, 1896; Dvořák, 1904), *Armide et Renaud* (Lully, 1686), *Armida abbandonata* (Vernizzi, 1623; Ruggieri, 1707; Buini, 1716; Falco, c.1719; Jommelli, 1770; Bioni, 1725; Bertoni, 1780; Cherubini, 1782; Mortellari, 1785; Prati, 1785), *Armida al campo (d'Egitto)* (Boniventi, 1708; Sarro, 1718; Vivaldi, 1718; Bioni, 1726), *Armida in Damasco* (Rampini, 1711), *Rinaldo* (Handel, 1711; Sacchini, 1783), *Armida delusa* (Buini, 1720), *Renaud, ou La suite d'Armide* (Desmarets, 1722), *Il trionfo di Armida* (Albinoni, 1726), *Armide* (Gluck, 1777), *Reinhold und Armida* (Winter, 1780), *Armida e Rinaldo* (Sarti, 1786; Andreozzi, 1802), *Rinaldo und Armida* (Paradis, 1797; André, 1799), *Rinaldo e Armida* (Mosca. 1799), *Renaud* (Häffner, 1801), *Armida Zauberin im Orient* (Gläser, 1825), *?La Déliverance de Renaud* (by ?), *La morte di Rinaldo* (Lualdi, 1920 dramatic scene). SEE ALSO: *La Gierusalemme liberata* (C. Pallavicino, 1687; Righini, 1803), *?Der Verstöhrung Jerusalem erster Theil, oder Die Eroberung des Tempels & Der Verstöhrung Jerusalem ander Theil, oder Die Eroberung der Burg Zion* (Conradi, 1692), *Gerusalemme distrutta* (Zingarelli, 1794), *?Selva incantata* (Righini, 1803), *Jérusalem délivrée* (Persuis, 1812)
¶OTHER: *Tancrède* (Campra, 1702 — background for Crusade, after Tasso; rivalry between the Saracens [i.e. Moslems] and Christian hero Tancred in Syracuse city-state 1005), *Tancredi* (?Baillou, 1777; Pavesi, 1812; Rossini, 1813), *I Lombardi alla prima Crociata* (Verdi, 1843; rev. as *Jérusalem*, 1847)

1100-1154   Roger I (d. 1101) King of Sicily; his son **Roger II** (1130-1154) King of Sicily, patron of science, literature, art; opposed both the papacy and Byzantine empire. 1108-1137: **Louis VI "Le Gros"** King of France.
Euryanthe (Weber, 1823 — incl. Louis VI), *Król Roger (King Roger)* (Szymanowski, 1926 — based on Euripedes *Bacchae* but features King Roger II; also version as *Roger de Sicile, ou Le roi troubadour* by H.-M. Berton, 1817)

1154-1189   **Henry II (b. 1133) King of England,** married to Eleanor of Aquitaine (d. 1185) and in love with Scottish-born **Rosamond Clifford**; 1170, murder of **Thomas à Becket,** Archbishop of Canterbury. 1129-1195: Henry II's son-in-law **Henry the Lion,** Duke of Saxony from 1142 and of Bavaria (1156-1180) — supported his cousin Frederic I Barbarosa in his campaigns in Italy.

¶*Henrico Leone* (Steffani, 1689), *Heinrich der Löwe* (Stegmann, 1792)
¶*Enrico II* (Nicolai, 1839). SEE ALSO: *Rosmonda* (C. Coccia, 1829), *Rosmunda d'Inghilterra* (Donizetti, 1834), *Il castello di Woodstock* (Tinassi & Collara, 1839), *Assassinio nelle cattedrale* (Pizzetti, 1958 — on Becket's murder)

1185   Defeat of **Prince Igor** of Novgorod-Seversk by the Polovtsi, a nomadic Turkic tribe. Also: **Shota Rustavelze** (late 12th or early 13th century) Georgian poet whose exploits became legendary.
¶*Knyaz Igor (Prince Igor)* (Borodin, perf. 1890)
¶*Tkmuleba Shota Rustavelze (The Legend of Shota Rustaveli)* (Arakishvili, 1919)

1189-1204   Third (1189-1192) and **Fourth Crusades** (1202-1204) — other political/religious conflicts. 1189-1199: **Richard I** King of England and a leader of Third Crusade; concludes treaty with his opponent **Saladin** (Salah Al-Dinid, d. 1193) sultan of Egypt and Syria and brother of **Malik al-Adil**. 1190-1197: **Henry VI** (son of Frederick I Barbarossa) Holy Roman Emperor.
¶*Riccardo I, re d'Inghilterra* (Handel, 1727), *Richard Coeur-de-Lion* (Grétry, 1784), *Richard en Palestine* (Adam, 1844). SEE ALSO: *Ivanhoe* (G. Pacini, 1832; Sullivan, 1891 — also as *Der Templer und die Jüdin* by Marschner, 1829; *Il templario* by Nicolai, 1840; *Rebecca* by Pisani, 1865; *Rébecca* by Castegnier, c.1882; see also Savi, 1863; Ciardi, 1888; Lewis, 1907), *I crociati a Tolemaide, ossia Malek-Adel* (G. Pacini, 1828), *Malek Adhel* (Costa, Grisi & Lablache, 1837), *Malek-Adel* (G. Nicolini, 1830; Poniatowski, 1846)
¶OTHER: *Il talismano* (Salieri & Rust, 1779; Salieri, 1788 — on Third Crusade), *Le Comte Ory* (Rossini, 1828 — on Fourth Crusade), *Il talismano, ovvero La terza crociata in Palestina* (G. Pacini, 1830), *Agnes von Hohenstaufen* (Spontini, 1837 — incl. Emperor Henry VI of Hohenstaufen & French King), *La battaglia di Legnano* (Verdi, 1848 — 12th-century Lombardy during invasion of Federico Barbarossa), *Fra Gherardo (Brother Gherardo)* (Pizzetti, 1928 — based on episode from the *Chronica* of Fra Salimbene de Parma, 1221-1287)

1206-1227   **Conquest of Ghenghis Khan (Temujin)**. Brought a large part of Asia and eastern Europe under Mongol sway.
Gengis-Kan (Anfossi, 1777). SEE ALSO: *Skazaniye o nevidimom grade Kitezhe i deve Fevronii (The Legend of the Invisible City of Kitezh and the Maiden Fevroniya)* (Rimsky-Korsakov, 1907 — combines history [Mongol invasion of 1223] with folklore and Christian mystery), *The Dark Blue Wolf* (Saburo Takata, 1973 — on Ghenghis Khan)

1212-1217   Period of **Fifth Crusade**; attempt to capture Egypt fails. 1213: assassination of Queen Gertrud of Meran, wife of King Andreas II of Hungary. 1220: German king **Frederick II** (d. 1250) crowned Holy Roman Emperor. 1226: death of **Saint Francis** of Assisi (b. 1182?), founder of Franciscan order. 1231: death of **St. Elisabeth**, daughter of Andreas II, married to son of Thuringian Landgrave — became patron saint of the poor.
¶*Il crociato in Egitto (The Crusader in Egypt)* (Meyerbeer, 1824), *Tannhäuser und der Sängerkrieg auf Wartburg* (Wagner, 1845; Mangold, 1846 — on German poets, crusaders, St. Elisabeth of Hungary), *Tannhäuser, oder Die Keilerei auf der*

Wartburg (anon., 1855), *Tannhauser el estanquero* (Giménez, 1890 *zarzuela*), *Tannhauser cesante* (Giménez, 1890 *zarzuela*). See also Binder, 1857 parody

¶*San Francesco d'Assisi* (Malipiero, 1921), *Saint Françoise d'Assise* (Messiaen, 1983)

¶*Bánk bán* (Erkel, 1861—murder of Queen Gertrud, Hungarian struggle against foreign despotism), *Die Legende von der heiligen Elisabeth* (Liszt, 1881—staged vers. of 1865 oratorio featuring St. Elisabeth)

1215   **Magna Carta.** Defined the rights of Englishmen and inspired their later struggles for liberty.

1228-1254   **Sixth Crusade** (1228-1229) led by Emperor Frederick II; **Seventh Crusade** (1248-1254) led by **Louis IX** (1226-1270) King of France—canonized 1297.

Louis IX en Egypte (Lemoyne, 1790), *Il Pirata* (Bellini, 1827—Seventh Crusade), *Oberto, Conte di Bonifacio* (Verdi, 1839—Sixth Crusade). SEE ALSO: *The Crusaders* (Benedict, 1846), *La schiava saracena, ovvero Il campo di Gerosolima* (Mercadante, 1848), ?*Saratsïn (The Saracen)* (Cui, 1899)

1263   Death of **Alexander Nevsky**—he defeated the Swedes at the river Neva and two years later halted the Teutonic Knights at Lake Peipus.

Alexander Nevsky (Prokofiev, 1938—dramatic cantata after his film score). SEE ALSO: *I Lituani (The Lithuanians)* (Ponchielli, 1874—on invasion of Lithuania [Marienburg] by Knights of the Teutonic Order)

1270-1300   **William Tell**; Swiss, Bohemian resistance to the Habsburgs.

¶BOHEMIA: *Branibori v Cechách (The Brandenburgers in Bohemia)* (Smetana, 1863)

¶SWITZERLAND: *Guillaume Tell* (Grétry, 1791; Rossini, 1829), *The Archers, or Mountaineers of Switzerland* (Carr, 1796). See also Baillou, 1797; B.A. Weber, 1795

1271-1295   **Travels of Marco Polo.** Polo's narrative greatly increased the interest of Europeans in the Far East.

Le istorie cinesi di Marco Polo (Ghisi, 1955 *pantomime sceniche*)

1275   **"Model Parliament" of Edward I.** A regularly elected Parliament which for the first time included representatives of all classes of the English people.

1282   **"Sicilian Vespers"** rebellion.

Die sicilianische Vesper (Lindpaintner, 1843), *Les vêpres siciliennes* (Verdi, 1855). See also Barth, 1841

1292   **Adolf, Count of Nassau** (?1250-1298) elected German king; crowned at Aix-la-Chapelle.

König Adolf von Nassau (Marschner, 1845)

1300   **Age of Dante** (1265-1321), **Petrarch** (1304-1374), **Boccaccio** (1313-1375). Period of **Guelph-Ghibelline** rivalries in northern Italy (13th & 14th centuries).

¶*Boccaccio* (Suppé, 1879)

¶*Dante e Beatrice* (Carrer, 1852), *Dante and Beatrice* (Philpot, 1889), *Dante et Béatrice* (Godard, 1890), *The Vision of Dante* (Foulds, 1904 concert opera), *Il sonetto di Dante* (Gastaldon, 1909), *Le Dante* (Noughuès, 1914)
¶*Francesca da Rimini*—after Dante's *Inferno*, based on historical characters incl. Giovanni Malatesta (Generali, 1829; Mercadante, 1831; Goetz, 1877; Cagnoni, 1878; Nápravník, 1903; Rachmaninoff, 1906; Zandonai, 1914), *Françoise de Rimini* (A. Thomas, 1882), *Paolo e Francesca* (Mancinelli, 1907), *Paolo és Francesca* (Ábrányi, 1907). See also Carlini, 1825; Staffa, 1831; Fournier-Gorre, 1832; Aspri, 1835; Borgatta, 1837; Morlacchi, 1839, inc; Devasini, 1841; Canetti, 1843; Brancaccio, 1844; Marcarini, 1871; Goetz, 1877; Moscuzza, 1877; Henreid, ?
¶OTHER: *Marino Faliero* (Donizetti, 1835—on the Doge of Venice executed in 1355; also Holstein, 1877, inc; Freudenberg, 1889), *Simon Boccanegra* (Verdi, 1857—14th-century Genoa), ?*Les Guelphs* (Godard, 1902), *Gianni Schicchi* (Puccini, 1918—Florence in 1299, derived from Dante)

1306   **End of Premyslid dynasty** begun by the legendary Czech leader who united tribes of Bohemia and founded Prague. (SEE ALSO c.870, above.)
Bretislav (Bendl, 1892—on the Premyslid feuds in early 1300s)

1309-1377   **"Babylonian Captivity" of the Papacy.** Removal of the popes to Avignon (France) weakened their political authority. 1347: **Cola di Rienzi**, tribune of the people, rules Rome; 1350, imprisoned in Prague; 1354, murdered in Rome after another attempt to establish tyranny.
Cola Rienzi, der Letzte der Tribunen (Wagner, 1842), *Rienzi* (A. Peri, 1862), *Cola di Rienzi* (Kashperov, 1863). See also Barnett, 1828; Conrad, 1839; Lucilla, 1872; Persichini, 1874

1337-1453   **Period of Hundred Years' War.** Reigns of **Joanna I** (1343-1382) and **Joanna II** (1414-1435) in Naples. 1340: **Alfonso XI** of Castile defeats Moslem army at Tarifa. 1347-1378: **Charles IV** of Luxembourg and hereditary king of Bohemia succeeds Louis IV of Bavaria as Habsburg emperor. 1348-1349: **Black Death** in Europe hastens decline of serfdom and emancipation of the peasantry. c.1349: **Dom Pedro** Infante of Portugal. 1381: **Wat Tyler**'s peasants' revolt in England. 1384: **Queen Jadviga** crowned in Poland. 1387-1400: **Geoffrey Chaucer** (1340-1400) writes *Canterbury Tales*. 1409-1480: **René, Duke of Anjou**, self-styled King of Naples and Sicily, whose daughter Margaret of Anjou married Henry VI of England. 1414: **Council of Constance**. 1415: **Henry V** victorious at Agincourt; marries Catherine de Valois, daughter of his defeated enemy **Charles VI "the Mad"** of France (1380-1422). Sir John **Fastolf** (1380-1459) knighted c. 1415. 1420: **Hussites** (followers of Jan Hus, 1369-1415) defeat Sigismund at Vysehrad. 1425: struggles in Bohemia between the Utraquists and the radical Taborites. 1431: death of **Joan of Arc** (b. 1412). 1440: execution of **Gilles de Rais** (b. 1404), French officer who fought

with Joan of Arc against the English & was made Marshall of
France at 25 after the Dauphin's coronation — historical source
for "**Blue-Beard**" stories as depicted by Charles Perrault (1697).
¶*La favorita* (Donizetti, 1839 — Castile 1340, period of Alfonso XI)
¶*Raoul Barbe Bleu* (Grétry, 1789), *Raoul di Crequi* (Mayr, 1809; Morlacchi, 1811;
Fioravanti, 1851), *Barbe-bleu* (Offenbach, 1866 operatic parody), *Barbableu* (Fron-
doni, 1868), *Ritter Blaubart* (Reznicek, 1920), *Ariane et Barbe-blue* (Dukas, 1907),
A Kékszakállú Herceg Vá (Duke Bluebeard's Castle) (Bartók, 1911 — time legendary)
¶*Karlštejn* (Novák, 1916 — on Charles IV)
¶*The Canterbury Pilgrims* (Stanford, 1884; De Koven, 1917 — featuring Chaucer,
pilgrims at Canterbury)
¶*Falstaff* (Salieri, 1799; Balfe, 1838; Adam, 1856; Verdi, 1893; Webber, 1928),
Falstaff, ossia Le tre burle (Salieri, 1799), *Sir John in Love* (Vaughan Williams,
1929), *Goodtime Johnny* (Gilbert, 1971 — on Shakespeare's *Merry Wives*), *Falstaff
In and Out of Love* (Rea, 1982), *Plump Jack* (Getty, 1987). SEE ALSO: *Le Vieux co-
quet, ou Les deux amies* (Papavoine, 1761 — also on Henry V), *Herne le chasseur*
(Philidor, 1773), *Die lustigen Weiber von Windsor* (P. Ritter, 1794); Ditters von Dit-
tersdorf, 1796 *Singspiel*; Nicolai, 1849), *The Merry Wives of Windsor* (Horn, 1824),
At the Boar's Head (Holst, 1925), *When the Cat's Away* (Swier, 1941 — on
Shakespeare's *Merry Wives*), *The Genuine Musical Hall Version of The Merry
Wives of Windsor* (Gilbert & Rogers, 1977), *Nevestele vesele din Windsor* (Alifantis,
1978). SEE ALSO HENRY V, following.
¶*La gioventù di Enrico V* (G. Mosca, 1817; G. Pacini, 1820; Moriacchi, 1823; Mer-
cadante, 1834), *La jeunesse de Henry V* (Hérold, 1815), *Henri V et ses compagnons*
(Adam, 1830 pasticcio), *Henry V* (Misterly, 1969, inc), *Good King Hal* (Barbie,
1979). SEE ALSO: *Agincourt* (Boughton, 1918)
¶*Die Hussiten vor Naumberg* (Salieri, 1803), *Dfte Tábora (The Child of Tabor)*
(Bendl, 1892 — on the Hussites at Naumburg)
¶*Ines de Castro* (G. Giordani, 1793; Andreozzi, 1793; Schall, 1804; Zingarelli,
Pavesi & Farinelli, 1806; Persiani, 1835; P.A. Coppola, 1841; Pasatieri, 1976 — on
Dom Pedro the Infante of Portugal and his secret wife, c.1349), *Don Pedro di
Portogallo* (Gibelli, 1849; Drigo, 1868)
¶*Jadwiga, królowa polska (Jadviga, Queen of Poland)* (Kurpinskì, 1814; Jarecki, 1886)
¶*Jeanne d'Arc à Orléans* (R. Kreutzer, 1790; Carafa, 1821), *Giovanna d'Arca ossia
La Pulcelle d'Orléans* (Andreozzi, 1789), *Giovanna d'Arco* (Vaccai, 1827; G. Pacini,
1830; Verdi, 1845), *Joan of Arc* (Balfe, 1837), *Johanna d'Arc* (Hoven, 1840), *Johanna
d'Arc* (Vesque von Püttlingen, 1840), *Orleanskava Dieva (The Maid of Orleans)*
(Tchaikovsky, 1881), *Die Jungfrau von Orleans* (Reznicek, 1887), *Jeanne d'Arc*
(Duprez, 1865; Mermet, 1876; Bruneau, 1878 *scène*; Chausson, 1880 *scène lyrique*;
Godard, 1891), *Jeanne d'Arc au bûcher* (Honegger, 1935 — oratorio for stage), *The
Triumph of St. Joan* (Dello Joio, 1959). See also Langert, 1862; Wamback, 1900;
Morera, 1907; Roza, 1911; Marsh, 1923; Anderson, 1934; Bastide, 1949;
Humphreys, 1968. SEE ALSO: ?*A Survival of St. Joan* (Ruffin & Ruffin, 1971 rock
musical), *Das Mädchen aus Domrémy* (Klebe, 1976)
¶*Giovanna Prima, regina di Napoli* (Coppola, 1840), *Giovanna II, regina di Napoli*
(C. Coccia, 1840), *Giovanna di Napoli* (Petrella, 1869)
¶*Wat Tyler* (Bush, 1951)
¶*Iolanta (Yolanda)* (Tchaikovsky, 1883 — on blind daughter of René Duke of
Anjou, sister of Margaret of Anjou)
¶OTHER: *Beatrice di Tenda* (Bellini, 1835 — on Beatrice Lascaris di Tenda, Italy
in 1418), *La Juive* (Halévy, 1835 — Council of Constance), *I due Foscari* (Verdi,
1844 — Venice & Milan in 1457, the Foscari, Carmagnola; see also *I Foscari* by

Zenger, 1863), *Il trovatore* (Verdi, 1853 – Spain at beginning of 15th century), *The King Goes Forth to France* (Sallinen, 1984 – incl. Battle of Crécy)

1395   Asiatic conqueror **Tamerlane** (Timur the Lame, ?1336-1405) defeats the Mongol "Golden Horde", moves into Russia reaching Moscow before his withdrawal. Overruns most of Ottoman Empire, defeating **Bajazet I** Emir of the Turks (1389-1403) at Ankara and taking him prisoner (1402).
Il gran Tamerlano (M.A. Ziani, 1689; A. Scarlatti, 1706; Lampugnani, 1746; Sarti, 1764), *Bajazeth und Tamerlan* (Förtsch, 1690), *Tamerlano* (Gasparini, 1710; Chelleri, 1720; Handel, 1725; Giai, 1727; Porpora, 1730; Vivaldi, 1735; Cocchi & Pescetti, 1754; Scolari, 1763; Sacchini, 1773; Mayr, 1813; Tadolini, 1818; Carafa, 1824; A. Sapienza, 1824), *Tamerlan* (Reichardt, 1800; Winter, 1802), *Timur, der Tartar Chan* (Seyfried, 1822). SEE ALSO: *Baiazete, imperator dei Turchi* (Leo, 1722), *Il Bajazet* (Bernasconi, 1742; G. Scarlatti, 1763), *Bajazet* (Andreozzi, 1783; Generali, 1814), *Les Turcs* (Hervé, 1869). See also Cocchi, 1746; Bertoni, 1765; Burghersh, 1821

1400s   **Medici** family dominant in Florence, Rome, incl. **Cosimo de'Medici** (Cosimo the Elder, 1389-1464); his son **Piero de'Medici** (Piero the Gouty, 1416-1469); and *his* sons **Lorenzo de'Medici** (*"magnifico signore"*, "the Magnificent", 1449-1492 – Florentine art patron and author) and **Guiliano de'Medici** (murdered in 1478). SEE ALSO 1500s, below. The Medici were denounced by reformer-preacher **Girolamo Savonarola** (1452-1498).
¶*?Isabella de'Medici* (F. Ricci, 1845), *Pierre de Médicis* (Poniatowski, 1860), *?I Medici* (Leoncavallo, 1888), *La cena delle beffe* (The Supper of Jests) (Giordano, 1920 – Florence at time of Lorenzo il Magnifico)
¶*Savonarola* (Stanford, 1884)

1451-1481   Mohammed II leader of the Ottoman Turks, captured Constantinople (1453) marking end of the Byzantine Empire.
Mahmuth II (R. Kaiser, 1696), *Maometto Secondo* (Winter, 1817; Rossini, 1820, rev. as *Le siège de Corinthe*, 1826, in which Mahommet II defeats the Greeks). SEE ALSO: *Palmira* (F. Stabile, 1836 – setting of Romani *Maometto* libretto), *The Siege of Corinth* (A. Cahen, 1890)

1491-1556   Ignatius Loyola founder of Jesuit Order.
Four Saints in Three Acts (Thomson, 1934 – loosely on Teresa of Avila & Ignatius Loyola)

1456-1526   Hungarian leaders include **János Hunyadi**, who repelled the Turkish army at Belgrade (1456); his sons **László** and **Mathias** (King of Hungary, 1458, of Bohemia 1469); Ladislas II (d. 1516); and Louis II (d. 1526). 1514: peasant revolt led by **György Dózsa**. 1521: Ottoman Sultan **Suleiman I "the Magnificent"** (1490-1566) captures Belgrade, beginning 150-year occupation of Hungary by the Turks. 1522: Suleiman takes Rhodes from Knights of St. John.
The Siege of Rhodes (Cooke, Lawes, Locke & Coleman, 1656), *Hunyadi László* (Erkel, 1844), *György Dózsa* (Erkel, 1867), *Dalibor* (Smetana, 1868 – opposition to

Ladislas II—also Knott, 1846), *Ritter Pásmán* (J. Strauss, 1892—on Mathias Hunyadi)

1461-1483   Louis XI (b. 1423) King of France. François **Villon** (1431-?1463), French poet.
The Vagabond King (Friml, 1925—musical show with Louis XI, Villon as characters)

1483-1485   Richard III (b. 1452) King of England.
Riccardo III (Salvayre, 1883; Testi, 1987), *König Richard der Dritte* (van Durme, 1961), *Richard III* (Turok, 1975), *Rikard III* (Kuljeric, 1987). See also Meiners, 1859; Canepa, 1879

1487   Cape of Good Hope rounded by **Bartholomeu Dias (Diaz)** (?1450-1500).

1489   Venice acquires island of Cyprus by putting pressure on **Caterina Cornaro,** self-styled "Queen of Cyprus".
La Reine de Chypre (Halévy, 1841), *Catharina Cornaro, Königin von Cypern* (F. Lachner, 1841), *Caterina Cornaro* (Donizetti, 1844), *The Daughter of St. Mark* (Balfe, 1844), *La regina di Cipro* (Pacini, 1846). SEE ALSO: *Otello, ossia Il moro di Venezia* (Rossini, 1818), *?Il mori di Venezia* (Ponchielli, 1879), *Otello* (Verdi, 1887), *Jago* (Bozic, 1968), *Catch My Soul* (White, 1968 rock musical—after Shakespeare's *Othello*). See also Zavodsky, 1945

1492   **Rodrigo Borgia (1431?-1503) elected as Pope Alexander VI.** His children included **Cesare** (1475-1507), Italian cardinal and political and military leader; and **Lucrezia** (1480-1519) Duchess of Ferrara, patron of the arts.
Lucrezia Borgia (Donizetti, 1833)

1492   **Christopher Columbus (1451-1506)—first voyage to the New World.** The Spanish conquer **Granada** and extinguish Moorish kingdom (SEE ALSO 711 above), consolidating monarchy of **Ferdinand of Aragon** and **Isabella of Castile.** Their younger daughter and mother of Charles V (see 1500s below), **Juana,** is declared insane and kept in confinement for nearly 50 years.
¶*Il Colombo* (Ottoboni, 1690), *Il Colombo overo L'India scoperta* (Pasquini, 1690), *Colombo* (Morlacchi, 1828; L. Ricci, 1829; Barbieri, 1848), *Colombo alla scoperta delle Indie* (Fioravanti, 1829), *Cristoforo Colombo* (Carnicer, 1831; Bottesini, 1847; Mela, 1857; Casella, 1865; Marcora, 1869; Franchetti, 1892), *Christophe Colomb* (Milhaud, 1930), *Columbus* (F. J. Skroup, 1855; Egk, 1933), *Christopher Columbus* (Vassilenko, 1933; Zador, 1939), *Cristobal Colon* (Balada, 1989). See also Schuller, 1968. SEE ALSO: *Bombo* (Romberg, 1921—musical farce in which Columbus buys Manhattan)
¶*Isabelle et Fernand, ou L'alcade de Zalaméa* (Champein, 1783), *Isabella d'Aragon* (Pedrotti, 1859)
¶*Juana La Loca* (Menotti, 1979)
¶ALSO: *Les abencérages, ou l'étendard de Grenade* (Cherubini, 1791-1813—on Almansor, last of Moorish Abenceragi warriors, and his final overthrow at Granada in 1492), *?La conquista di Granada* (G. Nicolini, 1820)

1498 **India reached by Vasco da Gama.** The Portuguese establish an ocean
passage from Europe round Africa to the Far East.
Dom Sébastien, roi de Portugal (Donizetti, 1843; includes as character Luis de
Camoëns — author of *The Lusiads*, a classic account of Da Gama's voyage and
other events in Portuguese history), *Il Vascello de Gama* (Mercadante, 1845),
L'Africaine (The African Maid) (Meyerbeer, 1860 — Vasco's adventures at
Madagascar and the "Cape of Storms"), *The Story of Vasco* (Crosse, 1974)

1500s Period of **High Renaissance in Italy** and continued dominance of
Medici family (SEE ALSO 1400s, above). The sons of Lorenzo
de'Medici "the Magnificent" were: **Piero de'Medici** (1472-1503),
Giovanni de'Medici (1475-1521; as Pope Leo X, 1513-1521 — the
patron of Raphael, Michelangelo etc) and **Giuliano de'Medici**
(1478-1516, Duke of Nemours). The son of Lorenzo's brother
Giuliano was **Giulio de'Medici** (1478-1534; as Pope Clement VII,
1523-1534, he refused to sanction the divorce of Henry VIII).
Giovanni (Pope Leo X) was the uncle of **Lorenzo de'Medici**
(1492-1519, Duke of Urbino), whose illegitimate son **Alessandro
de'Medici** (c.1510-1537) was murdered by a distant relative
Lorenzino de'Medici. Alessandro married **Margaret of Parma**
(1522-1586), daughter of Charles V of Spain, in 1533; in 1559 her
half-brother Philip II made her regent of the Netherlands.
Catherine de Medicis (1519-1589), daughter of Lorenzo II
Medici and a cousin of Pope Clement VII, married Henry II King
of France in 1533. ALSO: Leonardo **da Vinci** (1452-1519),
Michelangelo Buonarroti (1475-1564), **Titian** (1477-1576),
Raphael (1483-1520), Benvenuto **Cellini** (1500-1571), Giovanni
Pierluigi da **Palestrina** (1526?-1594). 1545-1563: **Council of
Trent,** an important agency in the Catholic Counter Reformation.
¶*Benvenuto Cellini* (Berlioz, 1838; F.P. Lachner, 1849; Diaz, 1890), *Cellini a Parigi*
(L. Rossi, 1845). See also Schlösser, 1845; Kern, 1854; Venzano, 1870; Bozzano,
1871; Orsini, 1875; Diaz, 1890; Tubi, 1906; Courvoisier, 1921. SEE ALSO: *As-
canio* (Saint-Saëns, 1890 — Cellini a principal character)
¶*Lorenzo de'Medici* (G. Pacini, 1845), *Lorenzaccio* (Bussotti, 1972 — on murder of
Alessandro de'Medici by Lorenzino)
¶?*Michel-Ange* (Isouard, 1802), *Luigi Rolla e Michelangelo* (F. Ricci, 1841)
¶*Palestrina* (Pfitzner, 1918)

1500s Period of **Charles V** (1500-1558; as Charles I King of Spain, 1516-
1556; as Holy Roman Emperor, 1519-1556) and **Philip II** (1527-
1598; as King of Spain, 1556-1598). 1513: Juan **Ponce de Leon** discovers Florida. 1567: reign of terror by the **Duke of Alba**, Philip's
agent in Flanders. 1588: defeat of **Spanish Armada** gives England
control of the sea and makes possible English colonization of
North America.
¶*Don Carlos* (Deshayes, 1799; Costa, 1844; Barth, 1859; Verdi, 1867), *Don Carlo*
(De Ferrari, 1854), *Karl V* (Krenek, 1938). See also "Don Carlos" settings by

Bona, 1847; Moscuzza, 1862; Nordal, 1843; Ferrara, 1863. SEE ALSO: *Ernani*
(Verdi, 1844 — Spain, Aix-la-Chapelle in 1519, featuring Charles V — see also *Her-*
nani by Mazzucato, 1843; also settings by Gabussi, 1834; Laudamo, 1849;
Hirschmann, 1909), *Elisabetta di Valois* (Buzzolla, 1850 — bride of Philip II)
¶*Il duca d'Alba* (G. Pacini, 1842), *Le duc d'Albe* (Donizetti, 1882). SEE ALSO: *Der*
Meergeuse (F.J. Skroup, 1851 — episode of Dutch revolt against Spanish rule).
See also *Egmont* settings by dell'Orefice, 1878; Salvayre, 1886; Meulemans, 1960
¶*Ponce de Léon* (Berton, 1797 *opéra bouffon*)

1509-1547   Henry VIII (b. 1491) King of England. John **Taverner** (1495-
1545), English composer.
¶*Henry VIII* (Saint-Saëns, 1883). SEE ALSO: *Anna Bolena* (Donizetti, 1830),
Caterina Howard (Lillo, 1849)
¶*Taverner* (Davies, 1972)

1511-1515   Painter Matthias Grünewald (b. 1455) creates the Isenheim
altar-piece in the Alsatian town of Colmar. 1512: Catholic annexa-
tion of Navarre — **Ferdinand** King of Frankfurt poisons the young
Navarrese king Francisco I ("Austin").
¶*Austin* (Marschner, 1852)
¶*Mathis der Maler* (Hindemith, 1938)

1515-1547   Francis I (b. 1494) King of France.
Rigoletto (Verdi, 1851 — "Duke of Mantua" modeled on Francis I), *The Wife of*
Martin Guerre (Bergsma, 1956 — disappearance of a French peasant and his
return eight years later in 16th-century France)

1517   Luther's 95 Theses posted. Beginning of Protestant Reformation in
Germany. 1525-1526: Peasants War in Germany partly inspired
by Luther. 1535: followers of Anabaptist **John of Leyden** put to
death.
Le Prophète (Meyerbeer, 1849 — on John of Leyden)

1519   Hernando Cortés (1485-1547), Spanish explorer and conqueror of
Montezuma and the Aztecs, reaches Mexico. 1525: death of
Cuauhtémoc (b. ?1502), last Aztec ruler.
Motezuma (Vivaldi, 1733; Majo, 1765; Mysliveczek, 1771; Galuppi. 1772; Sac-
chini, 1775; Anfossi, 1776), *Montezuma* (Graun, 1755; Zingarelli, 1781; Sessions,
1964), *Fernando nel Messico* (Portugal, 1798), *Montezuma, oder Tippo Saib*
(Seyfried, 1804), *Fernand Cortez ou La Conquête du Mexique* (Spontini, Jouy &
Esménard, 1809), *Cortez, or The Conquest of Mexico* (Bishop, 1823), *L'eroina del*
Messico, ovvero Fernando Cortez (L. Ricci, 1830), *Las Naves de Cortés* (Chapi y
Lorente, 1874). SEE ALSO: *La conquista del Messico* (Fioravanti, 1829), *Guatimot-*
zin (Ortega del Villar, 1871 — on Cuauhtémoc)

1519   Wedding of Hans Sachs (1494-1576), *Meistersinger* of Nürnberg.
Hans Sachs im vorgerückten Alter (Gyrowetz, 1834 *Singspiel*), *Hans Sachs* (Lortzing, 1840), *Die Meistersinger von Nürnberg* (Wagner, 1868), *Hans-Sachs-Spiele* (Be-
hrend, 1949 trilogy)

1519-1522   Ferdinand Magellan (?1480-1521) circumnavigates the globe.

1520   **Francisco Pizarro** (1470?-1541) – conquest of **Atahualpa** and the Incas.
Pizarre ou La conquête du Pérou (Candeille, 1785), *Pizarro* (Bianchi, 1787), *Pizarro* (Loder, c.1840), *Atahualpa* (C.E. Pasta, 1875; Cattelani, 1900). SEE ALSO: *The Cruelty of the Spaniards in Peru* (?, 1658), *Alzira* (Verdi, 1845 – an Inca princess; also *Gusmano de Valhor* by Generali, 1817 – on same subject)

1523   **Gustavus I (Gustavus Vasa, 1490-1560)**, proclaimed King of Sweden. 1524: Treaty of Malmö confirms independence of Sweden from Denmark.
Gustavo I, rè di Svezia (Galuppi, 1740), *Gustaf Wasa* (J.G. Naumann, 1786), *Gustav Wasa* (L. Kozeluch, c.1792), *Une nuit de Gustave Wasa* (Isouard & F. Gasse, 1825)

1547-1584   **Ivan IV Vasilievich "the Terrible" (b. 1530) first Tsar of Russia.** Massacre and destruction of Novgorod, c. 1570.
Ivan IV (Bizet, 1865), *Pskovityanka (The Maid of Pskov)* (Rimsky-Korsakov, 1872), *Oprichnik (The Guardsman)* (Tchaikovsky, 1874), *Kupec Kalashnikov (The Merchant Kalashnikov)* (A. Rubinstein, 1880 – in palace of Ivan the Terrible), *The Tsar's Bride* (Rimsky-Korsakov, 1899), *Ivan the Terrible* (Gunsbourg, 1910)

1553-1558   **Mary I** (b. 1516) Queen of England – eldest daughter of Henry VIII. 1553: **Lady Jane Grey** (b. 1537) proclaimed Queen of England, deposed nine days later – executed 1554.
¶*The Chronicle of Nine* (Rosner, 1984 – on Lady Jane Grey)
¶*Maria d'Inghilterra* (Ferrari, 1840), *Maria, regina d'Inghilterra* (G. Pacini, 1843), *Maria Tudor* (Kashperov, 1859; Gomes, 1879). See also Wagner-Regény, 1935

1558-1603   **Elizabeth I (b. 1533) Queen of England.** 1542-1587: **Mary Queen of Scots,** beheaded on charges of sedition against her cousin Elizabeth. 1564-1616: William **Shakespeare.** 1577-1580: **Drake's voyages** around the world.
¶*History of Sir Francis Drake* (?, 1659)
¶*Elisabetta, regina d'Inghilterra* (Pavesi, 1809; Rossini, 1815), *Elisabetta in Derbyshire, ossia Il castello di Fotheringhay* (Carafa, 1818), *Elisabeth von England* (Klenau, 1939), *Elisabeth Tudor* (Fortner, 1972). See also Giacometti, 1853; Walter, 1939. SEE ALSO: *Leicester* (Auber, 1823 – on Elizabeth, Leicester), *Il conte d'Essex* (Mercadante, 1833), *Roberto Devereux* (Donizetti, 1837), *Merrie England* (Hood, 1902 – musical show featuring Elizabeth, Essex, Sir Walter Raleigh), *Gloriana* (Britten, 1953)
¶*La gioventù di Shakespeare* (Lillo, 1851), *Guglielmo Shakespeare* (Benvenuti, 1861), *Shakespeare* (Serpette, 1899). SEE ALSO: *La Songe d'une nuit d'été* (Thomas, 1850 – in which Shakespeare, Queen Elizabeth, Falstaff appear)
¶*Maria Stuarda, ossia I carbonari di Scozia* (Sogner, 1815), *Maria Stuarda regina di Scozia* (Mercadante, 1821; C. Coccia, 1827), *Marie Stuart en Écosse* (Fétis, 1823), *Maria Stuarda* (Donizetti, 1840), *Marie Stuart* (Niedermeyer, 1844), *Marie Stuart au chateau de Lochleven* (Duprato, c.1863 opérette de salon), *Mary, Queen of Scots* (Musgrave, 1978), *Mariya Styuart (Mary Stuart)* (Slonimsky, 1981), *Maria Stuart* (Twardowski, 1981). See also P. Casella, 1813; Grazioli, 1828; Palumbo, 1874; Lavello, 1895; ?Moore, 1932; Fontrer, 1972; Virani, 1974; ?also as character in *David Riccio* by Capecalatro, c.1850, *Davide Rizzio* by Canepa, 1872

¶ALSO: *Eliza* (Arne, 1754 masque – peaceful Britons rally against Spanish Armada, 1588)

1560-1600   Europe in the 1560s-1590s. 1553-1615: **Marguérite de Valois.** 1562: King **Sebastian I** of Portugal killed at Alcazar during invasion of Morocco. 1572: **St. Bartholomew's Day massacre of the Huguenots**, during which Henry IV (Henry of Navarre) converted to Catholicism in order to save his life. **Henry III (Henry of Valois)** crowned King of Poland (1573), King of France (1574) – assassinated 1588. 1574: **siege of Leyden** (Holland). 1575: poet **Torquato Tasso** (1544-1595) writes *Gerusalemme liberata*, epic on the Crusades (SEE ALSO 1095, above.) 1576-1612: **Rudolf II** Holy Roman Emperor. 1589-1610: **Henry IV (Henry of Navarre,** b. 1553) King of France, first of Bourbon line; in 1598 issued Edict of Nantes – important step in direction of religious toleration.
¶*Henrico IV* (Mattheson, 1711), *Henri IV* (Martini, 1774), *Le jeune Henri* (Méhul, 1797), *Gabrielle d'Estrées ou Les Amours d'Henri IV* (Méhul, 1806), ?*Heinrich IV und d'Aubigné* (Marschner, 1820), *La caccia di Enrico IV* (Raimondi, 1822 comedy). SEE ALSO: *Vec Makropoulos (The Makropoulos Affair)* (Janácek, 1926 – opera singer remembers 300 years of history – also incl. Rudolf II)
¶*Le Roi malgré lui (The King in Spite of Himself)* (Chabrier, 1887 – crowning of Henry of Valois)
¶?*Le Pré aux clercs* (Hérold, 1829 – Marguérite de Valois engineers marriage between two lovers)
¶*La Mort de Tasse* (Garcia, 1821), *Torquato Tasso* (Donizetti, 1833 – on life of the poet)
¶ALSO: *Les Huguenots* (Meyerbeer, 1836), *Le siège de Leyde* (C.L.A. Vogel, 1847)

1598-1605   Boris Godunov (b. 1552) Tsar of Russia. 1605: succeeded by his son Feodor II; on entry of **"False Dmitri"** into Moscow, Feodor is assassinated and Dmitri is crowned Tsar. 1606: Dmitri assassinated by the boyar Vasili Shuisky, who is elected Tsar.
¶*Boris Goudenow, oder Der durch Verschlagenheit erlangte Trohn* (Mattheson, 1710), *Boris Godunov* (Mussorgsky, 1869)
¶*Dimitri* (Dvorák, 1882)

1600   Tycho Brahe (Danish astronomer, 1546-1601) and **Johannes Kepler** (German astronomer, physicist & mathematician, 1571-1630) work together at Prague.
Tycho Brahes Spaadom (Schalli, 1819 *Singspiel*), *Die Harmonie der Welt* (Hindemith, 1957 – on Johannes Kepler)

1607   Settlement of Jamestown. First permanent English colony in America. **Pocahontas** (1595-1617) befriends settlers, marries John Rolfe. 1620: Pilgrims arriving on *Mayflower* found **New England** colony at Plymouth.
¶*The Indian Princess* (Barker, 1808 – on Pocahontas)
¶*Merry Mount* (Hanson, 1934 – on New England Puritans, 1625), *The Crucible* (Ward, 1961 – on Salem witch trials, late 17th century)

1610-1643   **Louis XIII (b. 1601) King of France.** 1624-1642: Duc de **Richelieu** (Armand Jean du Plessis, French cardinal and statesman, b. 1585) chief minister of Louis XIII and virtual dictator. Jean-Baptiste **Lully** (1632-1687).

¶*Les trois ages de l'opéra (Le génie de l'opéra)* (Grétry, 1778 – incl. Lully as character), *Lully et Quinault ou Le déjeuner impossible* (Isouard, 1812), *La Jeunesse de Lully* (Larochejagu, 1846), *Lully och Quinault* (Berens, 1859 operetta), *Lully* (H. Hofmann, 1889)

¶?*Un duello sotto Richelieu* (F. Ricci, 1839), ?*Pierwsza wyprawa mlodego Richeliue* (Damse, 1844)

1613-1676   **The first Romanovs.** 1613-1645: **Michael I** (Mikhail Romanov, b. 1596?) Tsar of Russia, succeeded by **Alexis I** (1645-1676). 1671: execution of **Stenka Razin,** leader of Cossack and peasant rebellion in the Don and Volga regions.

¶*Ivan Susanin* (Cavos, 1815), *Zhizn za Tsarya (A Life for the Tsar)(Ivan Susanin)* (Glinka, 1836 – period of Michael I)

¶*Stenka Razin* (A. Rubinstein, 1852 – period of Alexis I)

¶*Nizhegorodtsï (The Nizhniy-Novgoroders)* (Nápravník, 1869 – mobilization of popular militia against the Poles, c.1612)

1618-1648   **Religious wars (Thirty Years' War),** ended by Peace of Westphalia. 1611-1632: **Gustavus II** (Gustavus Adolphus, b. 1594) King of Sweden. 1625: Albrecht von **Wallenstein** (1583-1634) made general of imperial forces by Emperor Ferdinand II – created Duke of Friedland. 1631: siege of Magdeburg. 1640: siege of Arras. 1647: Neapolitan revolt by Tommaso Aniello (**Masaniello**) against Spanish government. ALSO: Miguel de **Cervantes** Saavedra (1547-1616) Spanish author of *Don Quixote* (Part I, 1605; Part II, 1615); **El Greco** (Luriakos Theotokopoulos, ?1548-?1614), Cretan-Spanish painter; **Rembrandt van Rijn** (1606-1669) Dutch painter; Salvator **Rosa** (1615-1673), Spanish painter.

¶*Michel Cervantes* (E.G. Foignet, 1793), *El Manco de Lepanto* (Aceves & Llanos, 1867), *Le captif* (Lassen, 1865), *Das Spitzentuch der Königin* (J. Strauss, 1880), *Man of La Mancha* (Leigh, 1965 – musical show featuring Cervantes, Don Quixote)

¶*Cyrano* (Damrosch, 1913 – Paris c. 1640), *Cyrano de Bergerac* (V. Herbert, 1899 operetta; Alfano, 1936; Tambers, 1976; Twardowski, 1963), *Cyrano* (Lewis, 1973 musical show; Van Dijk, 1993 musical show)

¶*Konung Gustaf Adolphs Jagt (King Gustavus Adolphus's Hunting Party)* (Stenborg, 1777 "comedy with songs"). SEE ALSO: *Kung Carls jakt (King Charles's Hunting Party)* (Pacius, 1852)

¶*El Greco* (Harper, 1993)

¶*Masagniello furioso [oder] Die neapolitanische Fischer-Empörung* (Keiser, 1706), *Masaniello, ou Le pêcheur napolitain* (Carafa, 1827), *Le muette de Portici (The Dumb Girl of Portici)(Masaniello)* (Auber, 1828 – 1647 Neapolitan revolt against Spain). SEE ALSO: *Fenella, ovvero La muta di Portici* (Pavesi, 1831), *Salvator Rosa* (A.F. Doppler, 1855; Duprato, 1861; Gomes, 1874 – painter's involvement in 1647 Neapolitan revolt)

¶*Rembrandt van Rijn* (Klenau, 1937)

¶*Wallenstein* (Denza, 1876; Zafred, 1965), *Valdštejn* (Weinberger, 1937). See also Seyfried, 1813; Adelburg, c.1872; Musone, 1873; Ruiz, 1877; Shabelsky, 1950 ¶ALSO: *Der Freischütz* (Weber, 1821—Bohemia around 1650), *Friedenstag* (R. Strauss, 1938—day of the Westphalian Peace), *The Devils of Loudun* (Penderecki, 1969—trial of Father Grandier in 1634)

1643-1715   Louis XIV (b. 1638) King of France. 1704: battle of Blenheim ended attempts of Louis XIV to make France supreme in western Europe. 1688: death of **Frederick William the "Great Elector"** of Brandenburg.

La Roi l'a dit (The King Has Commanded It) (Delibes, 1873—set in court of Louis XIV), *Der Prinz von Homburg (The Prince of Homburg)* (Henze, 1960—Germany in 1675, battle of Fehrbellin, also featuring Friedrich Wilhelm)

1653-1658   Oliver Cromwell (b. 1599) Lord Protector of (British) Commonwealth. John **Milton** (1608-1674), author of *Paradise Lost.*

Milton (Spontini, 1804), *I Puritani* (Bellini, 1835)

1658   Leopold I (d. 1705) succeeds Ferdinand III as Holy Roman Emperor. 1660: sends army to check Turk advance. 1666: revolt of Hungarian noblemen. 1673: declares war on France. 1683: League of the Hague against France.

?*Die Türken vor Wien* (A. Müller, 1869)

1660-1685   Charles II (b. 1630) King of England

?*Die Liebe für den König oder Karl Stuart* (Süssmayr, 1785), ?*Merry Freaks in Troublous Times* (Nathan, 1843 comic opera on Charles II), *King Charles II* (MacFarren, 1849), *King Charles II* (Loder, 1849)

1667   Suleiman II (1642-1689) of Persia succeeds Shah Abbas II.

?*Solimano* (Perez, 1757; Galuppi, 1760; J.G. Naumann, 1773; G.M. Curcio, 1782), *Soliman den Anden (Soliman II)* (Sarti, 1770 "Syngespil"), *Zaide* (Mozart, 1779), *Soliman den II, eller De tre Sultaninnorna (Soliman II, or The three sultanas)* (Kraus, 1789), *Soliman der Zweite, oder Die drei Sultanninen* (Süssmayr, 1799), *Solilmano II* (L. Carlini, 1820)

1682   Murder(?) of Italian composer **Alessandro Stradella** (b. c.1642).

Il cantore di Venezia (Marchi, 1835), *Alessandro Stradella* (Flotow, 1844), *Alexander Stradellerl* (A. Müller, 1846 parody). See also Niedermeyer, 1837; Franck, 1844; Moscuzza, 1850; Sirico, 1863

1682-1725   Peter I "the Great" (b. 1672) Tsar of Russia, incl. regency of his older sister Sophia (1682-1689). Victory over **Charles XII** (1697-1718) King of Sweden, at Poltava.

Pierre le grand (Grétry, 1798), *Die Jungend Peter des Grossen* (Weigl, 1814), *Pietro il grande, ossia Un gelosa alla tortura* (Vaccai, 1824), *Pierre et Cathérine* (Adam, 1829; Flotow, 1835), *Pierre il Grand* (Jullien, 1852). See also Arapov, 1949; Frondoni, 1839. SEE ALSO: *The Czar* (Shield, 1790), *Frauenoert, oder der Kaiser als Zimmermann* (Lichtenstein, 1814), *The Burgomaster of Saardam* (Bishop, 1818 musical drama—the Tsar in Holland), *Il Falegname di Livonia* (Pacini, 1819), *Il Borgomastro di Saardam* (Donizetti, 1827), *Zar und Zimmerman* (Lortzing, 1837—the Tsar in Holland), *Il borgomastro di Schiedam* (L. Rossi, 1844), *L'Etoile du Nord*

(The North Star) (Meyerbeer, 1854 *opéra comique*—Peter disguised as a carpenter who plays the flute), *Mazeppa* (Pedrotti, 1861; F. Pedrell, 1878; Tchaikovsky, 1883; Minchejmer, 1899—Ukrainian cossack opposes the Tsar at Poltava; see also Maurer, 1837; Campana, 1850; Wietinghoff, 1859; Pourny, 1872; ?Jarecki, 1876; Grandval, 1892; Koczalski, 1905; Nerini, 1925), *Khovanschina* (Moussorgsky, perf. 1886—conflict between the Boyars and "Old Believers" representing mystic Russia, and the supporters of the "new" Russia sympathetic to western influences, during period of the regency), *Der Zarewitsch* (Lehár, 1927—operetta on Peter and his son Alexis), *Fregat "Pobeda" (The Frigate "Victory")* (Arapov, 1957), *The Blackamoor of Peter the Great* (Lourié, 1958). See also Mercadante, 1827

1687   **Newton's "Principia" published.** Seminal contribution to physical science.

1689-1702   William III (b. 1650) and Mary II (1662-1694) King and Queen of England. Samuel **Pepys** (1633-1703) English diarist and secretary of the admiralty.

¶*Lucia di Lammermoor* (Donizetti, 1835—though set in 1669; see also *Le Caleb de Walter Scott* by Adam, 1827; *Le nozze di Lammermoor* by Carafa, 1829; Rieschi, 1831; *Oblubienica z Lammermooru [The Bride of Lammermoor]* by Damse, 1832; *Bruden fra Lammermoor* by Brédal, 1832; *La fidanzata di Lammermoor* by Mazzucato, 1834)

¶*Samuel Pepys* (Coates, 1929)

¶*Wilhelm von Oranien* (H. Hofmann, 1882)

1700s   Armenians' struggle against Persian invaders in the 18th century. In **Hungary** anti-Habsburg revolts c.1700. 1711-1740: **Charles VI** (b.1685) Holy Roman Emperor, last male in Habsburg line; succeeded (1740) by his daughter Maria Theresa (SEE 1740-1786, below).

¶*?Die oesterreiche Grossmuth, oder Carolus VI* (Keiser, 1712), *Charles VI* (Halévy, 1841)

¶*David-Bek* (Tigranyan, 1949—Armenia)

¶*Czinka Panna* (Kodály, 1948—legendary gypsy musican during Hungarian revolt)

1702-1714   Anne (b. 1665) Queen of Great Britain and Ireland, daughter of James II.

Martha, oder Der Markt von Richmond (Martha, or Richmond Market (Flotow, 1847—England c. 1710, during time of Queen Anne)

1715-1774   Louis XV (b. 1710) King of France. Marquise de **Pompadour** (Jeanne Antoinette Poisson, 1721-1764), mistress of Louis XV. Period of regency of the Duke of Orléans (1715-1723). Adrienne **Lecouvreur** (1692-1730), actress. 1739: France declares war against the Holy Roman Emperor **Charles VI** (1685-1740).

¶*Adriana Lecouvreur* (Vera, 1856; Benvenuti, 1857; Perosio, 1889; Cilea, 1902)

¶*Le Postillon de Lonjumeau (The Postman of Lonjumeau)* (Adam, 1836—finding a tenor for Louis XV's court opera; see also *Giulio d'Este [Il postiglione di*

Longjumeau] by Campana, 1841), *La Pompadour* (Moór, 1902), *Madame Pompadour* (Fall, 1922—operetta on Marquise de Pompadour, Louis XV)
¶ALSO: *Manon Lescaut* (Auber, 1856; Puccini, 1893—incl. French investments in Louisiana*), *Manon* (Massenet, 1884—Amiens, Paris, L'Havre of c. 1721), *Le Portrait de Manon* (Massenet, 1894)

1733   **Stanislas Leszyczynski** (father-in-law of France's Louis XV) attempts to gain Polish throne on death of Augustus II (b. 1694), Elector of Saxony.
Stanislas Lesczinski, ou Le siège de Dantzick (Foignet, 1811), *Il finto Stanislao re di Polonia* (Mosca, 1812), *Il finto Stanislao* (Gyrowetz, 1818). SEE ALSO: *Un giorno di regno (Kingdom for a Day)* (Verdi, 1840), *Der Bettelstudent* (Millöcker, 1882)

1736   Baron **Theodore de Neuhoff** becomes King of Corsica.
Il re Teodoro in Venezia (Paisiello, 1784)

1740-1786   **Frederick II "the Great" (b. 1712) King of Prussia**, patron of artists and philosophers. 1694-1778: **Voltaire** (François Marie Arouet), French poet, dramatist, satirist, historian—admirer of Frederick II. 1717-1780: **Maria Theresa** Queen of Hungary and Bohemia and Archduchess of Austria; wife of the Austrian Emperor Francis I and mother of Marie Antoinette. 1740-1748: War of the Austrian Succession. **Wilhelm Friedemann Bach** ("Bach of Halle", 1710-1784), composer and eldest son of **Johann Sebastian Bach** (1685-1750). Johann Wolfgang von **Goethe** (1749-1832), German poet and dramatist. **Wolfgang Amadeus Mozart** (1756-1791). 1756-1763: **Seven Years' War**. Duke **Karl Eugen** of Württemberg fl. 1780s.
¶*Friedemann Bach* (Graener, 1931), *A Tamás templom karnagya (The Cantor of St. Thomas Church)* (Árányi, 1947—on Johann Sebastian Bach)
¶*Federico II re di Prussia* (Mosca, 1824)
¶*Maria Antoinette* (Carrer, 1884)
¶*Maria Theresa und ihr Kammerheizer* (A. Müller, 1868)
¶*Szenen aus Mozarts Leben* (Lortzing, 1832 *Singspiel*), *Mozart i Salieri (Mozart and Salieri)* (Rimsky-Korsakov, 1898), *Poslední akord, episoda z pobytu W.A. Mozarta v Praza (The Last Chord, an episode from Mozart's Stay in Prague)* (Moor, 1930), *W.A. Mozart* (Moor, 1934)
¶*Une Matinée de Voltaire, ou La famille Calas à Paris* (Solié, 1800 *opéra-comique*), *Voltaire* (F. Müller, before 1845)
¶ALSO: *I Masnadieri (The Robbers)* (Verdi, 1847; see also *Amelia, ossia Il bandito* by Zajc, 1860; *Die Räuber* by Klebe, 1957—references to Seven Years' War), *Luisa Miller* (Verdi, 1849; see also *Kabale und Liebe* by von Einem, 1977—incl. references to character modeled on Duke Karl Eugen of Württemberg), *Werther* (Massenet, 1892—near Frankfurt in 1780), *Der Rosenkavalier* (R. Strauss, 1911—Vienna during reign of Empress Maria Theresa), *Friederike* (Lehár, 1928—incl. Goethe as character)

---

*   Based on the Abbé Prévost novel of 1731; Puccini's version is set in 2nd half of 18th century, Massenet's in 1721.

1762-1796 Catherine II "the Great" (b. 1729) Empress of Russia.
La dame de pique (The Queen of Spades) (Halévy, 1850), *Pikovaya Dama (The Queen of Spades)* (Tchaikovsky, 1890—incl. appearance by Catherine). SEE ALSO: *Kazak stikhotvorets (The Cossack Poet)* (Cavos, 1812—on 18th-century Ukrainian soldier-poet Semyon Klimovsky)

1759 Ferdinand VI of Spain succeeded by Charles III.
El Barberillo de Lavapiés (The Little Barber of Lavapiés) (Barbieri, 1874 zarzuela—during reign of Carlos III, 1766)

1763 Peace of Paris. Ended the Seven Years' War and gave England a colonial empire in India and North America at the expense of France.

1776-1783 Period of American Revolution. 1776: Declaration of Independence. 1783: Peace of Paris and Versailles. 1787: U.S. Constitution framed.
1776 (Edwards, 1969—musical show on events leading to Declaration of Independence)

1771-1792 Gustavus III King of Sweden.
Gustave III ou Le bal masqué (Auber, 1833), *Il Reggente* (Mercadante, 1857—reset in 16th-century Scotland), *Un ballo in maschera* (Verdi, 1859—reset in colonial Boston)

1789-1815 Period of French Revolution and Napoleonic Empire. Giovanni Jacopo **Casanova** (1725-1798), Italian adventurer. Francisco José de **Goya** (1746-1828), Spanish artist. Domenico **Cimarosa** (1749-1801), Italian composer. Maximilien Françoise Marie Isidore de **Robespierre** (1758-1794), revolutionary leader. George Jacques **Danton** (1759-1794), lawyer and revolutionary leader. André Marie de **Chénier** (1762-1794), French poet. 1804-1815: **Napoleon I** (1769-1821) Emperor of the French. 1805: Horatio **Nelson** (1758-1805) defeats Franco-Spanish fleet at Trafalgar.
¶*Casanova* (Lortzing, 1841; Rózycki, 1922)
¶*Andrea Chenier* (Giordano, 1896)
¶*Cimarosa* (Isouard, 1808)
¶*Dantons Tod* (Einem, 1947), *Danton and Robespierre* (Eaton, c.1978)
¶*Pan y toros* (Barbieri, 1864 zarzuela in which Goya appears), *Goya* (Menotti, 1986)
¶*Kaiserin Josephine* (Kálmán, 1936—incl. Napoleon, Josephine as characters)
¶*L'Aiglon (The Eaglet)* (Honegger & Ibert, 1937—on the fate of Napoleon's only legitimate son "Napoleon II")
¶ALSO: *Bianca und Giuseppe, oder Dir Franzosen vor Nizza (Bianca and Giuseppe, or the French Before Nice)* (Kittle, 1848—Nice in Savoy at time of occupation by French Republican army, 1793), *La forza del destino* (Verdi, 1862—the war between Spain and Napoleon also breaks out in Italy), *Jakobin (The Jacobin)* (Dvořák, 1889), *Trafalgar* (Giménez, 1890 zarzuela), *Tosca* (Puccini, 1900—Rome in 1800), *Germania* (Franchetti, 1902—German resistance to Napoleon), *Thérèse* (Massenet, 1907—on the Girondists, Austrian War of 1792), *Madame Sans-Gêne* (Giordano, 1915; Dluski, early 20th cent.; Petit, 1947—on the wife of

Napoleon's marshall Lefèbvre; also as *The Duchess of Dantzic* by Caryll, 1903), *Il piccolo Marat (The Lesser Marat)* (Mascagni, 1921 — aristocrat forced to join revolutionary ranks, 1790), *Voyna i mir (War and Peace)* (Prokofiev, 1946 — Napoleon's invasion of Russia, 1812), *Billy Budd* (Ghedini, 1948; Britten, 1951 — British warship during year of the mutinies, 1797; see also *Billy,* musical show by Dante & Allan, 1969), *Dialogues des Carmelites* (Poulenc, 1957 — fate of Carmelite nuns during the Terror), *Tale of Two Cities* (Benjamin, 1957 — on the Terror), *The Ghosts of Versailles* (Corigliano, 1991 — Beaumarchais in love with Marie Antoinette)

1814-1815   Congress of Vienna. Remade the map of Europe after the revolutionary and Napoleonic eras.

ADDITIONAL

1815-1899   19th-Century (post-Napoleonic) world history. Nicolò **Paganini** (1782-1840), Italian violinist and composer. Latin American revolutionary **Simón Bolivar** (1783-1830), secures independence of Greater Colombia (1819). George Gordon, Lord **Byron** (1788-1824), English poet. Aleksandr Sergeyevich **Pushkin** (1799-1837), Russian poet. Elizabeth Barrett **Browning** (1806-1861) and Robert **Browning** (1812-1889), English poets. Frédéric François **Chopin** (1810-1849), Polish composer. **Carlota** (Marie Charlotte Amélie, 1840-1927), Empress of Mexico 1864-1867 and wife of Maximilian, Archduke of Austria. Edvard **Grieg** (1843-1907), Norwegian composer.

¶AUSTRIA: *Regina* (Lortzing, 1848 — revolutionary unrest in Vienna, 1848)
¶ENGLAND: *Robert and Elizabeth* (Grainer, 1964 — musical show on the Brownings, c.1845), *Lord Byron* (Giarda, 1910; Thomson, 1968), *The Rothschilds* (Bock, 1970 musical show)
¶ITALY: *Paganini* (Lehár, 1925)
¶MEXICO: *Maximilien* (Milhaud, 1932 — on Maximilian & Juarez), *Carlota* (Sandi, 1948)
¶NORWAY: *Song of Norway* (Wright & Forrest after Edvard Grieg, 1944 — musical show on Grieg)
¶POLAND: *Chopin* (G. Orefice, 1901)
¶RUSSIA: *The Death of Pushkin* (Kreitner, 1937 — inc), *Pushkin v Mikhaylovskom / Pushkin v izgnanii (Pushkin in Mikhaylovskuye / Pushkin in Exile)* (Shekhter, 1945-1958)
¶SIAM: *The King and I* (Rodgers, 1951 musical show — Anna Leonowers and King of Siam, 1860s)
¶SOUTH AMERICA: *Bolivar* (Milhaud, 1950)
¶SPAIN: *El poeta* (Moreno Torroba, 1980 — on episode in life of poet José Ignacio de Espronceda)

1800-1899   19th-Century U.S. 1861-1865: American Civil War. Daniel **Webster** (1782-1852), political leader, administrator and diplomat. Phineas Taylor **Barnum** (1810-1891), showman, circus

producer. Harriet **Tubman** (?1820-1913), black abolitionist
leader. Emily **Dickinson** (1830-1886), poet. Willam "Buffalo Bill"
Cody (1846-1917), frontiersman, scout and showman.

¶*Barnum* (Coleman, 1980 musical show)
¶*Eastward in Eden (Emily Dickinson)* (Meyerowitz, 1951)
¶*The Trial of Mary Lincoln* (Pasatieri, 1972)
¶*Annie Get Your Gun* (Berlin, 1946 musical show — incl. Annie Oakley, "Buffalo
Bill" Cody as characters)
¶*Harriet, the Woman Called Moses* (Musgrave, 1985)
¶*The Devil and Daniel Webster* (Moore, 1939)
¶ALSO: *The Man Without a Country* (Damrosch, 1937 — events of 1810-1860),
The Ballad of Baby Doe (Moore, 1956 — 19th-century Colorado), *Shenandoah*
(Geld, 1975 musical show — Virginia pacifist's family during Civil War)

1900-1993   20th-Century world history. 1914-1918: World War I. 1917:
Russian Revolution. 1939-1945: World War II.

¶ARGENTINA: *Evita* (Lloyd Webber, 1978 — musical show featuring Eva and
Juan Peron)
¶AUSTRIA: *The Sound of Music* (Rogers, 1959 musical show on Trapp Family
Singers, World War II)
¶INDIA: *Satyagraha* (Glass, 1981 — episode in life of Mohandas Gandhi, 1869-
1948)
¶ITALY: *Der Diktator* (Krenek, 1926 — parody of rise of fascism in Italy), *Napoli
milionaria* (Rota, 1977 — Neapolitan family at the end of World War II during Al-
lied occupation)
¶RUSSIA & SOVIET REPUBLICS: *Maryté* (Raciunas, 1953 — on Maryté
Melnikaité, a hero of the Soviet Union), *Rasputin* (Reise, 1988), *Tikhiy Don
(Quiet Flows the Don)* (Dzerzhinsky, 1934 — World War I, overthrow of the
Tsar), *Bronenosets Potyomkin (Battleship Potemkin)* (Chishko, 1937), *V buryu (Into
the Storm)* (Khrennikov, 1939 — on resistance to the communists in a rural Russian village, 1920-21), *V ogne (Into the Fire* (Kabalevsky, 1943 — on World War II
defence of Moscow), *Sem'ya Tarasa (The Taras Family)* (Kabalevsky, 1947 — on a
family living under occupation), *Velikaya druzhba (The Great Friendship)*
(Muradeli, 1947 — civil war in Northern Caucaus, character loosely based on
Stalin), *Sevil* (Amirov, 1953 — liberation of Azerbaijani women from Islamic
repression in 1918-1919; improved situation under Soviet rule 1929), *Nikita Ver-
shinin* (Kabalevsky, 1955 — Soviet power established in Far East during Civil
War), *1905 god (The Year 1905)* (Shekhter & Davidenko, 1955), *Oktyabr (October)*
(Muradeli, 1961 — Lenin, October Revolution), *Fiddler on the Roof* (Bock, 1964
musical show — persecution of Russian Jews in early 20th century)
¶ALSO: *Penelope* (Liebermann, 1954 — on a World War II incident)

1900-1993   20th-Century U.S. history. Susan B. **Anthony** (1820-1906),
feminist, leader in woman suffrage movement. Carry **Nation**
(1846-1911), reformer, temperance leader. Albert **Einstein** (1879-
1955) German-born American theoretical physicist. Fiorello H.
La Guardia (1882-1947), mayor of New York City (1934-1945).
Trial of Nicola **Sacco** (1891-1927) & Bartolomeo **Vanzetti** (1888-
1927, Italian-born political activists.

¶*The Mother of Us All* (Thomson, 1947 — Susan B. Anthony)
¶*Lizzie Borden: A Family Portrait* (Beeson, 1965 — celebrated murder case)

¶*Funny Girl* (Styne, 1964 musical show — entertainer Fannie Brice, impresario Florenz Ziegfeld Jr)

¶*George M* (Cohan, 1968 musical show — on composer George M. Cohan)

¶*Coco* (Previn, 1960 musical show — on fashion designer Coco Chanel)

¶*Einstein* (Dessau, 1973), *Einstein on the Beach* (Glass, 1976)

¶*Fiorello!* (Boch, 1959 musical show)

¶*Gypsy* (Styne, 1959 musical show — entertainer Gypsy Rose Lee)

¶*Marilyn* (Laderman, 1993 — on Marilyn Monroe)

¶*Carrie Nation* (Moore, 1968)

¶*Nixon in China* (Adams, 1987)

¶*Sacco and Vanzetti* (Blitzstein, 1964 — inc.)

¶*X, the Life and Times of Malcolm X* (Davis. 1986)

¶ALSO: *Call Me Madam* (Berlin, 1950 — musical show based on Perle Mesta as ambassador to Luxembourg), *Willie Stark* (Floyd, 1981 — inspired by Huey Long career)

SUPPLEMENTARY — ADDITIONAL TITLES
POSSIBLY/PROBABLY (?) ON HISTORICAL SUBJECTS

Adrasto re d'Egitto (Tarchi, 1792); *Amuratte II* (Raimondi, 1813); *Gli Aragonesi in Napoli* (C. Conti, 1827); *Atala* (G. Pacini, 1818; Gallignani, 1876); *Attalo Re di Bitinia* (Sarti, 1782); *Borislav* (Atanasov, 1910); *Caritea, regina di Spagna, ossia La morte di Don Alfonso re di Portogallo* (Mercadante, 1826 — also as *Donna Caritea; see also Donna Caritea, regina di Spagna* by Farinelli, 1814; C. Coccia, 1818); *Carlo re d'Alemagna* (Orlandini, 1713); *Carlo re d'Italia* (C. Pallavicino, 1682); *Cecilia* (Refice, 1923 *azione sacre* on legend of St. Cecilia and Valerian); *Charles de France ou Amour et Gloire* (Hérold & Boieldieu, 1816);

Don John of Austria (Nathan, 1847); *Don Juan de Austria* (Chapi y Lorente, 1903 *zarzuela*); *Die Druiden* (Seyfried, 1801); *Enrico* (Galuppi, 1743); *Enrico Quarto al passo della Marna* (Balfe, 1833); *Gerone tiranno di Siracusa* (A. Scarlatti, 1692); *Guernica* (P.A. Vidal, 1895); *István királsy (King Stefan)* (G. Erkel, c.1885 — on St Steven I, 997-1038, 1st king of Hungary); *Juan de Urbina* (F.A. Barbieri, 1876 *zarzuela*); *Der königliche Printz aus Pohlen Sigismundus, oder Das menschliche Leben wie ein Traum* (Conradi, 1693); *Kosakkerne (The Cossacks)* (Elling, 1897); *Krøl Lokietek czyli Wisliczani (King Lokietek, or the Women of Wislica)* (Elsner, 1818);

Il Manlii (G. Nicolini, 1801); *Matilda of Hungary* (Wallace, 1847); *Nitocri, regina d'Egitto* (Giacomelli, 1736); *I Normanni a Parigi* (Mercadante, 1832); *Novogorodskoy Bogatir Boyeslavich (Boyeslavich the Hero of Novgorod)* (Fomin, 1786); *El Olimpo en Narbona y Charles VI* (Garcia Robles, operetta); *Les Pêcheurs de Saint-Jean* (Widor, 1905); *Il Quinto Fabio* (Cherubini, 1783); *Re Enzo* (Respighi, 1905); *Le roi René, ou La Provence au XVe siècle* (Hérold, 1824);

on Saint Agatha (Caccini & da Gagliano, 1622); *Saint Louis, roi de France* (Milhaud, 1872 opera-oratorio); on Saint Ursula (da Gagliano, 1624); *San Bonifatio* (Mazzocchi, 1638); *Sant'Alessio (St. Alexis)* (Landi, 1631); *Sant'Alessio, vita, morte e miracoli* (Ghisi, 1957 *devozione scenica o per concerto* — from anon. medieval sources); *Il Sant'Eustachio* (Mazzocchi, 1643 — also opera on Saint Eustace by d'India, 1625); *Santa Teodora* (1635); *Starïy gusar, ili Pazhi Fridrikha II (The Old Hussar, or The Pages of Frederick II)* (Maurer, Genisha, Alyab'yev, Shol'ts & Isouard, 1831 *opéra-vaudeville*); *Tiberio imperator d'Oriente* (A. Scarlatti, 1702)

INDEX

*(References to countries, nationalities are selected;
see also individual persons, places, events, characters)*

Luna, Alvaro de, 101
Luna, Antonio de, 101
Luna, Count, 330
Luna, Count di, 101, 330
Luna, Count Fadrique de, 101
Luna, Cardinal Pedro de: see Pope
  Benedict XIII
Lusiads, The (Camoëns), 137
Luther, Martin, 141, 143, 145, 151, 152,
  155, 157, 159, 161, 177
Lutherans, 37
Lützen (place), 217
Luxembourg dynasty, 126
Luxembourg (Luxemburg), 98, 128
Lykov (boyar), 207
Lyon, cardinal of, 19
Lysiart (Count of Forêt), 66
Lysistrata (Lincke), 5
M. de Porceaugnac (Molière), 227
Ma Vlast (Smetana), 104
Macbeth (Scottish king), 55
Macbeth, Lady, 55
Macbeth (Bloch), 55, 56
Macbeth (Erskine), 55
Macbeth (Shakespeare), 55
Macbeth (Verdi), 55
MacDuff, 55
Macedonia, 6, 9
Machaerus, 17
Machaut, Guillaume de, 99
Machiavelli, Niccolò, 141
Madame Sans-Gêne (Giordano), 318, 321
Maddalena (in Andrea Chénier), 297
Madelaine, Countess (in Capriccio), 282
Madrid, 316
Madrigali guerrieri ed amorosi (Monteverdi), 64
Maeterlinck, Maurice, 115
Maffei, Andrea, 267
Magdeburg (place), 216, 217, 219
Magna Carta, 74
Mago, Simon, 25
Magus, Simon, 25
Magyars, 35, 50, 51
Mahler, Gustav, 144, 155
Mahomet, ou La Fanatisme (Voltaire), 124,
  253
Maid of Orleans, The (Tchaikovsky), 113
Maid of Pskov, The (Rimsky-Korsakov),
  206-208
Maino, Agnes di, 105
Mainz (place), 50, 61, 103, 129, 153
Majestic (ship), 308
Makropoulos, Hyeronymus, 203
Malabar Coast, 135

Malatesta, Giovanni (Gianciotto), 87, 89
Malcolm II (Scottish king), 55
Malcolm III (Scottish king), 55
Malesherbes (lawyer), 293
Malespini, Giannetto, 129
Malipiero, Gian Francesco, 13, 16, 25
Malipiero, Pasquale, 106
Maliuta, Grigory, 209
Malta, 310
Mamelukes (mercenaries), 310
Mamonov, 331
Mamontov, Savva, 207
Manfred (illegitimate son of Frederick II),
  78
Manfredo (in Montemezzi opera), 54
Mannheim (place), 268
Manon (Massenet), 231, 248
Manon Lescaut, 248
Manon Lescaut (Auber), 248
Manon Lescaut (Puccini), 248
Manrico (in Il trovatore), 101
Mantua (place), 77, 144, 149, 201
Mantua, Duke of, 148
Manuel I (King of Portugal), 135, 137, 138
Manzikert (place), 60
Maometto Secondo (Rossini), 124
Marat, Jean Paul, 289, 295
Marcel (Huguenot), 177
Marcellus II (Pope), 160
Marchfeld, battle at, 82, 83
Marcian (Emperor), 35
Marco Polo, 92
Marcus Antonius (Mark Antony), 13, 16
Marcus Aurelius (Emperor), 28
Marengo, battle at, 313, 314
Marenzio, Luca, 199
Margaret (Duchess of Parma), 172
Margaret (sister of Henry VIII), 189
Margaret (widow of James IV of Scot-
  land), 187
Margaret, St., 110
Margaret of Anjou, 112, 116, 117
Margherita di Savoia, 201
Margrave system, 44
Marguerite (French countess), 73
Marguerite de Valois, 176, 177, 200
Maria (Tsarina), 205
Maria Amalia of Saxony, 256
Maria-Aurora von Königsmark, Count-
  ess, 251
Maria Carolina (Queen of Naples—sister
  of Marie Antoinette), 262, 305-307, 313-
  316
Maria Luisa, 316
Maria Nagaya (Tsarina), 210

BIOGRAPHIES & COMPOSER STUDIES

ALKAN, REISSUE *by Ronald Smith.* Vol. 1: The Enigma. Vol. 2: The Music.

BEETHOVEN'S EMPIRE OF THE MIND *by John Crabbe.*

BÉLA BARTÓK: An Analysis of His Music *by Erno Lendvai.*

BÉLA BARTÓK: His Life in Pictures and Documents *by Ferenc Bónis.*

BERNARD STEVENS AND HIS MUSIC: A Symposium *edited by Bertha Stevens.*

JANÁCEK: Leaves from His Life *by Leos Janácek. Edited & transl. by Vilem & Margaret Tausky.*

JOHN FOULDS AND HIS MUSIC: An Introduction *by Malcolm MacDonald.*

LIPATTI *(Tanasescu & Bargauanu):* see PIANO, below.

LISZT AND HIS COUNTRY, 1869-1873 *by Deszo Legány.*

MASCAGNI: An Autobiography Compiled, Edited and Translated from Original Sources *by David Stivender.*

MICHAEL TIPPETT, O.M.: A Celebration *edited by Geraint Lewis. Fwd. by Peter Maxwell Davies.*

THE MUSIC OF SYZMANOWSKI *by Jim Samson.*

THE OPRICHNIK: An Opera in Four Acts by Peter Il'ich Tchaikovsky. *Transl. & notes by Philip Taylor.*

PERCY GRAINGER: The Man Behind the Music *by Eileen Dorum.*

PERCY GRAINGER: The Pictorial Biography *by Robert Simon. Fwd. by Frederick Fennell.*

RAVEL ACCORDING TO RAVEL *(Perlemuter & Jourdan-Morhange):* see PIANO, below.

RONALD STEVENSON: A Musical Biography *by Malcolm MacDonald.*

SCHUBERT'S MUSIC FOR PIANO FOUR-HANDS *(Weekly & Arganbright):* see PIANO, below.

SOMETHING ABOUT THE MUSIC 1: Landmarks of Twentieth-Century Music *by Nick Rossi.*

SOMETHING ABOUT THE MUSIC 2: Anthology of Critical Opinions *edited by Thomas P. Lewis.*

A SOURCE GUIDE TO THE MUSIC OF PERCY GRAINGER *edited by Thomas P. Lewis.*

THE SYMPHONIES OF HAVERGAL BRIAN *by Malcolm MacDonald.* Vol. 2: Symphonies 13-29. Vol. 3: Symphonies 30-32, Survey, and Summing-Up.

VERDI AND WAGNER *by Erno Lendvai.*

OTHER MUSIC TITLES AVAILABLE FROM
PRO/AM MUSIC RESOURCES, INC.

VILLA-LOBOS: The Music—An Analysis of His Style *by Lisa M. Peppercorn.*

THE WORKS OF ALAN HOVHANESS: A Catalog, Opus 1–Opus 360; with Supplement Through Opus 400*by Richard Howard.*

XENAKIS *by Nouritza Matossian.*

ZOLTAN KODALY: His Life in Pictures and Documents *by László Eosze.*

| GENERAL SUBJECTS |

ACOUSTICS AND THE PERFORMANCE OF MUSIC *by Jürgen Meyer.*

AMERICAN MINIMAL MUSIC *by Wim Mertens. Transl. by J. Hautekiet.*

A CONCISE HISTORY OF HUNGARIAN MUSIC, 2ND ENL. ED. *by Bence Szabolozi.*

EARLY MUSIC *by Denis Stevens.*

EXPRESSIVE RHYTHM IN EUROPEAN CLASSICAL MUSIC, 1700-1900: An Annotated Sourcebook and Performance Guide *transl. & edited with commentaries by David Montgomery.*

GOGOLIAN INTERLUDES; Gogol's Story "Christmas Eve" as the Subject of the Operas by Tchaikovsky and Rimsky-Korsakov *by Philip Taylor.*

HISTORY THROUGH THE OPERA GLASS *by George Jellinek.*

JOAN PEYSER ON MODERN MUSIC AND MUSIC MAKING 1: Twentieth Century Music—The Sense Behind the Sound, UPDATED 2ND ED.

JOAN PEYSER ON MODERN MUSIC AND MUSIC MAKING 2: Boulez—Composer, Conductor, Enigma, UPDATED ED.

JOAN PEYSER ON MODERN MUSIC AND MUSIC MAKING 3: The Music of My Time—Collected Essays and Articles.

MAKING MUSIC GUIDES: Making Four-Track Music *by John Peel.* What Bass, 2ND ED. *by Tony Bacon & Laurence Canty.* What Drum, 2ND ED. *by Geoff Nicholls & Andy Duncan.* What's Midi, 2ND ED. *by Andy Honeybone, Julian Colbeck, Ken Campbell & Paul Colbert.*

THE MUSICAL INSTRUMENT COLLECTOR, REVISED ED. *by J. Robert Willcutt & Kenneth R. Ball.*

THE MUSICAL STAMP DATE BOOK: with an Illustrated Guide to the Collecting of Musical Stamps *by Herbert Moore.*

A MUSICIAN'S GUIDE TO COPYRIGHT AND PUBLISHING, ENLARGED ED. *by Willis Wager.*

OTHER MUSIC TITLES AVAILABLE FROM
PRO/AM MUSIC RESOURCES, INC.

WHAT IS FLAMENCO? *Editorial cinterco.*
THE WIND CRIED: An American's Discovery of the World of Flamenco *by Paul Hecht.*

PERFORMANCE PRACTICE / "HOW-TO" INSTRUCTIONAL

THE BOTTOM LINE IS MONEY: Songwriting *by Jennifer Ember Pierce.*
GUIDE TO THE PRACTICAL STUDY OF HARMONY *by Peter Il'ich Tchaikovsky.*
HOW TO SELECT A BOW FOR VIOLIN FAMILY INSTRUMENTS *by Balthasar Planta.*
IMAGINATIONS: Tuneful Fun and Recital Pieces to Expand Early Grade Harp Skills *by Doris Davidson.*
THE JOY OF ORNAMENTATION: Being Giovanni Luca Conforto's *Treatise on Ornamentation* (Rome, 1593) *with a Preface by Sir Yehudi Menuhin and an Introduction by Denis Stevens.*
MAKING MUSICAL INSTRUMENTS *by Irving Sloane.*
THE MUSICIAN'S GUIDE TO MAPPING: A New Way to Learn Music *by Rebecca P. Shockley.*
THE MUSICIANS' THEORY BOOK: Reference to Fundamentals, Harmony, Counterpoint, Fugue and Form *by Asger Hamerik.*
ON BEYOND C *(Davidson):* see PIANO, below.
THE STUDENT'S DICTIONARY OF MUSICAL TERMS.
TENSIONS IN THE PERFORMANCE OF MUSIC: A Symposium, REV. & EXT. ED. *edited by Carola Grindea. Fwd. by Yehudi Menuhin.*
THE VIOLIN: Precepts and Observations *by Sourene Arakelian.*

PIANO/HARPSICHORD

THE ANATOMY OF A NEW YORK DEBUT RECITAL *by Carol Montparker.*
AT THE PIANO WITH FAURÉ *by Marguerite Long.*
EUROPEAN PIANO ATLAS *by H. K. Herzog.*
FRENCH PIANISM: An Historical Perspective *by Charles Timbrell.*
GLOSSARY OF HARPSICHORD TERMS *by Susanne Costa.*
KENTNER: A Symposium *edited by Harold Taylor. Fwd. by Yehudi Menuhin.*
LIPATTI *by Dragos Tanasescu & Grigore Bargauanu.*

OTHER MUSIC TITLES AVAILABLE FROM
PRO/AM MUSIC RESOURCES, INC.

ON BEYOND C: Tuneful Fun in Many Keys to Expand Early Grade Piano Skills *by Doris Davidson.*

THE PIANIST'S TALENT *by Harold Taylor. Fwd. by John Ogdon.*

THE PIANO AND HOW TO CARE FOR IT *by Otto Funke.*

THE PIANO HAMMER *by Walter Pfeifer.*

PIANO NOMENCLATURE, 2ND ED. *by Nikolaus Schimmel & H. K. Herzog.*

RAVEL ACCORDING TO RAVEL *by Vlado Perlemuter & Hélène Jouran-Morhange.*

SCHUBERT'S MUSIC FOR PIANO FOUR-HANDS *by Dallas Weekly & Nancy Arganbright.*

THE STEINWAY SERVICE MANUAL *by Max Matthias.*

TECHNIQUE OF PIANO PLAYING, 5TH ED. *by József Gát.*

THE TUNING OF MY HARPSICHORD *by Herbert Anton Kellner.*

See also above: ALKAN *(Smith)* — LISZT AND HIS COUNTRY *(Legnány)* — PERCY GRAINGER *(Dorum)* — PERCY GRAINGER *(Simon)* — RONALD STEVENSON *(MacDonald)* — SOURCE GUIDE TO THE MUSIC OF PERCY GRAINGER *(Lewis)* — TENSIONS IN THE PERFORMANCE OF MUSIC *(Grindea)*